Dissecting the Hack
Revised Edition

Dissecting the Hack
The F0rb1dd3n Network
Revised Edition

Jayson E. Street

Kent Nabors

Brian Baskin

Marcus Carey

Technical Editor
Dustin D. Trammell

ELSEVIER

AMSTERDAM • BOSTON • HEIDELBERG • LONDON
NEW YORK • OXFORD • PARIS • SAN DIEGO
SAN FRANCISCO • SINGAPORE • SYDNEY • TOKYO
Syngress is an imprint of Elsevier

Acquiring Editor: Rachel Roumeliotis
Development Editor: Matthew Cater; David Bevans
Project Manager: Julie Ochs
Designer: Alisa Andreola

Syngress is an imprint of Elsevier
30 Corporate Drive, Suite 400, Burlington, MA 01803, USA

Notices
Knowledge and best practice in this field are constantly changing. As new research and experience broaden our understanding, changes in research methods or professional practices, may become necessary. Practitioners and researchers must always rely on their own experience and knowledge in evaluating and using any information or methods described herein. In using such information or methods they should be mindful of their own safety and the safety of others, including parties for whom they have a professional responsibility.

To the fullest extent of the law, neither the Publisher nor the authors, contributors, or editors, assume any liability for any injury and/or damage to persons or property as a matter of products liability, negligence or otherwise, or from any use or operation of any methods, products, instructions, or ideas contained in the material herein.

Library of Congress Cataloging-in-Publication Data
Application submitted

British Library Cataloguing-in-Publication Data
A catalogue record for this book is available from the British Library.

ISBN: 978-1-59749-568-4

Printed in the United States of America
10 11 12 13 14   10 9 8 7 6 5 4 3 2 1

Typeset by: diacriTech, Chennai, India

Working together to grow
libraries in developing countries

www.elsevier.com | www.bookaid.org | www.sabre.org

ELSEVIER   BOOK AID International   Sabre Foundation

For information on all Syngress publications visit our website at www.syngress.com

Contents

PART 2   SECURITY THREATS ARE REAL (STAR) 2.0

Foreword

The world of hacking is a world of pain and frustration. Frustration for the hacker as he tries to figure out how to break the latest and greatest security device, and pain for the manufacturer or corporation that made or was relying on that device.

At least, that is the layman's view – the hacker is the "bad guy," set on doing evil and causing pain to those he comes up against, and interested only in one thing: destroying the security of the systems in front of him. The manufacturer is the innocent victim, trying to go about its business, but suffering unprovoked attacks. But it's not as simple as that. Hackers come in all shapes and sizes, some good and some bad, and they hack for all kinds of reasons, some benign and some selfish. Manufacturers also come in all shapes and sizes, and of course, the pain and frustration definitely comes in all shapes and sizes:

- The frustration of not getting your message across – trying and failing to make people understand not only what is wrong with their product but why it's important that they get it right.

- The pain of seeing your research buried under threats of lawsuits, even though you are right and the issue you've uncovered is there to be exploited.

- The frustration of dealing with manufacturers or commercial businesses that put profit or expedience over end-user safety and security.

- The pain of losing data or suffering an intrusion through an unpatched system...

The list goes on.

When I met Jayson, he didn't know it then, but he was going to experience pain and frustration in spades. He had come up with a brilliant scheme for overcoming all these obstacles, and it should have been a "no-brainer." Not only that, but he was enthusiastic, intelligent, personable, committed, and, most importantly, *on the right side*. He was one of us, one of the good guys, with something that was going to help solve the everlasting problem of how you get those with the power to make things change understand not only *what* needs to happen but *why* it needs to happen. In other words, how to engage them. Talk to me about marketing and my eyes will glaze over and I'll be a million miles away in a world of my own. Talk to most management about technical or security problems, and you'll have the same effect – they are off with the fairies and your wise words are going in one ear and out of the other.

However, Jayson had a plan. What do people like better than technical manuals and lectures on threat management or risk assessments? Stories, of course. Thrillers! Action! Secret agents taking on the forces of evil and winning!

Jayson and I meet about once a year in, of all places, Las Vegas. We both go there for the world's largest "hacker" conference, DEFCON. When I first met him, Jayson was excited. He had a book. This book. As soon as he explained the concept to me, I was sold. The idea that you could read a good book that not only entertained you but could then be flipped into a technical reference that showed you exactly how each of those neat hacks worked was a sure winner. Maybe this would be the way to get the "suits" to understand that this is not the stuff of fiction. This is real and it's happening to them, *right now*.

When I met him again the following year, he was still excited. Ideas were flowing, research was pouring in, and his book was progressing. He was now looking for a publisher. Things were looking good.

The year after that, he was still excited, but he was feeling the pain of rejection, and frustration as finding a publisher wasn't as easy as he'd first thought. But he was upbeat. He was a man on a mission. He had loads of new ideas so that just meant the book would be even better by the time it came out, so no problem... soldier on!

Three years on, and here he is again – still smiling and determined, but still frustrated and in pain. They just don't get it. The book gets better and better, but he's hitting a brick wall.

It could have ended there, but Jayson is no quitter. The other thing that impressed me about him when we first met was his determination to follow things through. He's never made me a promise that he hasn't kept (and we all know those are ten a penny at conferences... "Sure, I'll send you that stuff as soon as I get home..."), and he's always looking out for something he can do to benefit those around him. This book is all about sharing and learning, and that encapsulates the hacker ethos and, in particular, the DEFCON ethos. If you know something, share it. If you learn something, learn more. When you really know your stuff, teach it.

The publication of this book was a hard-won victory, and I hope you learn as much from it as Jayson did researching it, but most of all, I hope you enjoy it as much as I have and as much as it deserves to be enjoyed.

Adam Laurie
Dorset, UK, June 2009.

Acknowledgments

Thanks to Haki Berkeri for the pizza, Pepsi, and the good advice that kept me going when nothing else was.

I also owe thanks to Weldon for Wednesday, and Dee for all the days in between. I thank Rudy for the rides and for sticking with Hanzo. Big thanks to Marcus J. Carey for helping me off the ledge and introducing me to Brian. Thanks to Brian Baskin who created what should have been there in the first place, Jeff R. for helping out the iPhone guy, and David Letterman for letting me be on his show (and to Stephen Colbert for letting me on his I hope). Thanks to Del Rhea and Lee for their love of rodents who hang out at the mall. I thank Leon for being my first official fan, Rafe for his patience and tolerance of a wild and loud crazy roommate, Laura (she knows why), and Pam for leaving. I thank Crystal, Jason, and Sean for being good students, Marco for the experience in warehouse living, Leslie's mom for giving me Jackie (I'm taking good care of her), Capt. Tom Johnson for the loan of the gun (I was glad to give it back), Mrs. F. Collins for being the only teacher who encouraged me in learning and poetry, Stone for sweetly shipping me the sword from Shanghai (that was swell), and Sherry, Andrea, and Kris for all the help in the background with the book. Of course, thanks to Rachel for taking a chance on some geek on Twitter ☺. Also thanks to Syngress for making my dream a reality again (stay tuned - more to follow). Thanks to Ming and the Wuxi PWNAGE team for … well you figure it out ;-). Thanks to my family, whose fault it is that I am such a creative and unique individual. Oh yeah! And thanks to that person for that thing (yeah, you know who I'm talking about) - that was great.

A special shout out to Bastiaan de Boer from BRUCON, I can't wait to blow you up in the next book, thanks for supporting Hackers for Charity.

To Dan K., Johnny L., Jeff M., and Marcus R., thanks for believing in me and contributing to this revised version it means more to me than you know.

Last and by no means the least thanks to the INFOSEC and hacking communities, especially Tim Smith and all the great friends I have found on Twitter who have made my life a lot more interesting than it would have been if I had become a lawyer.

– Jayson

Lisa, Christina, and Margaret - thank you for giving me the time and inspiration to write. Mrs. Coffin, thank you for teaching me brevity.

– Kent

Thank you to my family and children for the time, freedom, and motivation to do what needed to be done. Thank you to all law enforcement agencies who work tirelessly every day to make this world a better place, and to the hackers who make their jobs more fun and interesting. Thanks for Jayson and Kent for putting together an excellent story. Thank you to Jayson for fighting through a major uphill battle, while learning of and climbing additional mountains along the way, and staying cheerful about it all, and to everyone who put it all on the line to make this book a success.

– Brian

H0w t0 R34d *Dissecting the Hack: The F0rb1dd3n Network*

Both sections of this book tell a single story. The adventures of Bob and Leon are more than just a fun read. They illustrate many very real threats to individuals, businesses, organizations, and even countries. The networked world is so interconnected; many don't realize how valuable a target they really are. The best and worst of humanity connected with the speed and power of modern technology comes together in a world of our own making that we do not yet understand.

"The F0rb1dd3n Network" tells the story of two kids caught up in an adventure they did not expect. Bob and Leon are most comfortable in a digital world but soon find that digital actions have physical consequences. Throughout their fictional story are real-world lessons.

"Security Threats Are Real" or STAR focuses on those real-world lessons. The hacks and tools in the fictional story are very real. STAR provides the details, sources, and references to learn more about the threats, defensive techniques, attacker techniques, and even cool toys of the fictional story.

"The F0rb1dd3n Network" can be read by itself as a story. It can also be read as an illustration of the issues described in STAR. Throughout "The F0rb1dd3n Network," you will find links that point to specific references in STAR where you can get more information about key concepts. Or if you read STAR, you will find links to "The F0rb1dd3n Network" where the story illustrates a scenario where very real tools and techniques are applied. Each section leans on the other. How you read them is entirely up to you.

For the more adventurous reader, "The F0rb1dd3n Network" contains "Easter eggs" as well. Woven throughout are references, hints, phrases, and more that will lead you to significant or trivial insights into hacker culture. Again, STAR will help you find out more about the Easter eggs. But not all the answers are given away. There must be some unsolved mystery to make hacking worth the time.

So read "The F0rb1dd3n Network" as a story. Read STAR as a reference work. Dig for Easter eggs in "The F0rb1dd3n Network." Or put it all together to learn more about the very real threats of the digital world we all live in.

Dissecting the Hack: The F0rb1dd3n Network can happen IRL.

About the Authors

Jayson E. Street   Jayson is not just an author of the book *Dissecting the Hack: The F0rb1dd3n Network*. His consultation with the FBI and Secret Service on attempted network breaches resulted in the capture and successful prosecution of the criminals involved. In 2007 he consulted with the Secret Service on the Wi-Fi security posture at the White House.

He has also spoken at DEFCON, BRUCON, UCON, and at several other 'CONs and colleges all over the world on a variety of Information Security subjects. He also was the co-founder and speaker of ExcaliburCon held in Wuxi China. He has also been a witness in civil & criminal cases.

He is a current member on the Board of Directors for the Oklahoma "InfraGard". He is also Vice President for ISSA OKC. Jayson has been a longtime member of the Netragard "SNOsoft" research team.

If you would like to find out more about him than even he cares to admit feel free to visit http://f0rb1dd3n.com/. Also note he is a highly carbonated speaker who has partaken of Pizza from Beijing to Brazil. He does not expect anybody to still be reading this far but if they are please be aware he was chosen as one of Time's persons of the year for 2006 FTW!

Kent Nabors   Kent Nabors serves as a Vice President of Information Security for a multibillion dollar financial institution. He has significant experience in both the banking and the IT industries. He has worked in bank examinations with the Federal Deposit Insurance Corporation and the Federal Reserve Bank.

Kent's background includes security policy development, systems implementation, incident response, and training development.

Kent is a graduate of the University of Oklahoma and Southern Nazarene University.

When he isn't thinking about locking down bits and bytes, he is usually trying to keep up with his wife and two daughters. Quiet time usually involves power tools or an eclectic reading list.

Brian Baskin   is a digital forensics professional employed by CSC and serves as the Deputy Lead Technical Engineer with the Defense Cyber Investigations Training Academy (DCITA), part of the Department of Defense Cyber Crime Center (DC3). For more than 10 years, Brian has worked with DCITA to research, develop, and teach forensic responses to growing cyber threats. Brian devotes much of his time to researching the evolving Internet crimes, network protocol analysis, and Linux and UNIX intrusion responses.

Brian also serves as a technical reviewer for DCITA. He helps to analyze content and procedures for more than two dozen cyber security courses for technical validity and relevance. For fun, he manages a content creation team that develops online Web-based incident response training that provides hands-on experience to military units stationed overseas. His team works with the various federal and military law enforcement groups for information sharing and collaboration on ongoing threats and best practices.

Brian has been involved with multiple book projects with Syngress Publishing, and he has also served as a subject matter expert for content development for the National White Collar Crime Center (NW3C) and the Federal Law Enforcement Training Center (FLETC).

Marcus J. Carey   is well known for being a compulsive mentor in the information security community. Marcus has more than 17 years of experience in the information security field, working in the military, federal, and private sectors. Marcus served more than 8 years active duty in the U.S. Navy Cryptologic Security Group. Marcus ended his naval service by being assigned to the National Security Agency (NSA) where he engineered, monitored, and defended the Department of Defense's secure networks. Marcus earned a Master of Science in Network Security from Capitol College in Laurel, Maryland.

Technical Editor

Dustin D. Trammell   is the founder of the Computer Academic Underground and cofounder of the Austin Hackers Association (AHA!). He has more than a decade of experience in various areas of information security including vulnerability assessment, penetration testing, secure network architecture, vulnerability research and exploit development, and security research in specific areas related to network protocols, network applications, steganography, and Voice over Internet Protocol (VoIP).

Over the years, Dustin has been involved with many security community projects such as the design and development of Sender Policy Framework (SPF) for e-mail (RFC 4408) and contributing as a core developer for the Metasploit Project. Dustin has also released numerous security tools such as the infamous PageIt! mass-paging application, the hcraft HTTP exploit-crafting framework, and the SteganRTP VoIP steganography tool.

He regularly releases vulnerability and exploit advisories, speaks at security-related events and conferences, and is on the Technical Advisory Board of the Voice over IP Security Alliance (VoIPSA).

Throughout Dustin's career, he has performed security research and development focused on attack vectors and exploitation methods for BreakingPoint Systems, VoIP security research for TippingPoint, and founded the VIPER Lab VoIP vulnerability research group at Sipera Systems. Before Sipera, Dustin was a Security Research Scientist for Citadel Security Software (acquired by McAfee) responsible for vulnerability analysis, research, and remediation within the scope of the Linux, Solaris, AIX, and HP/UX platforms.

F0rb1dd3n

Pr010gu3

A NEW ASSIGNMENT

Thursday, 9:24 a.m.

Stepan Senn looked up at the clear, blue sky of a fall morning. He could hear the crunch of dry grass beneath him as he turned his head slightly. The cool air on his face felt sharp against the hot blood that trickled from the corner of his mouth that was quickly swelling. He tried to sit up, but his body wouldn't obey. There was a sharp sound of metal on metal. The sound was familiar, but his mind wasn't working fast enough to recognize his situation. He craned his neck as he struggled to look above him. He saw legs, a hard face looking down at him, and a gun. The shape of the gun seemed to grow large enough to fill all he could see.

Everything began to spin in his mind. He closed his eyes hard against the image.

◐ ◐ ◐

"Sir? Excuse me, sir?" A hand touched Stepan on the shoulder and he jolted awake. "I'm sorry, I didn't mean to startle you."

"No problem." Stepan replied automatically as he picked up the briefcase he had just kicked over. He hadn't realized how tired he was after staying up late the last couple of nights.

"Sir, I believe your flight is boarding."

Stepan looked blearily at the Aeroflot gate agent. As his brain came back into focus, he stood.

"Thank you," he replied as he gathered his briefcase and coat. He made his way down the gangway and onto the plane in a mental fog. His clouded mind began to clear as it processed the surroundings he had awakened to find.

Stepan Senn's job had taken him all over the world. He had flown in many types of aircraft, but the Russian Tupolev 154 was not his favorite. He had flown on Aeroflot a couple of years after the collapse of the U.S.S.R. He remembered back then all the staff put on a good show, but the aircraft itself had looked tired. The exterior paint was faded and chipped. The interior was worn. Seats were dirty. Even the crew's

3

uniforms looked threadbare. Stepan hadn't been convinced then that the plane should have been in service.

Stepan also remembered when he was in Barcelona on business not that long ago and an Aeroflot pilot landed this same type of aircraft 250 meters to the right of the runway. Aeroflot just wasn't good enough for Stepan.

As he took his seat, this aircraft didn't improve his impression of the airline. The cabin was more cramped than similar-sized Boeing and Airbus planes Stepan had flown in. Its oval shape and low ceiling made sitting in a window seat particularly unpleasant. He was thankful that he wouldn't be repeating this journey.

But what should I expect when I'm flying to the second-poorest country in Europe? he thought to himself.

After they reached cruising altitude, Stepan relaxed again and closed his eyes. He began to think back to how he had ended up on this flight. He had been in Moscow. October trips to the Russian capital weren't a problem for a man from Switzerland. A Russian autumn was a nice change of pace, and his employer made sure he traveled well. Or that's what he had believed until now.

Stepan had been sent to hand-deliver a package to the office of one of his employer's partners. He didn't know the full story of what he had been carrying, but not knowing was a major part of his job. He had handed the envelope to the receptionist. Once she had sent an e-mail to his boss confirming delivery, Stepan left the office with his Moscow business complete. He knew better than to ask questions or, even worse, try to see what was on the disk he had guessed had been in the envelope.

It was a clear, cold day, so Stepan decided to walk back to the hotel. It only took about 25 minutes for the walk to the Rossiya Hotel. He even took the time to go past the east side of the Kremlin, turning at the Spasskaya Tower and on to the Rossiya. Once he entered his room, Stepan turned on his laptop and connected it to the hotel network. He typed in his overly long password, all the while wishing for some painful end for the skinny technician back at the office that insisted everyone had to memorize such nonsense just to gain access to their laptops.

Stepan pulled out his access token and typed in the six-digit random number from the token and the four-digit PIN he had memorized. Soon he had established an encrypted connection to the office back in Zurich, Switzerland (*p. 195). He opened his e-mail software and found the message waiting for him:

```
Your contact is waiting in Chisinau, Moldova. Your flight
arrangements have been made. You leave at 7:00 a.m. local time
tomorrow on Aeroflot. You are booked in the Hotel Dedeman Grand
Chisinau. There is a package for you at the front desk that you
need to deliver.

You will meet Simon Torgova at the outdoor café across from the
Central Garden on Columna Street the day you arrive at 3:00 p.m.
local time. Tell him his password is the same as your project
name. Report back here when an agreement is obtained.
```

This was Stepan's first project where he had been "let in" on more of the story. He had grown tired of the desk time he spent as a researcher for an international oil brokerage firm headquartered in his hometown. He had come up with an idea that could give his employer a huge advantage in the international trading game. In fact, he believed he had created a new product line for their brokerage activities: information. He had identified the target company and even found someone that might be easily influenced to assist them. When Stepan turned in all his research, he was told to do some courier jobs while preparations were made. It had been two months before this e-mail message from his boss told him it was time for action.

Stepan's boss had taken care of identifying an appropriate operative. Stepan didn't have any contacts that could help him with that part of the project. But this project started with his idea. He would be able to move out of research and maybe have a chance to be in on some of his employer's deals. But why Moldova, and where was that, anyway?

Stepan opened Google and typed in "Moldova." He thought he had seen a lot of the world, especially in the last two months of fieldwork, but backwater former Soviet territories had not been on any previous itinerary. *Land-locked, near the Black Sea, south of Ukraine and east of Romania. Why would anyone want to operate out of such a place?* he thought to himself.

◑ ◑ ◑

With a jolt, Stepan opened his eyes. He had fallen asleep again. As the plane's speed dissipated, over the bumpy runway in Chisinau, Stepan blinked his eyes and looked around. He made a promise to himself to either drink more coffee or sleep better on his next trip. It was time to begin his work in Moldova. He pulled his briefcase out from under the seat in front of him and waited for the plane to stop at the gate.

Stepan looked out the window of the aircraft. The side of the airport facing the tarmac was neglected and dingy. The plane finally stopped short of the terminal and stairs were rolled to the door. Stepan and his fellow travelers had to walk down the stairs, across the tarmac and into the airport. No covered automatic walkways with protection from the weather.

"Why Moldova?" Stepan mumbled to himself as he walked through the airport, his poor opinion of the little country now confirmed. The inside of the airport was a relic of past glory, although glory was hardly the word to describe it. The faces of the people sitting and waiting for flights seemed much happier than those of the arriving passengers. Stepan's countenance matched his fellow travelers as he waited for his one suitcase.

Once outside the airport, Stepan turned and looked at the front of the building. Its blue windows and bright red front entrance were a clean, modern-looking contrast to the run-down Cold War relic he had seen from the other side. Stepan shook his head as he was suddenly even more grateful for living in Switzerland. He soon found a taxi to take him to the Dedeman. The weather was warmer than Moscow, but still brisk.

"Welcome to the Dedeman, sir, how long will you be staying with us?"

"One night."

"All right, if you will fill out this information, I'll get a room for you."

The clerk passed a form and pen to Stepan. As Stepan completed the form, he asked, "Do you have a concierge?"

"Yes sir. His name is Viktor. He is right over there." The clerk pointed to an average-sized young man standing at a counter on the other side of the lobby.

"Thank you."

"And sir, I believe this is for you." The clerk turned and pulled a small, bulging envelope from a desk behind the counter and handed it to Stepan. Stepan collected the envelope and the key card for his room and walked across the lobby to Viktor.

"Welcome sir, what can I do for you?"

"I will be checking out in the morning. I'm in room 330. Please make sure I have a taxi ready at 8:00 a.m. for the airport."

"No problem, sir. Anything else?"

"Yes. Is that the Central Garden across the street?" Stepan asked as he pointed to the front of the hotel.

"Yes sir. It's not so pretty in the fall, but it is still a good place to start if you would like to take a walk around town."

As Stepan walked away, Viktor typed a note in the hotel's new guest information system so he would get a reminder in the morning to have the cab ready for Mr. Senn, room 330.

Stepan made his way to his room, set his suitcase and briefcase on the bed, and checked his watch. He was hungry and he had several hours before his meeting. He checked his pockets.

Envelope. Room key. Wallet. Phone. Okay, time for food, he told himself as the door closed behind him. He left the elevator, made his way through the lobby to the hotel restaurant. He was soon seated by an attractive, overeager hostess with bright eyes and a quick smile.

Okay, perhaps there are a few redeeming qualities to this country, he thought as he took the menu and returned the smile from the hostess.

Stepan took his time making a selection and then settled into a decent meal. Sitting still and eating was a pleasure compared to his flight.

Viktor watched from across the lobby as Stepan began to eat. He had worked as a concierge for the hotel for almost a year. It gave him an opportunity to practice his language skills and make the Lei needed to pay for school. The phone call Viktor was about to make would get him the Euros he needed for pocket money.

"I think your guest has arrived."

"Are you sure?"

"You said there would be a business man traveling alone; he would arrive this afternoon and only stay for one night. We've only had one man check in by himself today and he's scheduled to check out in the morning."

"Good job. We will be there shortly. Pay attention and let me know if he leaves the hotel."

Stepan finished his meal, charged it to his room account, and then walked out onto the street. Moldova wasn't much, but he would at least have a look while he had the time. He didn't notice how carefully Viktor watched his movement and noted the time as he left.

Two men entered the lobby a few minutes later. Vlad was middle-aged and tall, with cold, gray eyes and dark brown hair cut tight on the sides but just long enough on top to show a natural wave he brushed back as they came out of the breeze. He moved with the ease of an athlete but was dressed like a well-traveled businessman with a black open-collared shirt and silk sport coat. Pavel was younger and shorter. He had dirty blonde hair that was pulled into a short ponytail and a rather dingy backpack slung over one shoulder. He stooped under the weight of the load as they made their way across the lobby to the concierge.

Viktor was nervous as Vlad approached, but the presence of Pavel, Viktor's older brother helped him stay in control.

"Hello, Viktor. Thanks for the call."

"Sir, here is the room key you misplaced," Viktor said a little too loudly.

"Thank you. I always liked the service at this hotel. Your brother here is doing good work for me. Keep up your studies at university and maybe I'll have a job for you as well."

"Yes, sir. Your associate left just five minutes ago."

Vlad took the room key card and together with Pavel, made his way to Stepan's room. Inside, they found what they were looking for – a briefcase with a new IBM Thinkpad computer inside. It was one of those ultralight computers that doubled as an executive toy.

"Pavel, start with the laptop while I have a look around," Vlad ordered.

While Vlad walked around room, looking in drawers and sorting through Stepan's suitcase, Pavel lifted the computer deftly as someone who was comfortable with any device connected to a keyboard. He turned on the power and hit the default key combination to modify the boot settings. No power-on password. Pavel could always count on business types to not think of the basics. They always thought that spying was only targeted at governments (*p. 200).

Pavel enabled the laptop for booting from a USB device. He pulled out his key-chain and plugged the tiny storage device into the port on the right of the laptop case. Instead of the normal start-up screen that Stepan saw everyday, Pavel was greeted with a black screen with a few simple command options. This was a handy tool Pavel had picked up from a security Web site. It allowed him to reset any pass-word on a Windows system as long as he could control how the system started. Pavel didn't bother giving the administrator account a new password. He set it to a blank password, disconnected his USB device, and rebooted the machine. Soon the Windows XP "splash" screen appeared. He typed in "administrator" for the ID and no password and pressed the "Enter" key. He was in (*p. 239). Pavel turned the com-puter on the small desk and stood to give Vlad room to sit down.

"This is too easy. I wish he had used another hotel," Pavel said as Vlad sat in front of the now unlocked computer. "At least then it would have been a challenge."

"What challenge would you want?" asked Vlad.

"Viktor getting us into the room means that we got the laptop information, but now I don't need to do the Hotel Hack."

"The what?"

"At DEFCON, Major Malfunction presented a hack using a Linux box to break into hotel information systems through the TV set in a room. You can grab reservation information, TV movies they've watched, and sometimes even credit card information or read their e-mails."

"Who is Major Malfunction?"

"What? You don't know? He's the guy who wrote the hack!"

"Never heard of him," Vlad responded.

"You should really keep up with what the über-leet guys are doing if you want – "

Pavel saw a subtle firmness appear in Vlad's expression and he stopped himself.

"That's right, you were busy recruiting virus writers for one of your jobs. You missed out on some of the really skilled hackers." Pavel was pushing his luck with the way he talked to Vlad. But he knew he was right. If Vlad kept bringing in work like this, Pavel knew he needed to practice a variety of skills.

Vlad seemed to have had enough of the conversation. He removed a Swiss Army knife from his pocket. He opened a small connector from the knife, which fit neatly into the USB port on Stepan's laptop. Soon he was copying the "My Documents" folder from Stepan's laptop to his "pocket knife" (★p. 313).

"Only 10 megabytes. He must have another computer at his office or he keeps everything in e-mail," Pavel said as he looked over Vlad's shoulder.

A quick look from Vlad reminded Pavel that he was already getting on his employer's nerves. Pavel shut up and walked across the room and picked up the remote to the TV set.

Vlad ignored Pavel and kept his attention on the laptop. He looked in the default folder and quickly found the file he wanted. He copied the "outlook.pst" file to the pocket knife. This would give him a copy of all the e-mails Stepan had stored locally. With the e-mail secured, he looked up at Pavel (★p. 245).

"What are you doing?"

Pavel was looking at what appeared to be Stepan's room bill displayed on the TV.

"This guy hasn't had any time to pick out a movie and didn't use the Internet e-mail system offered by the hotel. But, he's got a request for a taxi at 8:00 a.m. tomorrow, and he paid for everything with an American Express card. Here's the number. I can't believe they didn't set this thing up to mask the digits on the display!"

"This could be useful," Vlad replied with a slight smile. Pavel was a resourceful young man to keep around, Vlad reminded himself, even if he was annoying at times.

"Now that you're done playing with the television, finish up on this laptop for me," Vlad ordered.

Pavel took Stepan's laptop from Vlad and blanked the three Windows event log files. Next, he changed the "last logged in user" registry key so that it would appear that Stepan's account was the last one used (★p. 269).

"Do you want me to reset the administrator password?" Pavel asked.

"No. You've done enough. This one won't ever know what he lost," Vlad answered as he walked toward the door.

Pavel powered down the computer, returned it to where he found it and followed his boss.

Vlad and Pavel strolled through the lobby without speaking. Vlad led the way as he walked across the street and into a small café. They took a table near the window where Vlad had a clear view of the hotel entrance in case Stepan returned.

"Set up your laptop. I want to see what we found," Vlad ordered.

Pavel complied and pulled his own sticker-covered laptop from his backpack and set it on the table between them. He logged in and took the pocketknife Vlad offered and connected it to a USB port.

Vlad took Pavel's laptop and looked over the list of files they had just acquired from Stepan's laptop. He didn't have much time, so he sorted the files by "Last Modified Date" and scanned the list. One file caught his eye immediately. It was called "Odysseus.doc" and was last updated just one day before (*p. 315).

"That would be too obvious," he said mostly to himself as he double-clicked on the file name.

After a quick scan of the first page, he said, "I've got what I need Pavel. You can take the rest of the day off. I'll call later if something comes up from the meeting. In the mean time, I'm going to be borrowing your laptop."

Pavel paused. He wasn't one to part with his laptop. He had too many tools there that he had spent months "acquiring." But he also knew that Vlad was not one to be disobeyed.

"Be careful with the laptop. I've been working on a potential new IE vulnerability and all my notes are stored there. Let me give you an account, so you can get to the tools you need without messing with all of my shortcuts."

Pavel took the laptop back from Vlad and created a new user account. He then did a "change user" command, typed "boss" for the user ID, and pushed the laptop back across the table.

"Your password is 'penguin.' Just call me and I'll come pick it up when you're done." Pavel stood from the table and walked away. At least Vlad was going to have to pay for his meal.

As Pavel left the hotel restaurant, Vlad began typing his password.

That kid never stops, he thought to himself as he finished typing the not-too-subtle reminder from Pavel that Vlad didn't really know how to use Linux even though he insisted on using it as his main operating system. Vlad found the document he had been reviewing and continued reading. It looked like Stepan had been given a research project by his employer. Stepan had filled this document with notes and information pulled from Web sites. He had started with a company called Data Mining, Inc. based in Raleigh-Durham, North Carolina. He had some information about a small firm in Houston, Texas called 3DNF, Inc. that had been acquired by Data Mining within the last six months. Vlad found some links from the U.S. Securities and Exchange Commission's Web site and the text from a press release about the acquisition (*p. 146).

Then Stepan had listed some names and e-mail addresses that belonged to the 3dnf.com domain. Vlad could only guess that Stepan had "googled" the domain name to harvest the addresses. If so, Stepan was a fairly resourceful researcher (*p. 138).

One of the names was in a red font instead of black like all the others. Michael Resol was someone of interest to Stepan. There were links to what appeared to be blog pages by Michael. There were even links to gambling sites. Then, there were some notes by Stepan:

```
Michael Resol is the best target. He is a network admin that
has worked at 3DNF for five years. He has been passed over for
promotions and he talks too much about his employer on his blog
site. Both his blog and Facebook sites reference his favorite
online gambling pages. I think he has some financial problems -
see link below.

Michael's tech position, length of time with 3DNF, and money
problems make him a good candidate for deployment of our
application (*p. 132).
```

"Interesting, but what is the 'application'?" Vlad muttered to himself. He had an idea based on the name of the file he was reading. Vlad looked at his watch. He needed to move along. He would have to fill in the gaps during his meeting with Stepan, and there were other files yet to read from Stepan's laptop.

Vlad shut down the laptop and stood to leave. He was in a good mood because of the progress so far. He left a large tip and paid for his and Pavel's meal. Outside, Vlad walked across Puskin Street and into the central garden at the middle of the town. He made his way down the tree-lined walk to the central fountain. On the far side of the fountain, he turned to his right and made his way to Columna Street. A left turn and one more block, and he could see the outdoor café.

As Vlad approached, he could see a small man in his thirties sitting alone at one of the four outdoor tables. He had blonde hair cut short, glasses, and sharp facial features. There was something about the way he moved that suggested to Vlad that whatever was around the next corner was sure to surprise this man. As Vlad approached, he saw that he was making a bad show of reading a newspaper.

"Impressive. You don't look like someone who can read Romanian," Vlad said in perfect English. In fact, every word Vlad said sounded as if it had been given individual consideration before it was spoken. He knew his baritone voice was a tool he could wield effectively.

"I can't," Stepan admitted nervously. "But I thought I should at least take a look and see if I could learn a little about the city." Stepan's Swiss accent was obvious to Vlad at once. He sat down in the empty chair across from Stepan. "Are you Simon?" Stepan asked.

"Yes," Vlad lied. As sloppy as Stepan had been securing his laptop, Vlad knew he would have exposed too much about his activities. *That's why you never use your real name*, he thought to himself.

"You must be Stepan."

"My employer tells me you come highly recommended."

"I finish my jobs efficiently if that is what you mean," Vlad responded.

"Uh, yes."

Stepan was obviously new at this business.

"What consultation does your firm require?" Vlad asked.

"We need someone who can install a certain program on a computer inside a company located in Houston, Texas, USA."

"What type of program, and what type of company?" Vlad responded.

"A rootkit to answer your first question, and a database consulting firm to answer your second." Stepan responded.

"That hardly seems like a task worth the cost of my skills," Vlad answered.

"We need to be certain that the program is installed on a particular system and we are willing to pay to ensure that it functions as designed. We need this to be done discretely and efficiently," Stepan answered.

"I can get that done. Is that all?"

"There are a few other steps to help ensure the information we need is accessible. The details are documented for you."

"Are you aware of my fees?" Vlad asked.

"Yes," Stepan answered.

Vlad took a pen and small piece of paper from his coat pocket and wrote "Volks-bank, 111-8-18-1-13-15-27-1" from memory. "Have the first half of the payment deposited here. I'll start as soon as I have confirmed the funds, and by the way, don't complain if you see any extra charges on your American Express card. I'll expect you to cover some of my travel costs" (*p. 315).

"Certainly. Do you have the necessary account information?"

Stepan's confused look was a pleasure to Vlad.

"I took the liberty of acquiring some financial information about you. Just a demonstration of the skills you are retaining," Vlad told him. *You're too inept to be doing this*, he thought to himself as he met Stepan's surprised gaze.

"Yes, well, of course, we will cover whatever expenses are required to complete the job." Stepan took an envelope out of his coat and slid it across the table. "My employer has also provided some background information on the job that you will find useful."

Vlad opened the sealed envelope. It contained a pen.

"What is the pen for?"

"It's a data storage device. If you pull the top off, you will see a USB connector for your computer (*p. 313). Inside is an encrypted file that details the instructions for your team, as well as the application we need installed on the target system. To access the files, you'll need the password – Odysseus."

Vlad allowed himself a small smile at that last piece of information.

"As I said, I'll begin when I have confirmed payment."

Stepan obviously wasn't sure what to do next. He began to gather up his news-paper and then paused.

"I have to ask – I understand you operate in many countries, so why Moldova? Are you from here?"

Vlad let out an honest laugh.

"No, I'm not from Moldova. But I do have some family ties here. I have found the legal environment of this country to be accommodating to my line of work. Local talent, although sometimes hard to find, is quite affordable. People from here are anxious to find work that gets them out of the country, and for the right skills, I can offer that."

"Oh, well, that does make sense. I'll make sure everything is in order." Stepan stood and walked away.

Vlad ordered a cup of coffee and then turned on Pavel's computer that he was still carrying. He logged in with the "boss" account Pavel had setup for him and connected the pen. He opened a window to review the files on the pen. Sure enough – two files. One was called "instructions.exe" and the other "files.exe." Vlad double-clicked on the file called "instructions.exe" and was greeted with an error message.

"Everyone assumes the whole world runs Windows," he muttered, missing the irony that he still retained Windows habits after he recently converted to Linux. Vlad looked through the program list on Pavel's Linux laptop. Sure enough – VMWare. Vlad launched the program and found that Pavel had several different Windows operating system images available. He clicked on the one Pavel had named "Surfing Win2K" and waited for it to boot. Vlad smiled – Pavel had modified that splash screen to show a penguin instead of the normal "Windows" welcome. It didn't require a password to open either. Vlad tried again to open the file. This time a window appeared asking for a password. He typed in "Odysseus." The program built a directory called "Transfer" on the desktop. Vlad opened the directory and inside were the files he expected. Vlad opened the one called "instructions.doc" and began to read.

Thirty minutes later, he was walking through town. It looked like he had to start his job a little sooner than expected. The last page of the file included instructions that he was to eliminate anyone who had complete knowledge of his activities – beginning with the individual who had delivered the instructions. At least there would be an extra payment for this service. He pulled out his cell phone and dialed a programmed number.

"Da?" The course voice sounded half asleep.

Vlad sighed disapprovingly as he answered in Russian, "Andrei, I need you to pick someone up tomorrow morning at 8:00 a.m. at the Dedeman Hotel in a taxi."

◑ ◑ ◑

Stepan was feeling pretty good the next morning. He had completed his first real "field assignment" without any problems. He also had finally put in motion an idea he had been working on for months. If Simon succeeded in setting up a reliable back door to the American company, he would be able to show his bosses a new revenue stream. Arbitrage of commodities had been lucrative to his firm for years, but it was old school. Arbitrage of information was how Stepan would become a partner.

Stepan knew a former partner of Mark Richardson had started his firm. The American had fled his home country after some questionable business dealings and set up an international trading company in Switzerland. Their new practice had been successful because of a willingness to deal with anyone. Stepan's plan would fit in just fine with such a firm.

Stepan finished packing and went down to the lobby. He walked over to Viktor at the concierge desk.

"Do you have that taxi ready for me?"

"Excuse me, sir, what room?"

"330."

"Oh yes. He is waiting for you just outside. Do you need help with your bag?"

"No." Stepan was ready to start making progress home. He walked out the door and met his ride.

"Good morning. I need to go to the airport."

"Yes, sir," was the response from the cabbie with a thick Russian accent. The cabbie took Stepan's suitcase and placed it in the trunk. Stepan got in the back seat and settled in for the brief ride back to the airport.

The day was clear and crisp. There was a slight breeze, but everyone on the street seemed to appreciate the sunshine. Stepan noticed more of the city as they drove than he had on the way in the day before. This time his attitude wasn't as gray and he was able to enjoy what he saw. He saw mostly old, Russian-made cars on the streets. He noticed the small shops that were starting to open for the day. The park he had walked through the afternoon before was mostly empty. A few people were walking through, probably on their way to work.

The traffic wasn't bad this morning. The drive down Bucuresti Street went quickly, and soon the city fell away and Stepan could see more of the landscape. Modest homes gradually yielded to countryside. The landscape seemed hard because of the coming winter, but the brightness of the day brought warmth in through the cab window. Suddenly Stepan's senses sharpened and he leaned forward in his seat.

"Is this the way to the airport?"

"Yes, sir," was the quick answer.

"This doesn't look like the way I came yesterday."

"Yes, sir."

"Do you speak English?" Stepan asked with growing concern.

"Yes sir."

That answer didn't convince Stepan. He leaned back in his seat and began to realize his problem. He was alone in a country he didn't know. His suitcase was in the trunk. He couldn't communicate with his driver. But the driver obviously had a destination planned. He thought about jumping out of the car. But that didn't make sense either. He would be abandoning his things, and he wouldn't know how to get back to the city or the airport.

The cabbie turned off the road suddenly. They pulled down a gravel road, turned right past some trees, and came to a stop beyond a little rise in the ground. Stepan looked around. He couldn't see the road. The cabbie turned off the car and got out. Stepan was too scared to even speak. His heart began to pound in his chest and his hands started shaking.

Andrei opened Stepan's door and caught him hard in the mouth with his fist. Stepan slumped. He wasn't unconscious – at least not quite. The shock of the act had the desired effect. Stepan stumbled as Andrei dragged him from the car and tossed him to the ground outside the car.

Stepan Senn looked up at the clear, blue sky of a fall morning. He could hear the crunch of dry grass beneath him as he turned his head slightly. The cool air on his face felt sharp against the hot blood that trickled from the corner of his mouth that was quickly swelling. He tried to sit up, but his body wouldn't obey. There was a sharp sound of metal on metal. The sound was familiar, but his mind wasn't working fast enough to recognize his situation. He craned his neck as he struggled to look above him. He saw legs, a hard face looking down at him, and a gun. The shape of the gun seemed to grow large enough to fill all he could see.

Andrei pulled the trigger and walked back to his car. He would collect his payment from Vlad that afternoon for another completed job. Vlad had been keeping Andrei busy lately.

0N3

PROBLEM SOLVED
Monday, 10:11 a.m.

"Yes! We've got the bastard!"

Mark pushed his chair back from the table and punched at the air. He had just spent the last four hours searching through piles of papers and books taken from Randolf Jamison's house the day before.

Randolf was sitting in a cell at the Houston federal prisoner transfer facility. He had been arrested on suspicion of trafficking in child pornography. Mark was the FBI agent from the Houston Computer Crime Task Force assigned to go through all of the hard drives taken from Randolf's three computers.

Unfortunately, Mark had hit a wall immediately. Most of the information on the computers looked normal, but on two of them, two-thirds of the storage space was filled with an encrypted volume. There would be no way to read the data, and what they had found in his house was not sufficient to keep him in custody. This case wasn't big enough to task some of the Bureau's special resources for such problems, so Mark had to find another way into these encrypted files.

"Try telling that to the little kids this pervert used to make his money!" Mark had snapped back at his supervisor when told he would have to find another way. Mark knew the math. There was no way he would be able to break into these drives - unless Randolf Jamison was stupid.

"If they were smart they wouldn't be doing this stuff in the first place," he told himself as he began. Mark went through every piece of paper they could find in his house. Sure enough, it was late-afternoon on his first day when Mark found it. Mark had been digging through magazines, bills, letters, books, and even saved junk mail trying to find a clue. For a pervert, Jamison kept a pretty plain-looking collection. They had only found a few pictures - just enough to confirm the statement they had from a probable victim's mother. But Mark finally noticed something that didn't belong. A Gideon Bible - obviously stolen from a hotel - stood out because it didn't fit the pattern of other material. There was a single piece of paper left inside the back cover. What Mark found there was the key to putting Jamison away.

"Thank God criminals can be so sloppy!" Mark exclaimed to the empty conference room. "If you record an encryption key, someone can always find it!"

Mark stood up from the table and started walking around the room. His body was moving on its own accord while his mind began to process what he had just found. Agent Jackson knew that he needed to start cataloging the contents of the once-encrypted drive he had been pounding on. But he had too much energy to be still. He started marching down the hall to get some coffee. Maybe he would run into someone on the Cyber-Crimes team he could talk to. After all, what's the use in solving a puzzle when you can't brag about it?

◖ ◖ ◖

"There he goes now," Special Agent Thompson said as he pointed at the glass wall of the conference room. The cluttered room had a large table running down the middle with two glass walls and hallways on either side. Mark was on his mission for hot caffeine on the opposite side when his boss noticed him. Agent Battle hardly had time to get a look at the blur as Mark disappeared down the hall.

"You'll find that Agent Jackson is a little...intense."

"Is he good?"

"One of the best investigators we have on the Cyber Crimes Task Force."

Special Agent Fredrick Thompson had been with the Bureau for nearly 20 years. After five years of fieldwork, he had shown the mental flexibility to adapt to technology better than most. That led to particular case assignments, the Houston Field office and, eventually, a command with orders to establish the Cyber Crimes Task Force for the South-Central United States.

For several years most of their work had been on drug cases. The Columbian and Mexican organizations bringing in drugs were constantly looking for an edge – and often that meant sophisticated communications gear and computers to track their business. But since 9/11, everyone in the Bureau was spending more time on anti-terror activities. And his team was no different. Agent Jackson's current case was almost a throwback with an old-fashioned pervert trafficking material across state lines. The only thing new was the technology used to hide the activity.

Thompson had a reputation in the Bureau for bringing together a strong team of more traditional FBI agents and technical talent he had personally recruited from the Air Force.

"Agent Jackson was one of my finds from the San Antonio Air Force Base 'Tiger Team.' They're an elite group of warrior-geeks who specialize in breaking into military networks and facilities to test security."

"That explains why he's so skinny. Does he know what to do with a gun?" Agent Battle asked with obvious skepticism.

"He's qualified for field work, but that's not his specialty. That's why you're here. Let me show you around some more. We'll catch up with your new partner in a while."

◖ ◖ ◖

"So have you met Battle yet?"

"No. Have you?" Agent Jackson replied as he sipped on his coffee.

"Yeah. Impressive. Marines, then NYPD. Battle's even spent some time on anti-terror work with our NYC office before Thompson decided we needed more muscle."

Mark was standing outside a cubicle talking to Agent Frank Adams, another member of the Cyber Crimes Task Force. Mark had just finished his tale of how he had found the encryption key that was going to send another pervert to jail. Frank hadn't been impressed. In fact, Frank had looked like he was holding something back as he listened to Mark. As soon as Mark had finished his story, Frank had cut him off to ask about Agent Battle. Mark even thought he saw a slight tension in Frank's face – kind of like a kid who had a secret.

"So what kind of name is 'Battle' anyway? Could there be any more testosterone than a Marine named 'Battle'?" Mark asked.

Frank smiled. "Probably not," he replied and started to turn back to his work with a slight shake of his shoulders. Mark wasn't done yet.

"More muscle is the last thing I need. I had my fill of jarheads when I was on the Tiger Team in San Antonio. I bet all Agent Battle could do with a hard drive is use it for target practice" (*p. 316).

"I think I'll take that bet, Jackson," Frank replied, careful not to look at Mark.

Mark turned to see his boss standing next to his new partner. As his brain tried to process what he saw, he could hear Frank suppressing a laugh as he shrank further into his cube. Standing next to Special Agent Thompson was a tall, athletically built woman. She stared slightly down at Mark as they measured each other with an intense stare. Agent Chris Battle clearly won as she had the element of surprise. Mark broke the eye-lock as Special Agent Thompson interrupted the slightly too-long silence.

"Agent Jackson, this is Agent Chris Battle. She is going to be joining the Cyber Crimes Task Force and will be your partner. Why don't you start bringing Battle up to speed by giving us a briefing on your progress on the Randolf Jamison case."

"Uh, yes sir. I was just heading back to the conference room. If we go back there I can show you what I found. I think we will have everything we need on Jamison before the end of the day."

As Mark led the way to the conference room he heard snickers from several cubes. He allowed himself one thought as his boss spoke. *Oh, this is going to be a long day.*

"Really? Is that why I saw you shooting out of the room so fast a while ago?" Thompson asked his subordinate.

"Yes sir. Well, I needed some coffee, actually. I just figured out the encryption key for Jamison's computers." Mark said as the three of them walked into the conference room.

"Good. Maybe the rest of us will get this room back, Jackson. How did you find it? This morning you told me we didn't have the tools to get to the data."

"We don't, sir. I spread all of this stuff out in the conference room to get a better perspective on what Jamison had in his house. An encryption key is the only way into the drives, and Jamison didn't strike me as very cautious. I made an assumption that he wrote down his key somewhere, just in case. Agent Battle, do you want to take a shot at this pile and see if you can find anything interesting?"

While Jackson had been talking, Battle had already started lifting magazines and books from the table. "Sure," she responded. As Agent Battle made it to the end of the table, she turned and asked, "I thought I heard you say earlier that Jamison was a pedophile. I don't see anything here but an average, boring single guy. What led you to him in the first place?"

"We got a tip from Perverted Justice. They're today's online version of the Guardian Angels from the 1970s. They got into a discussion with this pervert in a chat room. He claimed he had some "content" that he had personally created, and they talked him into giving a sample. When they got that, they called us. Jamison had given Perverted Justice a Yahoo! e-mail account (*p. 316). The Bureau checked it out and found that

REV 13:18
GEN   4:8
JDG 16:18
1SAM 17:4
MATT 2:16
MATT 26:47

account was last accessed from here in town. That's when I got the case. We sent an e-mail back to the account with a hidden embedded link to a Web page we controlled. When Jamison opened the e-mail, it forced his computer to hit our Web page and we were able to log his IP address," Mark explained.

"Why didn't you just subpoena his e-mail account?" Chris asked.

"We knew he was using an e-mail with a Russia-based e-mail server – it's a little hard to execute a subpoena over there. We already knew he was local. We used the IP address we recorded to identify his ISP and then we used the subpoena to get what we needed," Mark answered. "From that, we were able to track him down through his Internet Service Provider. Jamison had a DSL line under his own name. For all of his precautions on the encryption software, he didn't think about us tracking back through his e-mail."

"What about this?" Chris cut off Mark's story as she picked up the Gideon Bible.

"Not bad, Agent Battle." Mark said with a smile. "Why that?"

"If we are dealing with a pedophile, then this is the one book that doesn't belong here."

"You're close. But how do you find a pass phrase in there?" Mark asked.

"Agent Jackson, we're impressed you figured it out. Just tell us what you found so I can get back to work." Special Agent Thompson said impatiently.

"Yes, sir." Mark took the Bible from Chris and opened it. "My first clue was what Chris noticed. The Bible didn't belong here. And look. There was a handwritten list of verses folded and tucked in the back."

"So, every one of those verses makes up the encryption key? That doesn't make sense – it would be too much to remember or type, and most criminals are lazy." Agent Battle pointed out.

"You're right. I looked up all of the verses in the list and wrote them down. Here, look at the list." Mark handed Chris a sheet from a legal pad with a list of handwritten Bible verses. Throughout the verses were circled words, numbers, and lists of names scratched in the margin.

"So where is the secret in all of this?"

"The first thing I noticed was that the verses weren't in the order they come in the Bible. They looked random. That made me think there had to be something that they all had in common. I played with the numbers of the verses and chapters, but that didn't work. I highlighted all of the names and then noticed that all the verses had a 'bad guy' from a Bible story. In fact, Jamison had taken the time to put the verses in alphabetical order by the name of the bad guy. So I took all of the names and typed them in. I got it on my second try – he didn't use any capitalization for the names, and no spaces between. So his pass phrase was 'beastcaindelilahgoliath-herodjudas'."

"Clever Jackson. You and Agent Battle can clean up the mess you made of my conference room and then start going through the data Jamison was nice enough to save for us."

As their boss walked out of the room, the new partners looked at each other for a moment then they turned to opposite ends of the room and started stacking up the papers, magazines, books that Jackson had spread around the room.

"Do you always make this much of a mess?" Battle asked.

"I didn't think it was a mess. I was just trying to see if I could find a pattern."

"I can't think with clutter. I thought an Air Force guy would be a little more organized."

"I am organized, but that doesn't mean I'd pass inspection in a Marine barracks."

"No, you wouldn't. So where do we take all of this?"

"Back to the Cyber Crimes area. Come on, I'll show you where we work."

The two agents each made a couple of trips carrying boxes back to a large room. The space was filled with cubicles, all just high enough to give some privacy when seated.

"So what's with all of this junk on everyone's desks?" Battle asked.

"What do you mean?"

"This." Battle said as she picked up a can of Diet Pepsi wrapped in an R2-D2-shaped plastic holder.

"That's not junk, that's ambiance. I don't like this place to look too government-issue."

"Looks like none of you in this area are government-issue," Battle commented as she held the R2-D2 holder with one hand and pointed to a black T-shirt pinned to the inside of Jackson's cubicle just above the desk.

"What does 'I am the Fed' mean?" Battle asked as Jackson reclaimed his drink and took a swallow of the now-warm Pepsi.

"I was 'spotted' at DEFCON this summer" (*p. 317).

"You let your cover be blown?"

"I didn't have a 'cover.' I'm not a field agent, at least not in Las Vegas." Jackson sat down in his chair and looked at Battle. "So do you have a PC at home?"

"Yes."

"Figures. What operating system do you use?"

"Okay, I know where this is going. You want to know if I'm 'geek' enough to work here. I'll give you 10 questions, and then I'm done. But first, I want to ask you just two questions."

"I can handle that. What's your question?" Agent Jackson responded.

"Have you ever had to fire your sidearm in the field?"

"No."

Battle allowed her face to show her disappointment at the first answer. She also realized she didn't start at the beginning. "Have you even had to draw your sidearm in the field?"

"No."

With a roll of her eyes, Battle walked over and sat in the extra chair in Jackson's work area. "You're just what I expected. And if you want to ask, my answer to both of those would be 'Yes' – and both in my first week."

They stared at each other for a moment. Then Jackson broke the silence.

"How about if we just go get some pizza for lunch? I'll skip the geek questions."

GETTING STARTED

Tuesday, 3:30 p.m.

Pavel sat down at the desk in his room at the Houston JW Marriot. He knew this job was a big deal for Vlad because of the nice hotel room and the complicated logistics. Vlad had him fly to Houston by way of New York, then a day in Chicago just waiting in another hotel room. Now he was supposed to get settled in Houston and wait for Vlad to come pick him up the next day. Vlad had told him they would have a couple of others working with them on this job. Pavel's only other U.S. trip with Vlad had been DEFCON in Las Vegas. That was a simple, but long flight with no side trips.

Pavel knew that this was the continuation of the work they had done back in Chisinau a couple of weeks before. He didn't know what else Vlad had learned after he left him at the hotel that day. He also didn't know exactly what Vlad wanted him to do in Houston.

He was just told to bring whatever technical tools he needed for a network penetration. Pavel had an idea how to figure out some of the details.

Pavel reached into his backpack and pulled out an IBM Thinkpad. He pressed the power button and started fishing through his backpack while he waited to see what kind of operating system was loaded.

"Windows – typical," he mumbled to himself when the familiar splash screen appeared. He pulled out his CD case and started looking for his Ubuntu install disk. As he flipped through the case, his mind drifted. When Pavel left the hotel in Chisinau, he had to leave his laptop with Vlad. The next day they met at a coffee shop and Vlad returned his laptop, along with this Thinkpad.

"Consider this payment for the help in the hotel room," Vlad had told him. "Stepan won't be needing it."

Pavel knew what that meant as soon as he heard it. But now the reality started to settle in. Pavel was a hacker for Vlad. That meant writing custom Trojan code and root kits for Vlad's "projects." Pavel had even broken into several networks in the last couple of years. The trip to Las Vegas for DEFCON had been part payment from Vlad and part new assignment. Pavel had played tech-interpreter for his boss. Vlad could speak flawless English, but he couldn't last more than a few minutes talking "tech" with a true hacker.

So now I'm working for higher stakes, he said to himself. As soon as he said it he asked the next question. *How high are the stakes if people are dying?* This was the first job he worked on that he knew left people dead. Ever since Vlad recruited him, Pavel knew his employer was tough. Now he knew that he would kill. Pavel couldn't decide if he was excited, scared, or both by the rules of this game.

He blinked a few times and realized that he hadn't moved while his mind wandered. He turned his attention back to the laptop. He brought his hands to the keyboard and became aware of his heart beginning to beat harder in his chest. Just the idea of digging into Vlad's plan made him nervous. Actually beginning to do it had created an involuntary response in heart rate. He pushed on and fished through his backpack for his BackTrack 4 CD. As he worked, his hands began to sweat. After a few more keystrokes he paused again.

If I learn something and then let the wrong information slip in a conversation, I'm gone, he thought to himself. *I would be a 'loose end' for Vlad.* Vlad had trusted him more lately. The fact that he was sitting in the hotel room pointed to his greater confidence. *But is it worth the risk?*

Pavel chose caution. He ejected the BackTrack 4 CD and powered down the laptop. As he sat in the chair staring blankly at the wall, he could feel his heart rate slow and the nervous energy dissipate. "At least I should know some more about this place before we get started," he said aloud to himself. Pavel returned the CD to his backpack and pulled out his own laptop. Soon he was connected to the hotel Wi-Fi and doing Google searches for local television stations and newspapers. He spent the next hour trolling through local news stories, blog sites, and Twitter entries about Houston.

THE ACQUISITION
Wednesday, 12:05 p.m.

As Michael Resol approached his turn off the 610 loop, he gave a half-hearted shoulder check and then reached for his right turn indicator. His gaze came back to the front of the car, and he startled as his windshield wipers made a loud, dry rubbing sound in front of him. He brought his focus from the car in front of him to the motion of the wipers he had mistakenly turned on. Just then he saw the brake lights and telltale rise in the bumper of the car immediately in front of him as it quickly slowed. Michael slammed on his brakes and held on as his ABS took over and slowed him down. The sound of screeching tires from behind told him he was about to be hit. Michael watched as the nose of an old GMC pickup lurched down in his rear view mirror. And then – they all stopped. Michael put his head on his steering wheel as his wipers continued to count out a loud, dry, rubbing beat.

"Come on, pull yourself together Resol!" Michael said aloud. He turned off the wipers and started to slowly make his way off the highway.

Michael walked into the Starbucks at the appointed time. The efforts of an army of retail specialists to create a comfortable coffee shop were lost on him. He nervously scanned the patrons as he walked past the product displays and approached the counter. He noted a group of college-age kids gathered around an assortment of iPods, cell phones, and a laptop spread across a table in one corner. Nearby, two ladies were sipping their drinks and talking rather loudly about a movie they had just seen. In another corner was a man alone reading a newspaper. There was a cup of coffee and a book sitting on the table in front of him.

Was that the one? he thought. Staring wasn't an option. He'd check again as soon as he –

"What can I get for you today?"

"What? Oh…uh…just a coffee."

"Which one sir?"

"Uh…just your coffee of the day."

"Which one? We have three."

"The strongest you make."

"What size?"

"Right…large, no Venti, I guess."

"Room for cream?"

"No. Just coffee. Thanks." Michael tried to control himself and even managed a half-smile as he concluded the complicated $2 transaction. He was too nervous to even order a plain coffee. He fumbled with the cash as he paid, took his drink and turned to approach the man in the corner by himself.

There it is - 'Takedown', Michael confirmed for himself as he drew closer and could read the cover of the book on the table.

"That looks like an interesting book."

Vlad lowered the newspaper and smiled slightly. "It is a very interesting book. Have you heard of it before?"

"No," Michael answered as he pulled up a chair.

Vlad folded the newspaper neatly and placed it in an empty chair to his left. He slid the book slightly toward Michael. "It's a true story about a hacker who gets caught. Personally, I think the author embellishes too much. But it is still instructive. In fact, I have an idea for a variation on the hack used in the story."

"What do you mean?" Michael responded, concentrating carefully as he put his coffee on the table, trying to control the shaking in his hands.

"In the book, the hacker finds a program running on a computer. He used that program to connect to and manipulate the system. In fact, the computer he broke into was one owned by the man who eventually wrote the book. I want you to help me do something like that with your employer."

"That's going to be hard," Michael protested. "We got some kind of government contract last year and ever since then they've been installing firewalls, scanning our e-mail, and watching where we surf on the Internet. I even got in trouble for hitting a personal site on my lunch hour."

"That is not a problem. When someone installs strong defenses, the best method of attack is to just avoid them," Vlad answered confidently. He tapped the book lightly. "Look inside the book later. There are detailed instructions you will need. You will also find the first part of the agreed payment. I need you to use some of the payment to buy a wireless router. You will install it in your office building on the side closest to the parking lot. Just find an empty cubical and plug it into the network and hide it under the desk. Don't worry about any encryption settings. Be sure to change the SID from the default and don't allow it to broadcast. Like I said, just read the details I've left for you in there." Vlad explained with a casual wave of his hand toward the book.

"Next, you'll need this." Vlad reached in his sport coat pocket and pulled out a pen.

"There is a USB drive inside this pen - just pull the cap off and connect it to your boss's PC and run the program called 'svchost.exe'."

Michael's face screwed up in a nervous convulsion at the order. "There's no way I can run a program on my boss's computer! How am I supposed to get access to it?"

"That's your problem. Don't worry about his antivirus software. This is a custom-built Trojan that was made for this job - it's never been used in the wild."

Michael took the pen and the book. The pen went into his shirt pocket. He opened the book and found an envelope inside. He shoved it roughly into the back pocket of his blue jeans and stared at the cover of the book while he screwed up the courage for another question.

"I really don't know how to get this onto my boss's computer. What if I get caught?"

"Getting caught is your problem. Getting the job done is what you are paid for," Vlad responded.

Michael didn't have the sense to know that he shouldn't persist. "But they could trace this to me." Then he pressed just a little farther. "Wouldn't that lead back to you?"

Vlad's face was like stone. "It will lead back to no one." Vlad stared straight at Michael. Michael didn't perceive the danger in that response. Vlad then decided this one needed some help or the work would not get done.

"You know your boss's habits and temperament. Just watch and you will find an opportunity. The part you want to be careful about is installing the access point. You'll want to do that after hours. Tell me how you access your office."

"Access, uh, oh, how I get in?" Michael was trying to keep it together. "I have a badge. Here, I can show you." Michael pulled a credit card sized plastic badge out of his pocket and handed it to Vlad.

Vlad looked at the picture of Michael with his name at the bottom and the words "Network Support" at the top. He flipped the card over and then returned it to Michael.

"So you have a proximity access system?"

"Yeah, I just wave it at the sensor at each door."

"Is there a guard?"

"No. We have a receptionist at the front desk," Michael answered.

"Does anyone read the logs from your proximity card system?" Vlad continued.

"I think the security company might, I've never checked."

"So who is in charge of building security?"

"I think they outsource it," Michael answered.

"Since your company was recently acquired, have there been any new contractors working there?"

"How did you know about the acqui – uh, never mind. Yeah we've brought in some new techs lately. We've been getting rid of a bunch of our computers and installing new systems. They want us to match the big corporate standard."

"Can you get a badge for a contractor?" Vlad was getting weary of leading Michael along.

Michael sat for a moment and stared. "I think so. When they work late, they return them at the front desk. I might be able to get one after the receptionist leaves for the day."

"Use a contractor badge when you go in to make this change. That way if there is any suspicion, it will go back to the contracting firm" (*p. 203).

"Okay. I'll try that," Michael answered with no sound of confidence in his voice.

"Don't try it. Do it," Vlad corrected. "When you are done, we can meet here again in a week and I'll give you the rest of the payment."

"How will I know if I did everything right?" Michael asked.

"If I'm here next week at the same time, then you'll know you did everything right."

"And if you're not here, that means something didn't work?"

"If something doesn't work, I'll find you. But you don't want that to happen."

"What if I need to contact you?" Michael asked.

"There are instructions in that envelope. There is a number to call and a phrase to say. Then I'll call you. Write your cell phone number down." With that Vlad pushed a slip of paper toward Michael. He quickly complied.

Vlad picked up the paper and put it in his shirt pocket. "One other interesting point about your new book - the hacker gets caught in the end. Don't make that mistake, Michael."

With that, Vlad stood, picked up his newspaper and neatly returned the chair to its place at the table.

"By the way, make sure you don't leave any finger prints on the access point. That's the first thing they check."

Michael looked down, briefly trying to decide if paying off his gambling debt would be worth dealing with whoever "they" turned out to be. He looked up in time to see Vlad walk out the door of the coffee shop. Michael sat there staring at the coffee he had bought, but not touched.

TWO

JUST ANOTHER DAY

Friday, 5:00 p.m.

For the uninitiated, Bob Falken's bedroom looked like part-NASA control room and part high-tech junkyard. To Bob, it was both lab and sanctuary – the one place where he was in control of his world (*p. 318).

There was a constant hum from the combined sounds of cooling fans in nearly a dozen computers. There were various pieces of networking gear, cables, computer parts, and tools spread in even distribution across nearly all available space. Where there was an occasional gap, dirty clothes and DVD movie cases filled the void.

It was warmer in this room than in any other part of the house, and it smelled like a college dorm. For Bob, there was no better place to be. From here he could become anyone he wanted. He could travel anywhere in the world. For that matter, he could travel anywhere in a number of virtual worlds as well.

Outside of this room people ignored him, at best. More often they harassed him. In this space, he had power to control and remake himself.

Very few people were trusted to enter this part of Bob's world. In fact, only his dad and Leon were regular visitors. Bob's dad, George, was a retired engineer. He and his son lived in a middle-class neighborhood in Houston, Texas. Their neighborhood hadn't looked new since the 1970s when they moved there after George got his job. George had spent the majority of his life working on a variety of obscure pieces of the space program. Some of his designs had even orbited the earth in the forms of door components and panel covers. Nothing he designed had ever failed. If only his family had worked out as well.

He didn't know much about his son's activities. In fact, he was pretty sure that he didn't want to know all that happened in Bob's room. Since his wife had died when Bob was only 12, George had done all he could to encourage his son's interests.

Bob's natural affinity for anything digital pulled him farther into his own world. Only his friend Leon could bring Bob out into the "real" world as George called it. But to Bob, any time out of his room was just a distraction from his favorite reality. Bob carried scars from the loss of his mother. He and his dad were both very lonely, and neither knew how to help the other deal with the loss. That failure created other losses as they both drew into their own worlds. One world had been a plodding career that was really a self-sacrifice for the son. The other was a search for a connection and feeling of completeness that was stolen when he was too young.

The world Bob embraced was full of computers, networks, hacking, and the personas he created. For George, the closest he came to peace was when Bob was at home. His son was safe and appeared satisfied. *At least he's not running with more dangerous kids*, he had thought to himself on many an evening as he listened to the hum of computers and the clicking of a keyboard. George had spent quite a bit on computers for Bob over the years. But most of his spare cash flow for the last year and half had gone to Rice University where Bob was a sophomore. George knew that there was more gear in that room than what he had paid for. His son was supplementing his income somewhere, and it certainly wasn't from a regular job.

Drip...drip...drip...

The living room was silent except for the sound of the leaky kitchen faucet George kept meaning to fix. George sat in his favorite chair. His wife had bought the chair for him years ago as a Father's Day present. It was worn and dirty, but George would never replace it. He could sit in that chair and instantly remember the happier days when his wife was alive and his son was a little boy.

George turned the page of the year-old issue of *Popular Mechanics* he was perusing and then reached up to adjust his near-terminal combover. Right as his mouth opened in a yawn...

Slam! George startled and tore the page from the magazine at the sound of Bob's bedroom door closing.

"Gotta go, Dad – I'm late to meet Leon."

There was a blur as Bob rushed through the house and out the front door. George looked about, never quite catching up with the image that flew past him while his mind was still processing the sound from down the hall. His mouth opened to dispense some fatherly advice about being safe. But then it closed – no use talking to an already empty house. George held up the now-torn magazine page to finish the article as he heard his old car start.

Bob backed the 1986 Buick Electra Estate station wagon out of the driveway and started down the street. The white paint on the car had long ago acquired a dull, chalky patina. The faux-wood sides were peeling and rust created a kind of south Texas lace around all the edges of the car. For Bob, the beast of a machine was perfect. He had plenty of room for his pack-rat habits, including installing all manner of portable computer equipment in the car over the last couple of years. As he drove, he barely looked down the road while he turned on his old Toshiba Libretto laptop that was bolted to the dash of the car. Bob had a habit of wardriving whenever he could. He was constantly on the lookout for open wireless networks, and today was a good day to try out the new antenna he had installed the night before (*p. 175). Bob turned out onto Kirby Drive and drove down the street to the local Anime store. When he arrived, he suspended the laptop and made sure he locked the car.

Inside he met up with his best friend, Leon. They had relied on each other since high school. Both were equally bright, constantly testing themselves with anything they could hack. Leon had better people skills – to Bob's frustration since it meant he did better social hacks. Bob could hold his own on anything with a keyboard. The Anime store was the appointed meeting place for the day. Bob was a paranoid young man. His time online had taught him how easy it was to be traced. He didn't like leaving a trail in either the digital world or the physical one.

"Hey, did you drive yourself in circles over here?" Leon asked as he spotted Bob walking in the front door.

"You know I'm not going to let anyone follow me."

"Dude, no one is going to follow you just because they'd have to keep looking at the butt-ugly car you drive."

"Hey, the price was right! It was a freebie from my dad, and it's got plenty of room for my gear. Come on. I got that new directional antenna installed last night. I want to see if it works better than the Pringles can (*p. 183)." Bob started walking back to the front door. Leon followed after. They were soon crawling through Houston traffic on their way to the Galleria.

"So do you have the riddles worked out for 'Capture the Flag'?" Leon asked. "I've got some, but I need help to finish. I think it's going to take us a while to come up with 20 of them."

"No, I haven't got any done since yesterday," Bob responded as he drove and watched the Libretto screen. "We'll dream up the rest after we find eight more open access points. I've got 11 good ones we haven't used before already."

"That's only 19 access points. You just said there were 20 riddles. Aren't we going to plant 20 flags?" Leon asked.

"We're planting 20 flags. One of them is going to be at my house."

Leon turned with a surprised look. "Why would you want to have all of the 2600 hackers pounding on your network? Are you setting up a honeypot to track someone?"

"No. I need plausible deniability," Bob responded. "And don't you ever tell anyone I said that" (*p. 318).

"You need plausible deniability for what?"

"I want to try a hack on Groom Lake. Remember when Gary McKinnon was busted for breaking into U.S. government computers from London? I think he got a lot more information than what was told. I think he found a link between the NASA computers he hacked and the Groom Lake facility. I want to take a shot at the Groom Lake network, but I don't want it to be traceable to me and get Dad in trouble. By putting a flag at my house, I'll have a default system that's been hacked by 20-plus hackers from around town. Any one of them could have been the source!"

"Your plan sounds too clever," Leon answered. "I think you'd do better jacking into one of the country club houses with an open network."

"I'll try that as soon as I have a car that looks like it belongs in a country club," retorted Bob.

Leon turned quickly and looked behind them. "Hey, I think that's the second time I've seen that PT Cruiser since we left the store." Leon didn't care about who was near them, but he knew he could tweak his friend by playing on his paranoia.

"Don't start with me. We've had three PT Cruisers near us since we left – and no repeats." Bob answered. "Don't laugh." Bob pointed a finger at his friend. "There are people out there watching for people with skills like ours. If you don't start paying attention, you're going to find yourself in a room with no windows and a couple of NSA guys 'recruiting' you for a job."

"Bob, it's a scary enough world without your paranoia."

"It's not paranoia when they really are out to get you."

Leon knew there was no hope. This conversation was an old one. From there they went on mostly in silence. Bob drove, spending more time watching the cars behind him than the ones in front. Leon spent his time watching the number of unsecured wireless access points increment up on Bob's laptop.

They pulled into the Galleria parking garage and found a place to park. To Leon's continuing frustration, the space was in the opposite corner of the garage from the entrance to the mall. He knew that it wasn't worth asking Bob to find a closer space. This gave him a clear line-of-site to his car and gave him room to meander through the garage watching for eyes that might be tracking him. Bob was a good friend. Putting up with paranoia was the price Leon had to pay for that friendship.

Soon they were inside and making their way down to the food court. As they approached Ninfa Express, they could see that the usual crowd was supplemented with extra people this time. This was the monthly 2600 club meeting. Leon and Bob were regular attendees. Today, they were leading the prep for the first Capture the Flag war drive put on by the Houston chapter (*p. 319).

Leon sat down at an empty table. Bob walked to the center of their group of acquaintances (there weren't any real "friends" in this club). Leon always marveled that in this one setting Bob didn't have any problem talking to people. Leon looked around at the eclectic group of about 30 people. There were a couple of Goths, a Preppie, some geeky-looking teenagers, and even a Kicker. That was unique. Leon had spotted the thin guy in the cowboy hat at a couple of previous meetings. Leon got out of his chair and walked over and found him pounding on a Mac Power book with a DEFCON sticker on the top.

"How's it going'?" Leon asked as he sat down in the empty chair.

"Fine. Name's Jeb," he said while extending a hand. "I've seen you at all of the sessions I've been to."

"Yeah. Bob and I are regulars." Leon pointed to Bob at the table near the center of the group. "What brings you here?"

"I've been hacking on computers since my dad bought a PC to keep the books on our farm near Conroe," Jeb answered. "I don't want to be in the family business, so I've been trying to learn all I can so I can get a tech job."

"How'd you get the DEFCON sticker? Did you go this year?"

"No – I wish I could. I just picked it up from a guy I met at one of these meetings."

Leon started to comment on the Mac, but was interrupted by Bob who had now stood up.

"Hey everybody! Looks like we've got a pretty good crew. Today we're going to set the rules for Capture the Flag," Bob started. Slowly the talking stopped and everyone looked up from many different sticker-covered laptops to watch Bob (*p. 319).

"It looks like word got out since our last meeting. I don't recognize quite a few faces. If anyone here spots a Fed in the group, speak up" (*p. 317).

There was a moment of silence followed by a few snickers as everyone looked around and tried to take the measure of each other. Bob noted a couple of faces that he didn't recognize. One of them was Jeb. *Since when does a hacker wear a cowboy hat?* he thought to himself.

"All right. There are going to be 20 flags for the contest. The flag is a CyberBob icon file."

"What's a CyberBob?" came a rather meek question from the side of the gathering. There were a few more snickers as most of the crowd quickly noted the "newbie" in the group.

Bob was quick to respond. "It's another piece of the Hollywood conspiracy against me." This brought some eye rolls from a few "old timers" who knew Bob's reputation.

"Really, first they used my full name for the professor in *War Games.* Then they used my first name for this chat icon in *The Net.* And don't think I didn't get the message when they killed – " At that point Leon stood up.

"Like Bob said, it's an icon from the movie *The Net.* Just Google it, and don't worry about any conspiracies targeting our fearless leader here. I'll keep an eye on him."

Leon sat down, smiled and shook his head. Bob didn't seem to know he probably should have been embarrassed. He just kept going with the instructions.

"Leon is going to help me set up the contest and serve as the judge." Bob pointed at Leon as everyone in the meeting gave him one more look.

Bob continued. "Here are the rules. No damaging systems you find open. No dropping Trojans or using Trojans that you find already installed. We will only put the icon files in system folders, so don't go poking around where you don't belong. Don't hack into systems – we will only drop the files on boxes that have netbios running. They deserve to be used if they haven't at least locked that down. Finally, pull off the icon files you find. Don't leave a copy for someone who comes after you. There will only be 20 files out there, and the one who comes back here with the most wins.

"You will get 20 riddles to solve. Each one will give you a clue about the location of the unsecured access point. All flags will be located in Houston proper, so don't worry about suburbs. You can use whatever equipment you think you need. I suggest a good GPS, a good external antenna, and a copy of *NetStumbler*" (*p. 176).

Leon stood up again to add a little more. "Don't try to be clever and bring your own copy of the icon files. We're going to give each its own MD5 hash, so I will know if you have the genuine file."

"And no hacking the judge's PC for the MD5 hash files, or trying to work out a collision on your PS3," Bob added. "The contest will begin next Friday at 5:00 p.m. Meet here at noon next Saturday with the files you find. Leon and I have some more flags to drop still. We'll post the riddles on the Web site at the start time. But I'll give you one now to get you started" (*p. 320).

Bob passed out a piece of paper to everyone at the meeting. A single sentence was printed on each:

Look for the first flag between the sheriff and the Merry Men's leader.

"And don't try to find the file for this clue now. We won't drop the file at this location until Friday," Bob added before sitting back down.

With that, the meeting broke up into a dozen small conversations. An outsider would have seen only an odd group of people clustered around different tables. However, there was actually a self-organizing structure to the groups. The more stickers and the newer the laptop a person had, the more people seemed to be drawn to them. Bob and Leon spent some more time talking to people and looking at the new gear some had brought. Soon it was getting close to 8:00 p.m. and they still had work to do. They made their way back to the parking garage. Leon humored Bob and walked down and back one wing of the mall first, to make sure no one was following them.

"Can you do some more war-driving tonight?" Bob asked as he started the car.

"Sure. I'm good for a couple of hours."

At the end of the evening they had enough open access points in their list. They parked outside the Anime store where the day started and worked on riddles for an hour. Progress wasn't as fast as they liked.

"Let's knock off and try again tomorrow," Leon suggested. "I want to get back and put in some Halo time. How about I stop by tomorrow?"

"Sure, we can also get some more drive time in to see if we can find more open systems. Maybe we'll find some that are easier to write riddles to match," Bob agreed.

THE INSTALLATION
Saturday, 10:00 a.m.

Michael Resol walked out of the Wal-Mart with a new wireless access point. He had read through the instructions his contact had given him enough times in the last two days to memorize them. He had already spent most of the $25,000 that was in the envelope Vlad passed him in the coffee shop. He knew that he should have used more than just half of it to pay down his debts from gambling. "I can take care of the rest of my debt with the second installment next weekend," he told himself as he put the access point – and the new 30-inch HD flat screen monitor into the trunk of his car.

As Michael drove to the office, he thought about how lucky he had been the day before. He had spent all afternoon watching for an opportunity. At 3:45 p.m. he saw his chance. His boss got a call Michael guessed was from his wife. He heard something about a teacher conference at the school, a suspension and then the rush of wind as his boss stormed out of his office and out of the building. Michael waited for about five minutes, and then took some papers into his boss's office to leave on his desk. Sure enough – he hadn't locked his workstation. Michael made sure that no one was watching and sat down at the desk. He right-clicked on the desktop and selected "Properties." His boss had a password-protected screen saver set to go off after 20 minutes – just like company policy. Michael disabled the screensaver and turned off the monitor, then quickly walked out (*p. 243). He would take care of the Trojan on Saturday when there were fewer people in the office.

Michael pulled into the parking lot to find only a few cars there and a couple of motorcycles. As he walked to the front door, he pulled out the contractor badge he had found on Thursday afternoon. In fact, it had surprised Michael how easy it was to get. He had never noticed it before. The receptionist kept a box at the front desk with a slot in the top. Next to it was a sign for visitors who stayed after she left for the day that read "Please return badges here." A quick check by Michael revealed there was no lock on the box. He had found several visitor badges and two contractor badges.

His pulse quickened slightly as the door beeped and the light turned green when he swiped the badge. Michael first made his way to the break room for a soda, and then on to his desk. He tried to act as normal as he could as he walked to his part of the building.

On the way, he counted three people, all with heads-down, pounding on their keyboards. Michael did the same for a while.

After about half an hour with no one moving around the building, he got up quietly and walked into his boss's office. He slid into the chair and turned the monitor on. There it was – an open desktop. He pulled the pen out of his shirt pocket and removed the cap. The USB connector slid easily into the front of the PC. Soon a window popped up on the monitor with the contents of the new drive.

A sudden sound was enough to make him dive for the floor. Michael froze and listened…just someone at the copier down the hall. He took a deep breath, got slowly back into the chair, and scanned the cubicles around him. Nothing. "Where is Sydney Bristow when you need her?" he muttered to himself as he looked back to the monitor (*p. 320).

He double-clicked on the "svchost.exe" icon and waited. Nothing happened. *I hope that's what was supposed to happen*, he thought to himself. Next Michael had to cover up his change from the day before. He right-clicked on the desktop again and selected "Properties." He made sure to select the same screensaver that his boss had been running and re-enabled the password lockout at 20 minutes. He started to get up, and then remembered the papers he had placed on his boss's desk yesterday as a cover for his presence in the office. He gathered up the papers and walked out of the office. *It won't be smart to leave evidence that I was in here after he left*, he thought.

Michael went back to his desk and picked up his backpack. All was still pretty quiet in the office. He walked to the row of empty cubicles in his section. In the third one he checked, he found a spare network patch cord connected to the jack, but no PC. He set his backpack down and pulled out the access point, some duct tape, a rag, and his laptop. He powered on the laptop and connected it to the access point with the patch cord he had found. While he waited for his PC to boot, he connected the power cord to the outlet in the cubicle and powered up the access point. After his laptop was up, he opened his browser and logged into the access point with the default password. Out of his pocket he pulled the crumpled instructions that had been in the envelope he got on Thursday.

He followed the instructions, disabling the SID broadcast, changing the admin password to "penguin" and renaming the SID to "f0rb1dd3n." He made sure that logging was turned "off" on the access point. He then disconnected his laptop and plugged the access point into the empty network jack with the patch cord. Michael looked around – no movement, and he could hear some music coming from one of the programmer's cubicles. He crawled under the desk and wiped down the access point with the rag. He duct-taped the access point to the underside of the work surface and then took the time to wipe down the network cable as well.

Michael went back to his desk and worked for another hour. He had a hard time getting any real work done. His hands shook slightly as he typed. He was too excited thinking about how he was about to frame his boss, and make an easy $50,000.

THR33

IN COUNTRY

Saturday, 10:45 p.m.

As he stood outside the hotel waiting for Vlad, Pavel shifted restlessly under the weight of his backpack. He had only been there for five minutes and already he was sweating. The Houston night was humid and the temperature was still close to ninety degrees.

"Why do people want to live in a place like this?" Pavel muttered to himself as he tossed the last of a cigarette to the ground.

A blue, late-model van with no side or rear windows pulled through the circular hotel drive and stopped not far from where Pavel stood. Pavel walked casually across the drive and climbed in the side door after an unseen occupant opened it for him. As Pavel took his seat, he surveyed the occupants. Vlad was sitting in the seat next to him. Pavel recognized the driver – it was Andrei – whom he had little use for. As Pavel turned to the passenger in the front, Vlad started introductions in English.

"You know Andrei. This is Haki. He lives in the States and does occasional work for me. He was kind enough to arrange for our transportation and equipment on this job."

Haki turned in his seat to look at Pavel. Pavel's and Haki's eyes met and they both nodded a slight acknowledgement of the other. Pavel ignored Andrei, turned to Vlad and said in English, "Why did you bring the gorilla on this trip?"

"You better be careful. He's been studying English," Vlad answered with a slight smile. "You don't know what words he already understands."

Pavel looked at Andrei and saw no reaction.

"I know he can use a gun, but I don't see language skills in his future."

Vlad ignored Pavel, turned to Andrei and ordered in Russian, "Let's get started. We have a schedule to follow."

Andrei put the van in gear and pulled out of the drive as Haki punched in an address on a hand-held GPS.

Pavel turned to look at the back of the van. Behind him was a small work surface extending from one side of the van. An empty bucket was turned over and looked like it would serve as a chair.

"I thought you had a bigger budget for this job," Pavel commented.

"I do. The van will serve its purpose, and I want to make sure that we can abandon it quickly if necessary and not leave any gear behind."

Pavel continued his survey of the van as they drove, noticing that Vlad had a large duffle bag at his feet.

"How do I do this, on site?" Pavel asked.

"No, you'll need your wireless gear. You brought your antenna?" Vlad's question had the sound of an order.

"Always do," Pavel answered.

"Ding Ding. Prepare for a – right turn – in – point seven miles."

"So, if you've done so many field operations, why the GPS besides the pure geek factor?" Pavel asked.

"None of us have been in Houston before. Haki is based out of Dallas now. A little storm chased him out of New Orleans."

"That was no little storm. It was nothing like wha – " Haki tried to protest before Vlad allowed a slight grin and continued explaining to Pavel.

"We don't want to be wandering around town. A vehicle that is driving in circles will attract attention we don't need."

Pavel appeared to accept the explanation. But he knew Vlad liked high-tech toys enough to find an excuse to use gadgets like a GPS whenever he could. They rode along in silence for a few minutes. Haki and Andrei spoke briefly in Russian. Pavel listened quietly as Haki translated directions to Andrei as they drove.

After about 15 more minutes of driving, they turned into the parking lot of a small office park. The lot was surrounded by trees and nicely landscaped. There were a few cars clustered close to a couple of the low, white buildings, but for the most part, the lot was empty.

Andrei parked the van in the corner of the lot at the edge of the office park. They had a direct line of sight to the office where Michael had installed the wireless router just the day before. Near the roof at the corner of the building was a simple sign that read "3DNF, Inc."

Vlad began snapping orders in Russian, "Time to start. Andrei, Haki, I want you outside. Keep an eye on our perimeter, but don't draw any attention."

Vlad reached into his duffle bag and pulled out three small radios and gave one each to Andrei and Haki.

"Channel seven," Vlad noted as he adjusted his own radio.

Andrei and Haki did the same. Then, Haki opened the glove box in front of him and pulled out two Glock 19 pistols. He handed one to Andrei. They both checked the action of their firearms. Pavel noted that Andrei was quicker and moved with greater confidence.

After they both had left, Pavel pulled his backpack up from the floor in front of him. Several key chains, a small flashlight, and a broken USB thumb drive jangled on their lanyard clips hanging from the well-worn bag. Pavel pulled out his laptop. This was no ordinary laptop. An executive dashing through an airport would be left gasping for air in half a concourse if forced to carry this brick. Pavel had bought the custom-built machine after his first job with Vlad two years ago. It had two processors, two optical drives (one to burn CD's while the other played a DVD), more memory than most servers, and an odd collection of stickers.

Pavel maneuvered to the little work surface in the back of the van and sat down on the overturned bucket. As he waited for his laptop to boot, he dug around in his bag for a cable. He pulled out a small cable attached to a wide, flat piece of plastic about the size of a pocketknife. He connected the cable to a round jack on a card inside one of the accessory slots on the computer.

"Here – Can you get this near a window?" Pavel asked as he handed the other end of the cable to Vlad.

"Your cable isn't going to reach to a window," Vlad answered as he took the cable. He balanced the end on the back of the seat that Pavel had been sitting in and pointed it toward the front of the van – and the office building.

Pavel logged into his laptop and turned to Vlad. "You never answered my question about the gorilla. But first I want to know why we are here."

"You were there when we tossed Stepan Senn's room in Chisinau. The information we got off your new spare laptop, plus the instructions I got from Stepan were clear. This job requires a hands-on visit to ensure success."

"But I thought all we are doing is dropping a Trojan on a computer so we can remote in and steal some information. You've had me do that three times for different jobs just since we were in Stepan's hotel room. Why did we have to come all the way to Houston?"

Vlad drew a slow breath and looked at Pavel carefully. He was taking the measure of his young lieutenant. He wasn't ready to trust him – at least as much as Vlad was capable of trusting anyone.

"Stepan was working on a project for his employer to gain access to information that 3DNF is working on. 3DNF specializes in querying large sets of unstructured data."

"They were just bought by Kimeron, a large U.S. defense contractor. Kimeron wants them to get the brain power 3DNF has built up recently. Think about it – the U.S. government has the world's largest sets of unstructured data from all of their electronic eavesdropping. We are here because 3DNF is a doorway to that data. It's too risky to break into a U.S. government network. But 3DNF is a new acquisition for a defense contractor. The defense contractor is a trusted network – and that makes 3DNF the doorway we are going to use." Vlad could have continued, but Pavel cut him off.

"That doesn't sound like something worth a visit," Pavel noted.

Vlad was sharp in his response. "It is worth a visit. But your job isn't to decide what it is worth. Your job is to deal with the technical variables we will find. I need a reliable way into this network when we are done. That way in has to be undetected, and allow us to pull down a lot of data."

Vlad gave him a moment to be sure the point was understood, and then he continued. "Our front door is a wireless router and some duct tape under a desk. We will use that to jump from 3DNF to Kimeron. Once inside, we install a reliable back door that won't set off alarms."

"When we are done, there will be a nice payoff from Stepan's employer."

Pavel paused to be sure Vlad was done. Then he asked, "Is there anything else I need to know before I begin?"

"No. I'll make sure that you know what you need to as we go along," Vlad responded.

"What about my first question?" Pavel couldn't help himself.

"Andrei? I would think the answer to that one is obvious. Remember who the target is. I need backup with more skills than just a keyboard. Haki is good, but we need Andrei's talent...and temperament," Vlad added with a slight smile.

With that Pavel turned his attention to his laptop. He set his wireless connection to the settings Vlad had given him and waited for an IP address assignment.

"How long do you want to sit here?" Pavel asked.

Vlad understood the meaning behind Pavel's question to know he was asking if he wanted an aggressive and quick, or quiet and slow scan of the network.

"We won't have to sit here long. Don't run any kind of network scan," Vlad explained as he produced the familiar pocketknife from his sport coat pocket. Pavel could see the USB connector at one end.

"There are two files on this. Copy them both to your computer, and then run the one called 'Achilles.'

Pavel followed instructions and was greeted with a window that had a simple blank box and a 'Connect' button.

"Now what?" Pavel asked as his hands paused over the keyboard.

Vlad tossed a small, folded piece of paper onto the keyboard of Pavel's computer. "Enter the IP address on that," he ordered.

Pavel unfolded the paper and leaned it against the bottom corner of the laptop display. He typed in the address.

```
10.24.53.192
```

A black box filled most of the screen and then a Windows desktop appeared. Pavel turned to Vlad. "I'm sure this is a question I'm not supposed to ask, but how do you know where I should start?"

"Stepan wasn't the only resource on this project. I have other contacts that his firm is paying me to use," Vlad responded.

Pavel looked at Vlad for a moment and quickly saw he had used up his allowance of background questions.

"What do I do next?" Pavel asked as he turned his attention back to the computer he was remote controlling.

"Use the remote computer to pull the other file from your system. Then you will need to start carefully checking out the network for me," Vlad answered.

Pavel knew he was being sloppy, but no one was watching. He enabled the Windows server service on the remote computer, created a share of the root directory, and then went back to the desktop of his own laptop. From there he simply mapped a drive to the new shared folder that had appeared under the name of the target computer.

◑ ◑ ◑

Bob took a quick right and pulled into a small, twenty-four-hour convenience store.

"I need some more Diet Pepsi, and it looks like there is an office park over there." Bob pointed with one hand while he maneuvered the wagon into a space on the edge of parking lot. The car shuddered to a stop and Bob turned his attention to the Libretto bolted to the dash. They had been driving around for the last hour looking for more wireless networks for the scavenger hunt the next weekend. They had plenty of networks, but Leon was the one being difficult this time. He didn't think they had enough "interesting" targets, as he kept explaining with each new find.

Bob and Leon watched as several wireless networks appeared on the screen of the Libretto.

"Will any of these work?" Bob almost complained as he pointed to the NetStumbler display.

"I don't know yet. Let me look with Kismet. You don't see as much when you run just NetStumbler" (*p. 176).

"Let me know what you find. I'm going to go get a drink." The door creaked as Bob got out. Leon pressed the power button on his laptop and waited through the Ubuntu boot sequence. He clicked on his Kismet shortcut and waited for the application to load. He looked up from the laptop and scanned the parking lot. He saw only the usual traffic around a convenience store. Inside he could see Bob making his way to the back near the soft drinks.

Bob pulled two one-liter bottles of his favorite caffeine source from the cooler and walked over to the candy isle. He gave a quick scan of the sugar sources and selected a box of mints. He finished up his purchase and walked back to the wagon.

"Dude! We have our target!" Leon said too loudly as Bob climbed back in the car. Bob half-listened as he threw yet another empty Diet Pepsi bottle in the back seat and replaced it with one of the two he had just bought.

"What did you find?" Bob asked as he leaned over to see what was on Leon's screen. There were seven networks displayed. Four of them matched what Bob had detected on his computer. Three were not set to broadcast so Bob couldn't detect them. Of the new networks, one was not encrypted, and the name was "F0RB1DD3N."

"This one hadn't showed up because we were just running the scan with the Windows box. Kismet catches the ones that aren't broadcasting," Leon noted.

Bob had his chin down and was looking at Leon almost through his eyebrows with a "you don't need to tell me that" look. But instead of saying what he was really thinking, he just observed, "That's not a corporate network name."

"It's not a corporate name, but that doesn't mean it doesn't belong," Leon responded. "This place is full of little tech companies. There are plenty of nerds that work here that would set up something like that."

"Yeah, but why isn't it encrypted?"

"Let's find out," Leon answered as he changed his network settings to receive an IP address from the "F0RB1DD3N" network.

"Load Wireshark. I want to see what else is running on this network," Bob suggested as he reached in the back seat and grabbed his backpack with his main laptop inside. Bob and Leon quickly settled into a zone of typing and reading. The only sounds were from the people in the parking lot walking in and out of the convenience store.

Leon made more progress at first since he had a head start on Bob. Leon followed Bob's suggestion and had Wireshark running. This program would give him an idea of the traffic running on the local wireless network he and Bob were investigating. Leon quickly saw that they were not alone on the network. Someone was transferring a large binary file. He didn't say anything at first. Instead, he changed the settings for Wireshark to do a packet capture so he would have a copy of what was flowing through the network (*p. 207).

Bob didn't like the silence. His fingers began to fly across his keyboard. The sound of his typing was the nerd-equivalent of machine gun fire.

"What are you doing? You can't type that fast!" Leon squawked at Bob.

"Sorry, every hacker movie I've ever seen has the lead nerd pounding on his keyboard like that. I just wanted my scene for the movie."

"Like anyone would want to watch a couple of unemployed nerds drop CyberBob icons," Leon mumbled as he turned back to his monitor.

Bob shrugged and began to browse through his list of utility programs. He was about to click on the "T00Lz" folder when Leon spoke.

"Hey, I see a file transfer. Someone is working late tonight."

"What d'you see?" Bob asked as he leaned over to look at Leon's monitor.

"There's a computer on the wireless network with us. See, he's got a 192.168.1.2 address. I'm 192.168.1.3. He's transferring some kind of binary file to a box at 10.24.53.192. The ten network must be the corporate network."

"Are you doing a packet capture?" Bob asked. Leon looked at him with a 'do you think I'm an idiot' look and said, "Of course."

Bob went back to his "T00Lz" folder and clicked on the SuperScan icon (*p. 186). If someone was transferring a file to the .200 box, then there must be other interesting things in that network. This would be a good bonus site for the CyberBob icon. Once the program loaded, Bob started the scan to explore the 10.24.53.x network and see what he could find (*p. 321).

"What are you doing now?!" Leon yelled at Bob.

"What? I'm just running a network scan," Bob retorted.

"You're being sloppy! Dude, you lit up the subnet. Just because they leave the gate open doesn't mean you have to drive in with a bulldozer."

"If they're dumb enough to have an open Access Point, then they won't watch a SuperScan," Bob responded.

"Fine. I'll filter out your IP so we can see something besides your noise." Leon focused on his laptop. There was a brief quiet in the old Buick while each of them stared at their respective screens.

Bob's wrists looked like they were glued to the front of his laptop as he typed. His skin was so white from years indoors that it nearly glowed in the low light of his monitor. His fingers looked like two spiders reaching for prey as he typed. It took Bob only a few moments to produce a list of computers on the network he was scanning. He left the scan to run and opened a new window from his "Run" box at the bottom of the screen. He typed the first name of a computer that looked like a server followed by the default root path \\3D-FS1\C$ (*p. 249).

He was quickly rewarded with a listing of files and folders. He wasted no time in dragging a copy of the CyberBob icon from his desktop to this new window (*p. 321). He then confirmed with an updated file listing that now contained the bonus flag for their upcoming contest. Bob decided not to tell Leon yet. He wanted to look around a little more so he pulled the SuperScan window back on top to watch the results.

◑ ◑ ◑

Andrei and Haki had each walked in the opposite direction when they got out of the van. It didn't take long to see that the office park was mostly quiet. The few people there were not paying attention to their surroundings. They were on a mission to get to their offices or cars and on with their tasks.

Vlad's two "hired muscle" soon met up next to a grouping of small trees that stood in a landscaped island near the edge of the parking lot.

"Do you really think Vlad needs the protection on this job?" Haki asked in Russian.

"I've learned that when he calls me in on a job, I generally have work." Andrei answered.

"Watch for a while. I'm going to go get some smokes." Andrei pointed to a small store near the office park and started walking along the shadowed edge of the parking lot. Haki stayed in the shadow of the trees where he could see their van and the majority of the parking lot.

Andrei walked into the small store and up to the clerk at the counter.

"Marlboro," he said with a thick accent and held up two fingers. This was one American word he had learned a long time ago.

The clerk turned and retrieved two packs of the requested cigarettes from behind the counter.

"Thirteen seventy-three."

Andrei didn't really understand the clerk, but he fished a twenty-dollar bill out of his wallet from the allotment Vlad had given him earlier that day and slid it across the counter. The clerk gave him his change and Andrei walked out of the store. Andrei paused outside the door and opened the pack. He lit a cigarette and surveyed his surroundings while he took a first drag. There were two cars and a truck at the front of the store. The truck had a woman asleep in the passenger's seat. Both cars were empty, their owners wandering inside the store Andrei had just left. In the corner of the parking lot was an old, beat-up station wagon with two kids and a strange blue glow lighting their faces. Andrei had seen the same glow before when Vlad or Pavel were staring at a laptop screen in the dark. He pulled out a piece of paper and pen and wrote down the license plate number. Then he started back along the edge of the parking lot to where he had left Haki.

In just over a minute Andrei had covered half the distance with a determined gait. He didn't like that even this small exertion brought a few beads of sweat to his forehead in the sticky southern night. He took another drag on his cigarette causing a tiny dot of amber light to appear. Haki took note of the return and watched as Andrei approached.

"We need to talk to Vlad," Andrei announced as he approached.

"We just got here. I don't think it's smart to bother him."

"I'll take that chance."

Andrei didn't wait for a response. He changed his course back towards the van. Haki paused for a moment and then decided to follow behind Andrei. When Andrei reached the van, he gave a light knock on the side and then opened the driver's side door and sat down closing the door behind him. Haki was a couple of beats behind when he sat down and shut the passenger's door. Andrei was already talking.

"There is an old car parked at a small store just north of this lot," Andrei began as he pointed out the front of the window toward where they had just been. "There are two kids inside and they each have laptops running. They look like an American version of your little one," he said with a glance toward Pavel.

Vlad turned to Pavel. Vlad didn't need to say anything. Pavel gave just a moment to meet Andrei's look and then turned his attention back to his own computer. A few quick clicks and he had browsed through a menu and launched his copy of Nmap. He typed in the 192.168.1.x wireless subnet he was using to connect to the 3DNF network and began a scan.

Three seconds after the scan started, there were two other computers listed on the display that should not have been there (*p. 187).

◖ ◖ ◖

"Dude, now what are you doing?!" Bob yelled.

"What?" Leon answered as he turned toward Bob.

"Look!" Bob pointed to the flashing alert on his computer. His Comodo Firewall had popped a window in front of his SuperScan.

"Someone just scanned me!" Bob pulled his hands quickly off the keyboard as if he had been shocked (*p. 185).

"It wasn't me. I've just been looking at the ten-twenty-four corporate network," Leon answered.

◖ ◖ ◖

"We are not the only ones on the network," Pavel said as he turned the laptop around so Vlad could see the Nmap result.

"What can they see?" Vlad asked.

"If they are paying attention, who knows?" Pavel answered.

"Is the file transfer done?"

"I've got about 25% to go."

"Stop it," Vlad ordered.

Pavel shut down the transfer and killed his scan.

◑ ◑ ◑

"It stopped," Bob and Leon said in near unison. Bob had seen the network scan drop first, then Leon watched the screen stop scrolling on the packet capture.

"I've got a lot of data, but I don't think they were finished. It was all going to something that looks like a PC called 3M5763," Leon said.

"What now?" Bob asked.

"Let's just wait."

Leon and Bob sat quietly, each glancing from their respective computer displays to their surroundings. Two minutes crawled by filled with only the sound of quickened breathing from both of them.

"Look!" Bob almost squealed as parking lights on a van came on in the parking lot about 200 yards from their position. "That's got to be where this traffic came from!"

Leon and Bob watched, but there was no other activity from the van.

"Relax," Leon said. "There are several cars over there. That doesn't mean they were the ones."

"That has 'Fed' all over it! What if they were watching us, or maybe they were tracking something inside one of these offices?"

"We've got enough access points for the game. I'm going to pull out." Bob cranked up the old engine and put the car in gear. He didn't turn the headlights on, but slowly turned the car in the parking lot. As soon as they reached the street, the headlights of the van came on.

"I told you that's who we were watching!" Bob insisted.

"I don't think they're following us." Leon responded as he turned in his seat to see the van pull out onto the same street, now about a 100 yards back. He didn't sound quite convinced of his own words.

"Of course they are! There's no way the stuff we saw was from anywhere but that van!

They came up to a left-turn lane on Kirby Avenue. Bob finally turned on his headlights as they pulled up to the green protected left signal. Instead of going through, Bob stopped.

"What are you doing?" Leon asked as he looked back. Three cars separated them from the van. All were in the same turn lane.

"Proving that they are following us."

Horns started honking as Bob watched the light turn to yellow. As soon as it turned red, the cars on the perpendicular road got a green light for a protected left turn. Before the first car could take the turn, Bob punched the accelerator. The old V-8 engine roared and they lurched into the intersection. More horns blared as Bob cut off the surprised driver and led him across the intersection, continuing down Kirby.

"What are they doing?" Bob asked.

Leon watched behind them, bracing himself from the sudden motion.

"Oh my…you're right!" Leon watched as the van turned into the on-coming traffic lane and forced its way through the intersection. Horns blared again as the van cut off two cars that were trying to take their turn at the protected left.

"It's time for counter measures!" Bob yelled as he continued to accelerate past 50 miles per hour.

"That won't work," Leon complained. He had given his friend grief for the last year as he had watched him trick out the old wagon with more and more gadgets. 'Counter measures' was just his latest addition of weirdness from a paranoid mind.

"Shut up and hit the red button when I tell you to!" was Bob's reply.

Leon opened the glove box that revealed a piece of plywood mounted with three buttons crudely wired to cables extending into the dashboard through the back of the glove box. Two buttons were red and one was green.

"Which red button!?"

"The left one! Now wait for it! And whatever you do, don't hit the green button!" They continued down the road as the van swerved trying to make up the ground between them. Bob went through the next intersection on a green light – the van made it as well.

"They're gaining!" Leon shrieked. He had been pulled all the way into Bob's world.

"I told you it's not paranoia when they are trying to get you!"

Ahead Bob saw a Lexus RX350 SUV coming at them with its right-turn signal flashing. Bob accelerated and turned left across traffic onto the small side street lined with cars on each side, in front of the SUV.

"Now!"

Leon mashed the red button. He turned around to watch as the tailgate of the station wagon fell open. Four cans of white paint that had been rigged to fall came crashing out the back. Just as designed, each bounced once on the pavement, arced back into the air and emptied their contents onto the street in mid-flight.

Leon could see the lady driving the SUV toss her cell phone and grab the steering wheel with both hands. She gave the wheel a hard jerk and swung the SUV sideways as she slammed her breaks. Leon next saw several little league uniforms bounce around the back as the chaos faded into the distance. The nose of the SUV was now pointed askew to the direction of the street – neatly blocking any way around.

◗ ◗ ◗

Andrei nearly stood on the brake peddle of the van. The sound of screeching tires and a flood of heated words in three different languages filled the van as Andrei managed to stop just inches from the back of the SUV. Andrei threw the van in reverse and mashed the accelerator, skillfully driving backwards to the intersection where he threw the wheel hard to the right and spun the van completely around. Pavel grabbed at his backpack to protect the contents from taking flight across the back of the van.

◗ ◗ ◗

"Did you see that!?" Bob was hardly able to keep driving as he was so filled with adrenaline. His hands started shaking as he realized that his virtual world had just intersected with the real world. "I didn't think that would really work," he mumbled to himself.

Leon wasn't doing much better. "We are so screwed," he gasped.

◖ ◖ ◖

"One of you might be able to figure out where we should go next with this," Andrei said as he pulled the piece of paper from his shirt pocket. He handed Bob's license plate number to Vlad.

"What is this?" Vlad asked as he looked at the number.

"I wrote down the number to the car when I first spotted it. You and your little friend might have a way to find them with that number."

Vlad wasn't happy, but the information took some of the sting of failure away. Before Vlad could bark an order, Pavel slipped a data card into his laptop and hit the 'connect' icon to bring up a mobile Internet connection.

"Give me a few minutes," Pavel stated as his fingers flashed on the keyboard.

FOUR

IN REAL LIFE

Saturday, 11:53 p.m.

Bob pulled the car into an empty space at Wal-Mart. He turned off the engine and shared a collective expression of glazed disbelief with Leon. They knew that they had stepped across a line, but neither was ready to believe it. Even Bob, who had talked such a good story of paranoia, couldn't quite square the reality of a car chase with the imagined threats he had always seen around the next corner. Even so, Bob spoke first.

"I don't want to go home yet. We need to get some more information."

"Like what?"

"If they followed us, then they saw the license plate number. If they're Feds, then they probably will have someone sitting outside my house! Crap! Dad!" Bob realized the next step their pursuers would take.

"My dad is at home, or he was when I left!"

"It's only been a few minutes – just call him." Leon was trying to keep his friend calm, not realizing the volume he was using in his own response.

"And say what? 'Hey Dad, how's it goin'? By the way, has a van full of goons pulled up front yet? If so, it wasn't my fault. Oh, and whatever you do, don't let them in my lab.'"

"We've got some time," Leon said. He was starting to calm down and his brain was clearing a little.

"Let's assume the worst case scenario that they're Feds. We have to assume they know where you live from the car. That means we…"

"No!"

"What now?"

"My lab! It's going to end up in some evidence room with a bunch of bureaucratic nerds going through my data!"

"So do we go home now and see if we can beat them there?"

"Dude, you can't outrun a radio! The last time I checked the speed of light beats a Buick!"

Leon was getting frustrated as Bob became more agitated.

"Okay, calm down. Let's start over. We have to find a way to warn your dad. We can't protect all of your data – there's just no way to get back to the house safely."

Bob cut him off. "First we have to get rid of this car. We're a target as long as we are in this thing."

"How are we going to g – "

"Rudy!"

"What about him?"

"I bet he'd let us swap cars for a while. We don't need to tell him why; we just need a different set of wheels. We can give it back when this blows over, and if he gets stopped, he can't be linked to any of this. Give me your cell phone!"

Leon had no better suggestion so he just fished through his pockets for his cell. He handed it to Bob who started punching in the number.

"You have his number memorized?" Leon asked while Bob stared forward.

"Yeah, don't know why. It just stuck in my head after we worked on the last LAN party – Rudy! It's Bob…Yeah, we're about done with the Capture the Flag work. It's going to be great…Dude, I've got a favor to ask. We want to do some wardriving over in the River Oaks edition and my wagon will stick out for obvious reasons. Are you at work?…Cool. Can we stop by and swap cars for the night?…Yeah, Leon's with me… Okay, I promise he'll do the driving…Sheesh, I'm not that bad… I said yes I promise he'll drive…half an hour, sure. Thanks."

"Not bad – social engineer a hacker." Leon complimented Bob.

Bob didn't say anything, but he couldn't contain a self-congratulatory grin that spread across his face as he started the car and put it in gear.

"So what about warning your dad or saving your data?" Leon asked as he swayed with the rolling shocks of the old Buick that Bob was tossing around corners.

"Dude. I got nothin' okay?" Bob snapped.

Leon had no answer either. They drove in silence the rest of the way to the House of Pies twenty-four-hour diner. They did manage to calm down by the time Bob parked the car near the back of the parking lot close to the trash bins.

Inside, Bob and Leon had just gotten their drinks when Rudy walked up.

"So how many flags do you have left to plant?"

"Hey – how's it goin'?" Leon said as he slid over in the booth to make room for Rudy.

"Same old. I just finished working on a new boot screen for my PSP. Sousanator released a new prx you can use to make a custom startup."

"Cool – bring it to the next 2600. I'd like to see how you do that," Leon replied.

"We've got enough flags already, but we thought we ought to plant at least one in a country club. Most of the people playing will have cars as bad as mine, so this will make it a little more interesting."

"I understand. And thanks – that means I know at least one place to find a flag. I still haven't figured out your Merry Men clue."

"The clue wasn't about Merry Men. It's about the Merry Men's leader. Think about it, you'll get it. We need to get started if we are going to get this done."

"Thanks for letting us use the Mini." Leon said as Rudy put the keys on the table. "I promise I'll keep Bob away from the wheel."

Bob only half-smiled as he passed the keys to the Buick to Rudy.

"Can we meet tomorrow afternoon around five o'clock?" Rudy asked.

"Sure. How about back here?" Leon responded.

"And don't mess with any buttons!" Bob warned as Rudy stood up to leave.

"I won't. I'm afraid to think what mods you'd do to a car after seeing the stuff you bring to the meetings."

After Rudy left, Bob and Leon sat still for a few minutes staring around the restaurant. Bob's eyes lingered mostly outside, tracking the cars in and out of the parking lot. Bob suddenly got up, throwing three dollars on the table for the drinks and picking up his backpack.

"We've got to go. I know how we can check on my dad. I should have remembered sooner."

"What?" Leon asked as he followed Bob through the restaurant.

"My webcam. I keep the one over my main screen on feeding a password-protected Web site. We just need to find someone's network to jack into. Then I can see if anything's going on in my lab" (*p. 152).

Ten minutes later Bob and Leon were parked just inside the country club called River Oaks at the beginning of a cul-de-sac. The little Mini Cooper blended in with the occasional cars parked in driveways and on the street. The area was only partially lit with lights built into the brick mailboxes that lined both sides of the street.

Leon turned off the car and watched as Bob connected his laptop to an open wireless network from one of the houses around them.

"You'd think people would figure out to encrypt all of these older Linksys networks that everyone still uses," Leon commented as Bob waited for his browser to load the page from one of his Web servers (*p. 323).

"Something's wrong!" Bob exclaimed after a few seconds of tapping on the edges of his laptop.

"What?"

Bob rechecked a long URL he had just typed into his browser. "My Web server is down. I'm going to check my off-site box."

"What off-site box?"

"Uh, it's a server I found that I use to auto-FTP motion video clips from my room," Bob answered. "And besides, the professor at the university in Australia who runs the site teaches Medieval English Literature. It's not like he's ever noticed I've borrowed a gig. Or two."

Leon gave Bob a skeptical look.

"Okay, 30 gig, but he doesn't use the space they give him." Bob's fingers did their spider dance across the keyboard as Leon shook his head.

"Here it is," Bob said as he scanned the folder structure on the remote server. "I've got a file that was uploaded 20 minutes ago. That means someone was in my room." He clicked on the file name and his video player loaded. Leon looked close over his shoulder as the choppy video started. They both saw the door to Bob's lab open. First Bob's dad walked in, but he was followed by four other men.

"Crap! Feds! I told you they would find my house!"

There was no audio with the webcam, but they could figure out what was going on. Bob's dad was pushed into the room and was obviously confused and scared. The toughest looking of the three had his gun on George Falken. The well-dressed one who appeared to be in charge was standing near the door, and the youngest was looking at the monitors.

◗◗◗

Twenty Minutes Earlier...

"What was your son doing tonight?" Vlad asked George. Vlad's voice was calm, but forceful.

"I don't know. He was out with his friend." George, like his son, thought he was dealing with federal agents. He didn't know what was going on, but was convinced that Bob had finally crossed a line somewhere.

"We were investigating a corporate network break-in and found your son in the parking lot. We think he was involved."

"Bob wouldn't do something like that. He's a good kid." George was so focused on Vlad's questioning he didn't pay attention as Pavel walked around the room.

"Smile. We're on camera," Pavel said as he leaned close to look just above the 24-inch LCD in the middle of Bob's lab.

◗◗◗

Bob and Leon watched as Pavel's face nearly filled the screen. Pavel pulled back out of view and Vlad's gaze turned right at the camera. Andrei turned to the camera and in a swift motion brought his Glock away from Bob's dad and level with the camera. Bob and Leon both jumped as the screen went blank.

"Dad!" Bob yelled.

"Quiet! We don't want anyone to call the cops on us!" Leon insisted.

◗◗◗

George had thought his "visitors" were agents until Andrei shot the camera. He knew in an instant that whatever Bob had done, it wasn't the government he had offended.

"Watch him!" Vlad ordered Andrei – careful to use no names even in Russian. He then turned to Pavel. "Tell me what you can learn from this place."

Pavel had been admiring the setup since the moment they walked into Bob's room. He sat at the main desk that supported the seven monitors in the lab. "Chair" wasn't the right word to describe the seating. It was a large inflated ball of thick rubber resting on a round base with wheels and a support shaped kind of like E.T.'s head that formed the back of the "chair." It was a treasure Bob had found at a garage sale the year before and it fit the college-geek-dorm look of the room perfectly. The big flat screen was unharmed, but the camera that had been neatly mounted on the top was now little pieces of plastic spread on the bookshelf behind the monitors.

"This will take a lot of time. I see three different operating systems, a firewall console, an IDS console, and I think this is a wireless network detector," Pavel said as he pointed at the different displays.

He turned back to the main console. "This is a PGP passphrase screen - if he has anything valuable, it's going to be in this system, and we aren't going to get in" (*p. 229).

Vlad turned to George who had been standing quietly with Andrei's gun pointed at his chest. He grabbed George by the shoulders and pushed him down to the only other chair in the room.

"Let's start again. What was your son doing tonight? We saw him out with one other person near a company called 3DNF. We think they were trying to break into their network."

George's hands shook. He was scared enough when he thought he had federal agents in his house. Now he knew he was in as much trouble as Bob and Leon.

"I don't know who Bob was out with tonight. He told me he had a date."

"Thank you. Now I know what you look like when you're lying to me. This isn't the room of a young man who goes out on dates," Vlad replied calmly. He turned his back on George and began to walk around the room, inspecting the chaos of Bob's life. "He was in your car with another young man. We know they both had laptops with them, and we know they were connected to the company's network. This company was conducting special research for the government; we believe they were trying to steal information that would have been very valuable."

George leaned on the desk and put his head in his hands. Pavel was plugging in a USB drive to Bob's main computer next to him. Then George saw it. Spread among the clutter of Bob's desk, between science fiction action figures and spare computer parts was an Office Depot "Easy" button. He remembered when Bob had asked him for help modifying the marketing gimmick button to be a real electrical switch. Bob wouldn't tell his dad what he was going to do with it. Bob had just said that once it was hooked up, not to ever hit it if he ever came in the lab.

"I told you, Bob is a good kid. He wouldn't do anything illegal." As George talked, he shifted his weight slightly and leaned to his right, closer to the button.

"You don't expect me to believe you. I'm sure my assistant will find plenty of evidence of illegal activities in here. There is no way all of this gear came from a teenager with an innocent hobby."

George knew this was going to hurt, but he didn't know how else to protect his son. In a quick motion he brought the hand that had been supporting his forehead down on the button. Pavel saw the sudden motion and realized too late that George had a plan.

A female voice emanating from Bob's main computer filled the room.

"Sequence initiated."

A hum began to build.

Vlad grabbed George and threw him to the other side of the room.

"I told you to watch him!" he spat at Andrei.

Pavel pulled his USB drive out of the computer. He hit the "Easy" button, but nothing happened. The hum increased in intensity. Three of the seven displays flickered, and then showed a "no signal" message.

The female voice continued. "Sequence complete. Primary drives have been magnetically wiped. Sorry, Bob." A blue-white flash shot from the largest tower computer under the desk. The smell of burnt plastic filled the room.

Vlad took George by the arm, and then turned to Andrei. "Toss this room, then go break out a window in the back and make it look like a robbery."

Vlad forced George out of the room, through the house and out to the van. Pavel followed behind, looking around for anyone that might be watching them.

"Tie him up!" Vlad barked at Haki as he shoved George into the back of the van. Haki worked quickly to secure George while Vlad and Pavel got into the van. Andrei came along just shortly after.

"Done." Was all Andrei dared to say in Russian to Vlad.

George picked up on the language change. What had his son gotten involved in? Haki got back in the driver's seat and started the van.

"Start driving! Just get us away from here! Haki, do you have a place we can take our guest and not be disturbed?" Vlad asked in English.

"Yes. I have a place."

As they drove through the neighborhood, George sat quietly in the back, nursing the pain in his wrists where Haki had secured him to the side of the van. George made eye contact with Pavel. For a moment, he thought he detected remorse or doubt, or maybe just fear. But for George, his own fear filled his mind too much to allow him to fully process what he saw.

Vlad was watching Pavel. "We need to give our guest some time to think of a way to help us find his son and companion. On the off chance they were watching that camera, then they will be more difficult to find now."

◑ ◑ ◑

Leon was driving just to be moving. They didn't know where to go next. Bob wasn't speaking yet. He was still trying to process what they had seen on his webcam. Leon didn't mind the quiet. His body had already processed more adrenalin in the last few hours than it had seen in the last year. He had to concentrate just to keep the car at the speed limit. Intersections seemed to be too much information for his mind to assimilate.

"We need some cash," Bob broke the silence.

"What?"

"We need cash. We can't go home, and we have to take this car back to Rudy soon. We need to be able to buy ourselves some time."

"Do you have any?"

"Are you kidding? Any cash I get always ends up in my lab," Bob responded.

"Does your dad have any?"

"No."

"So where do you get the money for the lab?" Leon asked.

"I sell vulnerabilities I find to iDefense."

"You do? I've been selling to TippingPoint's ZDI!."

Bob shook his head. "Dude, you should go with iDefense. They throw better parties at DEFCON" (*p. 236).

The half-grin Leon managed with his friend's comment quickly faded. They drove along in silence, still with no purpose other than constant movement. They both stared blankly at the road ahead, barely seeing the traffic as they tried to cope with their situation.

Suddenly Bob looked up and exclaimed, "Turn back around! We need to go back!"

"Did you see something?" Leon asked as he scanned the traffic behind them.

"No. I just figured out where we can get some cash. You won't like it, but I don't think we have any choice."

"What's your idea?"

"It's more like where is my idea," Bob responded. "I'm going to get your laptop started and hook it up to my Wi-Fi antenna. We need to practice our Capture the Flag skills."

Ten minutes later Leon and Bob were driving slowly through the River Oaks development again. The price of the homes was evident by the number of unneeded chimneys each house had reaching into the warm and humid Houston sky.

"We can jack into a network here again and scan for trojans. There's got to be someone around here with more money than sense," Bob explained.

"You're right. I don't like it," Leon responded. "But I don't see many options right now. Anything we take we pay back, agreed?"

"Sure – if we live long enough."

Bob pulled up Kismet and watched the screen as Leon drove the Mini through the neighborhood; careful to avoid the section they had visited the first time. It didn't take long.

"I've got one," Bob said. "I think it's up ahead."

Leon drove past two more houses and turned off the headlights as he parked the car. The large Tudor-style house had no lights on inside. There were a few landscape lights, but no signs of activity.

"Okay, give me a minute," Bob said as he connected to the wireless network.

"I've got an IP – 192.168.1.103. I love it when they leave everything as defaults. This is a twelve o'clock person."

"What?" Leon asked.

"Twelve o'clock. You know, someone who's VCR is always flashing twelve o'clock because they have no clue how to reset it."

Leon managed a grin as he watched Bob work.

Leon opened up Bob's laptop and launched SuperScan and ran a quick scan of the subnet.

"Okay, you get mad at me for using that and now you pull that tool out," Bob observed before Leon had even started.

"Just give me a minute. I'd worry about a sensor tracking me if it were your house, but not here." Leon got a quick hit on 192.168.1.102.

"Here it is. The home computer is a Windows box and even has the SubSeven trojan running (*p. 212). I bet they have a teenage son who pulls down music on his dad's computer."

Leon opened the client application and connected to the IP address.

"Wow this version is old enough to have the 'not so secret' master password," Leon said (*p. 212).

"I know," was Bob's simple reply as he stopped what he was doing on Leon's computer and watched Leon work on his.

Leon quickly had a window open on Bob's computer that displayed the desktop of the computer in the target house. He browsed through several different directories and soon had a cached copy of the password used for an online brokerage account. A quick browser session confirmed that the password worked, and there was enough money in the account for their needs (*p. 216).

Next Leon opened an IRC session and was quickly logged into a carder site.

```
I need a quick cash out. $10K guaranteed 30/70 split. No rip-
pers. No Nigerians (*p. 251).
```

"This won't take long," Leon said as his fingers tapped on the side of the laptop. He and Bob watched as several posts came through over the next two minutes Bob leaned closer to Leon to see the posts.

"I'm going to check these out before I respond," Leon said as he typed.

"How did you learn about this channel?" Bob asked as Leon worked.

"I just picked up some chatter when I was trolling for some ideas on vulnerabilities that carders use to get their product – here's one we can use."

"What did you find?" Bob asked.

"Of the three responses, only one of these actually masked their IP address. I'd bet this one is the most professional. I'm going to do a PM," Leon said.

Leon opened a private message session on the IRC and started to make arrangements.

```
Can you do Western Union to Houston, TX?
Deal. Here is the account.
```

Leon swapped over to the browser window that was still logged into the online brokerage account. He ordered a transfer to the account requested by his new associate.

```
Done. Can you wire tomorrow?
If the funds clear, you can pick up your $7K tomorrow.
```

"That was too easy," Bob observed.

"Now for the hard part," Leon responded grimly.

Leon swapped back to the brokerage account and changed the password. He then went back to the desktop of the compromised computer. He opened up the word processing program and typed a message.

```
I'm sorry, but I needed to borrow $10,000 from your brokerage
account. I will arrange for repayment as soon as I can. I also
changed your password on the account to 's3cur1t33'. I suggest
you change it to something else as soon as you can. As soon
as you finish reading this, disconnect your computer from the
Internet and take it to a computer shop and have them restage it
for you. While you are there, have them tell you how to secure
your wireless network.
```

Leon then closed the connection to the compromised computer, leaving the message visible for the owner. He created a text file on Bob's desktop with the name and address of his "victim."

"That should scare him into being a little more careful," Bob observed as Leon started to pack up.

F1V3

STATUS CHECK
Sunday, 9:32 a.m.

The South Texas rain fell heavily on the 1970s vintage house. The small structure wore its 30-plus years of tropical storms, sun, humidity, and general neglect no better than the rest of the neighborhood. The only distinctive attribute of the house was the lack of cast-off items in the front yard. In fact, the only extra object in front was the blue van Andrei had deftly tossed around Houston the night before.

Inside the nearly empty house were Vlad and Pavel sitting at a small table in the kitchen. In the front room were Andrei and Haki. In one of the two bedrooms was George. He was sitting on a small wooden chair with his wrists locked firmly in handcuffs behind his back. A sturdy chain was looped through the cuffs to an eye bolt screwed straight into the wooden floor.

George had spent the night in the chair and his body ached. He hadn't been particularly abused, but the fear alone of the last 12 hours was enough to leave him nearly desperate. He had spent too long with his body prepared for fight or flight and no chance to do either. As he began to stop dozing and felt hunger and thirst build, he also started thinking a little more clearly. Bob was in trouble but not with any law enforcement agency. Bob must have been hacking into something he shouldn't have.

"I thought he was a good kid," George muttered quietly. He stared at the blank wall and the resolve of a father began to build.

"He is a good kid," he said a little more clearly.

◑ ◑ ◑

"So what did we get from our target last night?" Vlad asked as he sipped at a cup of coffee.

"Nothing yet. Your contact had good information. I got through the tunnel on the first PC and saw traffic from the government network."

"I want to go back today," Vlad said quietly.

"I don't think that would be a good idea," Pavel replied carefully. He surprised himself at the daring to disagree with Vlad. "We crossed into another network. We need to see if that tripped any alarms. We also don't know what those two others did on the network. They may have just been watching us, or they may have been tripping alarms."

"So...Michael isn't as disposable as I had planned. At least not yet," Vlad allowed the first smile Pavel had seen since they got to Houston. It was a smile that brought no comfort to Pavel. "We can just stay here for the day and give the father a chance to help us find those kids."

"What if they go to the police?" Pavel asked.

"After seeing how they acted last night, they won't go to the police." Vlad stared at Pavel while he thought through the next steps. Pavel shifted nervously under the gaze.

"I'll go talk to the father," Vlad announced. He picked up the coffee cup and tossed back the last of the drink as he stood. He set the cup down with a firm rap on the table.

Pavel let out a barely-audible sound. He wanted to speak, but thought better of it.

"What?" Vlad turned and held Pavel in his gaze again.

"Do we have to hurt him?"

Vlad smiled broadly this time. "Pain doesn't usually work that well, especially when family is involved. He just has to believe he can be hurt. Besides, the last thing we need is a bunch of screaming in a small house like this."

Pavel looked relieved, but didn't say anything as he watched Vlad.

"You wouldn't want to clean up the mess any way," Vlad said casually as he walked from the room.

Pavel's face lost a little color as he stared at his own cup of coffee.

"Andrei! With me." Vlad barked in Russian.

◑ ◑ ◑

"...four hundred...five hundred...six hundred...seven hundred...eight hundred... nine hundred...seven thousand," the clerk finished. "Is there anything else we can do for you?"

"No thank you," Leon replied as he gathered up the stack of bills and placed them quickly in his front pocket. He walked out of the Western Union office and got into the Mini Cooper where Bob was waiting.

"How can being evil be this easy?" Leon asked as he started the engine. "I could never make this kind of bank with a real job."

"You aren't crossing over are you?" Bob asked as he eyed his friend.

"No. I just see how much needs to be fixed so it's not that easy to be so bad. We need a place to stay. I'm not sleeping in a Mini and I'm tired of jacking into Wi-Fi networks."

Bob ignored the sleep comment – he could go longer than Leon without sleep. "I've been looking at the code from the stuff we captured last night. This stuff is over my head. We need to talk to Max St341."

"I don't remember that name," Leon responded. He drove aimlessly just working to obey every speed limit sign and not draw any attention in their direction.

"I used him to help on some code on one of my exploits from last year," Bob responded.

Leon drove quietly for a block. "Those guys sure didn't seem like Feds to me. Shouldn't we go to the cops or someone?"

"I am not taking that chance! For all I know my dad is in Bagram Air Force Base right now. You don't know what a Fed looks like any more. They can be harder to spot in the real world than in Vegas."

There was another too long silence as they both considered what to do next. Bob spoke first.

"Let's get to a hotel that's got Wi-Fi. You can crash for a while and I can contact Max."

◐ ◐ ◐

The cubicle at 3DNF sat empty. It was too early for the employees who kept normal hours and too late for the programmers. There were four computers whirring and six monitors glowing with no one to watch. The desk was cluttered with scribbled IP addresses, discarded meeting agendas, and an empty Mountain Dew bottle.

The middle and largest monitor was unlocked. It displayed the aggregated data from the few network intrusion detection sensors deployed in the company network. Near the top of the screen, the oldest entries sat unread. Steadily, new entries appeared at the top of the list. In the middle, a grouping of entries in red slipped a little lower. Chance would determine how far down the list, or even off the screen, they would be by morning on Monday when the analyst came in (*p. 157).

◐ ◐ ◐

"How do we find your son?"

Nothing in George's history prepared him for this. The face that stared back at him was strong and intense. George hadn't been abused, at least beyond being yanked from his house, tossed in the back of a van, and chained to the floor in a small, dark room. During the lonely hours he had just spent with the handcuffs cutting into his wrists, George had prepared himself for resisting. But in the moment of looking into his questioner's eyes, he chose differently. He knew he wouldn't last long. His son's best hope wasn't in how long George could take a beating. Bob was smart and George had to trust that.

"He doesn't carry a cell phone."

"What about his friends?" Vlad asked with a steady tone that told George he had chosen right.

"No. He never told me their numbers. You have to wait for him to call me."

"And how would he know to call you?" Vlad asked.

"I bet he knows his computers have been destroyed. He'll want to know what happened at the house."

"But how will he contact you then?" Vlad asked, as he grew impatient and leaned in over George's face.

"He – he doesn't carry a cell phone. But back at the house, Bob keeps a cell phone in a drawer. The battery isn't in it. Whenever Bob stays out real late with his friends, I would put the battery in the phone and turn it on. Bob would call and let me know he was okay."

"We detected your son connected to a wireless network he shouldn't have. What was he doing?"

"Bob usually doesn't tell me what he is up to."

"I didn't ask what he usually does. What was he doing?"

"I don't know. I…well, it could have been Capture the Flag."

"What?" Vlad was getting impatient and his body language changed from confident control to in-your-face threat.

"C-capture the – it's a game I think – at least that's what I heard him talking about last week."

"Continue," Vlad said as George tried to shift his weight in the chair and Vlad drew even closer.

George quickly brought his eyes back to his questioner. He had allowed himself a quick glance at the quiet man who looked even more menacing and was standing guard at the door. "They plant an icon file inside networks and then leave clues for their friends to find them."

"What icon file?"

"I never saw it. But I heard him mention something called 'Cyber Bob' once when he was doing a video chat with a friend."

"One more thing – where is the cell phone?"

"In the kitchen. There is a drawer near the…"

George didn't get a chance to finish as Vlad spun on his heel and walked out of the room. He could soon hear his questioner's voice in another language through the walls.

Is that Russian? He doesn't sound happy, George thought to himself.

George allowed himself a snicker at the thought. Bob has always had the gift of being able to get under someone's skin quickly but he had outdone himself this time. He went still, though, realizing the consequences of it this time.

"Andrei!" Vlad snapped as soon as he shut the door to the little bedroom where George was chained.

"Go back to the house. Be careful. I don't want you walking into the police. In a drawer in the kitchen is a cell phone. Bring me that phone. And make sure you get the battery; it will be in the same drawer. And don't draw any attention to yourself. That van is already at risk because of the way you were driving last night."

Andrei's only response was to turn and walk to the door. He knew better than to ask questions when Vlad was barking orders as fast as he could think of them.

"Don't put the battery in the phone – just bring it to me!" Vlad called as Andrei started to close the door behind him. Andrei paused and looked back, giving a nod of acknowledgement before leaving.

◑ ◑ ◑

Leon tried to doze for a while but sleep wouldn't come. Part of it was the stress, part of it the noise from Bob that kept pulling him back from sleep. Bob sat at the little desk in the hotel room illuminated by the glow of a monitor. He was working on "the Beast" – the name he had given his oversized, sticker-covered laptop. He had just finishing setting it up and getting it connected to the hotel Internet service. Leon got off the bed and walked over to Bob. He looked over his shoulder and watched as Bob loaded World of Warcraft. Soon his character was running down a stone road in the middle of a dark forest. There was no one around, but occasionally there was movement off to either side. Bob ignored the motion and kept running like he was on a mission.

"I thought we came here so you could get some help from Max," Leon asked as he pulled a chair up next to Bob.

"We did, and that's exactly what I'm about to do."

"It looks to me like you're playing a game when you ought to be making a phone call."

Bob didn't take his eyes off the laptop. "There's no way I'd call him. This has to be done out of band" (★p. 224).

Bob hit a function key and checked his friends list. "Look, he's on," he said as he pointed to the fourth name down the list. "Just let me do a whisper."

```
I need to meet in the place. We need to talk. Code Alpha 9!
Again with the codes! Is Alpha 9 an emergency or did you finally
get a girlfriend?
```

"I like this guy already!" Leon said. "He knows you pretty well, too." Bob ignored Leon and just kept typing.

```
Just meet me!
I'm dropping out of a group to do this, so it better be good. OMW.
```

Bob didn't run anymore. A green glow enveloped his hands as they began to move. Suddenly, he was standing inside an inn in Stormwind City.

"If you could have done that all along, why were you running?" Leon asked.

"I wanted to get away from the area where I had finished my last session just to make sure I was alone," Bob responded.

He ran through the streets, ignoring guards and other players. He crossed over a bridge and ran along a canal. After a few turns, he crossed a bridge again and continued to follow the water.

"Dude, are you running in circles?" Leon asked.

"Just a minute – I always get lost here." Bob tapped a key and a map appeared on the screen. He leaned in toward the monitor and mumbled something.

"There it is," Bob said clearly as he leaned back in his chair and changed the display back to Stormwind City. Bob crossed the canal one more time and then ran more deliberately. "This is the trade district..." Bob continued to run, ignoring less powerful characters around him. "Now the Mage Quarter..." Bob turned right after another bridge. "That's the Meeting Stone." The area grew darker as he passed into a room. "And this is the Stockade." Bob ran downstairs and came to an opening surrounded by a spinning blue light. He walked through the portal and a "loading…" screen appeared.

"Now we are in our own instance," Bob explained.

"Our own what?" Leon asked.

"Instance. We just entered an area where we can chat with Max on an instance server," Bob said as he tapped a few keys. "I'm going to do a shadow meld."

"So what did you do that for if this is private?" Leon asked.

"I still have trust issues," Bob replied with a smile.

They stared at the screen for only a few moments before another character appeared through the portal. "That's Max," Bob observed as he typed another command.

```
Shadowmeld. Really? Show off :-P.
```

Bob moved his character and it became solid. He turned and faced Max.

```
Better?
It didn't matter to me - I could still see you.
Yeah, Yeah, but I think it's cool - like a Ninja.
Why do you always want to meet here?
It's as private as we can get without a Vent server. Why don't
you just get on the Vent server?
```

"What's a Vent server?" Leon asked.

"Man you need to game more," Bob sighed. "It's like an IP telephone. You can use the speakers and microphone on your computer to talk to other players in a dedicated channel. It's way faster to communicate than typing. I don't know why but Max will never get on one."

```
What do you need?
I need help looking at some code. It's too hot for the Net. Need
to meet in person.
I told you before. I know we live in the same city, but I don't
meet IRL.
```

"What's IRL?" Leon asked.

Bob looked at him like he was an idiot. "In Real Life. You should really game more. You are missing out on an entire subset of our culture."

"Hacker Speak is easier than your WOW slang," Leon responded.

```
I'll give you $500 cash if you will just look at the code.
What makes this code so special?
I picked it up on a wireless sniff. I don't know what it is but
it was something being pushed into a network not pulled out.
```

There was a pause. Max was thinking about the offer and the challenge.

```
Where do you want to meet?
In front of Brother's Pizza in the Greenspoint Mall. How do I
recognize you?
Look for the one wearing the iDefense shirt. I'm Hearthing back
to the Outlands. Time?
Tomorrow at noon.
```

The hands on Max's character began to glow green. There was a flash of white light, and Bob's character was alone. Leon walked across the room and sat down on the bed.

"So tell me how all of that was 'out of band.' None of that conversation was encrypted," Leon demanded.

"Sometimes obscurity is good enough security. Tell me what Fed would be able to convince his boss to let him play World of Warcraft on the government clock until he had a player that would know how to get around the world like this. Besides, terrorists would think this is a depravity of the West. They wouldn't use it so that means the Feds wouldn't care to look into it."

Leon accepted the logic of Bob's reasoning. For all of his paranoia, he had a smart and unique way of thinking outside the box.

"I'm going to get some sleep," Leon said as he fell back on the bed.

"I'll do the same in a few. I want to look around Stormwind City a bit and make sure we were really alone." With that Bob turned back to the monitor of his laptop. Leon sighed.

"How can you tell if anyone was watching you? Can't they just transport out just like you could?"

Leon watched as Bob's character climbed up the stairs and walked back out towards the canal. Bob ignored Leon's comment.

LOG REVIEW

Monday, 9:37 a.m.

Jonathan Tao sat his Mountain Dew on the work surface of his cubical and sat heavily into the chair. Jonathan hated Mondays. Monday mornings never brought good news. Most of his attitude was from self-inflicted sleep deprivation each weekend mixed with an over-application of caffeine. He opened up the laptop backpack and pulled out his main work computer. He alternated between unlocking the monitoring stations on his desk and connecting the cables to his laptop. The dance was an amusing ritual of imbibing caffeine, typing passwords, reading logs, and rubbing tired eyes. Eventually, Jonathan's attention turned to the large display at the middle of his set of monitors. He kept this screen on and logged in all the time. It was used mostly to display logs from the firewall and the few network sensors recently deployed at 3DNF.

Jonathan took a couple more swigs of his carbonated breakfast as he scanned the entries on the Snort console. He was rarely fully awake for this weekly ritual, but he performed it faithfully. Usually, if he found anything of interest, it only merited a call to the network support team because a server went down. Jonathan squinted his eyes as he scanned through Friday evening then into Saturday. His expression didn't change except for the breaks for additional swallows of breakfast. Suddenly at 11:06 p.m. on Saturday, there was a string of alerts. Someone had run a network scan from inside the company. He nearly missed the desk as he sat up abruptly and slammed down his drink (*p. 157).

"What the frack is this?" he asked aloud to himself. None of the caffeine he had consumed could bring about the same level alertness as what was just done with a few lines of log entries. His eyes tracked through the rows of text until 11:09 p.m. when the entries stopped. Jonathan got up and trotted off to the receptionist.

"Hey Susan, who can check the logs from our badges?"

"We can get those from the building management company. I can call and ask for you. What do you need?" she responded efficiently.

"I need to know everyone who was in the building Saturday." Jonathan's hand tapped out an impatient rhythm on the counter between them.

"I can have them send it to you," Susan volunteered.

Jonathan quickly responded, "Oh, I can just wait for it."

Susan turned, looking a little annoyed. She looked through the contact list on her computer and then dialed a number on the phone.

"Yes, this is Susan at 3DNF… Yes Alice, the weekend was nice, and yours?"

Jonathan's tapping on the counter approached a drumbeat as he watched Susan listen to Alice's response.

"Uh, Alice, I'm sorry to be quick, but can we get a copy of the building access logs from Saturday?…Just e-mail it to me when you get it…Thanks for the help. Oh, and tell your sister I got the catalog she sent me – " thump – thump – thump. "I'll talk to you later. Thanks."

"Thanks, Susan, I really appreciate it." Jonathan didn't wait for a response as he started to walk away. "Just forward the e-mail you get from Alice, as soon as you can – it's important," he said as he disappeared behind the door out of the lobby.

"Hey Jonathan, why the hurry?" Michael asked as Jonathan scurried past his work area and into the general manager's office. Michael didn't get an answer. He sat there trying not to stare, but wondering what was going on. There were very few offices at 3DNF. Since their product was software, they had mostly cubicles for the developers. There were a couple of conference rooms and a few offices. All these had at least one wall of glass opening into the common area. The company had built its reputation on the creative power of some very smart people. Closed offices didn't fit the culture. Neither did the closed door to Alex Henderson's office where Jonathan sat behind a glass wall talking. Michael could see the expression on his boss's face change and his posture go from a relaxed slouch to a stiffened upright, then to standing. Michael looked down as the door opened.

"Michael, come here," Alex ordered.

"Sure," Michael responded as he locked his workstation and walked to his boss's office. He was suddenly 13 years old again and on his way to the principle's office after getting caught committing some prank. Michael sat gingerly in the chair next to Jonathan as Alex closed the door behind him.

"Jonathan, why don't you start by explaining to Michael what you just told me?"

Michael listened and tried to produce an appropriately surprised expression as Jonathan described the log entries he had reviewed. Thoughts came to mind too fast to answer. *Am I busted? Is this from what I did? I thought they didn't want to get caught? Am I supposed to say something?* Michael suddenly realized both Alex and Jonathan were waiting for his response.

"How do you know it came from inside the network?" Michael started.

"The IP address was internal, and the firewall didn't show any strange activity," Jonathan explained.

"Was it just a programmer doing an experiment?" Michael offered.

"It didn't look like an experiment to me. It was a noisy scan," Jonathan responded.

"Could this be related to the buyout?" Alex asked looking at Michael.

"What do you mean sir?" he responded.

"We just about wrapped the sale and I know people are nervous. Everything I've been told is we are going to all keep our jobs, and probably make out pretty well. But if someone has doubts, they might be looking around for ways to make Kimeron back out. Guys – do some homework on this. I want to know what's going on, but I don't want to raise any suspicions. If this is someone inside, then we need to keep everything quiet. We don't want to be the ones that screw up this deal. Give me a report tomorrow morning on what you learn."

Michael and Jonathan looked at each other briefly and both stood. They knew they had been dismissed. Alex turned his attention to the papers on his desk. The two walked out quickly.

Jonathan started talking as soon as they cleared the door to the office. "I want to look over some logs. I'll stop by later and we can talk."

Michael was grateful for the answer. He walked straight for his cube and did his best Invisible Man impersonation.

Jonathan was soon pouring over all the logs he could.

"I knew we should have put more money into the sensors than this," he complained to himself as he read. He moved his focus from screen to screen. Anyone watching would not have been able to discern any pattern. To Jonathan, he was checking off each sensor and control point until he had a clear picture of what he knew and what he didn't. He rummaged through his desk drawer and pulled out a business card. "He said they wanted to build relationships with the community," Jonathan mumbled as he picked up the phone and dialed the number on the card.

"Houston FBI, may I help you?"

"Huh, yes. Agent Mark Jackson please."

There was no acknowledgement as the line went silent for a moment.

"This is Mark."

"Hey, uh hello. This is Jonathan Tao at 3DNF. We met at the InfraGard meeting a couple of weeks ago" (*p. 323).

"Yes, I remember."

"You said in your presentation that the FBI was looking for ways to build relationship with infrastructure companies," Jonathan tried to get started.

"Yes."

"I know we are just a software company, but I have an issue here at the office that you might be interested in."

"Try me."

Wow - very concise - can this guy be any more Fed? Jonathan thought.

"I detected a noisy network scan that originated from inside our network over the weekend. We are about to be bought out by Kimeron."

"The defense contractor?" Mark asked.

Okay, now he's a little interested, Jonathan guessed to himself.

"Yeah. My boss is suspicious that there may be an employee who is trying to disrupt the purchase. He asked me to look into it further. I've been digging through our logs and I can't get a clear picture of what was done. Do you have anyone that could help me take a look?"

"Just a minute, let me check something on my calendar."

The line went silent for less than half a minute.

Mark came back on the line. "Can I stop by this afternoon?"

"Sure, that would be great." Jonathan responded. *I hope I'm doing the right thing,* he thought.

Chris Battle looked up from her paperwork with a poker face as Agent Jackson hung up the phone.

"Chris, I've got a project for us."

"What?"

"One of the contacts I made at the last Infragard meeting has some suspicious activity on their network and they want some help looking at it," Mark explained.

"What is Infragard?"

"It's a program the FBI set up several years ago to build contacts with organizations that control national infrastructure. Banks, utilities, local government agencies, even food producers participate in the program. They get together once a month for presentations and to get to know each other. It's better if something bad happens that people don't have to waste time swapping business cards."

"So this contact - have they had a loss?" Chris asked.

"He hasn't found one yet. He works for a software company that is being acquired by a national defense contractor. That definitely qualifies them as "infrastructure," Mark answered.

"I thought there had to be at least $30,000 in loss before it qualified for our involvement on business issues," Chris continued her questioning.

"It does. But this is building contacts. You never know who knows who in this business. This is how I build our network. We're probably just going to calm down an administrator at a software company. Some guy sitting in the corner who sees the

FBI walk in will suddenly realize they shouldn't poke around the network. And we can get out of the office for a couple of hours."

"It sounds like a waste of time, but you're the one doing the training. What time?"

"About 1300. Let's get some lunch on the way," Mark answered as he filed the last of the papers he had spread on his desk and then stood.

◐ ◐ ◐

"Hey Michael, I got some help for us." Jonathan had startled Michael as he tried to look like he was working. Michael took a slow breath, turned to face Jonathan, and leaned back slightly in his chair.

"What do you mean?"

"Remember I told you I went to that Infragard meeting last month?" Michael asked as he set his now warm Mountain Dew bottle on Michael's desk.

"Sort of – wasn't it something about pandemic flu?"

"Well, that was the main presentation. They have different topics every month from public and private organizations," Jonathan explained.

"Is that all? I would think the FBI has some other reasons," Michael asked.

"Oh I'm sure they do. I bet they are better at asking questions than telling what they know. Anyway, I just got off the phone with one of their agents."

Michael was pretty sure he felt a heart palpitation. "What did they say?"

"He's going to be here this afternoon to help us look over the logs. If we have to give Alex an answer tomorrow, maybe he can give us some ideas about how to figure this out," Jonathan answered.

"Let's not tell Alex," Michael volunteered. He was going to lose control of this situation soon.

"Okay, why?" Jonathan asked.

"You heard what he said. We better not be the ones who mess up the merger! That's why he's so nervous about this network scan. Anything that could mess up the deal will look bad on him and cost him a pile of money." Michael was making this up as fast as he could.

"Makes sense," Jonathan agreed. "We still have to give him a report tomorrow, and by then maybe the FBI will have some ideas."

"Cool. Uh, I think I better wrap up the new Dev server install, so I'll have some time to help." Michael hoped this would get him some quiet time to make a phone call.

"Sure. I'll come get you when he gets here." Jonathan picked up his drink and wandered off.

Michael was fairly successful in keeping his movements to a near-normal speed as he reached for a desk drawer and pulled out a now-crumpled manila envelope. He looked over the instructions again and then dialed a number.

"Pizza Hut, may I help you?"

"Sorry, wrong number," Michael responded and quickly hung up.

"This is way over my head! Though the money is good and I no longer have any other options."

Michael sat with his head down near his knees and took a few deep breaths. He jerked back up at the sudden ring of his cell phone. He mashed the "talk" button and brought the phone to his ear.

"What do you need?" Vlad started abruptly. Michael gave a quick summary of the morning as quietly as he could. There was a moment of silence as Vlad processed the information.

"This will work out well," Vlad answered. Michael couldn't think of any way this would work out in his favor.

Vlad continued. "I have your Lee Harvey Oswald."

"What?" Michael didn't see any connection between an assassin and his hacking problems.

On the other end of the conversation, Vlad smiled as he started to explain.

S1X

THE MEETING
Monday, 11:47 a.m.

Leon and Bob walked into the Greenspoint Mall. They had covered little distance when Bob turned to the arcade at their right and pulled Leon in with him.

"I thought we were going to the pizza place?" Leon protested as Bob walked to the change machine.

"We are. But I want to look around first." Bob pulled a few crumpled bills from his jeans pocket and walked over to the token machine while Leon loitered near the front and made a feeble attempt to look inconspicuous. Bob quickly returned and passed a handful of tokens to Leon.

"You play a game here near the entrance. I want to see if anyone is tailing us."

Leon had stopped joking about his friend's paranoia. Now he was thankful for it. He dutifully slipped a token into one of the games and played while Bob leaned next to the machine and watched. He didn't see anyone showing any interest in them as he scanned the entrance to the arcade or the main hallway of the mall. After a few minutes, he was satisfied.

"We will be late. Let's go," Bob said as he started to walk. Leon left the game running and followed Bob. As they walked through the food court, Bob stayed to the right so he could survey the open space.

"I don't see the T-shirt yet," Leon observed.

"Keep looking," Bob responded as he looked.

Leon was first. "Your Max friend is cold. He's got his sister to be a decoy for him."

"What do you mean? Where?" Bob asked. He followed Leon's nod toward a table on the far side of the food court. A thin, college-age brunette sat with her back to them. He couldn't see a face, but her shape was nothing like the nerd acquaintances Bob knew.

"How do you know she's his sister?" Bob asked.

"She's hot. No geek would have a girlfriend that looked like that," Leon observed.

"Good point."

"Do we take the bait?" Leon asked.

"Do we have a choice? Just watch out for pepper spray. You go left, I'll take right." Bob started walking. Leon followed the lead and headed around the food court in the opposite direction. They both reached the round table at the same time and sat down in unison. The girl didn't startle at all.

Bob started. "Your brother should have told you not to sit with your back to the crowd."

"Then how would you have seen the iDefense T-shirt?" she responded. The logic caught Bob off guard, but Leon quickly smiled at their new acquaintance.

"Beside the point," Bob recovered. "Where is your brother?"

The girl flipped her hair out of her eyes – succeeding in revealing only one striking brown eye that contrasted with the shock of dyed, bright blue hair that covered the other one. Her attractive, vaguely Asian features were enough to cause Leon pause, and keep Bob off balance.

"Why are you asking me about a brother? I don't have a brother. You wanted to meet me."

Bob wasn't convinced. "Sure. Where is Max? Do we have to go somewhere to meet him? We don't have much time."

"I'm Max."

"Right. We need help fast. Where do we find him?" Bob continued. Leon just sat with a half-grin watching the parlay.

"You find him right here. What do you want?"

"Okay, how do I know you're Max?" Bob challenged.

"In WOW, you have a pet Scorpion you named 'Snookums'."

Leon chuckled as Bob answered exasperated. "That's pretty good, but anyone who plays WOW could know that."

"Okay, I'm the one that showed you how to pop the sled on that buffer for the browser bug you were working on about a month ago. Since I didn't get any credit in the shout out, I know you didn't tell anyone how I helped," Max responded.

Leon laughed and turned to Bob. "Dude, you are so busted. You told me you came up with that bug on your own!"

Bob's mouth hung open like a flytrap for a moment before he recovered. "That's beside the point!" he protested to Max. "Dude, you're not a dude!"

Max was quick. "Get over it. It's the Internet! The guys are guys. The girls are guys. And the 14-year-olds are FBI agents! What do you expect?"

Leon looked straight at Bob. "I am starting to like her," he confessed and then turned to Max. "Okay, we need some help. Let's delete the awkward introduction. Bob's a little harder to deal with IRL."

"You're paying, so what's the job?" Max asked.

Bob finally started to get his footing. "We need you to go back to our hotel."

"Whatever, what do you think I am?" Max protested.

"I thought you were a dude with enough candle power to help! Here, I'll show you some of it." Bob reached down and opened his ever-present backpack. He pulled out his older machine and booted it. While it was coming up, Leon pulled a USB thumb drive from his pocket and slipped it into the side of the computer. Bob typed for a moment and then turned the laptop to face Max.

"Here is a Wireshark capture we did when we were planting icons for a wireless Capture the Flag game. We saw this code and we think it has something to do with the Feds. What do you see?"

"Max looked for less than a minute. "This is serious. Whoever was planting, this was deliberate. Your capture doesn't show any scan from the source of the code. They knew what their target was."

Bob looked at Leon. "Why didn't you see that?"

Max looked at Bob. "I'll go look at what else you have, but I've got pepper spray."

Leon just smiled as Bob took the laptop and handed the thumb drive back to Leon. The three got up and Bob led the way they came toward the arcade. Max assumed they were walking toward the exit when Bob took a quick turn to the right and opened an unmarked door where there was no shop. Max gave Leon a questioning look but he just followed along without hesitation. Max did likewise. They were walking along a maintenance hall behind the food court restaurants. They came to a branch that went to a door marked "Exit" but Bob continued straight ahead.

"Have you been here before?" Max asked as they walked.

"I wouldn't have suggested a meeting here if I hadn't," Bob answered as he led them to another door. He opened it and they were back in another main hallway of the mall. It wasn't crowded, but there were enough people there for them to quickly blend in. Bob marched across the hallway, past a Sears, and opened another unmarked door on the other side. Leon and Max just kept pace as they went down the brick-walled space. They came to another branch, and this time, Bob veered left. He pushed open the door into the daylight of the parking lot.

As they approached the Mini, Leon pulled out his keys. Max looked at the car and quickly spoke up, "I'm not getting in a stolen car with you two."

Bob turned. "Why do you think it's stolen?"

"I wasn't sure until you just answered that way," Max responded. "You two don't look like you could afford a real car."

Leon took this one. "It's not stolen. We borrowed it from a friend."

"Borrowed doesn't sound too safe," Max responded as she looked at the line of police cars parked near them at the Houston PD Mall substation. "For a car of question-able source and two guys scared of Feds, why are you parking by so many cops?"

"The closer to danger, the farther from harm," responded Leon smugly.

"Huh – Tolkien fan," Max observed. "Shotgun!"

Leon smiled as he watched Bob acquiesce and fold himself into the back seat. As Leon turned the key in the ignition, Max turned back to look at Bob.

"And one more thing – IRL my name is Hannah."

Bob didn't have a response. He just gave a sigh. Leon watched his face in the rear view mirror and then turned to his passenger. "Nice to meet you, Hannah. Thanks for helping us." Leon pulled out of their parking space and patiently made his way out of the mall parking lot. Bob processed his online acquaintance's real-life identity in silence.

FIRST LEAD

Monday, 1:01 p.m.

"Good afternoon, how may I help you?" Susan asked as a man and woman walked in the door at 3DNF.

"I am Agent Jackson and this is Agent Battle. We have an appointment with Jonathan Tao," Mark responded dryly as he and Chris both displayed their badges.

Their identification could have come from a cereal box. Susan was so taken aback when she saw the letters "FBI" that she saw nothing else. She said nothing more and quickly turned to the phone in front of her and dialed Jonathan's number.

"This is Jonathan."

"You have a couple of visitors from the FBI," Susan reported with a halting voice as she looked up at the two standing in front of her.

"Great, I'll be right there." Susan heard the click and set the phone down. "He'll be with you in just a moment," she reported as she continued to stare. She had never seen FBI agents at the office. Most of their visitors were strangely dressed programmers, some rumpled academics, and vendors. Lately, there had been an influx of lawyers with the buyout. *They look more like lawyers than agents*, she thought as the shock wore off and they turned and surveyed the entrance behind them.

Very shortly, the door to the office opened and Jonathan appeared. "Great. Agent Jackson, I'm Jonathan," he said as he extended a hand.

"Call me Mark. And this is my partner Chris," Mark responded as he finished the handshake.

Agent Battle didn't look too pleased with her partner as she shook Jonathan's hand as well.

"Let's start at my desk," Jonathan led the way through the door and past the rows of cluttered desks and large monitors.

"This looks like your kind of place," Chris commented to Mark as they walked. She muttered, "There probably hasn't been talk of a date around here since this place opened for business."

Mark allowed a couple of steps worth of space to open between him and Jonathan as he responded. "Just because we're bright doesn't mean we don't mate."

"Great now I won't get that image out of my head," Chris responded as they walked.

Jonathan pulled a couple of chairs over to his work area and tossed an empty Mountain Dew bottle in the trash. Chris gave a quick glance around the area before she sat down. She noted one set of eyes that marked her movement. Michael quickly leaned forward in his chair out of their line of sight. Jonathan was already talking and Mark was listening intently when Chris turned her attention to the monitors in the work area.

"So what I don't get is why they were doing such an obvious scan," Jonathan was stating. "I looked at our main servers and didn't find anything out of the ordinary. But then I found this." Jonathan's right hand was driving a mouse and clicking quickly as windows appeared on the main screen. He pointed to a server called 3D-FS1 and double-clicked. Another flurry of clicks and soon, a window appeared listing the contents of directories.

"Here in the root of one of our file servers is an icon file called 'CyberBoB'." It doesn't tie to any executables. The time stamp shows that the file was placed here right in the middle of the scan traffic that started all of this."

Mark leaned forward and stared intently at the screen for a moment. "Can I have a printout of this listing?" he asked.

"Sure." Jonathan clicked some more. "It will be on the main printer." He started to get up before Mark interrupted.

"Do you have a wireless network here?"

"No. We used to do subcontract work for a defense contractor and now that they are buying us, they don't want any wireless. I have to run a check every couple of weeks just to make sure."

"How do you do that?" Mark asked.

"Let me show you." Jonathan opened up the wireless options window on his Windows XP system and clicked the "scan for available networks" options. The three of them watched as it returned a blank window. "Nothing. I'm kind of surprised, I haven't picked up anything lately from some of the other businesses around here either" (*p. 176). Jonathan stood up. "I'll get that printout for you." He left Mark and Chris in the cubicle.

"What are you thinking?" Chris asked.

"Not yet." Mark answered and turned as Jonathan reappeared quickly with a sheet of paper.

"Jonathan, have you had any staff turn over lately? You mentioned a buyout," Mark questioned.

"No, we haven't. If the deal goes through, I think most of us will make out pretty well. They are buying the company for the brainpower anyway."

"Have you had any temps around? I noticed a lot of new computer boxes piled up as we walked in," Mark continued.

"Yeah a couple of kids. We've been getting new equipment. Alex, my boss, said we are supposed to have everything matching the new company's standards. He had Michael bring in help."

"Who is Michael?"

"Oh – Michael Resol. He runs our infrastructure. He had to get some help for the equipment staging work," Jonathan explained.

"Did they come from an agency?"

"No. I think they were friends or relatives of one of our programmers."

"Did you do background checks on them?" Mark continued.

"I don't know. Hey Michael!" Jonathan called across the hall. Michael looked like a prairie dog popping out of his hole as he jumped a little too fast at the mention of his name.

"Yeah?" came the reply with a voice that cracked on the single word.

"Do you remember the names of the temps you had in to do the PC installs?"

Michael walked over to the group. "Uh, there was John Aggarwal and Robert something. I think it was Focker. No, Falken."

Michael's eyes met Agent Battle and he instantly looked away. Mark followed up. "Do you have any paperwork on these people?"

"No. I should have, but they were friends of friends. They were just kids and it was just for a few hours. I paid them with old gear we were going to get rid of anyway."

Mark made some notes on a pad he carried. "Do you have a way to reach them?"

"Do you think they did the scan?" Michael asked.

Mark looked at Jonathan expectantly. "It's okay, Michael and I are the ones who are supposed to be looking into this," Jonathan volunteered.

Mark looked back at Michael. "I don't have a theory. I just want to make sure I get the facts."

"Sure. I don't have anything for John, but the Robert guy gave me an address and phone number. Just a sec." Michael went back to his desk and pulled a Post-It note off the top of a pad. He had just written down the info that morning from Vlad.

"Here you go." Michael handed the note to Mark. Chris noted a slight tremor in Michael's hand at the exchange.

"One of the days they were here Robert was wearing some kind of geek or hacking shirt," Michael volunteered.

"Interesting. Thanks for the help." Mark stood and Chris followed the lead. "We need to check a couple of things out. Can I call you tomorrow?" Mark asked Jonathan.

"Sure. If you have any ideas, let me know. We're supposed to report to our boss in the afternoon," Jonathan responded.

"No problem." Mark started to turn for the entrance.

"Do you need to look through the server logs or anything else?" Jonathan asked.

"I've got what I think I need for now," Mark answered. I might have some follow-up questions, but first I want to check a couple of ideas and we'll be in touch.

"I don't trust that Michael guy," Chris observed as soon as they closed the doors to the car.

"He's scared, but it could just be because we were there," Mark observed.

"What's your theory? You knew something with that icon thing," Chris asked.

"I think they have some sloppy network security and just got used for a hacking game."

"A game? They are about to get bought by a major defense contractor, and some strange network scan happens and your theory is a game?"

"Yeah. I don't have enough to get a warrant, but it's worth our time to go for a drive."

"A drive? Where to?"

"I think I know who this Robert is. If I'm right, then I can use this defense contractor connection as a reason to look at a network I've been wanting to see for several months."

"What network?" Chris was not following any of this.

"There is a group of local hackers that I've been trying to build a relationship with. One of the brightest is named Bob, and I think this looks like something he would have done. I don't think he did anything malicious here, but he might have just given me a way to get a look inside his home network. I'm betting we will find some leads on other things that will be interesting," Mark explained.

"Home network?" Chris asked.

"Sure. Guys like him have some pretty impressive networks that they use to do research."

"And do you have one?" Chris asked.

"Of course. It's not too big. Just a few servers, two laptops, my main PC, and of course the gaming machine. You should come over some time and – "

"You did not just invite me over."

Mark gave Chris a confused look. "What?"

"You did not just invite me to your place," Chris clarified for her slow partner.

Mark shook his head as he turned his eyes back the road.

"No. I invited you over to see my lab." Mark curtly replied clearly put off. "It's just as well – it would be lost on you."

THE DISCOVERY

Monday, 5:32 p.m.

"What do you think we can do without a warrant? Are you going to just ask him to show you his network?" Chris asked as they drove through the dreary neighborhood to the Falken house.

"I don't know yet," Mark answered as he finished the turn and started scanning for house numbers. He started to slow the car and eased toward the curb as he approached. "Right now I just want to talk to him and see what he can tell me. It might lead us to," Mark's voice dropped off as he set the car in "park."

He pointed down the left side of the house. "The gate to the backyard is wide open. Let's do this together," Mark said as he gave a quick look up and down the street and pulled out his revolver. Chris was already ahead of him and had her door open first. Mark wanted to take the lead, but Chris was around the front of the car and making her way up the driveway before Mark could gather himself.

"Front door looks normal," Chris noted as she walked past the left corner of the attached garage and started to walk through the gate. Mark followed along the house, watching down the street before following into the backyard. No one noted the visitors.

There were no windows along the side of the house as they reached the back corner. Chris gave a pause for Mark to catch up. She gave a quick look around the small rectangle of overgrown Bermuda and a lone spindly tree in the backyard. The first window was about shoulder-high. Chris glanced in the corner. She didn't say anything, but Mark noticed she bent down quickly and her hands flexed on the grip of her gun. A few steps and she paused at a glass patio door that was standing pushed open with a bent handle. The matching door frame that once held the lock was bent.

Mark noted a crowbar tossed on the patio before he caught Chris's eyes as she got ready to go in.

"Hello? FBI! Anyone home?" Mark announced. Chris swept the room from right to left and saw no movement. She moved across the cluttered family room to her left toward a hallway as Mark came in behind and gave another look to the kitchen to the right. It had obviously been tossed. This was what Chris must have seen through the window. Mark turned to his left and saw Chris paused at the hallway waiting for him. He covered the distance in three quick steps and Chris then turned into the hallway and held her gun straight ahead of her.

"Clear!"

Mark moved behind Chris and checked a small front foyer and living room. It was neat and unoccupied.

"Clear!" Mark responded as he turned back to find Chris proceeding down the hallway. Mark followed with his gun held low. Chris checked a bathroom to the right while Mark checked a small neat room to the left. The room was too neat compared to the house they had seen so far. Mark's gaze took in a sewing machine, a cutting table, perfect curtains in the window and –

"Something burned in here!" Chris noted as she positioned herself by a closed door at the end of the hall. Instead of going in, she looked to her right at the open door to George's bedroom. Mark took Chris's place in the hall as she proceeded into the room and did a quick sweep of the bedroom and small bathroom. Chris came back as Mark opened the door to Bob's bedroom/lab. It was hard to see if anything was out of place or the mess was a normal state. Mark noted the acrid smell of burnt electronics as he holstered his gun and scanned the room.

"Is this how you people live?" Chris asked. "I'm going to go see why the kitchen was tossed." Chris was only one step down the hall when Mark stopped her.

"This might be part of it." Chris turned back as Mark held up the largest piece of a shattered webcam and then pointed at the top of the largest of the many monitors arrayed at the makeshift desk. Chris followed Mark's gaze and then saw the hole in the wall.

"So why did someone break into this geek's house, shoot a camera, and toss a kitchen?" Chris asked. This makes no sense. And what is that smell?

"Something fried the electronics in here," Mark said as he tapped a couple of keyboards with the tip of a pen he had pulled out of his pocket. Nothing is working in here. I bet the kid wiped everything.

"Your kid wasn't here when this happened," Chris answered.

"How do you know that?"

"That kitchen was tossed like someone was searching for something," Chris explained as she walked around the room. "I don't see why they would shoot the camera, but whoever came in didn't think anyone was home. They would have made too much noise with the crowbar and the patio door."

"I don't know," Mark doubted as he walked over and checked the two small windows in Bob's room. "They're both locked. He didn't get out this way."

"Let's see what the kitchen has to say," Chris said as she walked down the hallway.

"Why would the kitchen be so interesting?" Chris asked as they surveyed the mess. Most of the cabinet doors were still closed, but every drawer starting from the right side of the room was tossed on the floor with its contents spread evenly about. About a third of the way around the room, the mess stopped. "Whoever it was found what they were looking for in this drawer," Chris observed as she stood over the last tossed drawer.

Mark surveyed the dumped contents on the floor. Most looked like typical kitchen contents with silverware, measuring cups, and other utensils. But the pile of stuff at the center under the last open drawer was different. There were an unusual amount of batteries, small nails, spare change, pieces of paper, coupons, pens, and even a tossed deck of cards.

"Whatever they were looking for was in the kitchen junk drawer," Mark observed.

"I've never seen a house without one of those," Chris noted. That just means we can't figure out what they were looking for from here. It could have been anything."

Mark pulled out his phone and hit the speed dial for the office. He gave a sigh thinking about the time he was going to be spending trying to get some data off of those cooked hard disks in Bob's lab.

An hour later, Chris and Mark were getting back in their car.

"So am I going to have to sit at the office tomorrow and watch you do your geek thing with all those computers the guys are back there tagging?" Chris asked.

"Probably not. I do that work alone, and I bet it won't reveal much. Bob is a bright guy and if he wanted information wiped, then it's wiped."

Mark pulled out of the neighborhood and headed for the highway.

"Where are you going? I thought the office was north of here," Chris asked as Mark made the turn onto the entrance ramp.

"I'm not done with this. There are three guys who hang out with Bob at the 2600 meetings. I know where two of them work, so I want to go ask some questions."

◐ ◐ ◐

Twenty minutes later, Mark parked the car outside of a Bellaire strip center in front of a store called LightSpeedSystems.

"Just let me talk," Mark cautioned as they got out of the car.

"Of course – like I even speak the language," Chris answered as she held the door open for Mark.

Chris was just inside the door behind Mark when a large unkempt guy with dark eyes and sloppy red hair called out.

"Hey Jeb, if that really is your name, why are you bringing a Fed with you?"

"Sorry, my name is Mark Jackson and this is – "

"I know who you are. You are the kicker who calls himself 'Jeb' at the 2600 meetings. You clean up pretty good. She's a Fed, so I'm betting you are, too."

Mark gave up. "Chris, this is Dobbs. He's a friend of Bob from the 2600 meetings."

"I knew it!" Dobbs exclaimed. "You guys and your Patriot Act are watching all of us!"

Mark revealed a look of exasperation and annoyance as he raised both his hands slightly towards Dobbs. "I'm just a tech who has learned it's best not to tell everyone where I work."

"That's crap! I bet you are part of a whole program made just to watch people like us. You just need to put some faces with all the data you've been scraping with Echelon!" (*p. 324)

"I'm not going to convince you. I just need a few answers." Mark said almost pleading.

Chris suppressed a laugh as she surveyed the store and watched Mark blow his own cover.

"Like I'm going to give you guys answers. You don't need answers anyway. I bet you've been using your wire taps on – "

"Dobbs, give it a rest. I just want to know if you can help me find Bob," Mark interrupted now losing patience playing "good cop."

Dobbs stopped talking and looked down at his shorter visitors for a moment. "Okay, I'll confess." Dobbs sighed. "Bob and I have been building a small nuclear device. We had to scrape the glowy stuff off of about 1700 watch faces we found at flea markets to get enough fissile material."

Mark leaned on the counter with both hands and just bowed his head slightly. "Dobbs, you need to understand I think Bob is in trouble and I want to help."

Mark held Dobbs' gaze for a three-count and then Dobbs looked away.

"I haven't talked to him since the meeting. You know as much as I do. He was still working on the Capture the Flag setup.

"Can you get in touch with him?" Mark asked.

"He's the only person I know who's more careful than me," Dobbs responded reluctantly. "I don't even have an e-mail address."

Mark reached in his pocket and pulled out a business card. Dobbs gave a flinch at the motion before he saw the white paper.

"Here is my card. If you hear from him, call me."

Dobbs looked at the card and saw "Federal Bureau of Investigation." "Why would I need to call you? If I hear from Bob, you'll probably have it all on tape…"

"Dobbs, the last thing we have time for or care about is tapping your lines," Mark interrupted him as he turned to walk out.

"Why not? All I need is a detonator and my watch-bomb could take out half the Gulf!"

Mark paused at the door. "And what would you have to hack then?" Mark gave a grin and walked out before there was a reply. Usually, no one got the last word on Dobbs at the 2600 meetings.

"So that is what we work so hard to protect from terrorists?" Chris asked with disgust as they got back in the car. "That must be what happens when Dan Haggerty goes geek."

"Dobbs is one of the smartest ones at the 2600 meetings. I swear if you put a keyboard on a '57 Chevy he could write a Perl script to improve the gas mileage."

"What's a pearl script?" Chris asked (*p. 324).

Mark just gave a sigh and started the car. "We have one more visit to make."

❮❮❮

"House of Pies?" Chris asked as they turned into the parking lot. "If these guys are so smart, why don't they have better jobs?"

"A lot of them work just to feed their computer habit," Mark answered. They walked in and paused at the "Please Wait to Be Seated" sign. A young, African-American man approached with two menus. He wore the same polyester slacks and polo as the rest of the staff, but Chris saw the flash of a Tag Heuer watch. She also noted some very nice looking black D&G rimless glasses.

"Would you two agents like a booth or table?" he asked.

Chris gave an annoyed look to Mark.

"What do you mean?" Mark asked.

"You talk to one hacker, you talk to all. Information wants to be free. And you two look just like Dobbs described." Mark noticed the iPhone secured to the waiters' belt.

"I just want to ask if you know where Bob is."

"I haven't seen him or Leon since they left the 2600 meeting to do more wardriving. I thought with all your spying at our meetings, you would be able to find him if you want." Rudy gave his best angry look, but it wasn't as convincing as Dobbs had been.

"So there were two of them." Mark saw an opportunity. He reached out with his left hand and placed it on Rudy's shoulder and gently guided him to the closest booth. Rudy sat down and Mark slid into the booth beside him and Chris took a seat across from them.

"Listen, if you were paying attention at all of those meetings, I'm just as much a propeller-head as you guys. Bob never seemed like someone who would go bad. I just know he's in trouble and he needs help. Please, tell me what you know." Mark responded earnestly.

Chris wouldn't admit it, but she was impressed. Mark had picked the right technique at the right time. She saw Rudy's expression ease just enough as he took in a long breath.

"Bob was here with Leon last night," Rudy started.

Mark gave a slight knowing glance toward Chris, and then turned back to Rudy. "What did they tell you?"

"Not much." Rudy looked at Mark, then across at Chris. He didn't trust her, so he turned back to Mark.

"Anything you have will help," Mark encouraged. Mark and Chris waited for Rudy to fill the silence.

"They needed a car."

"I thought Bob had a car."

"It's not that. They needed a car for the wardriving. They wanted to scope out some places in a country club. Bob said he wanted to find a spot that a regular hacker wouldn't fit in," Rudy explained.

Chris allowed herself a nod of agreement at the logic.

"So what car do they have right now?" Mark asked.

"They took mine. I've got Bob's wagon parked in the back. He and Leon have my Mini Cooper."

"That's a pretty good ride for a waiter," Chris observed. "That watch doesn't look like it belongs here either." She said inquisitively.

Rudy and Mark both gave Chris a look.

"My dad agreed to pay for my college and car as long as I keep an hourly-wage job. He said everyone should respect hard work," Rudy responded in a somewhat haughty tone, and then looked back to Mark who gave a slight helpless shrug of his shoulders.

"Can you give me the license number?" Mark asked as he handed Rudy a piece of paper and a pen. Rudy just nodded and started writing.

"I hope you didn't let Bob drive your car," Mark added as he collected the paper and pen from Rudy trying to lighten the mood.

Rudy seemed to perk up at the comment. "No way – I made Leon promise he would drive."

"Rudy, you did good. We want to help Bob, too," Mark said as he got out of the booth. Mark looked to the front of the restaurant and then at Rudy. "You've got customers. We will be in touch." He shook hands and presented his card in hopes of possibly more information in the future from Rudy.

It wasn't until Mark reached to turn the ignition in the car that Chris spoke.

"You did good."

Mark paused and turned to look at Chris. "You sound surprised."

"I am."

"The best hacks are human, not technical. Rudy needed to tell someone. I just gave him the right 'someone' so he could help his friend."

"So do you have any other leads – or do we get to call it a day?"

"You can call in the bolo on the Mini." Mark handed the slip of paper to Chris. "Tomorrow I'll see if there is anything left on the gear from Bob's house. Right now that's the only path I see."

S3V3N

CODE REVIEW

Tuesday, 3:19 a.m.

Leon wanted to stay awake. He had enjoyed watching Hannah work as she parsed through the code they had captured from 3DNF. He sat in an uncomfortable hotel chair between Bob and Hannah as they worked. Hannah's hands moved across the keyboard with the flair of a pianist. After each command was completed, there was a certain virtuoso quality to the way she finished off the strike on the "Enter" key. As Leon watched his two companions, every blink of his eyes took a little longer to open. His breathing slowed and his body relaxed slightly. One deep breath and –

"What!?" Bob had punched Leon on the shoulder.

"I told you they were Feds!"

"What?" Leon still couldn't command any more words.

"I told you they were Feds!" Bob tried again.

"We don't know that," Leon responded and then yawned. "That's just what Dobbs said in his Twitter. Did you find anything in the code?" (*p. 136)

Hannah jumped in. "Whatever you guys caught, it wasn't amateur. I found references to IPs that tie back to Germany, Russia, Switzerland, and China. There's no way to know where the command and control for this is. I tried looking at these IPs and they are all black holes. They either don't exist or they have some good source filtering" (*p. 255).

"What does the code do?" Leon asked.

"We can't tell. But there is more about where the code was going when you caught this copy. You guys were too quick looking at the packet capture. Here," Hannah pointed at the display on her laptop. " – the file was going to 10.24.53.192."

"Yeah, we knew that," Leon said. He turned to Bob and wondered aloud to Bob brooding in his chair, "Since when are you so quiet?"

"But did you see this?" Hannah continued scrolling down a couple of screens worth of captured data and pointed again. "Whoever was on the wireless network with you was also talking to 10.43.84.143."

"Okay, so they hopped to another private network," Bob responded. Leon noted the slight annoyance in Bob's tone.

"What were they doing?" Leon turned back to Hannah.

"Well, it's a different subnet. So I'd sure like to know if it just hopped through a switch, or if it is going through a router to an internal segment, or DMZ, or out to another extranet. We just can't tell if this is in the same general network or not. Since the person you were eavesdropping on went straight to the first IP, they knew what they wanted." Hannah turned to Bob. "You didn't see any scanning before you started this capture, did you?"

"No – this is the only interesting part of the traffic we saw," Bob responded.

Hannah continued, "I bet if they are good guys or bad, they were placing some kind of command and control on at least one box, maybe two."

"Feds!" Bob loudly concluded.

"We don't know that," Leon pointed out trying to break Bob out of his funk.

"They've got my dad!" Bob responded, his voice close to cracking.

"What?" Hannah turned to Leon. "That's more than the code review I signed on for."

Leon didn't want to lose the new help. "Listen, we think – but we don't know – the people who were on the network were Feds."

"Of course, they were – you guys saw Dobbs's DM when they went to his shop." Bob was getting his voice back. He turned to Hannah. "Max, I had a camera in my lab. It was tied to a motion sensor and sent a video file to a remote server I use. We pulled down the file and saw three people in my lab with my dad. They had a gun on him and one of them shot out my camera. None of my stuff is live on the web anymore."

"That doesn't sound like the Feds," Hannah responded.

Bob looked almost wounded with her answer, but he didn't stop. "Dobbs. He's from 2600, he – wait a minute – you were lurking at the meeting last month, weren't you!"

"I was watching," Hannah confessed defiantly.

"Where?" Leon jumped in.

"I was hanging out close enough to listen to what was going on. I knew if I sat down and started talking, I'd probably get pulled in and then I'd have to come up with some complicated real-world story."

Bob shook his head, a little mad at himself for not connecting the dots before now. "Anyway, two Feds showed up at Dobbs's shop yesterday. They were asking about me!"

Hannah started to ask a question, but Bob cut her off.

"And get this – one of the Feds has been going to 2600!"

"Who?" Hannah asked.

"Jeb – the kicker. He was in a suit at Dobbs's place. They've been watching us all along!"

"Listen, if they are Feds, they won't get you for anything more than listening to an unsecured wireless. I've looked at the logs and you don't have anything other than a radio broadcast someone was dumb enough to not encrypt properly. But, if these guys are bad – you don't know how far they will go. If they have your dad, I say go to the Feds now and take your chances."

Bob was shaking his head in disagreement before Hannah even finished. Leon was a little slower to come to a conclusion. Everyone had exhausted his or her arguments. They sat in silence with each looking at a different random object in the room. After a few sighs and shifts in a seat, Leon tentatively broke the silence.

"I think Hannah's right. We need someone on our side and I think it's worth taking the chance." Leon paused, expecting the push back from Bob, but it didn't come. Instead, he just looked expectantly at Leon to see if he had more. Leon continued his thought.

"If Jeb – or whatever his name is – has been watching us, then at least he knows we aren't that bad. If he's been paying attention in the 2600 meetings, we don't teach people to do evil." Leon paused for a breath and Bob let him continue.

"Let's set up a meet at some neutral place. Maybe they can help."

Bob sat and considered the idea. He knew his friends were right, he just had to break the momentum of his own distrust of anyone in a position of authority.

"Okay, let's send a text to Jeb. I've got his cell number from Dobbs."

"Don't use your phone," Hannah volunteered.

Bob gave her an incredulous look. "Of course, not. I don't carry a phone – and I'm not going to use Leon's and give them a way to trace us. I'll use a VMware browser appliance through Tor to a Web site that sends texts" (*p. 256). Bob turned and reached for his laptop, balanced it on his knees, and started typing.

Hannah looked a little embarrassed at the answer and leaned back in her chair while Bob worked. Leon leaned over Bob's shoulder as he typed.

```
I hear you are asking around about us. Meet at Galleria parking
garage, where we exit from 2600 meetings at 17:30 today. Don't
bring goons. Bob.
```

"I don't think 'goons' is a way to make a friend," Leon suggested.

"Tough. I don't want any extras," Bob answered still agitated with no tangible target to lash out at, then he clicked the "Send" button on the screen. "Now, we need a different car. The Mini works for wardriving, but we may need to blend into the crowd now. Max, do you have a car?"

"Uh, yeah. But I don't want every cop on the street looking for it." Max said taken aback at the abrupt transition.

"What do you have?" Bob asked, ignoring Hannah's concern.

"It's a Ford Taurus my dad gave me after he wore it out driving to work for years."

"Perfect. We'll need you to drive to the meet by yourself and be our way out. We will need to ditch the Mini. If the Feds have been talking to Rudy, then they probably know we have his car," Bob deduced.

"I'm not sure. I don't think Rudy would tell them," Leon suggested.

"We can't take that chance – Rudy has more to lose than we do. We've got to assume the Mini isn't safe. Besides, we left the wagon in the parking lot, remember?"

Leon nodded in agreement, but Hannah wasn't satisfied with her part.

"I just said I don't want to have cops looking for – "

"Max, we don't have a choice. We need to get out of there and you are the only way," Bob responded. "Besides, we won't be followed. They won't ever see us get into your car – that's why we picked the location."

Hannah still wasn't convinced. She looked at Bob and started to speak. Just as she took a breath, Leon cut her off.

"Hannah, please," was all he said quietly. She looked at Leon and her expression softened just slightly.

"We arrive at different times, and I don't park anywhere near you."

"Deal," was all Bob said.

Leon smiled slightly at Hannah and nodded his head. "Okay, now we are a team." He turned back to Bob. "So what do we need for the meet?"

"Let's see…" Bob leaned back in his chair and stared at the ceiling with his hands behind his head. "We'll need my iPaq to check for heat, my laptop with the code, and, uh, and that's probably it." I don't want to take more and risk losing it."

Two hours later, Leon and Bob pulled into the Galleria parking garage slowly. Leon started up the ramp while watching the environment for threats. Bob had his iPaq running WiFiFoFum. The software gave him a radar-like display of wireless access points in the area (*p. 177).

"We're clear so far – no cops in this part of the garage." Bob leaned over and showed the display to Leon. A single dot appeared near the edge of the screen.

Leon understood. The display showed sources of wireless network signals and estimated their distance. The Houston police department, like a few others around the country, had begun using wireless signals between their squad cars and repeater stations set on traffic signals. The resulting network gave them a high-speed data link back to their headquarters, so they could retrieve datalike lookups on license plates or pull up videos on certain public area surveillance cameras. The problem with the system was that they hadn't considered how easy it was to detect the wireless signal. Even though it was encrypted, it still warned of their presence. Even when they went on silent runs, they were emitting a Wi-Fi networking signal (*p. 180).

Leon turned back to watching the cars slowly pass as they drove up the ramp. Just as they made the turn passed the second-level stairwell entrance, neither of them noticed the man step out of the door. As Leon and Bob proceeded up the ramp, Andrei strode calmly across the ramp and over to an older-model sedan. He needed something that wouldn't have an alarm. The well-practice move was only visible to someone directly in front of Andrei. He slipped the tool between the window and the rubber gasket of the door and with a deft move, caught the lock and pulled. The door was open and Andrei quickly went to work on the ignition.

Mark and Chris were already standing by their car on the third level. As agreed, in the texts they received, they were positioned on the opposite end of the level from the stairwell. Neither spoke as they watched the full parking lot. There was a lull in foot traffic, but they could hear the sound of cars and people on the other levels. Chris caught the motion first and tapped Mark's arm as she turned.

Leon pulled the Mini Cooper up the ramp and continued around up to the fourth level. Chris followed the movement of the car while Mark watched where it came from.

"Is that our contact?" Chris asked as she tracked the movement.

"Yeah. Watch for them to walk in. They'll either come from behind us or that stairwell," Mark motioned across the parking garage to the metal door that had no window. They stood scanning the area for only a couple of quiet minutes before the door to the stairwell opened slowly. Two college-age kids walked out. The shorter leaned forward slightly to compensate for the weight of the backpack he carried.

"We don't need to worry about them running," Chris noted.

Leon paused for a moment, but Bob never broke stride. Both of them were scanning the area. Bob went straight to the first space between a parked car behind him and an SUV in front. Leon was close behind. From their position, they could see the door to the stairwell, were a few paces from the ramp up to the next level, and had a clear line of sight to the two "Feds" who were the objective of the day. The hood of the SUV gave more protection from their biggest threat.

"Dobbs was right – that's Jeb from the 2600 meetings," Bob observed. He could see both of Mark's hands, but the lady stood with her side facing them. Her left hand was visible resting on the hood of a car, but her right arm was held close to her side, hiding her hand. "I think she has a gun," Bob noted while trying to deny the reality at the same time. Leon nodded half in agreement but didn't speak.

"Bob. What were you guys doing at 3DNF Saturday night?" Mark started the conversation.

Bob didn't give Leon a chance to speak. "I'd rather know what you guys were doing there!"

"Bob, we weren't there. We got a call that they found a CyberBob icon file on one of their servers. That sounds like you were planting stuff for the Capture the Flag."

"You were there!" Bob retorted without answering Mark's question. "We were minding our own business at a convenience store and detected you guys planting a Trojan on their network!" Bob yelled accusingly.

Leon winced and gave Bob a look since he had just confessed to eavesdropping on a network to a federal agent. However, "Dude, shut up!" was all that came out.

"Bob, I don't know what you are talking about. We weren't there."

"We have proof you were dropping files on a private company's network!" Bob took a breath and decided to play his only card. "I'll give all that up if you will just let my dad go! He had nothing to do with it and didn't know where I was!"

There was a pause while Mark and Chris exchanged confused looks.

"Bob, let's go somewhere to finish this conversation in private. I think you don't understand – "

Mark stopped talking as a car pulled behind Bob and Leon's position. It was coming up from the lower level and passed in front of the stairwell entrance. Leon caught the motion and turned. Chris saw the car, and then saw the taller of the two kids move rather quickly.

In the same moment, Andrei pulled behind Bob and Leon. He smoothly raised his gun up from the passenger's seat, where it was laying with his hand on the grip.

Leon felt the first shot more than he heard it. The sound of a gunshot inside the parking garage reverberated and then a ringing sound began to grow inside his head.

Before he could decide if he was hit, he saw Bob go down. The bullet hit Bob directly in the middle of his backpack. The impact slammed him forward and his face caught the passenger's side mirror on a Chevy Tahoe as he fell. For a half-count, Leon saw Bob hit the ground and saw the back of his backpack stained a dark color, looking like it was wet. Leon yelled for his friend and ducked low at the side of the SUV and tried to get to Bob.

From there, the experiences of the two friends diverged. For Leon, he was suddenly amazed to find Bob struggling to get back up and begin barking orders at him. For Bob, the gunshot impact, the face-plant into the SUV, and Leon's shouting blurred into a surreal world of soldiers and gunfire.

"What are you looking at?!" Bob barked with a voice of authority. Before Leon could process the fact that his friend was standing, more orders followed.

"Cover my left while I find where they're coming from!" Bob crouched down, opened the Velcro cover on the case attached to his belt and pulled out his PDA. Leon saw Bob's WiFiFoFum wireless scanner. But it was clear that Bob saw something different.

By now, Andrei had continued in the car up the ramp to the next level. As soon as his first shot hit, he tried two more that Leon never heard. Both shots missed. They traveled passed Bob and Leon towards Mark and Chris. From Chris's position, the fire appeared to come from the kids. Mark was down behind the engine block of their car while Chris stayed up just high enough to return fire. She did little more than inflict even more damage on the Tahoe protecting Bob and Leon.

"What are you doing!?" Mark yelled at Chris.

"One of your geeks is shooting at us!"

"That's not them - do you think they know anything about - " Mark stopped talking as he followed the motion of Andrei's car around the curve to the next level. Andrei had kept his gun pointed out the driver's side window as he pulled away from Bob and Leon. As he saw Chris duck first, he fired again. Andrei needed to keep them pinned down as he drove by. Mark wasn't as quick to react. He had his weapon out by this time, but he hadn't fired. The moment of decision had already passed and he had not acted. Chris was already moving. As she went down behind the car, she reached with her left hand and grabbed Mark's jacket. Her momentum pulled Mark down in just enough time for Andrei's shots to miss.

"I've been here for less than a week and you already owe me!" Chris yelled as she turned to follow the motion of Andrei's car up the ramp. There was no angle for a shot.

"We've got two in the area, but we should make it to the LZ. Cover the left and stay low!" Bob was just starting to get his feet under him when Leon grabbed his backpack. Bob jerked back with the sudden hindrance and spun at Leon.

"Dude, you follow an order when - " Leon's open hand met Bob's left cheek with a smart pop.

"Bob! Shut up!"

Bob's eyes went glassy for a moment as if the landscape around him was changing.

"This isn't a game, it's a parking garage and you just got shot!"

Bob's voice was shaky this time. "I – I'm okay."

"We've got to get to the car and stop the bleeding!" Leon barked.

"Stop the what?"

"Just stay low!" Leon grabbed Bob and began to drag him toward the stairwell.

Mark stood and looked up the ramp in the direction Andrei had gone. Chris lowered her weapon and turned her attention from Mark to Bob and Leon. She looked just in time to see Leon nearly toss Bob into the open stairwell door and follow him in. They ran two levels down and came out at the ground floor. Bob stumbled more than ran as the adrenalin was wearing off, and he found he had less control over his arms and legs. They made it across a corner of the garage over a sidewalk and into the stairwell of the adjacent garage. Bob was convinced the stairs were steeper here. He was getting weaker and had to force his body up to the third level behind Leon's lead. By the time they reached the car, the outline of a Chevy Tahoe mirror was obvious on Bob's face.

By now, Andrei was strolling through the mall. He had already jumped out of the car with it still in gear. The car had continued into a grey Mazda Miata, leaving a knot of metal and the wail of a car alarm. Andrei had left the chaos and walked calmly through the door to the stairwell. He paused at the sound of footsteps. He hadn't realized he was nearly close enough for another shot at Bob and Leon, who were dashing down to the first level. As the sound faded, Andrei had moved steadily down, but at the second landing turned instead for the mall entrance. He was clear before Bob, Leon, Mark, and Chris had a chance to conclude who had been doing the shooting. As far as Andrei knew, he had taken out one of his two targets. That should be enough for now. It wasn't worth the risk of staying around to finish the work. There would be another chance.

"What happened?" Hannah asked when they opened the two passenger doors on the old Ford Taurus. Hannah couldn't understand the answer because Bob and Leon were both yelling. She heard a "Go!" in the torrent of words and hit the accelerator as they both pulled the doors closed.

"No! Not here! Take the other exit!" Bob yelled and Hannah gave the wheel a quick right flick and all of them crumpled to the left with the force of the turn. Hannah was on the accelerator again and the engine responded as best as it could. On the turn, there was just enough force to break the tires loose from the concrete parking garage surface. They squealed and fishtailed before Hannah hit the breaks hard for the next right. Bob hit the back of the seat in front of him and groaned in pain while Leon was greeted with the dash since neither had a chance to put on a seat belt. Another lunge to the left as the car squealed right and then there was daylight.

"Slow down!" Bob ordered as he pulled himself upright. Still trying to process what happened to him "We need to blend in. Just get on the highway!"

Leon turned in his seat to look at Bob. "Why are you alive? I saw you get hit!"

Leon hung over the seat and reached for Bob's backpack. "Just lay down while I see the damage."

Bob complied as best he could while Hannah began to drive slowly and submerged into the Houston traffic. Leon managed to get the backpack off and raised Bob's shirt to find the beginning of a massive bruise – and nothing else.

Leon started to laugh. With a mix of shock and relief he said, "Dude, you're gonna have the biggest bruise I've ever seen!"

"What?" Bob managed as he started to sit back up. He reached for his backpack and some quick rummaging was followed by "Damn it! They killed the Beast!" Bob started to pull his Toughbook from his backpack, but only got it part way out before he exclaimed. "Ow!"

"What?" Leon watched as the Toughbook landed on the seat beside Bob.

They both watched as the laptop hissed and smoked. Bob wiped his now wet and stinging hand on his pants.

"I think it hit the battery. That was a lot of heat." He bent his arm around and felt his back. "And I think he popped my Pepsi bottle too. Bob looked in his backpack. "Yeah, I think some of the other stuff in my bag must have slowed it down enough so it didn't go all the way through. I'm glad Beauty's got her own bag."

◑ ◑ ◑

George's body was beginning to stiffen and ache from the hours spent tied in the same position. He shifted as much as he could to vary the pressure on his back against the unpadded chair. It had been a while since he had heard any voices in the house. He wasn't sure who was left there to guard him. Then it hit him - maybe it had been too quiet. Was anyone actually left? He had to test before he started making some real noise for help.

"Hey, can I get some water?" ...Nothing.

"Come on, it's been hours. Just a drink!" he exclaimed a little louder with more defiance.

The pause was long enough for George to think there was no one left. He took a breath and hopped his chair as far in the direction of the window that the chain would allow. On his second try to stretch a little further, he heard a chair leg scrape on the floor in the other room. It was followed by footsteps, then the sound of water from the tap. George was motionless and held his breath. He still had company. Now to see who it was.

Pavel opened the door carrying a plastic cup with water.

"I suggest you don't ask for things when the boss gets back," Pavel said as he brought the cup to George's mouth. George took a long drink, leaving about half the water down the front of his shirt.

"Thanks for the drink, and thanks for the advice. He didn't seem like a very helpful type."

Pavel managed a slight smirk as he turned and began to leave the room.

"You seem like a smart, young man." *Will he talk?* George asked himself.

Pavel paused and turned to look at George but said nothing.

"So why don't you tell me about your retirement plan?" George had already concluded that Pavel was the best of the group to target for making a personal connection. If he could find a way to get the young man to relate to him, then George would have a better chance of surviving this ordeal.

"My skills are my retirement plan," Pavel responded with false bravado pointing at his laptop that could be seen on the table through the open door.

"Those skills will serve you well as long as you get a chance to live long enough," George countered.

"I don't have any reason to think I won't," Pavel answered. He didn't seem as confident as his answer.

"You are putting a lot of faith in the good will of you partner."

"He's not my partner – I just work for him."

"So how long do you think you will work for him?" *Set the hook.*

"I haven't thought about it much," Pavel answered as he shifted in his chair and looked directly at George for the first time in this conversation.

"I used to not think about retirement," George leaned forward slightly as he answered. "The problem is, life seems to go faster the older you get. You will be surprised how it sneaks up on you. And you will look around and realize a lot of little decisions you made without thinking have woven themselves into a rope you can't break."

"What do you mean?" Pavel asked.

Don't jerk too hard on the line… "It makes sense to work for someone like your boss right now. You're smart, I assume the pay is good, and I bet you get lots of time off."

"It's been worth it so far," Pavel confessed.

"But I bet he doesn't like his secrets to be out of his control," George responded.

"I've proven myself to him." Pavel countered a lot less confident.

Almost there… "So you know things he probably wouldn't trust to be shared?" George asked.

"I guess so." Pavel slowly responded as he saw where this conversation was going.

"So what happens if you decide to do something a little less risky?"

Pavel paused, and then took a breath to respond. The sound of a car door outside ended the moment. He didn't say another word but turned quickly and walked out of the room, quietly closing the door.

Damn. A few more minutes and I might have had a chance, George thought.

Pavel returned to his chair in the kitchen in front of his laptop. He slouched slightly and rested his chin on one hand and began randomly surfing on some hacking sites. He didn't want Vlad to walk into the house and find him talking to their "guest." Pavel tried to look relaxed. After only a few minutes of feinted interest in browsing, he realized that the car door wasn't Vlad.

It must have been someone next door, he thought to himself after he began to relax again. Pavel sat and stared blankly at the wall. He processed the conversation he had just had with George. He thought about what he had done at 3DNF, about Stepan's laptop that Vlad had given him… "The laptop," he said aloud as he nearly jumped from his chair. Pavel went into the front room where he had left his backpack. He dug around the big main compartment and pulled out the Lenovo ThinkPad. Pavel had hardly touched the laptop since Vlad had given it to him. That one time in the hotel, he had almost gone through the drive to see what other information about his current job was still there. This time he would go through with the forensics. He was determined to see what Vlad wasn't telling him about their work.

Pavel fished through a couple of pockets in his backpack and came out with a handful of CD cases. He shuffled through the pile and settled on a disk that had the words "BackTrack 4" handwritten on it.

"Let's see what Vlad left behind on this laptop," Pavel mumbled as he waited for the box to boot. He was soon greeted with a Windows login screen. He hit the "Enter" key since the last time he had worked on the laptop, he had reset the administrator account to have a blank password. He was logged in.

"Wait, this is different," he observed. Vlad had apparently reinstalled Windows on top of the image Stepan had used. Pavel saw that Stepan's custom wallpaper was gone and had been replaced with the default Windows "grassy hill" screen. He browsed the Programs menu and found that everything was default.

"Okay, so I have to work for this," he observed as he slid the BT4 disk into the laptop and hit the power button. Soon Pavel was in a zone of file fragments and remnants of e-mails. His mind was trying to process the global reach of what he was working on. This was bigger than anything Vlad had ever given him before. This information cost Stepan his life. Would Pavel have to pay a price too? What would it be?

After an hour, he heard the car door, but it took a couple beats before he realized that sound was most likely Vlad. He didn't have time to shut everything down properly. He just hit the power button on the ThinkPad and shoved it into his backpack along with his pile of CDs and a portable USB hard drive he had been using for file images. He just managed to turn back to his other laptop and pull up the SANS Internet Storm Center page before he heard the front door open (*p. 236).

"Has it been quiet?" Vlad asked.

"Yeah. Just doing some surfing," Pavel offered as he sat up straighter and stretched.

"Good. Andrei and Haki should be back soon. Andrei can handle all manner of situations, but he will need Haki to survive this Houston traffic and not create an incident for us."

Vlad poured himself a cup of coffee and sat down opposite Pavel.

"Since we have some quiet, we need to talk about what you will be doing at our next visit to 3DNF."

E1GHT

BATTLE PLANS

Wednesday, 11:37 a.m.

Bob, Leon, and Hannah walked into the front of the bookstore. Leon turned to go to the coffee area but Bob snagged his sleeve.

"Perimeter," was all he said and turned to his left. Leon understood and this time with no eye roll, dutifully changed his path to go past the coffee and toward the back of the store. Hannah lingered at the "Newly Published" table and watched the entrance while Bob and Leon finished their sweep. As they made their way back, Hannah drifted toward the barista and ordered an espresso.

"That will be $2.76."

"Thank you," Hannah said as she gathered the drink. "He will pay for it," she answered and gave a nod and a wink to Leon. Hannah walked to a table and took the chair with her back to the wall.

"What can I get you?" the barista asked Bob. Bob was off his game again as he watched Hannah take his chair.

"Uh…just a bottle of water," Bob mumbled and walked off without claiming his drink.

"Coffee." Leon was still smiling from the wink he just received as he pulled out the money to pay and gathered his cup and Bob's bottle of water. Leon arrived at the table to find Bob shifting his chair back against the wall, leaving Leon to put his faith in his friends.

"You know if the Feds are really after you, you shouldn't sit there with your face on that camera," Hannah nodded to the security camera dome in the ceiling. Bob started to look in the direction of her glance, then thought better and pivoted his chair to face Hannah.

"So who do we trust now?" Hannah asked. Her voice was less confident now.

"No one," Bob responded with a dismissive wave of his hand. He leaned back and held his hands to his head. He looked like he was trying to keep something from leaking from his ears.

"We can't fix this ourselves," Leon stated. "We never got to finish talking to the FB – er, Jeb," Leon corrected as he leaned forward and lowered his voice.

"Of course not – we were getting SHOT," Bob countered with the loudest whisper he dared.

"We don't know who was shooting," Leon answered. "If we have to trust someone, I say we pick someone we know has to follow the rules."

"Rules," Bob scoffed. "Since when does the government follow rules?"

Leon looked straight at Bob. "I'm not saying Jeb is a Senator – he's an agent. I'd trust an agent over whoever it was in that van Saturday night – or the shooter today!"

Bob turned to Hannah, trying to find an ally. "Max, you've got to see we are in this alone."

"I'm not sure I'm quite as much a 'we' as you want. I think Leon has a point."

Bob was cut. He leaned forward and was more careful to keep his voice down. "Look, let's assume we need to trust the Feds. Even if we go to them now, we don't have enough to buy our freedom. All we have is the partial code we captured, a wild story about a car chase, and my missing dad." He paused, but there were no protests from his companions as they processed the observation. "We need the rest of the code that the guys in the van were pushing into 3DNF. And we don't have much time. For all we know, they could have already gone back and finished the job!"

Leon was starting to agree, but he wasn't ready to give in. "So now what, we camp out at 3DNF?"

"Yes! But we need some help," Bob answered.

"So now you want to trust someone else? That doesn't make sense," Hannah observed.

Bob looked at Leon but answered Hannah's question. "The 2600 LAN party crew. If I would trust them on my home network, then I trust them to help us. And besides, they don't need to know what they are helping us do. We just need their labor and some of their gear."

Hannah looked at her watch and then changed the subject. "I've been off the grid too long. I need to make a few calls before people start to look for me." She looked at Bob. "Don't worry, I won't tell anyone what I'm really doing." She got up from the table and took her drink to another table next to theirs and pulled out her cell phone.

Leon watched as Bob reached into his small green ShmooCon satchel and pulled out "Beauty" – his small EeePC – and fished out a power cord. "So how do we get the help?"

"That's what I'm doing now. I'm going to check a few things, and then I'm going to send some DMs on Twitter. I don't want to do a tweet in case the Feds – or whoever is chasing us – is listening" (★p. 136).

Leon sat in relative peace for a few minutes. He shifted his attention from sweeps of the bookstore to futile attempts to eavesdrop on Hannah's quiet phone conversations. "Who is she talking to?" he thought. He finally spoke to Bob. "So who do you think will help?"

"I thought I'd start with 0hm and M00d1mus. They've been working on a Yagi rifle that we can use for a distant wireless hookup" (★p. 183).

"Did they finally get that working? The last time I heard it was still giving them problems."

Bob didn't look up from his typing. "Yeah, it's working. At least that's what 0hm bragged about last week."

"Anyone else?" Leon asked.

"Yeah. R10t and Rudy have been doing some cool stuff with Bluetooth we might be able to use. I figure we can do a meet up at Dobbs's place".

"But the Feds know about Rudy and Dobbs. They've even been to Dobbs's shop." This time Leon thought he was the cautious one.

"That's the point. They've already been there. We will only be there for a few hours and the Feds will be looking for the next place to check, not where they've already been." Bob leaned in a little closer to Leon. With a nod of his head toward Hannah, he said in part command and part plea, "Make sure she doesn't say anything to Rudy about his car."

◑ ◑ ◑

Vlad and Pavel were again sitting at the small kitchen table. He took another sip of his coffee while Pavel continued to surf aimlessly. Then Pavel decided to use the moment to get a little more information.

"Where are the other two?" Pavel asked.

"Wetwork," was all Vlad offered with a quieter voice than usual.

Pavel's face tightened slightly. "So do we go back to that company tonight?"

"Yes. We need to get this finished. You need to be sure you know what your steps are when we get there. We are going to be quick and efficient. No wasted time at the location."

"All right. Is there anything besides the file I was dropping the last time?" Pavel asked.

"Yes. 3DNF is just a front door. We are creating a way further inside. The file I need you to drop is on a target another hop in on a government system.

"So what do I do?" Pavel asked.

"Do you still have the target IP I gave you?"

"Yes."

"Good, that will be what you target as soon as we arrive. Next, we need a more standard malware that we can drop on a couple of systems inside 3DNF."

"Won't this just set off alarms?" Pavel protested.

"I just want a couple, and they will be enough to make it look like they were sloppy with their surfing habits – which I'm sure they are. That way they won't be looking for external activity."

"All right. I've got a copy of the gh0stRAT," Pavel offered.

"Good – everyone loves to blame the Chinese. The Americans will spend their time looking in the wrong place," Vlad agreed. "It is usually easy to make them look for the wrong enemy" (*p. 325).

◑ ◑ ◑

The back of Dobbs's computer shop looked like it once was a place of order. There was no window. A door led into the room from the shop, another led to a small bathroom, and a third to the alley in the back. The walls were lined with shelves filled with computers and related gear in various stages of repair. There were a few pegboards covered with so many different parts and cables that only Dobbs could make sense of the clutter. In the middle of the room was a large table. Lunch from that day and the day before had been shoved to the side and replaced with a pile of gear. The owners of the pile looked on in pride at their work – a pride only they would understand since it looked like a flea market display.

Dobbs, R10t, 0hm, and M00d1mus had just started going through their inventory when the front door chimed. Dobbs looked toward the front of the shop and saw Leon and Hannah walking in the door. Bob lingered outside a moment and then came in as well. As Bob walked in the shop, Dobbs got a good look at Bob's face. He immediately walked over to Bob.

"Dude, you get the license plate of the car that hit you?" Dobbs asked.

Bob didn't say a word. Leon smirked and said, "Actually it was an SUV."

Dobbs looked at Bob expecting more of a story, but Bob ignored him and scanned the shop before leading the way to the back.

"Where's Rudy?" Bob finally asked when he walked into the work area and saw the rest of the crew.

"I don't know, he called and said he had car problems and wouldn't make it," M00d1mus answered.

Bob and Leon just gave each other a quick glance but said nothing.

"So what are you guys up to?" Dobbs asked in the general direction of Leon while never taking his eyes off Hannah. Bob plopped his backpack on the table and started pulling out equipment of his own to add to the pile.

"We have a project that requires your skills," Bob cut in.

"Hi, I'm Dobbs," Dobbs extended his hand with a flourish to Hannah.

"Hi, I'm Max," she responded.

"You're cute for a Max."

"Careful – she could own you seven ways before you had a chance to patch," Leon said a little too defensively.

"Wait, are you Max St341?" R10t asked.

"Yeah, that's me."

"Dude!" was all that 0hm could manage before Bob cut him off.

"We need some help with surveillance. Is this Yagi rifle working?" Bob asked as he picked up a blend of Old West and Buck Rogers. The device was the stock from an old shotgun. The barrel had been replaced with a length of handle from an old broom. Mounted to the contraption was a mass of wires and what appeared to be a small antenna at the end of the "barrel".

"Yup, we've been playing with it for the last week. We can connect to a wireless network from a quarter mile just like we were inside," 0hm answered. "What do you need it for?"

"We need to connect to a network from about a quarter mile away," Bob answered with a half-grin.

"What network?" M00d1mus asked.

"You don't want to know," Leon jumped in. "We just need some help getting ready and we'll bring your gear back when we are done tomorrow."

"This thing is pretty touchy, I think you'll need some help."

"You don't want to go there," Hannah cut in. She started to say something else but Bob cut her off.

"R10t, did you bring the Bluetooth gear?"

"Sure. It's working fine," R10t responded as he turned the small EeePC toward Bob. R10t picked up a small dongle cabled to the laptop. "With this and the Bluesnarf software we configured, you can use this either to detect a Bluetooth device in the area, or to even jack in on some of the older models" (*p. 190).

"Very nice," Bob answered intrigued as he looked at the display. "Show me how it works."

Bob and R10t descended into a conversation about the laptop. Hannah started walking around the room, looking at the gear and quietly continuing to assess the talent at the table. Leon picked up the yagi rifle.

"So show me how this works," Leon said to M00d1mus.

Soon the room was filled with an even buzz of tech-speak and keyboarding. In half an hour, the two groups were done. Bob had mastered the yagi rifle and Leon had even managed to listen in on a phone conversation from outside the shop by an unsuspecting passerby.

Hannah used the lull in the discussions to point at a monitor that displayed four black-and-white video feeds of the store.

"Dobbs, what cameras do you use for this?" she asked.

Dobbs almost jumped in response to the question and attention from "Max."

"It's just cheap stuff," he said as he pointed to the camera mounted near the ceiling pointing at the back door. "I do have a cool set of wireless cameras that actually run on a 9 volt," he volunteered as he began rummaging around one of the shelves.

Bob put down the yagi rifle he had been holding and turned. "Dude, we need those! That's perfect," Bob looked at Leon. Hannah shook her head as she caught Leon's eye. Bob just kept going as he caught up with Hannah's idea. "We can use those to establish a perimeter! What's the range on these things?"

"A few hundred feet," Dobbs offered. "Why do you need a perimeter?"

"Again, don't ask," Leon responded starting to tire of questions he couldn't answer.

Soon Bob was finishing packing the extra gear in his backpack. Leon picked up the yagi rifle.

"Dobbs, thanks for the help," Leon offered as the trio got ready to leave.

"No problem. Does this mean we get a head start in the Capture the Flag?"

Bob let out a weak laugh. "This means you might be running the Capture the Flag if you don't hear from us tomorrow."

Dobbs gave a laugh that was cut short when he realized that Leon and Max didn't see the humor. "Be careful," Dobbs then offered.

"As long as you guys did the hacks on this gear right, we'll be fine," Bob answered and turned for the door. Bob, Leon, and Hannah left the shop with Bob leading the way, scanning for faces or cars that they should avoid. The rest of the crew made their way back into the public part of the shop and lingered around the counter.

"Max was cute, but she hardly said anything. Why do you think she was with them?" Dobbs asked.

"I've seen some of Max – uh, her work on Milw0rm.com," R10t volunteered. If she's the same one, I can see why Bob is putting up with her – she has skills."

"Yeah, but she still looks too good to be hanging around with either one of them," 0hm observed.

DATA COLLECTION

Wednesday, 11:46 p.m.

"Don't go straight to the 3DNF parking lot," Bob directed from the back seat of Hannah's car. He hadn't even looked up as he was going through all the gear they had packed into duffle bags a few hours earlier at Dobbs's shop.

"Why not?" Hannah asked. "I think we can set up far enough away with the – "

"I have another idea," Bob cut her off. "Turn just before the convenience store. There is another office building on this side of the parking lot that I think is empty. I bet we can get inside and use it for cover."

Hannah complied and turned right off of the access road just before the small shop where Bob and Leon had sat just a couple of days before dropping a CyberBob icon for a game. She drove down the street and pulled to the front of an empty three-story office building. It was dark outside, so once she turned off the headlights, they were well obscured by shadows (*p. 321).

"At least whoever owns this building didn't pay the electricity bill," Leon observed. He pointed at the lights for this section of the parking lot – they were all turned off. Leon looked toward Bob in the back seat. "Hand me one of the bags."

"Not yet," Bob answered as he scanned the area. "We need to give it a few minutes to make sure there isn't any movement around here. Bob pulled out his wireless scanner and watched the screen while Leon and Hannah looked for any motion around them or signs of activity in the building.

"Okay," Bob said as he returned the PDA to the holster on his belt. "No cops around and no other obvious wireless activity. I think we walk the perimeter and see if we can find an open door or some landscaping place that gives us cover and line-of-site to 3DNF on the other side."

The three gathered up their gear and got out of the car quickly. If anyone were paying attention, they would have seen the brief, dim dome light in the car flash on as they piled out and then three muffled door closings as they all tried to be as stealthy as possible. Bob led the way to the corner of the building.

"Aren't you at least going to try the front door?" Hannah asked as they walked.

"No. That's the only one that would be locked," Bob answered as he approached the side of the building. "Besides, it's harder to pick the lock on a glass door. They are secured from the inside."

The surface of the building was grey stucco that gave a soft glow in the low ambient light of the area. Halfway down the side of the building was a metal door. Bob gave the door a try and was rewarded with an unlocked doorknob – but the door was held fast with a deadbolt lock. "Okay, I can work with this. Watch out for me."

Bob knelt on one knee and began to rummage through his backpack. "I've been playing with bumping locks and I'm getting pretty good at it" (★p. 325).

"I hope 'pretty good' means we can get inside before we're spotted," Hannah responded. Bob ignored the comment while he began to work on the deadbolt. "Leon, hold the doorknob for me while I do this." Leon held the doorknob turned all the way open while Bob squeezed in beside him to work on bumping the deadbolt lock. It was a little awkward, as Bob had to have both hands working on the lock at the same time Leon held the doorknob turned.

Hannah stood back and watched. After just over a minute of unsuccessful tries and a little grunting she asked, "Do you think the bad guys or whoever they are would think to use this building too?"

Leon took a deep breath and turned back to Hannah. Bob gave one more hit and pressure on the lock and it finally yielded. "Yeah, they might. That's why we better hurry up," Bob said as he slipped into the dark hallway. Leon turned back to get a duffle bag while Hannah followed Bob inside. Leon gave one last scan of the area and began to close the door. Just then Bob came back down the hallway and squeezed past Leon.

"What?" was all Leon could get out before Bob cut him off.

"Just hold the door. If we are going to be inside, then we need to monitor the perimeter. Bob knelt down and fished through his backpack. He pulled out one of the wireless cameras from Dobbs's shop and switched it on.

"Watch the area for me," Bob whispered as he ducked back outside. He stopped at some shrubs and found a sturdy branch to balance the camera on. He checked to make sure he had set it with a good line of site to the door and went back inside. Leon pulled the door, too, and all three of them made their way down the hallway.

Once they reached the middle of the building, they came to an open atrium with a large stairway trimmed in glass and chrome that circled around the space to the second and then the third floor. They quickly and quietly went straight to the third floor. From there, they selected an office at the back of the building with a clear view of the target corner of 3DNF.

"Let me have that other camera," Leon asked Bob. "I'll set it down a hall on the second floor looking back at the stairs. That will give us one more warning if someone comes this way."

Bob pulled out the other camera and handed it to Leon. Leon started to walk out of the office while he flipped the camera on. Nothing happened. Leon stopped in the hallway and played with the switch. Nothing. He pulled open the back cover and found the batteries were corroded. "This one's worthless," he said as he turned back toward Bob and Hannah.

"I've got another option," Bob offered. "That's why I brought R10t's laptop as well." He was setting his laptop on a credenza near the window. "Remember, he had Bluesnarf on here. If anyone comes by with a Bluetooth headset, we'll see them coming."

"Yeah, but how do we know they are going to use a Bluetooth headset?" Hannah asked with a hint of doubt in her voice.

Bob didn't look up from his laptop. He just responded, "Because I saw at least two of the guys in my webcam video had them when they were in my room."

Hannah made eye contact with Leon. Leon just shook his head with a look of admiration for his friend. "You sure you're not related to A.C. Doyle somehow? You catch way too many details."

Bob still didn't turn from his laptop screen. He just mumbled, "Elementary."

◑ ◑ ◑

"Do not waste any time," Vlad directed his order at Pavel. You know what your steps are, we just need to get them done quickly."

Pavel didn't protest at being told the obvious. Vlad was in "commander" mode and had been barking orders through most of the drive from the safe house back to 3DNF.

"Andrei – you and Haki keep in touch. I need a good perimeter and eyes on anything that happens inside it," Vlad continued.

Haki nodded his head and turned to Andrei. The four were all still sitting in the same van, parked in nearly the same place as their last "visit." Haki's only comment to Andrei was "Let's go" in Russian before he opened the driver's door and began to walk back to the cover of the few trees at the edge of the parking lot. Andrei followed. Once they reached the cover, Haki finally spoke.

"It's not safe in there until the kid gets the work done on the computer. Until then, our safest place is out here. You take this side of the parking lot and watch the access road. I'll walk toward the back and make sure any area that has line-of-sight to their position is secured. Don't use the radio. If you need to talk to me, use the cell. We don't want to bother Vlad unless we have to." Andrei agreed and without a word turned and walked away toward the convenience store again to make sure that area was clear. Haki stood for a moment and just watched the area for activity. He didn't see any movement. There were a few lights on in the 3DNF building. The same odd collection of vehicles as before was in the parking lot. Haki pulled out a cigarette and lit it. He took a drag, creating a single red glow for just a moment. He then decided to begin walking slowly in the general direction of the building now occupied solely by Bob, Leon, and Hannah.

Pavel was soon situated at the back of the van again. His laptop was on the makeshift table. He was sitting on the overturned bucket. Vlad had pulled the cable for the external Wi-Fi antenna so that the end hung over the seat in front of Pavel.

As Pavel prepared to connect to the 3DNF network, Vlad pulled his laptop out from a bag he had brought. Pavel stopped and watched as Vlad brought the machine out of "sleep" mode and began to tweak the wireless settings. Vlad noticed Pavel watching and turned in his seat.

"You aren't the only one with a technical task on this part of the project," Vlad noted wryly.

"Is there something I can help with?" Pavel offered.

"No. I want you to proceed," Vlad responded. "I will need to verify that I can connect into the network myself once you are finished. "We have to have confirmation we can provide to the buyers that this connection works. It does not make sense for you to be the only one with the ability to get in on this connection from the outside." Vlad turned back in his seat and focused on the laptop display.

Pavel sat still for a moment while his mind raced. *If Vlad can get into the network by himself, then what does he need me for? Stepan stopped being useful and look what happened to him.* Pavel glanced down at his open backpack and noticed the black outline of Stepan's Thinkpad. He quickly added up the conversation with George, the information he had pulled from Stepan's laptop, and Vlad's comment. Pavel realized it was time to look out for himself.

Pavel made his connection to the 3DNF network. He was more cautious this time. He started by opening Wireshark, so he could watch any traffic on the same network segment as his connection, including Vlad's. He watched the screen and saw nothing.

"I know you told me to be quick, but I'd like to watch the network for a few minutes and make sure we are alone," Pavel offered.

Vlad sighed and turned in his seat to look at Pavel again. He held Pavel's look for a moment and then decided he was right. "Very well. Five minutes." Vlad sat his laptop on the floor of the van and turned back in his seat after checking his watch to mark the time.

Pavel turned back to his laptop and the now-open copy of Wireshark. He was immediately greeted with traffic on the network. It was directed at an IP address next to his on the subnet. He didn't say anything but just watched.

"Tell me if you see anything," Vlad said still sitting with his back to Pavel.

"I will. It's quiet right now," Pavel responded nonchalantly as he stared at the screen.

◑ ◑ ◑

The office was dark except for the slight glow from two laptops – one for Bob and one for Leon. Leon was seated in front of his laptop. Bob and Hannah stood over his shoulders while he worked. Bob had run the antenna cable from the laptop to the yagi rifle, which now rested next to his own laptop on an empty credenza near the window. The end of the yagi rifle was balanced atop a couple of abandoned phone books Bob had found piled on the floor just outside the office. Occasionally, Bob and Hannah would look away from Leon's screen to inspect the single image on Bob's laptop showing the grainy picture of the side door. There was also a window showing Bluetooth activity in the area. Both indicated they were alone.

"So whose computer is this?" Leon asked as the three of them stared at the screen where he had just pointed.

"I think it's worth the risk to check," Hannah tentatively replied.

"Be careful," was all Bob offered.

Leon loaded nmap and began a profile scan of the single IP address. It didn't take long for the application to identify the target host as an unpatched installation of Fedora Core.

"Look, they've got SNMP running on the box," Leon again pointed triumphantly at the screen. Before Leon could get the mouse over to the folder to get his next tool, Bob pronounced "Use Metasploit".

"Just a sec," Leon sounded mildly annoyed as he pulled up the app and directed an exploit at the target. It took just a few seconds for the remote shell to launch. Soon Leon was typing away as he explored the directory structure of the system (*p. 260).

"Look at this!" Leon said loud enough for Hannah to shush him. Leon just kept going, however. "This is as good as the 'F0RB1DD3N' network name."

"What?" Bob asked leaning in closer to see the window Leon was pointing at on the display.

"This folder under the home directory – it's called 'Odysseus.'" That's got to be some interesting reading. Leon pointed his cursor over the folder but Bob stopped him.

"Dude, just grab the whole home directory. You can read it later."

"You're right," Leon agreed. It took only a couple of minutes to begin copying back the home directory from the Fedora computer, bring along the interesting folder full of Open Office documents and a contacts file.

◑ ◑ ◑

"Have you seen anything yet?" Vlad asked.

"No, I think we're alone," Pavel lied as he minimized his Wireshark window, ensuring Vlad wouldn't be able to see the log of traffic he had just captured that included someone pulling data off of Vlad's laptop.

"Then it is time to get started," Vlad responded as he reached to the floor of the van and picked up his laptop. Pavel understood he couldn't delay any more and began to work on his target host.

◑ ◑ ◑

"I think this is one of the Feds!" Bob said a little too loudly for Hannah's comfort. She immediately "shushed" him.

"What? No one else is here," Bob observed pointing at his laptop.

"It just doesn't feel right is all," Hannah observed.

"I don't think we can tell who it is yet," Leon offered as he started browsing through the files he had copied. "Besides, I didn't think a fresh install of Fedora Core or Open Office is a standard issue for a three-letter agency."

◑ ◑ ◑

Haki and Andrei had continued to walk their assigned sections of the perimeter. The area was relatively quiet. The parking lot of the convenience store had a little traffic. Haki walked past the store along the edge of the office parking lot.

There were no cars in this area. An occasional tree planted along the property line provided sufficient shadows to hide his presence to all but the sharpest eyes. Haki wasn't being particularly careful. His occasional drags on the cigarette created a red glow to contrast with the occasional blue light from his cell phone headset.

As he walked along the edge of the abandoned office occupied by Bob, Leon, and Hannah, he noticed a slight glow from one of the office windows and an occasional moving shadow. *That is not right*, he thought. He looked back toward the van with Vlad and Pavel. The window above had a perfect view of their position. He continued along the back edge of the building and paused at the corner. He checked behind him, and then glanced around the corner of the building. It was clear. He could see the same door the kids had used a little while earlier. A few quick steps and he was in front of the door. He tried the knob – it was not locked.

◑ ◑ ◑

Bob and Hannah were still watching over Leon's shoulders as he looked through the files he had just finished copying from Vlad's laptop. The display on Bob's laptop clearly showed both a Bluetooth device in the area, and the figure of someone at the side door. Hannah looked up just in time to see the door close.

"What was that!?" She nearly squealed.

"What?" "Quiet." Bob and Leon spoke over each other.

"Someone just came in the back door!" Hannah was pointing at Bob's laptop as Bob covered the space to his laptop with one large jump. Bob pointed at the display and where the Bluetooth headset signal was clearly visible.

"We aren't alone!"

Leon moved first. He grabbed the yagi rifle and yanked out the antenna cable. Bob and Hannah both scanned the room trying to decide where to go next.

"On the floor behind the desk," Leon ordered. He took up a position just behind the door that was slightly ajar. "And shut the lid on the laptops – we don't want any light in here."

Bob complied and closed both laptops and carried them with him to the far side of the desk where Hannah was already crouching. They didn't quite fit in the space but did their best.

Everything was suddenly quiet. Each could hear little more than their own heart beating out a quick beat that filled their ears. Leon thought he heard something and waved at the other two to get lower. There was some wiggling of a shadow, but they didn't succeed in shrinking down any further. Leon brought his finger to his lips and they all tried not to breathe.

There it was again. A footstep on the hard floor near the stairs. Someone was definitely coming. Leon's hands tightened around the stock of the yagi rifle. Now he wished it were good for its original design and not the tech mod they had been using.

Haki started to go past the door. He was trying to guess which office matched to the one that had a glow when he was standing outside. *What was that?* he thought.

Did something move? Haki brought his pistol up as he walked into the room. Andrei wouldn't have approved. Haki had led his way into the room with the pistol. Leon saw the shape and was ready. Haki's attention was on the desk and he walked straight to it before he realized there was a shape slightly behind and to his right. Leon brought the yagi rifle down and put the end right in the middle of Haki's back.

"Drop it!" Leon shouted and shoved the end of the yagi rifle hard into Haki's back. The quick bite of pain, noise, and surprise wasn't enough. Haki took a breath and tried to decide his next move. Because it was dark outside, the office window reflected what little light was in the office. He could see the rough shape of Leon and what appeared to be a rifle pointing at him. He couldn't move fast enough, so he complied and dropped the pistol.

Bob saw his chance and came out from behind the desk with what was left of his favorite laptop – "the Beast." He caught Haki in the forehead with the Toughbook and dropped him with one hit. Hannah started to come out from behind the desk.

"What did you do with my dad!? Where is he? What do you want from us!? That's what you get for shooting my best laptop!" With the last line, Bob brandished his Toughbook in the air one more time and then dropped it on the unconscious Haki's forehead.

Bob kept ranting, but Leon ignored him. He bent down and pulled out Haki's wallet. He looked through it and found a typical Texas driver's license, a couple of credit cards, and a little cash. Leon was so focused on looking at the documents he didn't notice as Bob stopped talking and bent down. He started to pick up Haki's gun. He managed to stand only part way up before he accidentally fired the weapon. The bullet went through the side of Haki's left leg. Haki groaned at the pain and moved slightly, but he didn't come around.

"What are you doing!?" Leon jumped to his feet, checking himself for holes. Bob dropped the gun and Hannah jumped back behind the desk as it landed, this time with only a metallic clatter.

Leon looked at the weapon but didn't want to touch it. "Get the gear together now! We can't stay here – someone probably noticed we just shot somebody!" Leon directed the last two words at Bob who turned and started shoving laptops in his backpack. He even retrieved what was left of his favorite "Beast" that had been lying beside Haki's head.

Leon looked back at the gun and put his foot on the top of it and gave it a well-aimed shove down the hall. He was rewarded with the clatter of the gun bouncing down the first flight of stairs in the atrium outside the office.

"Come on!" Leon said as he turned back to see Bob and Hannah already packed up and heading towards him. As quickly as they could, they ran out of the office, down the stairs, through the hallway, and out the side door. They quickly piled into Hannah's car and drove away.

◑ ◑ ◑

The sound had been muffled, but Andrei knew what it was. He scanned the parking lot and could see no disturbance. He didn't want to use the radio yet. He pulled out his cell and dialed Haki's number. Nothing. Now he had to tell Vlad. He pulled out the radio. "I'm coming your way. I think I heard something and now Haki is not answering."

Vlad didn't respond to Andrei's message. Instead, he immediately shut the top on his laptop and turned to Pavel.

"You keep working. I'm going to see what is going on. Stay here until you are finished. If I don't come back, use the GPS to get back to the house. You have to finish. That path into 3DNF and the target IP I gave you has to be working."

"How are you getting back?" Pavel asked.

"I can take care of myself," Vlad answered as he finished shoving his laptop into his bag and clipping the radio to his belt. "The question is, can you?" Vlad challenged. "Send me an e-mail when you're finished before you leave here. I need to know when the work is done. If you don't hear from me, stay at the house for no more than a day. After that, you are on your own." With that, Vlad climbed out of the van. He scanned the area and saw Andrei walking quickly in his direction.

Pavel crawled up to the passenger seat and carefully looked out the side window. He could see Vlad and Andrei walking slowly away from the van toward the convenience store.

"So how much am I worth to him after he gets that e-mail from me?" Pavel asked himself aloud. He moved back to his laptop and the first thing he did was save a copy of the Wireshark traffic capture he had of someone hacking Vlad's laptop. "I have an idea who was doing this, but I might need a copy, too." Pavel then opened a remote shell session on a box he controlled on a server at a local Houston university. He and Vlad had decided any local command and control testing should originate locally so that the true source of the activity would be hidden while they were in the country. A little more typing and soon, Pavel was rewarded with another shell, this time over an SSL session. He typed a single word.

```
patefacio
```

Soon he was rewarded with a rush of data across his screen. The data flow was so fast that he checked his network connection properties and realized it had saturated his connection. "Damn," Pavel muttered to himself. He paused his display occasionally and traced his finger down the screen as he read. He saw documents, spreadsheets, audio files, video clips, query strings. It went on and on while he scanned, losing track of his surroundings. "It works, but Vlad doesn't need to know quite yet," Pavel observed.

"I wonder if this is a concentrator of U.S. agency data. This must be what Vlad is going to sell access to. No wonder he wants to make sure he can get in by himself."

Pavel realized he wasn't tracking time. He looked around and made sure he was still alone. A quick look out the front and side windows confirmed no movement around him. He went back to his laptop and shut down all of his connections. If Vlad wasn't back by now, it was better to return to the safe house as ordered. Vlad and Andrei could take care of themselves. Pavel slid into the driver's seat and searched through the GPS. The safe house coordinates were there. He would take his time to make sure he didn't draw any attention.

N1N3

DATA ANALYSIS

Thursday, 1:45 a.m.

Bob, Leon, and Hannah were gathered around the small desk in their hotel room. Leon was seated in front of his laptop, looking over the files they had pulled from the Fedora Core computer. The room was mostly quiet except for exclamations of disbelief when they finally came to the document containing Vlad's instructions. The file had traveled through three countries and four computers. It began as an opportunity for Stepan to improve his position in his company. Then it was an opportunity for his employer to add to their profits. Then, for Vlad, it was another job. Now for Bob, Leon, and Hannah they had a way to finally tell good guy from bad. They had their way to stop running.

"This is scary!" Hannah exclaimed as they all took some time to sit back and consider what they had just finished reading. "This means that these 'bad guys' – whoever they really are - have a way to spy on us without anyone knowing about it. They get to just sit back and let data pour into their collector."

"So what do they do with this information?" Leon asked.

"Any damn thing they want to!" Bob answered as he stood up. "It's bad enough our government is sucking up all of this information. For all we know data about us is in this 'Concentrator' thing. But I'd rather the 'bad guys' be the ones we know in our own country - not the ones we don't know in another." Bob was pacing around the room now. "If this kind of data is the target, then the rules are totally different. This would mean – DAD!"

Leon and Hannah didn't say anything. Leon had already reached the conclusion that Bob had tumbled to. "We'll figure something out," Leon offered.

"If this is what is at stake, then my dad is DEAD!" There were veins tracing their path along Bob's temples now.

"He's got to be okay for now," Leon answered as he stood and put both hands on Bob's shoulders trying to comfort and calm him down. "They must have grabbed your dad to find us. That means as long as we are still on the run, then they need him. They think your dad knows how to find us. When that van chased us, they didn't know what we knew - or didn't know at the time. We have to figure out what to do before they decide he can't help them."

Bob sat back down and put his head in his hands. He just worked at breathing.

"Bob, we can hack this," Hannah suggested. Both Bob and Leon looked over at Hannah. "Well, come on. You guys can social people, you can break systems. This is just a system and people. Bob, you've got Max to help, remember?" Bob managed a small grin. It was enough to pull him back to the puzzle they had to solve.

SHRINKING TEAM

Thursday, 8:03 a.m.

George's body was stiff and he ached everywhere. He had just enough slack in the chain that looped over the handcuffs and attached to the floor to almost stand. He was able to get out of the chair and lie on the floor just to put his body in a different position. But his hands were still behind his back, so no matter how he turned, eventually he would cut off the blood flow to one arm or the other and awake to prickling numbness.

Something was going on again. He had heard people returning the night before. He couldn't tell how many were in the house this time. With the daylight he saw only the young one he had spoken with earlier. Pavel had uncuffed George long enough for a visit to the bathroom, given him a few bites of a sandwich, and then returned him to his chair and chain. This time Pavel didn't speak at all. George concluded it wasn't safe to try since they were not alone in the house. George had tried to look around, but the voices he could hear came from a room he couldn't see.

Now George was alone again. He sat trying to move his legs and arms as best he could to relieve the pain. *How much longer is this going to last? Is Bob okay? What has he gotten himself into?* They were the same questions that tormented him in the dark hours when he couldn't sleep. There still were no answers.

Pavel was sitting at the kitchen table again when Vlad and Andrei walked into the room. Pavel looked up and watched them both while they took a seat. He hadn't heard what they had been discussing while he was taking care of their "guest."

"We have to assume this place is compromised," Vlad announced.

"So where is Haki?" Pavel asked. Their local contact had never returned from the trip to 3DNF. Pavel had come back in the van.

"I do not know," Vlad said curtly. "If he has decided to care for himself, then we can no longer trust any arrangements he made for us."

"Why did you let him go?" Pavel challenged Andrei in Russian. It was the first time Pavel had spoken directly to Andrei during the whole trip.

Andrei didn't respond with words. Instead, he was out of his chair so quickly that it flew back from where he had sat. Andrei reached across the table toward Pavel but Vlad caught his hand.

"Not now. Besides, he has a point." Vlad caught Andrei's gaze and held it for a moment. Andrei thought better of any more action if his boss was going to step in. But he couldn't let the little one be disrespectful.

"I told you, we split up to cover area. He disappeared and all I heard was a gun shot," Andrei protested.

"You think you heard," Pavel responded with a snort. He snapped back, even though he knew he would be dead if Vlad wasn't there.

"Enough!" Vlad ended it. "Pavel, I did not receive an e-mail from you last night. Since you are sitting here, I assume that you were successful with your assignment?"

"Yes. Of course." Pavel's voice had just the hint of a defiant attitude. Vlad assumed it was emotion left from the outburst Pavel had directed at Andrei. Since the conversation had changed to English, Andrei understood he wasn't needed. He walked over to the counter and got some coffee. He stood leaning against the kitchen counter testing himself to see how much of the conversation he could follow.

"Why did you not tell me when you confirmed it was working?" Vlad said in a relaxed tone that instantly put Pavel on his guard.

"I was worried about the attention we had drawn and wanted to get out of there as quickly as I could," Pavel lied.

Vlad appeared to accept the explanation. He leaned back in his chair. "You need to go pack up," he told Pavel. "I don't know where we will be going yet, but we will not stay here long."

"So where did the extra cars come from?" Pavel asked with a head nod toward the front of the house.

Vlad turned and looked at Andrei as he responded. "Andrei had to steal one to get back. You will be getting rid of that shortly." Andrei nodded an acknowledgement.

"The other is legitimate. I had a spare I had bought on my own in case I needed to make other travel arrangements."

Pavel looked at Vlad, wondering if he would have a part in those travel arrangements or not.

◑ ◑ ◑

TENUOUS CONNECTIONS

Thursday, 8:20 a.m.

Bob's eyes were open, but it took a while for his brain to begin processing the large dark shape before them. *Where am I? What day is it? What is* - Bob remembered falling into bed sometime in the early hours of the morning. Hannah took the other bed in the hotel room, so Bob decided it was better to use just the edge of the bed where Leon was already snoring away. But now he awoke to find himself rolled over with his face next to Leon's back. Bob's brain engaged and he was instantly out of bed and making his way to his laptop that was sitting on the hotel desk.

The sudden movement woke Leon who rolled over and struggled to sit up. The water was running in the bathroom - Hannah was already up. Leon looked at his watch and pulled himself to the edge of the bed. After a few stretches he was ready to start the day…once the bathroom wasn't occupied.

"This could take a while," Leon mumbled and pointed at the bathroom. "Is it time yet?" he asked.

Bob didn't even turn from his laptop. "No. We have some time. I think Max woke me up when she got up."

Leon stared at the back of Bob's chair for a moment before he realized he had nothing to say. He made his way to the bathroom, paused, and then raised his hand to knock on the door. Instead of knocking, Leon swung lightly at air as Hannah opened the door and a small cloud of steam billowed toward him. She was obviously wide-awake and ready for the day. Her bright eyes, mischievous smile, and still-wet hair made her look like she had slept much longer than she actually had.

"Good morning," Hannah offered as she slipped past Leon.

Leon managed little better than a muffled sound that approximated "Eh uh huh." He began to process how vibrant she looked and what a mess he must be at that moment.

"You look terrible," Hannah grinned as she played off Leon's fogged facial expression. "Perhaps you need to keep better company at night."

Leon's jaw dropped slightly and his eyes opened just a little wider. "Uh, yeah."

"A girl could get jealous with the way you two cuddled up last night."

With that Leon retreated to the bathroom and shut the door before he had to look at Hannah – or let Hannah look at him – any more. "Idiot!" Leon mumbled to himself.

"What was that?" Hannah asked through the door.

Leon spun around to face the now-closed door. "Nothing!" Leon turned to look in the mirror. "So when did she get so hot?" he whispered to himself in the mirror. He looked at the door, but there was no voice from the other side this time.

Hannah went over to her bag and pulled out her laptop. She quietly sat back on the bed and started surfing and checking e-mail. She and Bob each went about their own digital business. The room was relatively quiet with only occasional clicking, typing, and the sound of Leon trying to get cleaned up in the bathroom. After 10 minutes of awkward silence, Bob and Hannah were relieved when Leon reappeared, looking marginally more awake.

◑ ◑ ◑

Agent Jackson arrived at his desk to find his partner already there. "Sorry I'm a little behind this morning. Are you ready to go?"

"Of course," Agent Battle responded. She opened her drawer and pulled out her sidearm. "How are we going to do this?"

"I think it will go better if they don't know we're coming." Mark picked up a small notebook from his desk and made sure he had his pen. "Okay, let's go."

◑ ◑ ◑

Jonathan picked up the phone on the second ring, giving him time to put down the half-empty bottle of Mountain Dew.

"Hello?" Jonathan managed after swallowing his last gulp of breakfast.

"Hi Jonathan – this is Susan. Do you know where Michael is?"

"He's here somewhere. He's probably just getting coffee. What's up?"

"He has a couple of visitors up here – the same two agents who stopped by on Monday." Susan dropped her voice for the second part of her statement and turned away from Mark and Chris who were standing near her desk.

"Really? Okay, I'll see if I can find him and come up front. Thanks." Jonathan got up and took two steps before turning around and going back to his desk to leave the drink behind. He stopped at the break room first. He was right.

"Hey Michael – we have company again."

"Who?" Michael asked as he turned around from the coffee machine.

"The two FBI agents who stopped by on Monday. Susan just called me and said they were up front."

"Did you call them?" Michael asked.

"No. I was going to ask if you did. I haven't heard anything from them since they called on Wednesday with those follow-up questions. You gave them everything they asked for, right?"

"Of course," Michael offered almost offended, sloshing some of his coffee as he motioned with the same hand holding his cup.

"How about you clean that up and I'll go get them," Jonathan offered, looking disapprovingly at the mess on the floor. "I'll just bring them back to our area."

Michael tossed out his coffee in the sink and made a weak attempt at wiping up what he had dumped on the floor. Jonathan disappeared down the hall toward the front door.

"What can I do for you today?" Jonathan asked when he met up with Mark and Chris. "Did you find out anything from the logs we gave you?"

"Not yet." Mark answered. "But we do have a few more questions. "Is Michael here today, too?"

"Sure. Is he in trouble?" Jonathan asked, wondering why the Network guy was getting so much interest and not him.

"No, it's not that," Mark assured him. "We just want to make sure we keep every-one on this up to speed."

"No problem. He's probably on his way back to his desk now. I just saw him in the break room. Come on back."

Michael was already at his desk when Jonathan and the visitors arrived. Michael had just finished a spell of controlled breathing trying to calm down.

"Hi Michael, how are you doing today?" Mark asked as he offered his hand. Michael stood quickly.

"Great. What can we do for you?"

"We wanted to check on that wireless sweep you were going to do yesterday. Did you find anything?"

"Oh sure. No. Uh, no we didn't find anything. We walked all through the building and outside like you suggested and never found anything new. There's one wireless signal from the company next door, but they've got the connection secured – I could see the little padlock on my laptop."

"Interesting," Mark offered sounding almost disinterested. "Based on the IP address information you gave us, that would have been a logical source. We could try – " RING – RING "…I'm sorry, excuse me for a moment." Mark pulled his cell phone off of his belt and turned slightly away from the other three to take the call.

"This is Mark…Yes, we are…Okay, just a sec." Mark wedged his cell phone between his chin and shoulder and pulled his notebook and pen out of his jacket pocket. "What kind of proof?…Okay, really? You'll have to prove that…, okay, I believe you, what was the name you saw on that?…Brad?…Oh, I'm sorry, Vlad. V-L-A-D right?… Listen, this is good info, but I need to see the evidence.…We need to meet…Yes, yes we will help you find your dad. Here, I've got an idea, let's meet at the Arboretum at…" Mark checked his watch. "…5:00 p.m.…Yeah, I know about the traffic, that's the point. It'll be safer for you." Mark gave Chris a questioning look, and she nodded. Jonathan and Michael just watched, trying to figure out what the conversation was about. "Okay, good…The open area near the middle…Yeah it's been a while but I know where it is, sure…No, it will just be me and Agent Battle. I promise after last time we will make sure we are alone." Mark chuckled and looked over at Chris. "Yeah, that one. See ya' then."

"Who was that?" Michael asked as Mark pocketed his notebook and holstered his phone.

"Just someone we need to speak with." Mark knew he hadn't given enough information to satisfy Michael.

"Was that about our case?" Michael tried one more time.

"3DNF isn't really a case at this point," Chris suggested, giving a non-answer. She watched Michael – he didn't like the answer, but didn't have the nerve to follow it up.

"Well, we're done here," Mark noted affably. "We just wanted to see if the wireless angle worked out." He took a step away from Michael's cube. "We don't want to be a bother. You both know how to reach me or Agent Battle if you see any more strange traffic, right?"

"Sure," Jonathan offered. "Are you sure you don't want anything else?"

Chris noticed the quick, sideways glance Michael gave Jonathan at that question.

"No, I think we're good for now. Your defenses look good. You have some issues with temps – I think you just had someone looking around who shouldn't have. They'll probably stop with word getting out that we came by. Chris, anything else?"

"No. We're good," Chris offered dismissively as she started to walk away.

"Here, let me walk you guys out," Jonathan offered.

As soon as Jonathan and the agents were down the hall, Michael nearly dove for his phone. He picked up the handset and put it to his ear before he realized he didn't know the number. He wedged the handset between his ear and shoulder and started fishing through his pockets. He made a mess dumping empty candy wrappers, keys, change, and an ATM receipt on his desk before he found the number. He tapped it in and waited for the answer.

"Pizza Hut, may I help you?"

"Sorry, wrong number," Michael responded and nearly tossed the handset across his desk, missing the base when he tried to hang it up. He got the phone back in its right place and laid his head on his desk.

"Are you okay?" Jonathan asked as he returned from the front of the office. Michael sat up abruptly.

"Yeah, I think so. I'm gonn – " Michael's cell phone rang. Michael stood up quickly and swept the contents of his pockets that he had spread onto his desk back into his hand and shoved them back in his pocket. He raised a hand to wave at Jonathan as he started walking away and answered his phone.

"Hello?"

"Why did you call?" Vlad asked.

"We need to talk. I can't – well, not right now. Can you call me back in a sec?"

"No. Just walk out of your office, I'll wait."

"Okay," Michael answered as he made his way past Susan and then out the front door. "Okay. The FBI was just here."

"What did they want?"

"They said they wanted to know if the wireless checks we did found anything."

"What did you tell them?" Vlad asked.

"Exactly what you told me to. But that's not the point. While they were here, one of them got a phone call. I could hear half of the conversation and he said something about a person named 'Vlad' and a meeting today."

"Did they say who Vlad is?" Vlad asked, trying to remember if he had ever let Michael know his real name.

"They didn't say. But they did say something about a meeting today at 5:00 p.m. at the Arboretum."

"And why do you think you need to tell me all of this?" Vlad asked, trying to see just what Michael knew.

"I just think they were on to something. I asked if the call was about 3DNF, but they wouldn't say. I think they know something about what's going on." Michael's words were spewing out so fast his cell phone needed a good wipe down.

"Relax," Vlad instructed. "You have done better work than you realize. The access point was successful. I think we need to meet so I can pay you the rest of the money. In fact, I'll have a bonus for you. If you want, I can put you in touch with someone that can help you with travel documents if you feel like taking a trip for a while until things calm down." Vlad finished in a relaxed tone.

"Wow, that's great," Michael responded, starting to finally control his breathing. Responding to the assurances from Vlad. "Where do we meet?"

"Do you know where Sharpstown Mall is?" Vlad asked.

"Uh, yeah. Are you sure you want to meet there – it's kind of rough."

"It is a busy place – we need a crowd where we can talk," Vlad answered. "Can you be there in 30 minutes?"

"Well, they'll miss me at work," was the nervous response.

"I don't think you need to worry about that job. Your bonus will buy you some time to find something better."

"You're right. I'll be there. Where do we meet?" Michael asked.

"There is a large entrance sign at the southeast corner, near where they have the carnival set up in the parking lot. I'll be there waiting for you."

"Okay I – " CLICK. Vlad hung up the phone and Michael was talking to air. Michael looked around and realized he had been standing in the middle of an empty section of the parking lot – and nowhere near his car. He looked around and saw no one else. He quickly made his way to his car and drove off.

RING – "Hello?" Michael answered as he pulled out onto the highway.

"Hey, it's Jonathan. Are you okay?"

"Yeah, I'll be alright. I decided to go get a drink, but I don't feel too good. I'm going to go home and lay down for a while." Michael lied.

"All right. The boss wanted a briefing on our visitors. I'll let him know how it went. Do you want me to cover for you?"

"Sure. Thanks for the help. I'll see ya." Michael hung up quickly before his nerves failed completely and settled in for the drive to Sharpstown Mall.

LOOSE ENDS

Thursday, 12:11 p.m.

Michael made his way down Bellaire Boulevard and drove past the large south entrance to the mall parking lot. He turned into the Taco Cabana across the street and walked over to the intersection to cross the street. The crossing turned out to be the most dangerous part of his trip from 3DNF. A few car honks and a dash and Michael was standing in front of the large yellow arch-shaped sign for the mall. As promised, his contact from the Starbucks was standing to one side of the sign.

Michael walked toward Vlad. Vlad matched Michael's stride and said, "Let's just walk along the edge of the street carnival here. I like to stay where we can both see what is going on around us." Michael didn't answer, but obeyed.

After a few steps, Vlad began. "As I said earlier, you have done better work than you realize. By the time they find the access point, you won't care. And your boss will have some explaining to do because of what is now on his computer."

"Cool. Uh, so it all worked out and I can get paid then?" Michael asked as he walked beside Vlad, watching his own feet and paying no attention to the crowd around him.

"Oh yes. But there are a few questions I have for you first." Vlad stopped walking and turned to face Michael. "First, is there anything else about the phone call you have not already told me?"

Michael looked away for a moment, thinking through what he had heard. "The agent said something about finding a dad. That part didn't make any sense."

Vlad had to make a focused effort to keep his facial expression neutral. *That confirms it*, he thought. "Anything else about the call?"

This time Michael was a little quicker with his answer. "No, that was it."

"All right. Next question, what happened with the wireless scan the FBI asked you to do?"

"It worked just like you said. We ran the scan with just a Windows laptop and nothing showed up," Michael reported.

"Good. Did they ask you any more about the name I gave you?" Vlad continued. He also started walking again, this time back in the general direction of the entrance sign. They had to split up for a moment because of all the people walking along the sidewalk towards the carnival.

"They didn't say anything about that today. They just said it looked like we had some issues with our temp help. I don't know if they did any more checking on that."

Vlad paused from the walking and looked at Michael as if he were checking to make sure he was telling everything he knew. "Did they say anything else about their investigation?" Vlad asked more sternly.

"Well, when they were done with that phone call, I asked if it was about the 3DNF case. One of the agents said that 3DNF wasn't really a case. That might mean they don't think anything happened."

Vlad paused for a moment, deciding what he should do next. The extra long look from Vlad made Michael look away at the crowd. "Well, we should get to the part you care about. I didn't want to bring cash with me for this payment," Vlad said in a more casual and relaxed tone. He took a step closer and put his hand on Michael's shoulder and guided him over to a tree at the edge of the parking lot next to the carnival. "I will set up a bank account for you off shore. You will get an e-mail with all of the instructions to access the account. You can do it remotely, but I suggest you visit in person. It is much easier if you don't bring any of your profit back into the United States."

Michael's head was spinning. He couldn't believe it had worked out so well. He was going to be out of debt, travel a little bit, and his old boss was going to be in trouble.

"So did that name they mentioned – Vlad – mean anything? Do they have a lead back to us?" Michael asked.

"I have not heard of anyone named Vlad. I think that was not related to your assistance in any way. That had to be either another case, or a dead end." Vlad's assurance was enough for Michael. Vlad surveyed the edge of the carnival in the mall parking lot in front of them. People were milling around in every direction. "This is a good place to complete our business." Vlad pointed back to the main entrance sign where they had first met. He walked in that direction and Michael followed.

After a few quiet steps Vlad began again, "I need to leave, and it is best if we do not take the same route. I believe when you arrived you parked across the street."

"Yeah, that's right," Michael, confirmed.

"Then I want you to go ahead and cross over, but instead of going back to your car, sit at that bus stop," Vlad motioned with a nod.

"What for?" As soon as the words were out of Michael's mouth he realized he should probably just shut up and obey.

"You will sit at that bus stop for at least five minutes. We need to leave separately, and you need to pay attention and make sure you do not see anyone that may have been trying to follow you."

That way you will have the opportunity to watch the crowd and make sure no one took note of our meeting," Vlad stated like he was schooling a child on the need for table manners.

Michael was even more compliant after Vlad's firm instruction. "Sure. Uh, thanks for the job. Let me know if there is another chance like this in the future."

"I will know how to find you," Vlad assured him with just a hint of a smile and walked away.

Michael looked up and down the street and saw no one that would make eye contact with him. He could see his car in the parking lot across the street. He followed instructions and crossed Bellaire and turned to his right. He walked over and sat on the bench of the bus stop and began to watch the people walking up and down the sidewalk.

Vlad turned north and walked straight across the parking lot, towards the mall entrance. The blue light of his active Bluetooth headset gave a soft glow. He had kept an open call going the whole time he was with Michael. One word was enough for the next step. "Da."

Andrei was stationed on the second level of the parking garage, northeast of Michael's bus stop. He was alone standing in front of the car he had stolen the night before. Through the scope of his rifle he could see Michael sitting and watching up and down the street. Andrei waited for a clear shot. "Breathe in, breathe out, hold, squeeze." There was a slight muzzle flash, but the silencer took care of most of the sound.

A man sitting next to Michael on the bench caught the unnatural movement next to him in his peripheral vision and turned. Michael gave a raspy grunt and slumped backwards. The small hole in his chest was much cleaner than the mess on his back where the bullet had begun to tumble as it exited his body. It had gone through the bench where Michael sat and continued in the direction of the abandoned Circuit City store behind them.

The man jumped up and began to look around. Nothing looked unusual. No one was running, no one stopped to look, no tires squealed. He looked down and saw he had blood splattered on his shirt. "Help! Hey, HELP!" People began to stop and then a few screamed. Some ran away, others hid their faces and just walked quickly by. No one ran toward Michael. The awkward position of Michael's lifeless body told the story.

◖ ◖ ◖

"Are you done?" Vlad strolled through the mall.

"Yes."

"Are you clear?"

"Not yet." Andrei had managed to disassemble his rifle and return it to its case before Vlad had asked for an update. The case was padded and looked more like a large sports bag. Andrei pulled a rag from his pocket and rubbed down the outside of the trunk and then walked to the driver's side door. He slipped back in the seat and wiped down the surfaces he had touched. He rolled down the window, covering the handle with the rag, and got out. He fished in his pocket, pulled out a couple of fifty-dollar bills and tossed them in the seat and began to walk away.

"On my way," Andrei spoke into his headset.

"Did you leave the bait?" Vlad asked as he exited the north side of the mall and made his way to his car.

"Yes. Whoever gets in to get the cash will leave their prints."

"Find another van. I'll meet you back at the house." Vlad hung up.

Andrei kept walking and gave a sigh and shake of his head. He scanned the area and looked for an older-model vehicle that met his boss's requirements.

EXPENDABLE ASSETS

2:11 p.m.

Pavel was sitting on the couch in the front room. He had his laptop balanced on his outstretched legs. He was looking at international flight options and trying to decide if he should fly out of Houston or rent a car and drive to New Orleans or Dallas. He had decided it was time to have his own contingency plan. The sound of a car door out front announced Vlad's return. Pavel surfed to the Black Hat conference site and then cleared his browser cache before Vlad walked in (*p. 277).

"Has it been quiet?" Vlad asked.

"Yes. How did it go?"

"Fine. We have one problem solved, but we are not yet done."

"I thought we had the file transfer process working, so we were ready to go now." Pavel put his laptop down and noticed Vlad checking the display to see what was open on the screen.

"We still have to find those kids that were at 3DNF. We have to make sure they don't pass anything to authorities. And we have to take care of our guest." Vlad answered with a nod to the back of the house where George still sat alone.

"We don't know if they have anything, and that connection we set up will be quiet as long as we want. Even if they scan their network traffic, it won't show up. It's just going to look like normal Web traffic on the way out."

Vlad's voice got louder than Pavel expected. "We cannot have anything left behind!"

"I understand, but we haven't left any – "

"You do NOT understand," Vlad pointed at Pavel. Pavel leaned back in his seat at the gesture. "We are not just working for Stepan's employer," Vlad stated impatiently.

Pavel gave Vlad a confused look and sat upright on the couch. "I don't understand."

"This data...This access is too valuable to just sell back once. The file I gave you to install was not what we received from Stepan. I had it customized," Vlad began.

"Why didn't you let me – "

Vlad just held a hand up for silence.

"This was custom work like you have never seen," Vlad started. He sat down on the chair next to the couch. "The volume of information processed through this feed is massive. Stepan's employer isn't the only one who is interested in this. I have others I answer to on this job.

Pavel wasn't catching on. "So who is in charge of this? I thought you were working as a contractor for Stepan's employer."

"I am. But that was just what led to the job. They are clients, but I have an employer. A more, um, exacting employer who is also interested. They do not tolerate failure well, and they are very – well, that is something for you to learn on your own. For now, you need to understand that I have to make a clean exit out of the country or I – we – all fail."

Pavel started to form another question but the door opened. It was Andrei. Vlad turned when he walked in the door, carrying his bag.

"Everything clear?"

"Yes."

"Good. Get your gear packed." Then Vlad turned to Pavel. "You too. We need to be ready to move, within the hour."

◑ ◑ ◑

Hannah parked the car outside the IHOP and turned off the engine. "So is it time?" she asked.

Leon checked his watch. "Yeah, I think we should do it now." He turned to look at Bob in the back seat. "Are you going to be okay while I do this?"

"Yeah, whatever. You do the better non-geek social attacks anyway," Bob responded. He was slouched in the back seat leaning to one side on the pile of backpacks. Leon, Hannah, and Bob had tossed all their gear in the back after checking out of the hotel a couple of hours earlier.

"All right. Just keep quiet so I can concentrate." Leon pulled out his cell phone and scrolled down to the number he had saved into his contact list earlier that morning and hit "Send."

Andrei was in the back of the house packing up his gear as Vlad had instructed when his cell phone rang.

"Da – Haki?" Andrei had seen the local number and assumed Haki was finally making contact.

"Hello?" Leon wasn't sure he understood what the voice on the other end had said. "Da?"

"Hey Andrei, listen, I just need to talk to Vlad."

Andrei's face revealed genuine surprise as he held the phone out from his ear and looked at the caller ID again. He walked into the kitchen where Vlad and Pavel were hunched over Pavel's laptop.

"I do not know who this is, but they know my name and yours and they speak English." Andrei handed the phone to Vlad.

Vlad slid his chair back from the table, took the phone, and walked into the front room. "Yes?"

"Hey, Vlad?" Leon asked.

"Who is this?"

"I'm one of the guys you chased Saturday night."

"How did you get this number?" Vlad was genuinely surprised at this development.

"I got it because you're sloppy. When you went back to the F0RB1DD3N network, your system got owned. Word of advice, if you go on a hostile network, don't use a Linux box that hasn't been patched in forever. I've got a copy of everything of interest on your laptop, including your contact list."

"Since you called me, what do you want?" Vlad asked, his voice sounding terse as he tried to gain control of the conversation.

"I want you to let George go free."

"I do not know who or what you are talking about," Vlad answered cooly. He needed to see what else this caller knew.

"I know you took George from his house. I know you trashed his house. And I have a video tape of you and your goons – "

Bob leaned forward from the back seat. "You let my dad go! You let him go NOW or we – "

Leon held the phone away from his ear and looked back at Bob, "Shut Up!"

"It sounds like you have a rather emotional associate," Vlad dryly observed.

"Yeah, but he has some skills you don't want turned against you. Now put George on the phone so I know he is alive!" Leon said with an edge creeping into his voice.

"And why would I do that?" Vlad asked unfazed by the boy's emotional state.

"If you don't, then I have no reason to make a deal with you, and my next call is to the FBI," Leon answered simply.

"Very well. One moment." Vlad walked back past Pavel and Andrei in the kitchen and down the hall to George's room. He threw the door open quickly and startled George. Vlad covered the phone with his free hand and leaned his face in right next to George's. "You will tell your son you are alive and nothing else. One more word and I do not have a reason to keep you." Vlad put the phone next to George's face. "Speak!"

"B-Bob, is that you? I'm okay. What di – "

Vlad pulled the phone away. He could hear the voice on the other end of the call speaking to someone – "He's alive."

"Now if I return George, how do I know I can trust you to not turn everything over to the government?" Vlad asked.

"You have my word."

"I do not know what your word is worth," Vlad countered with a low growl.

"Then I give you my word that you will have a bunch of Feds all over you before this day is finished. You don't have a choice but to trust me and let George go." Leon said.

Vlad didn't see much of an alternative. "So where do we meet?"

"The Arboretum today at 6:00 p.m. at the start of the Inner Loop Trail."

A grin spread across Vlad's face and he suppressed a chuckle. *That's how they think they are going to take me down*, he thought amazed at his good fortune.

"And if I bring George, what will you be bringing me?" Vlad asked.

"We will have the last copy of all of the data we collected on a USB drive," Leon answered.

"Not quite good enough. You bring your laptops with you. If you are as clever as you say, you might keep copies of the data."

Leon looked at Bob for a second in the back seat. "Agreed." The line went dead as Vlad hung up.

Bob looked at the pair in the front seat. "What? So you think I was a little over the top?" he said waiting to hear his review.

◑ ◑ ◑

Vlad walked back into the kitchen where Pavel and Andrei were sitting.

"Are you done packing?"

They both nodded in agreement.

"Good. We have had a development that will make our exit easier. The kids from the parking lot have overplayed their hand and they want to meet," Vlad started to explain.

"How did they get Andrei's number?" Pavel asked trying to act confused.

Vlad's face got a little harder as he turned to Pavel. "Apparently you are not giving me good advice on securing my laptop."

"What do you mean?" Pavel asked, feigning surprise.

"They got into my system and have a copy of the instruction documents for this job and my contacts file." Vlad answered. "They claim if we bring them our guest, they will delete everything."

"You didn't agree to that did you?" Pavel asked.

"Of course I did," Vlad answered. "I would have agreed to anything to get them to show up. Because, they want to meet at 6:00 p.m. at an arboretum, but Michael from 3DNF told me that he heard the FBI agents setting up a meeting with someone at the Arboretum at 5:00 p.m. These American kids think they can set us up." Vlad uttered the last sentence with contempt.

Pavel leaned back in his chair and put his hands over his face, trying to figure out if he was ever going to get home alive. Pavel put his hands back down and looked at Vlad. "How are we going to deal with the FBI and – "

"Relax. We have the advantage because we know where and when everyone is meeting. Everyone that is a threat to us is going to be conveniently in the same place an hour before our meeting. We just need to show up early for that first meeting and remove all threats." Vlad looked at Andrei with a satisfied smile. "I need your services one more time before we can go home."

"Understood."

T3N

CHOOSING SIDES

Thursday, 4:05 p.m.

Vlad surveyed up and down the street as he threw the last of their bags into the trunk and closed the lid. There was no one watching. He turned to Andrei. "Go get our guest and put him in the van." Andrei took two steps before Vlad turned back to him. "And take off the cuffs. We do not want some neighbor calling the police because they see him restrained." Andrei nodded and returned to the house.

Pavel was already sitting in the passenger's seat of the van. Vlad got in his car and waited. Soon Andrei came out holding George Falken firmly by one arm. George was too tired to have any fight left in him. The deprivations and fears of the past days had made him compliant. He did his best to stumble along where Andrei led and fell into the van when Andrei gave him a light push. Andrei stepped in behind and locked the seatbelt across George.

Pavel turned to face George. He held his gaze for a moment and just before the driver's door opened, George saw a wink and the hint of a smile as Pavel turned around.

Andrei got into the driver's seat and tapped the Bluetooth headset to answer Vlad's call. "Just follow me and take your time," Vlad instructed. It took just over 40 minutes before they approached the turn off where Memorial Drive passed under a railroad bridge. At this point, Vlad called Andrei again. "Just pull over on the right before the tracks and have Pavel drive the rest of the way."

"Understood," Andrei answered. He gradually slowed the van and pulled off the road. He put the van in 'Park' and turned to Pavel. "Hand me that bag." Andrei growled and pointed at his bag at George's feet. Pavel struggled to pick it up and pass it to Andrei. "Keep track of the 'guest,'" Andrei instructed menacingly as he got out of the van.

Pavel didn't respond. Instead he slipped into the driver's seat and after a couple of tries, managed to merge back into the crowded and slow-moving traffic. He continued along the gentle curve of Memorial Drive until he reached the entrance of the arboretum.

Andrei hiked up the gentle embankment to the railroad tracks and followed them straight south along the eastern edge of the arboretum. Just as they had planned when they looked at the map on Pavel's laptop earlier that afternoon, there was a place where the trees of the park thinned and there was a view of an opening that surrounded a small pond with a little tree-covered island in the middle. Andrei found a place under a tree and low brush at the edge of the arboretum grounds that gave him a clear view of the Inner Loop trail. He knelt down and pulled the parts of his rifle out of the bag.

He paused a moment as he lifted the stock. *The one thing Haki did right was getting this Blaser R93*, he thought to himself. He quickly assembled the weapon and began to attach the silencer at the end of the barrel. *It was a lot smoother this afternoon with the other American than my old Dragonov SVD.*

Vlad had followed the winding drive up to the main entrance ahead of Pavel. By the time Pavel got there, he could see Vlad's empty car. He parked the van and sat still, just staring toward the main building where Vlad must have gone in a couple minutes before.

George decided he had one more chance. "You know," his voice was raspy from lack of rest and food, "I think you could make it out of here now."

Pavel turned in his seat and looked at George, holding his gaze. "Yeah, I think you're almost right," Pavel agreed reassuringly. Pavel had been thinking about this since his first conversation with George. He didn't like his chances of getting out of the country if he stuck with Vlad's plan. Vlad would take care of himself, and so would Andrei. Pavel had to do the same. "I want to watch the area for a little while first. We have a few minutes."

Pavel turned back to George. In a genuinely concerned voice he asked, "If we have to get out and move, do you think you can make it?"

"I – I don't know." George was still using his hands to hold himself upright. "I'm sorry I think I would slow you down."

"I think we can stay in the van. I just wanted to be sure," Pavel answered as he turned his attention back to the situation around them. Since it was just at the end of the business day, the parking lot was not crowded. There were a few cars, the expected mix of SUVs, sedans, and one nice sports car. One mom was walking up to the main building with a couple of kids in tow. He spotted one sedan with a couple of people still sitting inside, talking. "It's time to get out of here and get some help," Pavel announced.

"What about my son? Aren't we here to meet him?" George perked up as the instinct of fatherhood overrode the one for self-preservation.

"The best way to help your son is to get out of here and contact the police," Pavel answered. He started the van and pulled out of the parking space. He hit the accelerator a little hard and the van lurched as he turned the steering wheel sharply to point the van back toward the entrance. George did his best not to fall over as the van leaned with each curve.

◑ ◑ ◑

"I see them," Andrei whispered to Vlad on the open call.

"Where are they?" Vlad asked sharply as he made his way along the wooded trail. The area was quiet as he continued along through the trees.

"They are on the north side of the pond facing away from my position. If you approach from the west trail, then that will turn them toward me."

"How many?" Vlad asked.

"There are five. I have seen four of them before, but the new one is just a girl. She looks like a civilian. The two adults are not."

"Anyone else around?" Vlad checked again to be sure.

"No. It looks clear." Andrei looked back behind his position to verify. As far as he could tell, he was alone.

"Good. Keep your aim on the agents. The kids are mine. Do not do anything until I tell you to."

"Understood."

Vlad reached the end of the tree-covered portion of the trail. He could see the people Andrei had described just ahead of him. He paused to check the surroundings. "Get ready for my word," he whispered to Andrei on the call. "I need to know what they know first."

Andrei shifted in his position and eased up to the scope on the rifle. He began to pan along the pond to cover his main target. The cross hairs rested dead center on Agent Battle.

Vlad walked out of the cover from the trees and approached the group, keeping a tactical separation and making sure that he did not get in Andrei's way. As soon as he was visible on the trail, the female agent tapped the shoulder of the other agent. He had kept his attention on the only other trail into the clearing. That motion was enough to cause the three kids to look back as he approached.

"I see you are the ones I should be dealing with instead of these children," Vlad began. He was certain he could see a weapon on each of the agents beneath their jackets. The kids showed no evidence of a threat.

Snap. A camouflaged figure, hidden in the shadows of some nearby trees shifted his weight slightly to watch Vlad's appearance in the clearing. The noise wasn't that loud, but it was enough. Andrei looked behind his position again and this time saw the movement of at least one figure. The rifle was too slow. In a smooth motion, Andrei dropped his rifle, rose out of his kneeling position and pulled out his Glock. As he began to pull the weapon level he heard someone from behind him yell "Gun!"

Seven rounds hit Andrei from unseen opponents before he even had a chance to respond. Andrei's lifeless body dropped to the ground. One camouflaged man ran to cover Andrei; two others broke their cover and moved into the clearing.

The sound of the gunfire surprised Vlad most of all. He expected to hear nothing from Andrei's silenced rifle when he chose to give the order to shoot. Instead, he pivoted around to the new threat and pulled his own weapon out in the same motion. Vlad squeezed off two rounds at the two agents moving into the clearing. Both shots missed, but the fire was enough to cause them to drop for cover. Their shots at Vlad were just as effective. He had already started to pivot, keeping his profile to his opponents as small as possible.

Mark and Chris both had their weapons out. Mark saw past Vlad and realized the agent checking Andrei's position was in his line. Chris saw only Vlad. Her shot caught his left arm. The searing pain and impact startled Vlad, throwing him off balance.

Vlad was hit and had counted at least four weapons with him in the middle. He had lost the initiative. Now it was just revenge. He turned back to those meddling kids that had shattered all of his careful planning.

At the first sound of gunfire, Hannah had dropped to her knees. Leon managed two steps in Hannah's direction, between her and Vlad. In the rush, he didn't see her duck. As he planted his foot for the next step, one of Vlad's next rounds hit Leon in the chest. The impact felt like someone had hit him with the full swing of a hammer. Leon had no control of his legs. He dropped hard, catching Hannah's shoulder in his back on the way down. His head snapped back and then found the packed gravel of the trail. His mouth filled with blood. All he could do was try to breath, but his lungs were not obeying. Everything went dark.

"LEON!" Hannah screamed.

Satisfied for the moment with two of the targets down, Vlad's next target was Chris. His left arm was hanging limp at his side, but the weapon in his right hand was still moving in a smooth motion. Chris's first shot was just to Vlad's right.

Vlad's movement had kept his profile to Chris small, but it left his chest uncovered to Mark who was a few feet right of Chris. Mark's shot hit center of mass. The impact jerked Vlad's arms out and his last shot went wildly high. Chris's next shot hit the side of Vlad's chest under his now-raised arm.

Vlad fell onto his back, disappearing into the grass just off the trail. With each attempt at a breath, he could hear a gurgling sound where air escaped his lungs from the holes in his chest.

Vlad looked up and saw the deep blue of the afternoon Houston sky through the trees. He could hear the crunch of dry grass beneath him as he turned his head slightly. The hot, humid air and sticky blood filling his mouth mingled to give a sensation of drowning. He tried to sit up, but his body wouldn't obey. There was a sharp sound of metal on metal. The sound was familiar, but his mind wasn't working fast enough to recognize his situation. He craned his neck as he struggled to look above him. He saw legs, a hard face looking down at him, and a gun. The shape of the gun seemed to grow large enough to fill all he could see – and then nothing.

Chris knelt down and checked for a pulse. "He's gone! How are the kids?!" She yelled over to Mark.

Hannah jerked Leon. "LEON!" She ripped open his shirt, tears clouding her vision as she fumbled with the straps of the bulletproof vest. Afraid of what she might find.

Leon took a couple of gasping breaths. "Gahh THAT HURT! And I busted my lip!"

"Well why'd you jump in front of me and take the bullet then!?" Hannah answered with fear and joy and relief all woven together.

Hannah began to pull off her own shirt, revealing a bulletproof vest.

"I thought that's what I was supposed to do!" Leon answered, not noticing the hint of tears in Hannah's eyes. He finished getting the vest off and wiped his bloody lip on the back of his hand.

"DAD!" Bob yelled. Somehow he was the only one of the five that remained standing through the whole shoot out. Even though he had had the most bullets fly past.

He was untouched. Once he realized everything was clear, he took off running down the trail towards the main building.

"Bob! Wait!" Mark did his best to keep up, but Bob had the greater motivation and stayed ahead of him.

Bob blew through the building and out into the parking lot. There he found a collection of police cars, an ambulance, some unmarked vans, and a large collection of people walking about in black jackets that had "FBI" on the back.

"DAD!" Bob yelled.

"Son, come over here." Special Agent Thompson was walking toward Bob. "I've got someone that wants to talk to you."

Bob paused, and then walked over to the tall man with salt-and-pepper hair combed straight back and black sunglasses.

"Bob, it's okay," Mark said between deep breaths as he caught up with Bob.

"Where's my dad!?"

"Right over here, son." Special Agent Thompson put his hand on Bob's shoulder and guided him over toward an ambulance. Bob ran ahead when he realized he was being led to the ambulance.

"Dad – are you al – "

George was sitting on the back bumper of the ambulance while an EMT checked his blood pressure. When George saw his son, he found strength he didn't think he had left and jumped up to wrap his son up in a hug. As soon as he did, his legs started to give. Bob and the EMT eased him back down on the bumper.

"Bob, you're okay. You're okay. I was so – " He couldn't stop the tears that started to fall. Bob tried to reassure his dad, but he couldn't form any words. He just held his dad. For the first time in too many years, they just held on to each other. Neither was alone any more.

Mark found an EMT without a patient. "We've got someone back there that needs to be checked out. He took a bullet in his vest."

"Who was hit?" Bob asked, starting to pull back and let his dad get some air.

"Leon, but he's goin – "

"What? Why didn't you tell me? Dad, I'll be back." And Bob was running back toward where he had just come from. The EMT picked up his bag and just let Bob lead the way. They only made it as far as the gift shop inside the main building when they came to Leon leaning on Hannah's shoulder.

"Are you okay?" Bob asked trying to hold back tears.

"Sure. How about your dad, is he – "

"He's fine. What happened?" Bob assured and asked in one breath.

"I don't know. I heard the shooting behind us, then in front of us and the next thing I knew I was on the ground and Oh THAT HURT!" Leon exclaimed.

"Oh man up," Hannah said as she continued to help Leon walk. Her concerned look not matching her words.

"I thought that's what I did when I took your bullet," Leon said with an added grimace of pain for effect.

"I didn't say I didn't appreciate the gesture," she said allowing a slight grin and squeezing him a little tighter.

Leon gasped slightly, not sure if it was from pleasure or pain.

"Sir, let's get you back to the ambulance. I want to get you checked out," the EMT instructed. Bob and Hannah made sure Leon made it the rest of the way.

Soon Leon was sitting at the back of the ambulance. George had found the strength to stand, helped by a candy bar and sports drink one of the agents brought from the gift shop.

"So where is the kid that helped me?" George asked Special Agent Thompson.

"We're holding him over near where we picked you two up at the entrance. He'll be going back to our office for some questioning."

"For what it's worth, I think he's a good kid who got in over his head. He was helping me escape when you stopped us. He didn't want to be with the other two."

"Sir, we will take your statement once these guys finish checking you out, and we will take that into consideration," Agent Thompson assured him.

Mark offered his hand to George. "Mr. Falken," he said as they began to shake hands, "you have one ingenious son. And he has a couple of very smart friends." All three of the kids smiled at each other.

George was feeling a little stronger as the sugar from the candy bar kicked in, and the feeling of being safe settled on him. "I still don't understand how everyone ended up here."

Leon and Bob started talking at once, then stopped. "You go ahead," Leon offered.

Bob took a breath. "Leon managed to hack into Vlad's laptop. He was the main guy who took you."

"Where is he?" George asked.

"Sir, he will not be a problem for anyone again," Mark said with conviction.

Bob continued. "Anyway, when we were at 3DNF Wednesday night, Leon hacked Vlad's laptop and got a copy of all of his contact information. We had to get more information to figure out who took you. We staked out the place across from 3DNF and tracked the bad guys when they came back. It got a little scary when I shot one of them."

"What!?" both George and Mark responded together.

"You didn't tell me about that part," Mark said.

Bob put his hands up. "I'll get to that in a second. We found out from the data on Vlad's laptop that he was trying to set up a back door into some U.S. government computers through their connection to 3DNF."

"Son, why don't you skip over that part," Special Agent Thompson advised. We can go over that back at the office in 'private.'"

Just a week ago Bob would have responded to the suggestion with as much attitude as Dobbs showed Mark and Chris when they visited. Instead, Bob understood now that some things were not for public disclosure.

"Vlad's laptop had a set of instructions, a contacts file, and," Bob looked at Thompson, "some stuff that could jeopardize a certain unnamed country on it. We got the phone numbers of people he was working with and used that to set him up."

Mark broke in. "So that's when you called me early this morning to set up that call while Chris and I were at 3DNF."

"That's right. Mark and I set up a call so Michael – he was also in the contact list as an employee of 3DNF – would overhear a conversation about a meeting today at 5:00 p.m."

"Who's Michael?" George asked.

"Michael was the employee who was helping Vlad," Mark answered quickly.

"What do you mean 'was'?" Leon asked but already dreading the answer.

"Michael called Vlad like we thought he would. They had a meeting today just after noon when we left 3DNF. We put a bolo on him, but we didn't have the time to put a tail on him. We got a call from the HPD that he was shot by a rifle."

"A rifle!?" Leon exclaimed. "These vests you gave us wouldn't have stopped a rifle!"

Mark continued, "We weren't counting on the vests to protect you from that shooter. We knew from our last meeting at the Galleria that there was someone else. We made sure to have people staking out his position. Remember, I picked the place. I knew there was only one clear shot into that area. We had a spotter across the railroad tracks and three other agents surrounding him in the arboretum area. The vests were to protect you from Vlad."

"But how did you get Vlad to bring me here?" George asked. This still doesn't make sense.

"I'm not finished yet, Dad," Bob continued, still euphoric from surviving the shootout. "There's more. Leon called Vlad. Well, he called the shooter – Andrei. We had his number from Vlad's contact list. Leon told him we would meet at 6:00 p.m. at the same place where Michael thought we were meeting the FBI at 5:00 p.m. Since Vlad and Michael would talk, we knew Vlad would think it was a setup and he would come early to trap us at 5:00 p.m. He didn't know we had a trap in his trap!"

George looked at the very self-satisfied expressions on everyone's faces. "I think I've got it. Bob, you'll probably need to tell me that again after I've slept for a day. And probably with diagrams."

Bob turned to Leon. A smile spread across his face as the enormity of the story he had just told sunk in. "Dude, do you know what we just did? We just saved the United States! That's bigger than saving the Internet! That means we're bigger than Dan Kaminsky! Or Tony Watson!"

Leon looked exasperated. "Bob, we aren't even up there with GOBBLES. Or n3t-d3v for that matter."

Bob's shoulders dropped a little and he asked almost plaintively, "Well then won't we at least get an interview with Stephen Colbert?"

"Sorry, Dude, I wouldn't be expecting a call even from Letterman," Leon responded with a satisfied smile as things got back to normal (*p. 281).

The EMT stepped in and broke up the conversation. "Mr. Falken, and you," he pointed at Leon. "Both of you need to leave now. You need to get checked out at the hospital."

"I'm going with him," Hannah chimed in. She hadn't let go of Leon since she had helped him get his vest off and walk back from the shooting.

"That's fine, but no one else in the rig," the EMT answered.

"I'll bring Bob and we'll catch up with you at the hospital," Mark offered. "Bob, let's talk for a second." Mark led Bob a few steps away from the ambulance as the EMT shut the doors. "You guys did some really clever work on this. You don't know, heck, I don't even know how many lives you saved today. I just want to throw this out there. I think you and Leon could do good work with our unit."

"No way." Bob's head was shaking before Mark had finished. "There is no way I can work with you guys." He started counting off on his fingers, "I'd never pass a background check. I don't look like a Fed. I'll NEVER wear a suit. I won't even tuck in my shirt. And I'll never work on a computer where the only sticker is an asset tag for some bean counter to track a requisition."

Mark stopped him before he began on the other hand. "It's not that bad," Mark assured with a laugh. "Just think about it for a little bit. Once everything calms down you might consider it. Besides, you wouldn't be an agent. We have consultants and contractors who would be interested in your talents. And come on, you'd probably prefer walking in through the front door instead of an unmarked van just snatching you off the street some day to 'recruit' you."

"You wouldn't," Bob responded, partly as a statement and partly as a question.

Mark laughed again. "The FBI doesn't snatch citizens off the street." Then Mark added with a sly grin, "But I might know someone who would."

3P1L0GU3

END PROCESS

Friday, 2:00 p.m., St. Petersburg

RING…RING…

A woman reached her hand to answer the phone. Her hand paused over the receiver. She knew this line was never supposed to ring. "This is not going to end well," she said aloud just before she picked up the line.

Security Threats Are Real (STAR) 2.0

2

Recon

In a quick and dirty nutshell, reconnaissance is the ability to quietly locate a target that would be worth attacking. In the physical world, this process is centuries old and well perfected throughout the ages by both attackers and defenders.

A criminal has many targets that he or she can exploit in a day. While many exploits result in very few treasures, a lucky payoff can make the entire attack process worthwhile. In the physical world, reconnaissance would mean keeping a watchful eye out for a potential target, while focusing your efforts on a target with low risk and a high payoff. What started with bandits hiding high in the trees over trade routes evolved into using technological advances, such as telescopes and binoculars, to scout from a distance. Furthermore, technological leaps allowed for remotely operated surveillance cameras, wireless detection devices, and infrared heat scanners. The dawn of the social age has made the job even easier, as you can follow along as your favorite targets use Twitter and Facebook to describe their upcoming vacation plans, and monitor FourSquare accounts for instant, automatic location updates. This last example was recently showcased with the site www.PleaseRobMe.com, a site that automatically listed user accounts that used Twitter and FourSquare to show that they were away from their homes.

In the digital world, many of the reconnaissance actions are actually very similar. An attacker is scouting for targets that suffer from easily exploitable vulnerabilities and may hold valuable information. Whether it is credit cards, passwords, or helicopter schematics, an attacker has a certain goal in mind and is constantly on the prowl for targets to prey on. Regardless of your company's business or product, there will be at least one person in the world who would love to get his or her hands on your internal data.

This chapter will cover all of the aspects of reconnaissance that were introduced in the story and explore how you, your company, or your organization can protect against attackers scoping out your assets.

> **NOTE**
>
> We created an alternate reality for the Security Threats Are Real (STAR) section online. You can follow along and walk through reconnaissance against 3DNF. Many of the characters have presences across the Internet also. You will be able to find plenty of background information for the company and characters. Don't forget to substitute your company, name, and others close to you.
>
> Flip to the end of this chapter to follow along with how to hack 3DNF yourself!
>
> 3DNF corporate presence:
>
> - www.3dnf.net
> - http://blog.3dnf.net
> - http://twitter.com/3dnf
>
> Characters from Dissecting the Hack on Twitter:
>
> - http://twitter.com/Underground_Bob
> - http://twitter.com/I_30N
> - http://twitter.com/M4x_St34L
> - http://twitter.com/Rudy_HTown
> - http://twitter.com/Da_Dobbs
> - http://twitter.com/P4v3l
> - http://twitter.com/MResol

SOCIAL NETWORKING

> **THE HACK DISSECTED**
>
> *One of the names was in a red font instead of black like all the others. Michael Resol was someone of interest to Stepan. There were links to what appeared to be blog pages by Michael. There were even links to gambling sites. Then, there were some notes by Stepan:*
>
> *Michael Resol is the best target. He is a network admin that has worked at 3DNF for five years. He has been passed over for promotions and he talks too much about his employer on his blog site. Both his blog and Facebook sites reference his favorite online gambling pages. I think he has some financial problems – see link below.*
>
> *Michael's tech position, length of time with 3DNF, and money problems make him a good candidate for deployment of our application. (p. 10)*

Performing an attack (either physical or virtual) on a company is a very risky process. There are many angles of defeat for the attackers unless they have a bulletproof plan. However, there is an ace in the hole that many attackers have learned to utilize: the insider. In many instances, an insider within the target company can provide copious amounts of information to help with the attack, even unknowingly.

In our story, Vlad and his associates were able to take advantage of a 3DNF insider, Michael Resol, to set the stage for their attack. Michael made a few critical security mistakes that left him open to persuasion: he's a compulsive gambler, he keeps a detailed public presence about his work, and he has made public comments about his disgruntlement with his employer. He has now become a target for Vlad and will prove to be the enabler for much of what is to come.

This represents an ever-growing issue in our modern times. Not only are more people using the Internet on a daily basis, but also more are using it to form and join communities with others. This movement has been accelerated by acceptance of Facebook and Twitter, which allow users to publish their thoughts and ideas with no experience or skill in Web authoring. In the earlier days of the Internet, there was real skill and practice required to have an online presence. You would need to find a server to host your Web pages. You would need to learn how to code in Hypertext Markup Language (HTML) and learn how to manually upload your content to the Internet through complex tools and utilities. The creation of hosts like GeoCities made the process easier, but it wasn't until the dawn of sites like MySpace and Blogger that the skill level dropped enough to make Web publishing available to all users.

This dawn of Web publishing allowed users to update the world with details of their lives and experiences, paragraphs at a time, and proved successful in launching the online careers of many people. For some users, though, writing a paragraph or two at a time proved too high of a hurdle to leap. When the micro-blogging service (Twitter) came along, their prayers were answered. Now, users can send quick updates about their lives in small, 140-character messages to the world.

Exploit Techniques

When we discuss exploiting this material, it is in the context of being able to quickly view and search an employee's public persona to find the information that can be used for an attack. The type of material that can be found could be directly used for an attack, such as information about construction projects, new physical security hardware, or new policies in place. It could also be information that leads to an employee of the company that could be turned.

Exploiting an Employee

In our story, Vlad was able to use publicly available information about the company to find and exploit one of the network administrators within 3DNF, Michael Resol. Michael is not unusual or unique; he faces trials that many others in the world face. He's addicted to online gambling and is dissatisfied with his job. There are times when all of us are dissatisfied with our jobs, but the period usually passes and gets better. Michael's downfall was not just that he posted material online, but that he made himself a target for exploitation, and lacked the constitution to avoid temptation. He needed money to pay off his gambling debts, and when approached with an offer to pay off his gambling debts by simply acting out against an employer that he didn't like, he jumped on the chance.

Attackers typically look for model employees with a large chink in their armor. A good citizen with a particularly embarrassing past can be used for blackmail. For example, a deacon in the local church with a passion for online pornography, a C-level executive escaping from a past of drug addiction, or an unlucky network technician with an addiction to online gambling.

Michael's situation is a bit more straightforward than the others as a simple money payment can make his current debts go away, but Vlad could have just as easily threatened him with turning the information over to his employer. Many employers are hesitant to hire employees with extraordinary debt. In fact, it is one of the key factors looked at when applying for a government security clearance. Individuals with large amounts of debt can find themselves in a position of weighing their patriotism against their overburdening debt, and the debt usually wins the fight.

Once the attacker has an employee under his thumb, he can continue to press them for further information and actions. Many blackmailed employees are unaware that they're entering a one-way transaction. Even if they enter an agreement willingly for money, as Michael has in the story, there is no way out. If he comes down with cold feet and wants to reconsider the agreement, the money will be stripped away. Vlad would then immediately threaten Michael with disclosing details of the corporate espionage to his employer. In practical terms, this wouldn't work out best for Vlad, but it's a very effective scare tactic that puts the victim in a position to decide between his personal safety and his company.

Exploiting the Company

Even easier for the attacker than exploiting an employee is to just sit back and wait for the employee to leak information all over the Internet. This is becoming a common occurrence as employees take to the Internet to air their grievances with their employers or business partners. Confusing privacy controls on popular social networking sites like Facebook complicate the problem as many users are unaware that their private messages are actually being aired publicly for the entire world to see. Although many of the messages may seem innocent to the author, an attacker targeting their company can use information to form an idea on internal business matters. Consider the following messages:

> *Employee 1: "New exploit released for Windows Server... oh, this is going to suck"*

> *Company Press Release: "We will have a scheduled downtime this weekend to perform maintenance on our servers."*

> *Employee 2: "Just got an email that I have to work through the weekend. So much for my fishing trip!"*

Each of these messages, on its own, is just an innocent posting on the Internet. Companies take down their servers all of the time for regular maintenance. However, an attacker who is cyber-stalking employees of the company can put the pieces together to see that the company's servers are vulnerable to a newly released exploit and that they are waiting until the weekend to install patches. This is a process known as *inference*, and it is a common attack vector in the information security field simply because of the vast amounts of data being released on a regular basis.

Posts made online can even come back to haunt an employee long after a security event has taken place. In early 2010, a civil action lawsuit was filed against a school district in Pennsylvania over the misuse of laptops distributed to its students.[1] The laptops contained surveillance software that allowed the school system to turn on each camera at any time and take pictures from the user-facing webcam. This activity led to an incident in which a student was disciplined for allegedly using illegal drugs, later reported to be a box of Mike and Ike candy. Although the case itself is interesting in its own merits, of particular note here is the online persona of the school's network technician and his role in the situation. According to one independent researcher, the network technician maintains his own blog and has "a large online Web forum footprint,"[2] meaning that he is easily found across many online discussion forums. The technician has made many public postings and interviews about his involvement with the laptop webcams. At the very least, the online information shows his fascination and passion for using the technology to spy on students and catch those performing illegal acts. The decision of who was right and wrong is still undecided in this case as of the time of this printing, but the amount of material publicly posted by a technician involved with the case has made the school's legal defense much harder to prove.

Facebook

THE HACK DISSECTED

Michael Resol is the best target. He is a network admin that has worked at 3DNF for five years. He has been passed over for promotions and he talks too much about his employer on his blog site. Both his blog and Facebook sites reference his favorite online gambling pages. (p. 10)

Facebook has become the elephant in the room for many organizations. Once seen as yet another blogging site on the same level as MySpace, Facebook has grown to be one of the most immense and powerful sites in the world. It is hard to visualize the true size and scope of what Facebook does. On their own statistics site they've released the following statistics[3] as of March 2010:

NOTE

- More than 400 million active users
- 50% of our active users log on to Facebook in any given day
- More than 35 million users update their status each day
- More than 60 million status updates posted each day
- More than 3 billion photos uploaded to the site each month
- More than 5 billion pieces of content (web links, news stories, blog posts, notes, photo albums, etc.) shared each week
- Average user has 130 friends on the site
- Average user spends more than 55 minutes per day on Facebook
- Average user writes 25 comments on Facebook content each month
- Average user is a member of 13 groups

Reading through this information should paint a clear picture as to your users' activities on such a site. The average user spends nearly an hour a day on Facebook, many logging in while at work. The average user also writes 25 comments each month to their contacts about their daily lives.

The danger with Facebook isn't just with the content that's posted, but also to whom it's posted. Most users do not understand the security settings of Facebook, or how to limit content to just their close friends. Additionally, Facebook has gone out of the way to confuse its users into changing their accounts to publish material to "Everyone." One recent privacy modification to Facebook in December 2009 confused many users into changing their settings to allow material be published to everyone.

One example of the danger of such changes came with the suspension of a college professor in Pennsylvania in early 2010 for posting alleged threats against her students.[4] The professor kept a very private Facebook profile, limiting her discussions only to her friends. She was also habitually denying friend connections with her students, keeping her professional life separate from her personal life. Changes to her privacy setting, chosen without her understanding, allowed her students to peek in at her private profile to see derogatory remarks made against them.

Twitter

THE HACK DISSECTED

"I told you they were Feds!" Bob tried again.

"We don't know that," Leon responded and then yawned. "That's just what Dobbs said in his Twitter. Did you find anything in the code?" (p. 81)

***

"That's what I'm doing now. I'm going to check a few things, and then I'm going to send some DMs on Twitter. I don't want to do a tweet in case the Feds – or whoever is chasing us – is listening." (p. 92)

Although nowhere near the immense size of Facebook, Twitter has become a micro-blogging site that surprised many Internet analysts. While being ridiculed by many, it has quickly grown to be one of the most popular community-building sites.

Twitter allows for people to post messages publicly to the world in small, 140-character status updates. Users can also follow others that they are interested in, creating a myopic world of celebrity where many users are judged by how many followers they have. All status updates, or "tweets," that users make are published freely for anyone to read or search for. The exception to this is when users set their profile to "Protected." At that point, anyone can see the users' basic profile information, along with the users' friends, but not their actual tweets.

Twitter has become the new form of instant messaging among friends and colleagues. Unlike standard Instant Messaging (IM) clients, such as Microsoft Messenger and AOL Instant Messenger, there is no stateful connection to Twitter. The recipient of your message does not need to be online to receive your message. They will simply read it when they decide to view their messages. There is no way of knowing exactly when someone is on Twitter and when they're not, except by noting the times of their tweets. It is often compared with the world's largest chat room where everyone is lurking away from their keyboard.

In our story, Dobbs used Twitter to send a message to Leon about his recent visit from the Federal Bureau of Investigation (FBI). Later, Bob uses Twitter to send private direct messages (DMs) to his friend to seek help. DMs are sent privately from one user to another on Twitter without anyone else being able to read them. It is one of the few privacy restrictions used on the service.

Best Practices

There is no way to completely prevent your employees from posting anything to the Internet for the public to see. However, there are effective ways to mitigate the risk through your company's hiring process and through its internal security education efforts.

Background Checks

To avoid attacks against its employees, a company will have to employ additional security measures to ensure the character of the people they are hiring. However, this is harder than it sounds. Many corporations do not make reference calls for new applicants and make their decisions solely off of the applicant's own experiences. Even fewer companies take advantage of background checks to look into an applicant's background before they are hired, to see if they could be susceptible to bribery or exploitation. Further, only a small percentage actually sponsor a full security clearance check.

Education

As far as reducing information being leaked out against your company, much of this can be alleviated by educating your users and employees. Education needs to go farther than a simple "abstinence" plan and a few statements of "don't do that." Modern users will post information online and will resent any limitation of their privilege to do so. Instead, work with them as peers. Show all users the actual cases of information being leaked out from companies and walk through how to mitigate the risk. In the example messages shown earlier, Employee 1 could have segregated the exploit from his personal work just by stating that an exploit was released without the exclamation. Attackers are constantly seeking ways to link innocent messages to personal activities in a person's life. Don't do their work for them by publicly stating that a security issue is going to affect you.

Educate your peers on proper online privacy controls. If they use Twitter, they may want to consider "protecting" their account to keep details private except from friends. If they are on Facebook, walk through the privacy settings and explain each in detail. For each type of data that can be posted to Facebook, there is a setting that controls who is allowed to view it. These controls limit viewing of your data to Everyone, Friends of Friends, Just Friends, or a customized group.[5] Explain and demonstrate why they should not have any privacy setting set to show information to "Everyone."

SUMMARY OF SOCIAL NETWORKING

As demonstrated in the story, the entire chain reaction of events all started with a susceptible employee posting too many personal details about himself and his work to the Internet for all to see. Vlad and his associates picked up on these details and targeted the employee with a large bribe to perform a few simple tasks within the 3DNF office.

The issue of online leaks of corporate and personal information is a growing one as millions of people publish daily updates of their life and work habits. It can lead to exploitation of both employees and the companies that they work for. The best mitigation for these attacks is to prevent them from occurring in the first place. Use better employee screening in your hiring process to avoid bringing in susceptible employees. Educate your users on the dangers of posting public material online. Also, educate them on proper privacy controls for the online systems that they use on a regular basis.

FOR MORE INFORMATION

Social networking is an ever-evolving and growing world. Some sites change dramatically over the years, and current security policies will grow to meet the increasing risks. To give you more material on securing your information and network, we've provided additional reading links below. These links provide resources on proper security actions that you can implement today, as well as help guide you toward experts in the field who can assist with your security struggles.

- The Security Twits Twitter directory: https://twitter.com/securitytwits/lists
- This you?? What's the point of phishing a Twitter account?: www.f-secure.com/weblog/archives/00001893.html
- US-CERT: Staying Safe on Social Network Sites: www.us-cert.gov/cas/tips/ST06-003.html
- Sophos Social Media Threat Beaters: www.sophos.com/lp/threatbeaters/
- Social Media Security Podcast: http://socialmediasecurity.com
- "How cybercriminals invade social networks, companies": www.usatoday.com/tech/news/computersecurity/2010-03-04-1Anetsecurity04_CV_N.htm

GOOGLE HACKING

> **THE HACK DISSECTED**
>
> *Then Stepan had listed some names and e-mail addresses that belonged to the 3dnf.net domain. Vlad could only guess that Stepan had "googled" the domain name to harvest the addresses. If so, Stepan was a fairly resourceful researcher. (p. 10)*

Nearly everyone in the information security industry has been made aware of the issue of Google Hacking. But even though "Google" has become an acceptable verb in our common speech, the concept of Google Hacking is still a new concept to many outside the industry.

Google Hacking is a concept coined and perfected by Johnny Long, a well-known security researcher and founder of "Hackers for Charity," and author of a line of Google Hacking books, the latest being *Google Hacking for Penetration Testers, Volume 2* (ISBN: 978-1-59749-176-1, Syngress). Upon discovering that carefully crafted Google search queries could return results that showed that the target is running vulnerable software ripe for attack, Johnny created the Google Hacking Database (GHDB) at www.hackersforcharity.org/ghdb/, which quickly grew from hundreds of submissions by Johnny and teams of volunteers.

Google Hacking relies on certain keywords or phrases that only exist within Web sites that are running vulnerable software. It also targets keywords of sensitive data itself, such as credit card numbers and social security numbers. In some cases, the specific Google search queries even allow a user to bypass the security controls over a Web site and login directly as an administrator.

Although Google Hacking itself deals specifically with locating vulnerabilities and data leakage, it is now commonly used to reference any type of search query used to dig up information about a person or company that may not have been intended for public disclosure, and the usage doesn't stop with Google. Google may have originally been the only search engine that supported such complex queries, but now Yahoo! and Bing support many of the same operators and can perform the same search functions. For the sake of simplicity, we will call the act Google Hacking, but realize that most operations will work on your favorite search engine.

Exploit Techniques

Google, and all major search engines, have very powerful capabilities that can search within and across a trillion Web pages. We will cover a variety of ways to use Google to perform reconnaissance on a target in this section, focusing on the attempts used in the story. In the story, Stepan provided a list of names and e-mail addresses from 3DNF to Vlad, which had impressed the hardened criminal. Vlad refers to Stepan "Googling" 3DNF to locate the information, which is actually possible as we'll show you here.

Advanced Search Operators

The main Google Hacking technique involves understanding the nuances of the various advanced search operators supported by a search engine. Everyone knows the basic search operators, such as + and −. If you want to make sure a word is there, you precede it with a +, such as *+Hacking*. Likewise, if you don't want a particular word to show up, you can precede it with a −, such as *−Google*. A query of *+Hacking −Google* will bring up any page that refers to hacking but does not include the word "Google."

If you want to search for a phrase or sentence, you would include it in quotes, such as *Hack the Planet*, a quote that some may remember from the movie *Hackers*. The results of this search will display pages dedicated to the "Hack the Planet" concept formed by computer researcher Wes Felter.[6]

These basic operators work fine for the majority of Internet users, but lack the subtle capabilities required by a master searcher. Crafting search queries that take trillions of potential Web results and limits them to exactly the results that you are looking for is an art that takes practice and diligence. To harness this power, you will need additional search operators, such as the ones shown in Table 1.1.

You can try out all these operators on your own as you're reading along. Feel free to take a break from reading and explore Google using your newfound powers. The first operator we'll take a look at is the *site:* operator. This operator will limit your results to just the domain name that you specify. So, if you perform a basic search for *site:microsoft.com*, you will receive a list of Web results that all come from www.microsoft.com and its various subdomains. If you wanted to further limit it to a subdomain, such as http://store.microsoft.com, you can adjust your search query to read *site:store.microsoft.com*. You can then search for a particular item that you're interested in, knowing that only results from the Microsoft Store will appear. Try this search for Microsoft Flight Simulator: *site:store.microsoft.com Flight Simulator*.

The *inurl:* operator will prove to be immensely helpful for many searchers. Sometimes, the data we're looking for is not just the text in a page, but instead the text that appears in the Uniform Resource Locator (URL) for a particular page. If looking for the e-mail addresses, physical addresses, or telephone numbers of a site, you could try looking directly for a common page named "contact." Depending

Table 1.1 Common Advanced Search Operators

Search Operator	Description
site:	Limits all search results to a single domain name and the pages contained within it
inurl:	Searches for the keyword in the Web page's Uniform Resource Locator (URL)
intitle:	Searches for the keyword in the title of the Web page
intext:	Specifies that the keyword *must* appear within the text of the Web page
inanchor:	Searches for the keyword only within HyperText Markup Language (HTML) anchors (page links)
link:	Searches for Web pages that point to the specified URL
ext:	Searches for Web documents that have the specified file extension
cache:	Searches for the specified URL in Google's archived cache

on the software used by the Web server, this file could have differing extensions, such as: contact.htm, contact.html, contact.asp, contact.php, and so forth. A generic search for *inurl:contact* will return all of these results. Some sites have differing names for this particular page, with some calling it "aboutus." Such a query for pages with "contact" in their names would miss these differently named pages.

Switch over to Google and search for *inurl:aboutus.htm*. You should receive back more than 750,000 results to parse through. Let's try combining search operators here to limit the results. Let's pretend that we only want to search for United States Government agencies with this page: *inurl:aboutus.htm site:gov*. In this example, we're using the *site:* operator to limit results to the top-level domain of *.gov.* Let's limit it even more by searching for government agencies with addresses within Washington, DC by using the search query *inurl:aboutus.htm site:gov "Washington, DC"* and you will notice the results to be much more manageable, as shown in Figure 1.1.

Google's capabilities have grown greatly over the years. Although they originally limited themselves to just search plain text documents and Web pages, they now have the power to index media-rich file formats such as Microsoft Word documents,

FIGURE 1.1

Google Search Results Using Advanced Operators

spreadsheets, and Adobe Portable Document Format (PDF) documents. Years ago, it was these search queries that uncovered many sensitive and classified documents being publicly posted all across the Internet. For example, consider spreadsheets, which are used to store large amounts of organized information, and provide the power to perform on-the-fly computations for prices and numbers. In short, spreadsheets are typically used for internal data calculations and are not commonly shared outside of an organization. Using the *ext:* operator, we can focus our results directly on a particular type of file, such as Microsoft Excel spreadsheets. Try searching for *ext:xls site:mil* or *ext:xlsx site:mil.* This search query will search for all public Excel .xls and .xlsx spreadsheets located on military ".mil" Web servers. Although the results of this query will return mostly innocuous material, it proved a black eye for many organizations in their early years of Internet use, as critical information was being inadvertently posted and leaked out.

Archived Web Pages

While searching Web pages for the information needed in an attack, it is important to realize the impact that time has on a Web page. The page that you see today may not be the same that was shown yesterday, or last year. Information changes on a constant basis and some sites simply start reducing the information they share on their sites for fear of an attack. However, this reduction doesn't help them against Web archive services, such as Google and the Internet Archive's Wayback Machine, located at www.archive.org/web/web.php.

The Google Cache service stores Google's latest copy of a Web site on their servers and is incredibly useful in instances when a Web site goes down for maintenance. It can also be used by online searchers to pull up information that may have just been removed or modified on a Web site, before Google has the opportunity to reindex the Web site and change its cached version.

To view a cached version of a Web site, you can simply search for the page in question and click the **Cached** link directly below the result, as shown in Figure 1.2. By clicking this link, you will be shown the Web page, but it'll be served directly from Google's servers instead of the actual Web site's server. If that statement made you tingle inside, you probably saw a great reconnaissance opportunity here.

By connecting directly to a company's Web site, as we've discussed throughout this section, you are giving up tell-tale signs of your approach. There is an ongoing Web log maintained by the company's Web server on every single page reviewed and the Internet Protocol (IP) address of the machine that requested it. Most attackers will find ways to obscure their source IP by browsing the Web through relaying proxies, but we could also the Google Cache service for this. By focusing our search queries on the Google Cache, we can mine a ton of information from the target without ever accessing the target's server. However, this isn't completely foolproof. Google only caches the actual text content of the page, not images or multimedia; those are still directly hosted from the target's server, and even viewing the Google Cache will relay back your presence to the target as you attempt to download graphics and videos. When you view the Google Cache version of a page, you will notice a large banner at

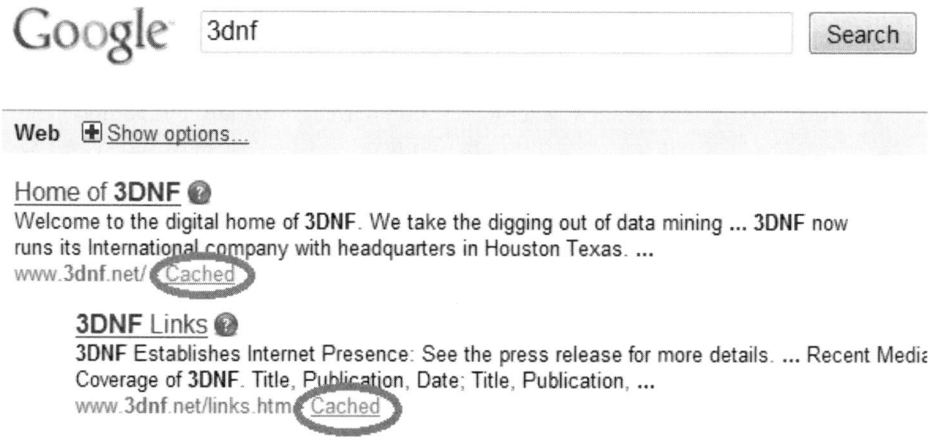

Google 3dnf   Search

Web ⊞ Show options...

Home of **3DNF** ❓
Welcome to the digital home of **3DNF**. We take the digging out of data mining ... **3DNF** now
runs its International company with headquarters in Houston Texas. ...
www.3dnf.net/ Cached

3DNF Links ❓
3DNF Establishes Internet Presence: See the press release for more details. ... Recent Media
Coverage of **3DNF**. Title, Publication, Date; Title, Publication, ...
www.3dnf.net/links.htm Cached

FIGURE 1.2

Google Cache Link

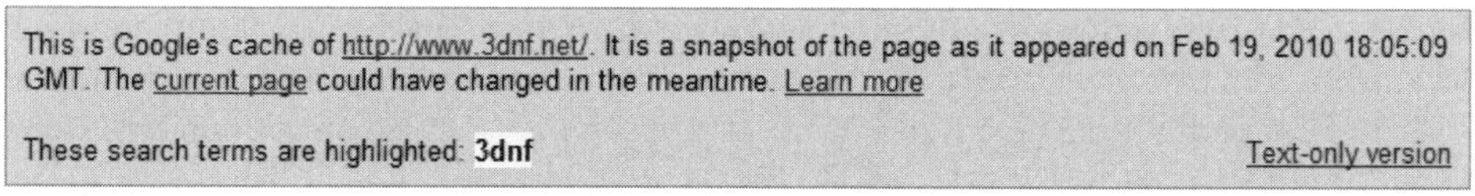

This is Google's cache of http://www.3dnf.net/. It is a snapshot of the page as it appeared on Feb 19, 2010 18:05:09
GMT. The current page could have changed in the meantime. Learn more

These search terms are highlighted: **3dnf**   Text-only version

FIGURE 1.3

Google Cache Page Banner Showing Text-Only Link

the top of the page, as shown in Figure 1.3. At the bottom-right corner of this banner
is a link that will take you to a text-only version of the page. By clicking this link, you
will see only the text itself of the page, directly from Google's servers. It is not completely segregated for some sites, but chances are that on a majority of Web sites, you
can passively view the page details without ever accessing the target's servers.

This action can also be taken manually without clicking through the various
Google links. You can directly pull up the Google Cache version of a Web site by
Google searching with the *cache:* operator. For example, search for *cache:3DNF.net*
and you'll be taken directly to the cached version. If you then want to strip out the
images and leave just the text, click in the Web browser's address bar and add the
following argument to the end of the URL text: *&strip=1*. This text will tell Google
to reshow the page but strip out all images and multimedia. Performing these actions
manually causes you to access the real Web page's server during the first cache request
while obtaining the search query to modify, thus defeating the point of stripping the
content hosted on the real Web page's server during the second, stripped request.
These actions can however also be performed automatically through a variety of Web
browser add-ons, such as the Passive Cache add-on for Mozilla Firefox, which allows
you to right-click on a URL and immediately bring up the stripped cache version of it,

resulting in never having actually accessed the real Web site's server. Passive Cache can be found at https://addons.mozilla.org/en-US/firefox/addon/977.

It is also possible to view more archaic details of a site through its entry in the Internet Archive's Wayback Machine, a site with more than 150 billion pages archived based on their address and date. With it, you can view Apple's Web site from 1996, years before they gained their international popularity. You can probably guess at the power of this search engine. In their early days, many businesses will post incredibly detailed information on their Web pages, trying to coax more business to their stores. Over time, the need for operational security outweighs their need to bring in new, casual business, so details start to drop off their Web pages. Using Archive.org's Wayback Machine, you can also find details on pages that have been seemingly removed from the Internet.

One notable example was from a United States Postal Service (USPS) data leak in 2004, in which a USPS Supervisor installed Kazaa on his work computer and inadvertently shared out the entire hard drive.[7] This information was collected by a random P2P user, who downloaded hundreds of pages of disciplinary write-ups full of personal information. This information was then posted to a public forum and viewed by all. Over time, the Web site went down and the forum was pulled. This site is no longer retrievable and does not exist anywhere … except in the Wayback Machine. By placing the URL into Wayback, we can view a cached version of the entire forum posting and read all of the details, as shown in Figure 1.4. This functionality is also automated by the Passive Cache add-on for Mozilla Firefox.

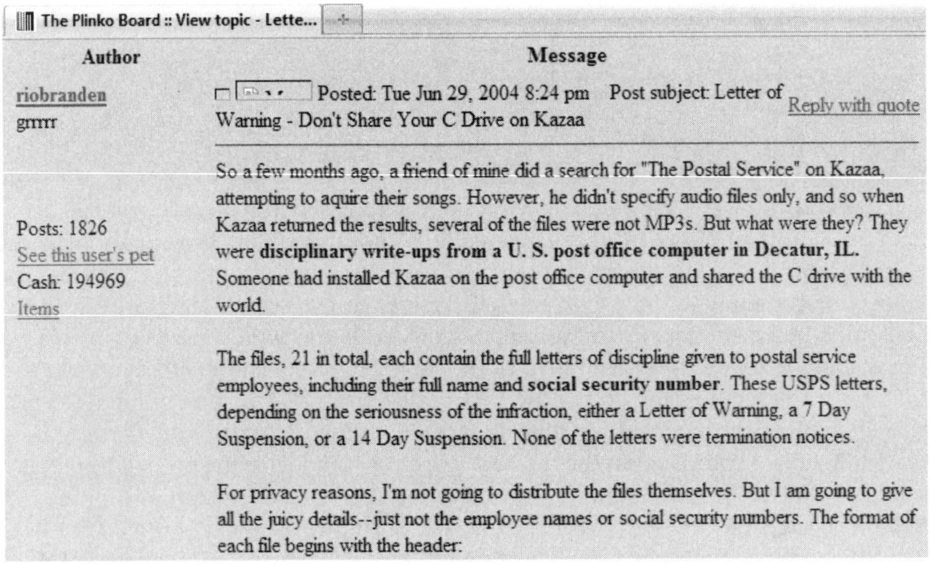

FIGURE 1.4

Archive.org Display of a Deleted Web Site

Advanced Dork

Although the immediate tool required for these actions would be your search engine of choice, there are a few additional software tools that can help speed up the process and make it easier to complete. Many of these applications are actually just free add-ons to Web browsers to include additional functionality, as the entire Google Hacking world exists within a Web browser.

One notable add-on is Advanced Dork for Mozilla Firefox, developed by CP, and downloaded from https://addons.mozilla.org/en-US/firefox/addon/2144. CP is also coauthor on the popular *Google Hacking for Penetration Testers, Volume 2* (ISBN: 978-1-59749-176-1, Syngress). Advanced Dork allows you to quickly right-click on any URL in a Web site and be presented with a custom set of Google advanced search operators to start tailoring a search query. You can also right-click on a selected string of text and use it in your queries, as shown in Figure 1.5.

Best Practices

As a business, you will need to expect that someone will use the vastness of material on the Internet against you. As a practice, you should be Google Hacking your own business on a regular basis to gauge what type of material is being displayed to the public on the Internet. Search on particular keywords of your business products and limit the results to just your domain using the *site:* operator. Search on details of your employees on your own site to see how easily available their information is. And don't forget to search through archived pages on the Archive.org Wayback Machine to see if there is critical information still made available.

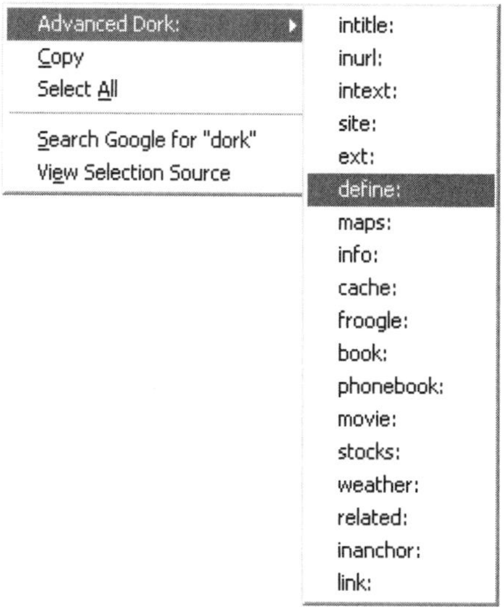

FIGURE 1.5

Advanced Dork Extension for Mozilla Firefox

SUMMARY OF GOOGLE HACKING

As the size of the Internet grows, through trillions of Web pages, the scope and power of search engines such as Google will continue to grow. A well-crafted search query can help return very exact and specific results for the information that you are seeking, turning Google Hacking into a surgical skill for some. To be proficient at it, a searcher will need to become comfortable and practiced at using the various advanced search operators available within the Google, Yahoo!, and Bing search engines.

FOR MORE INFORMATION

Google Hacking has grown into a very complex and very efficient way of searching for publicly disclosed information on the Internet. For the scope of this book, we only focused on a very small portion of its power. There are many more references available, some shown below, that will assist you in helping to craft specific Google search terms to look for material about your site.

- *Google Hacking for Penetration Testers, Volume 2* (ISBN: 978-1-59749-176-1, Syngress)

- GHDB: www.hackersforcharity.org/ghdb/

- Google Guide: Search Operators: www.googleguide.com/advanced_operators.html

- Google Help: Cheat Sheet: www.google.com/help/cheatsheet.html

DEEP WEB SEARCHING

THE HACK DISSECTED

He had some information about a small firm in Houston, Texas called 3DNF, Inc. that had been acquired by Data Mining within the last six months. Vlad found some links from the U.S. Securities and Exchange Commission Web site and the text from a press release about the acquisition. (p. 9)

Businesses of all types are facing a constant and persistent threat from hackers these days. While the well-known hacking attempts are targeting entities in the financial and defense industries, there is absolutely no business that is safe from attack. There is no company that should feel protected from attack simply because their business would not interest an attacker, as many small companies and businesses are hacked simply to become a relay point for further attacks against better targets. By having a business on the Internet, you will inevitably face a threat from hackers in the current environment.

Once an attacker has singled out a business to focus upon, the first stages of reconnaissance include finding every public detail about the company and its employees. This information would include all of the physical business locations, contact phone numbers, and lists of employees and partners. Your first thought, as someone within the company, may be to just limit every possible detail about the company on the Internet. This is a sensible thought. If your building's address is not posted anywhere on the Internet, then it is impossible for an attacker to find it, right? However, it is nearly impossible for any organization to remain completely secret. Anyone can find the headquarters of the Central intelligence Agency (CIA), and many knowingly pass the National Security Agency (NSA) "black glass building" Headquarters in Fort Meade, Maryland daily.

Someone knows that your company exists, and you cannot hide from the Internal Revenue Service. There are numerous databases across the world that store critical details about businesses, their operations, and their employees in an online world known as the *Deep Web*. Such details are required when filing for a business license within the United States. These databases are also placed online for public disclosure, even if they are not directly indexed by Google or other search engines. There is little effort in a hacker manually searching through such databases to find details on their chosen target.

This section will cover areas in the story in which such databases were used by the actors to gather details on their target. It will also cover additional ways in which you can search to see what information can be gathered about yourself or your company.

Exploit Techniques

In terms of an exploit, these online databases are normally open and available to the public. Even databases with basic security controls will usually allow access through registered accounts or well-crafted queries. These databases themselves are open to attack to simply gather details on the hacker's real target.

At this stage of an attack, any information that can be gathered will be sought out. Although the public search results discussed earlier can get a large amount of the publicly available information, a well-motivated attacker will use numerous database engines to search for further details.

United States Securities and Exchange Commission

One critical site used for many reconnaissance pursuits is the Electronic Data-Gathering, Analysis, and Retrieval (EDGAR) database managed by the United States Securities and Exchange Commission (SEC) at www.sec.gov/edgar.shtml. All publicly traded companies are required to submit regular updates regarding their business operations to the SEC to ensure that they are operating honestly and legally. As these companies are publicly traded, all of this material is made available to the public for free, with no registered accounts required.

There are hundreds of record types stored by the SEC, each with their own specific purpose and role. The most basic purpose is simply to locate the company's business and mailing addresses and its list of senior staff, such as the entry for Microsoft

MICROSOFT CORP (0000789019)

SIC: 7372 - Services-Prepackaged Software
State location: WA | State of Inc.: **WA** | Fiscal Year End: 0630

Business Address
ONE MICROSOFT WAY
REDMOND WA 98052-6399
425-882-8080

Mailing Address
ONE MICROSOFT WAY
REDMOND WA 98052-6399

Ownership Reports from: (Click on owner name to see other issuer holdings for the owner, or CIK for owner filings.)

Owner	Filings	Transaction Date	Type of Owner
DUBLON DINA	0001160193	2010-02-18	director
GATES WILLIAM H III	0000902012	2010-02-18	director, 10 percent owner, officer: Chairman of the Board
GILMARTIN RAYMOND V	0001181176	2010-02-18	director
HASTINGS REED	0001033331	2010-02-18	director
Klawe Maria	0001458332	2010-02-18	director
MARQUARDT DAVID F	0001193109	2010-02-18	director
NOSKI CHARLES H	0001039894	2010-02-18	director
PANKE HELMUT	0001268397	2010-02-18	director
ELOP STEPHEN A	0001198785	2010-01-21	officer: President, Business Division
Lu Qi	0001454755	2010-01-05	officer: President, Online Services
BACH ROBERT J	0001193099	2009-12-28	officer: Senior Vice President
MUNDIE CRAIG J	0001193111	2009-12-24	officer: Senior Vice President
Klein Peter S	0001478007	2009-11-24	officer: Chief Financial Officer

FIGURE 1.6

SEC Filing Records for Microsoft

Corporation shown in Figure 1.6. Gathering a list of employees can be quite attractive for an attacker. Why spend weeks breaking into a company when you can simply steal a laptop from the car of a senior director and just access the corporate network through Virtual Private Network (VPN), or steal data directly off the laptop.

Equally interesting submissions that can be found are the 10-K (annual report) and 10-Q (quarterly report) that break down the total income and expenses of the company. Additional searches for CORRESP (correspondence) forms allow for viewing messages sent from the company to the SEC, and vice versa. These messages may seem mundane for many, but they open additional avenues of reconnaissance for an attacker. For example, in 2009, Apple Inc. sent multiple correspondences[8] to the SEC regarding a confidential treatment request for one of its reports. Such requests allow for the report to be shielded from Freedom of Information Act (FOIA) inquiries for 10 years. The summary of the report made note of agreements between Apple, Google, and Genentech. In the realm of large corporations, such reports are not very unusual. However, with smaller companies, such details could point to potential partners of your targeted company. As we'll discuss later in this section, determining the active partners of your target can allow for additional avenues of attack.

Searches such as this are not limited to just the United States. Many countries have their own systems in place for tracking their traded companies. Canada's version of EDGAR is their System for Electronic Document Analysis and Retrieval (SEDAR) found at www.sedar.com.

State Taxation Databases

On the state level, there are numerous irregularities to the information that you may find. Unlike a central federal repository, like the SEC EDGAR, each state can choose how to store its own information. This can prove to be a frustration to many attackers, as they have to continually seek out new and updated databases for each state to use in their information gathering pursuits.

Maryland's Department of Assessments and Taxation (MDAT), for example, hosts a publicly searchable database system in which addresses can be searched to determine their ownership. Their site can be found at www.dat.state.md.us. If a search through the SEC EDGAR database shows that your target has a business address within Maryland, then the MDAT would allow for you to pull up additional details that it stores regarding the company like the search results shown in Figure 1.7.

Such search abilities are fine for the shut-in doing all of his work from the basement of his family's home. However, there are additional search capabilities for the more active scout. Through basic online searches, the attacker has found a human target and decided to "tail" him throughout the day. The target drives across town to a commercial district full of various manufacturing businesses. He parks in front of a nondescript, unlabeled office and enters for a few hours. Although there are no telltale clues on the building or office to describe what it could be, the MDAT site can help tell us. By performing a property search for a particular street, the site will return the results on the homes or businesses found on that street.

Even with this capability, the true results may be shielded through various parent corporations and holdings. For example, the search result in Figure 1.8 shows the

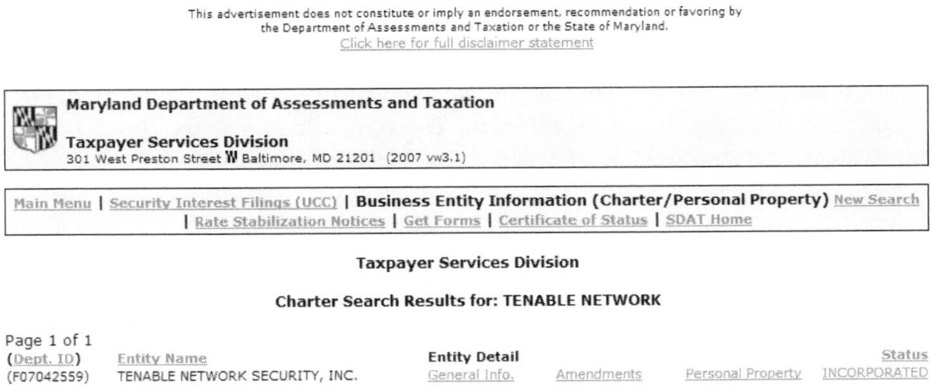

This advertisement does not constitute or imply an endorsement, recommendation or favoring by
the Department of Assessments and Taxation or the State of Maryland.
Click here for full disclaimer statement

Maryland Department of Assessments and Taxation

Taxpayer Services Division
301 West Preston Street W Baltimore, MD 21201 (2007 vw3.1)

Main Menu | Security Interest Filings (UCC) | **Business Entity Information (Charter/Personal Property)** New Search
| Rate Stabilization Notices | Get Forms | Certificate of Status | SDAT Home

Taxpayer Services Division

Charter Search Results for: TENABLE NETWORK

Page 1 of 1 (Dept. ID)	Entity Name	Entity Detail			Status
(F07042559)	TENABLE NETWORK SECURITY, INC.	General Info.	Amendments	Personal Property	INCORPORATED

FIGURE 1.7

Maryland Report for Business Filing

Maryland Department of Assessments and Taxation HARFORD COUNTY Real Property Data Search (2007 vw5.1d)					Go Back View Map New Search	

Page 1 of 1

Name	Account	Street	OWN OCC	Map	Parcel
S3 LLC	01 302744	1400 HANDLIR DRIVE	N	57	304
HARFORD HOTEL LLC	01 302736	1420 HANDLIR DRIVE	N	57	304
MANSI ENTERPRISES	01 302728	1435 HANDLIR DRIVE	N	57	304
CS REMAINDER II L	01 302698	1440 HANDLIR DRIVE	N	57	304

FIGURE 1.8

Maryland Report for Property Ownership – Street Search

businesses on one small street directly off of Interstate 95. What appears to be a list of unknown businesses is actually just the true owners of two major chain hotels: a Pizza Hut and a Cracker Barrel restaurant.

Additionally, it's even possible to track a target to his home and use this online database to determine when the home was purchased, for how much, and from whom. For the more aspiring attacker willing to break into a home, like Vlad and Andrei, contacting the previous owner of the home can lead to learning about the home layout, security systems, and other important security details.

Press Releases

Although there are numerous online Web sites that can be searched to dig up details on your target, a great source of information is the target itself. Many companies will publish numerous press releases detailing their business proceedings. Such press releases can include details on new partnerships, ground breakings on new facilities, or new software solutions being developed. This is especially true for publicly traded companies that rely on a favorable public presence to keep investors happy, as they tend to publish all major innovations and movements that would look favorably on the company in a press release.

Press releases are sure to contain the latest industry buzz words in the exact ratio required to both awe investors and make the competition jealous. However, this information also provides additional ammunition for an attacker.

Partnerships

Throughout this section, we've been discussing material that can be found directly about a company that can be used to plan an attack at a later point. However, there's another avenue of attack that could be just as profitable: attacking the target's partners.

This threat became real for Microsoft in early 2004 when portions of their Windows 2000 and Windows NT operating system source code were leaked onto the Internet.[9] The files were not stolen from Microsoft. Instead, they were obtained from

Mainsoft, a long-time partner with Microsoft.[10] Mainsoft was allowed portions of the Windows source code, which they posted on their secure File Transfer Protocol (FTP) server. However, the FTP server was vulnerable to a number of exploits, which allowed attackers to connect and siphon off all of the data.

Understanding Listed Material

Viewing the public information in Deep Web databases is not intricately complicated. Much of the material is placed online in a structure that can be easily browsed by nontechnical viewers that work in the financial and government sectors. The material itself is even available in more technical formats such as HTML and Extensible Markup Language (XML) for easier processing and inclusion into customized applications.

The specialization, though, is in understanding the language and appropriateness of the material available on these sites. A first-time user will undoubtedly spend hours reading through long, boring, and very technical documents about the accounting processes of corporations before they find something of value. Even in that situation, many attackers without an understanding of the financial or legal system may not realize that they're holding a gold mine even when they're directly staring at it. An attacker would need a basic level of understanding of the market, or have a friend on tap that could guide them to the right locations.

Best Practices

As a company, the number one mission is to turn a profit every year. As such, it is impossible to expect a company to lie permanently invisible from sight. Information about their physical and human resources will eventually be found by an aspiring hacker on the Internet. However, there are some safeguards that can be put in place to slow or obfuscate the reconnaissance process used by an attacker.

Many companies are inherently part of a larger umbrella organization. This allows for ownership of physical properties to be used in both ways. A small company may use its parent organization as a property owner in its public filings. Conversely, a large organization may be able to hide its ownership of an office or project under the name of one of its subsidiaries. An attacker would have to know all of the various bits of ownership involved in your company, which can be extremely difficult for larger organizations that may own dozens of subsidiaries.

The need to put out regular press releases and news interviews is important for a publicly owned business to keep its investors aware and interested in the company's progression. In the typical process of developing a press release, there are often many individuals who are involved as wordsmiths to ensure that the release says exactly what is required without making any unnecessary promises or expectations. It is important in this process to gain the input of your organization's Chief Security Officer (CSO) and Chief Information Security Officer (CISO). This could help you avoid posting a press release about your brand new data center and include details about its specific location and security protections.

SUMMARY OF DEEP WEB SEARCHING

There's more to the Internet than what can be found on its surface. Google and other major search engines can only scratch so deep into online sites and are specifically limited from grabbing details from many of the online database systems. Sometimes, a manual approach must be taken to search and interpret results directly from the sites by the attacker.

Once an attacker has chosen a target, he or she will use every piece of publicly available information to gather as many details as possible about the target's physical location, network capabilities, and employee staff. All of these items can be scanned further to search for additional areas of vulnerability that can be used later in the attack process.

The first area of searching for details about a company is determining if it is a publicly traded company, and using the SEC to monitor all of its public filings. This would help the attacker to understand the full scope of the company and its business, as well as provide physical location details and possibly lists of senior employees who could be targeted.

FOR MORE INFORMATION

Performing Deep Web searches requires a great amount of skill and knowledge. There are literally tens of thousands of online databases that can be tapped to provide information for any particular topic. The difficulty comes in determining how to find these databases and when to use them for a particular attack or defense. While we couldn't possibly list every resource, below are some references from Fravia, a well-known Web searcher, to help lead you on your journey.

- Recon 2005 – Fravia – Wizard searching: reversing the commercial Web for fun and knowledge: www.archive.org/details/Recon2005_Fravia

- Web Searchlores: www.searchlores.org

PHYSICAL SURVEILLANCE

THE HACK DISSECTED

"We've got to go. I know how we can check on my dad. I should have remembered sooner."

"What?" Leon asked as he followed Bob through the restaurant.

"My webcam. I keep the one over my main screen on feeding a password-protected Web site. We just need to find someone's network to jack into. Then I can see if anything's going on in my lab."
(p. 49)

An integral part to reconnaissance is keeping steady surveillance of your targets and your surroundings. As an attacker, this would involve watching the physical facilities of your target, as well as keeping tails on notable employees. When do most employees arrive for work? When do most leave for the day? Do they go out for lunch or eat in? Are there employees working overnight? At what time does the main entrance go on lock down and when does it reopen?

As you could imagine, it is impossible for a single person to survey all of these items themselves. And, even if they could, they would undoubtedly be singled out as a suspicious person of interest. However, technology has to come in to automate the process through security cameras and webcams.

Remember that as we discuss reconnaissance, we should not forget that it is also used as a defensive mechanism. Defenders must be just as vigilant to monitor their physical facilities against attacks. This held true in our story as Bob was able to monitor the webcam in his computer lair to witness Vlad and his gang trashing the room. The prominence of webcams has made physical surveillance extremely inexpensive and easy to setup. However, there are areas where a webcam can fail you, or even turn against you.

Exploit Techniques

As you would already expect, establishing a physical surveillance plan is important for both attackers and defenders. Each side wages war by detecting surveillance used by the other side and destroying or obfuscating it at every possibility. Hiding surveillance equipment has grown into an art in recent years as the technology allowed for smaller and cheaper equipment, and the market has grown even larger with a variety of "Nanny Cams." How would you like an earth-tone hollow rock with a daytime and nighttime video camera and a built-in digital video recorder that can take up to 160 h of surveillance footage on battery power? Such devices are now available through Internet stores and can be hidden in the landscaping of a business facility by either the company or the attackers. There really isn't enough space in this book to cover all the types of covert surveillance equipment available for purchase through the Internet. It is worth the time to go "window shopping" on the Internet to see the variety of incredibly normal items that contain surveillance equipment of all types.

Monitoring Public Webcams

For many reasons, businesses and individuals are surrounding themselves with webcams. Public-facing businesses use them to give an air of transparency to their customers. Others use cameras to help showcase their development efforts, especially when dealing with wealthy clients. They have numerous cameras around their facilities that track employees and millions of dollars worth of parts movements throughout the day.

By watching and recording webcams, an attacker can determine critical information about a facility's personnel and security such as the following: What time do employees show up? Who sits in which offices? Where do the managers and executives sit? Are parts tracked with a barcode scanner when they're moved? Where is the alarm panel?

Webcam Hacking

Although the idea of installing a covert camera within a target's facility may sound cool, it is also a very risky maneuver. At times, it may not even be worth the hassle, especially if the company has already done it for you. Hollywood glamorizes the ability to tap into a building's existing security system and instantly control it, but the capability is still out of the hands of the common attacker.

With the right tools, and the right know-how, it is possible to take over some Internet-based IP cameras that are being used by many organizations. This capability was demonstrated by two researchers with Voice over IP Exploit Research (VIPER) Lab at DEFCON 17.[11] In a presentation called "Advancing Video Application Attacks with Video Interception, Recording, and Replay," the duo gave a live demonstration on taking over an existing IP-based surveillance camera and "overwriting" its live stream with a pre-selected video. More details on this exploit, along with a video example, can be found at www.wired.com/threatlevel/2009/07/video-hijack/. They unveiled new versions of their free UCSniff (http://ucsniff.sourceforge.net) and VideoJak (http://videojak.source-forge.net) tools, allowing for the audience to follow along from home. Their results were shocking enough to credit them with an inclusion in the United States' Homeland Security Daily Open Source Infrastructure Report, viewable at www.globalsecurity.org/security/library/news/2009/08/dhs_daily_report_2009-08-04.pdf (PDF).

For some cameras, such dramatic efforts may not even be necessary. With a few well-known Google Hacking search terms, it is possible to locate publicly accessible webcams that have been indexed by Google. Many of these webcams have a Web-based interface for their users to access to view the live video footage and, of course, these interfaces contain expectable keywords that can be searched upon. There are dozens of search queries that you can use to locate these, with many found on the GHDB at www.hackersforcharity.org/ghdb/. Here's one that you can start using immediately to start scouring the Internet tubes for webcams:

- inurl:indexFrame.shtml?newstyle=Quad Axis

This query, when entered into Google, will return a few dozen public webcams running the popular AXIS Video Server.

There are many similar search methods to locate webcam sites, especially when you combine them with the *site:* operator to run each through the domain of your target.

Beyond using Google Hacking techniques, it is possible to search for Internet surveillance cameras using the recently created SHODAN Computer Search Engine at www.shodanhq.com. SHODAN is a search engine that focuses on the types of Web servers instead of the content being hosted. It can be used to find sites that run particular software, such as the unique applications used for Internet surveillance cameras.[12] As a demonstration of the results shown by SHODAN, you can submit a simple query for video by entering the following URL: www.shodanhq.com/?q=video

As many people in the information security industry know, most computer people are looking for ways to simplify their work and are more than willing to let someone else do the work for them. The best way to do this, besides tapping into someone else's webcam footage, is to find their archive of captured images. Most webcam applications will allow for each image taken to be exported out as a JPEG graphic file to the hard drive. It's actually common to find a folder with months of webcam footage, especially if the camera uses motion-detection to record. In our story, Bob made a wise security choice by backing up all of his webcam images to an off-site server over the FTP. So even with a bullet through his camera and computer, he was still able to view the feeds up until the time his equipment was destroyed. However, in this situation, his security is only as good as that of the FTP server. Even if someone is not able to directly view his camera footage, they could stumble on the cache of webcam images and monitor the office from there.

Best Practices

As with all security devices, proper planning needs to be performed to ensure that your facility is kept secure from intruders and attackers. While a common Certified Information Systems Security Professional (CISSP) can rattle off the industry standards for where surveillance equipment should be installed, each implementation will be unique and will require appropriate study. It may be preferable to install very noticeable surveillance equipment on the exterior of your facility to give the impression of strong security and ward off vandals and common criminals.

Some facility managers like to use this same implementation on the interior, but that's an area for discussion. If you just want to scare someone off, noticeable cameras and a loud alarm would vacate the common criminal. However, a more advanced attacker will expect them and learn ways to work around them. Some businesses prefer hidden internal cameras and silent alarms to goad criminals into a false sense of security, giving a greater chance for law enforcement to catch them in the act.

Surveillance Tracking

Being on the defense side, it is advantageous to search for surveillance equipment that may be concealed in or around your property. For this, there is a specialty skill used for military and government operations known as technical surveillance countermeasure, or just TSCM. Unique detection equipment is used to search for a variety of surveillance "bugs" through a very slow, methodical, and expensive process. However, if your paranoia level is at the right level, a good bug sweep could help ease your anxieties and ensure that your facility is well protected.

Storage Requirements

This may seem like a funny, offhand suggestion, but it is a critical concern. Your surveillance cameras require storage to store the images or video feeds throughout the day. If storage space runs out, which is very common with "forgettable" items like cameras, you may stop storing footage. This is basically a self-inflicted denial of service attack.

Ten years ago, in the winter of 1999, one of the authors of this book worked in a small data center. As the first person to arrive on a Monday morning at 5:00 A.M., the author noticed the rear office entrance slightly open with the door handle missing. The area was sealed off as the police and relevant federal law enforcement were called to investigate. A criminal had broken into an adjacent medical facility and then cut a large hole through the drywall to enter the main office atrium. The door knobs and dead bolts were pried off the office rear access door, allowing the criminal access to the office suite. The storage closet was broken into, and a floor safe was lying open on the floor.

After a full inventory, the intruder had made off with … about $10 worth of change from the soda vending machine. All that was in the safe was software licenses and service contracts, each in a sealed, unopened envelope. The network investigation was managed by an outside agency.

During the interviews, it dawned on IT staff to check the surveillance camera: a hidden, digital camera in the main hallway. Upon pulling up the folder view, they were perplexed. There were videos leading up until the prior Wednesday, and none after. It was at this point that the last member of the technical team arrived for work, the person in charge of backing up the camera videos to CD-ROM and then deleting them off the hard drive. He admitted that he had gotten so busy that he had forgotten to do that for a few weeks.

With no physical evidence left at the scene, and no trace of computer use, the case never went any further and for weeks everyone was self-perplexed about how easily they let a criminal walk free … with a pocket full of coins.

Encrypted Backups

As discussed earlier, there is a great need for backups of all surveillance images and video footage. It's common to keep at least a year's worth of video footage, if not longer, within reach for any internal security-related issues. Just like any other backup that you would have of data, the surveillance backups should be encrypted and kept in a secure facility. Losing a single month's worth of surveillance to an attacker can give away many crucial details of your staff and facility procedures.

SUMMARY OF PHYSICAL SURVEILLANCE

Physical surveillance is often the first line of defense against a physical attack or against intrusion into your facility. However, the technology can also be used against you with intruders installing their own surveillance equipment to watch your facility. Even worse, using some well-publicized exploits, attackers could turn your own cameras against you!

An attacker will use every possible physical resource at their disposal to survey their targets, even public webcams and urban cameras. Many of these cameras can be found readily with a few common Google search terms, listed at Johnny Long's GHDB. Using attacks released at DEFCON, attackers can even take over a company's IP-based cameras and substitute their own footage in place of the live stream.[11]

Companies should implement comprehensive surveillance of their facility, internally as well as externally, which provides for proper maintenance of the cameras. Proper security doesn't stop with the cameras itself; backups should be encrypted and kept off-site to prevent their theft and use by criminals.

FOR MORE INFORMATION

In this section, we covered the basics of physical surveillance and some of the security pitfalls that exist within its industry. As with any security industry, physical surveillance devices are evolving at a very fast rate, providing for smaller and more powerful camera equipment. Below, you will find Internet references to help you understand differing views on physical surveillance, as well as track the latest news and updates.

- Hack N Mod Surveillance Hacks: http://hacknmod.com/tag/surveillance/

- CCTV DVR Security Camera Blog: http://cctv-dvr.blogspot.com/

- Schneier on Security: On London's Surveillance Cameras: www.schneier.com/blog/archives/2009/08/on_londons_surv.html

LOG ANALYSIS

THE HACK DISSECTED

The middle and largest monitor was unlocked. It displayed the aggregated data from the few network intrusion detection sensors deployed in the company network. Near the top of the screen, the oldest entries sat unread. Steadily, new entries appeared at the top of the list. In the middle, a grouping of entries in red slipped a little lower. Chance would determine how far down the list, or even off the screen, they would be by morning on Monday when the analyst came in. (p. 59)

***

Jonathan took a couple more swigs of his carbonated breakfast as he scanned the entries on the Snort console. He was rarely fully awake for this weekly ritual, but he performed it faithfully. Usually, if he found anything of interest, it only merited a call to the network support team because a server went down. Jonathan squinted his eyes as he scanned through Friday evening then into Saturday. His expression didn't change except for the breaks for additional swallows of breakfast. Suddenly at 11:06 P.M. on Saturday, there was a string of alerts. Someone had run a network scan from inside the company. He nearly missed the desk as he sat up abruptly and slammed down his drink. (pp. 63–64)

As a network defender, security logs are your first line of defense against an intruder. Multiple network-monitoring devices act like surveillance cameras on your network's perimeter, tracking packets coming through ingress and, hopefully, egress points. As it is physically impossible to monitor each and every single packet going through your network manually, the process to identify suspicious or malicious packets has become fairly automated. Each packet is profiled by comparing its data against a set of custom rules that look for suspicious identifiers. If a positive result is found, an alert is raised and the entry is logged for follow-up, as was demonstrated in our story.

Jonathan Tao, one of the network administrators at 3DNF, was running a security event logger on one of his machines. By reviewing the entries from the past weekend, he was able to see a number of packets alerted upon by the automated scanner, showing a port scan within the network.

Having access to critical, just-in-time log data is paramount to defending your network's data. You must be continually looking at what is happening now at your network's borders and preparing for an assault, which might occur at any moment.

Exploit Techniques

Anyone who has seen the television show "CSI" can testify to the quote "every contact leaves a trace."[13] Whether it is through fingerprints, DNA samples, or a slick lock of hair, there is almost always something left behind to run a trace on. And while in TV land the samples are screened and returned within hours, in the real world it takes months of sitting through a backlog before you see any actionable evidence to work from. Inside your network, every action has a trace. If a network attack takes place, it must occur in the form of packets sent across the network. The problem is in finding these pieces of evidence. Searching for a single bad packet in a capture file of millions of packets is literally like searching for a needle in a haystack. But be assured they're there, and once found can be singled out and placed into a firewall or intrusion detection system (IDS) rule so that later traffic can be acted upon before they result in exploitation.

Best Practices

A well-secured business should be in the position to expect a network intrusion at any possible moment and have an appropriate response and mitigation plan in place. Above all else, a proper border detection system needs to be put in place to monitor for a security event underway. But, take heart; this is a large business sector with dozens of vendors willing to sell you services to secure your network. Or take advantage of the numerous free and open-source applications available for monitoring your network's gateways. Take note though, these tools are completely useless without a dedicated security member or team monitoring their log output on a constant basis with a daily log review. These security members should also have the proper training to recognize a suspicious incident and escalate it to a proper authority for review.

Snort Rules

One such free and open-source border monitoring tool is Snort, the most popular IDS currently in use. It is a free, open-source application that is developed by Sourcefire, Inc., and it can be found at www.snort.org. Snort can be implemented into various locations across your network to provide early detection of unauthorized traffic so that administrators can curtail it before it gets out of control. Snort rules for most common applications and network traffic types can be found across the Internet, with some provided below for integration into existing Snort sensors.

Writing custom rules for Snort is a science, as well as an art. It requires a fundamental understanding of your network infrastructure, as well as the common packets that are expected to flow across it. Your network security team should have a good finger on the pulse of your traffic by regularly reviewing firewall logs and even monitoring live captures with a network protocol analyzer like Wireshark, which can be found at www.wireshark.org.

Although this section will not attempt to teach you how to write Snort rules, it will show you just how simple they can be to develop. All rules follow the structure of:

```
action proto src_ip src_port direction dst_ip dst_port (options)
```

So, if you wanted a simple rule to notify you when people go to Google's Web site, you could write a rule similar to the following:

```
alert tcp any any -> 66.249.90.104 80 (msg:"Someone is trying to
    Google something!";)
```

Another quick example is to detect if anyone is trying to connect to an external Simple Mail Transfer Protocol (SMTP) mail server, on Transmission Control Protocol (TCP) port 25:

```
alert tcp any any -> any 25 (msg:"Someone is trying to email
    something!";)
```

In our story, what alerts Jonathan Tao, one of the network administrators, is a port scan alert from Snort. This operation is actually built into Snort with a preprocessor called *sfportscan*, which can be configured for particular styles of port scans. It was a well-configured Snort rule set that allowed for 3DNF's network monitors to display the correct alerts for the scan that occurred. If only Jonathan had been reviewing the logs over the weekend …

Nagios

Although Snort is one of the best tools for monitoring your network for intrusion attempts and suspicious traffic, good administrators would also monitor each of their servers and services within the network. While many security engineers would scoff at such a tool for security monitoring, this is a highly relevant tool to have in your bag. One of the first symptoms of many amateur intrusions is a network service or system that crashes and is no longer available. Even if an attacker has been on your network for months, many occurrences are not noticed until a critical server crashes and a technician investigates. The authors have responded to intrusions that were discovered just this way. That doesn't include the number of servers that get hacked and crash, get wiped and reinstalled by a technician, then hacked again. Unlike Snort, which focuses solely on the traffic flowing across your network, Nagios is like a triage nurse for your systems, keeping constant check of their vital signs and overall health.

Log Visualization

Although log analysis is a critical portion of your network defense strategy, it is a highly technical skill that requires an advanced level of knowledge of your network systems and overall network traffic. At times, the person best equipped to monitor your logs for intrusions is too highly skilled for the job, and is off saving the world. At other times, a credible attack takes place, but the security individuals cannot clearly enunciate the issue to the management team to get their buy-in to make changes. Visualization can help solve both of these issues.

Visualization is a technique to graphically display your network logs to show, in a very simple picture, the full scope and impact of a network issue. Take Figure 1.9, an output from the Port Scan Attack Detector (psad) tool that shows the effect of a compromised host within a network. That single internal system, the central box at the bottom, is beaconing to hundreds of external computers to spread malicious data. Although this concept is pretty easy to explain, an image has greater impact as it can be imprinted into someone's mind for easier remembrance. It also makes it easier for security engineers to do their job, as tracing lines of connections between graphical images can be more effective that comparing long lists of IP addresses from a text log.

The psad tool mentioned earlier is a free application that can take the log output from other logging applications, and even directly through Snort rules, and output graphical images such as the one in Figure 1.9. For more information on psad, visit the Web page at www.cipherdyne.org.

Security visualization is a growing discipline in the information security field, and there is a fine art to displaying the most appropriate graph for the traffic that you are viewing. One of the best community Web sites for visualization is SecViz (www.SecViz .org). Of particular note about the Web site is their graph exchange, which includes hundreds of network visualization graphs for many styles of attacks and intrusions, providing quick inspiration for how to best demonstrate your own security incidents to your C-level executives.

SUMMARY OF LOG ANALYSIS

Although surveillance cameras may be the first line of defense against an attack on your front door, proper log analysis is the first line of defense against a network intrusion. Every attempt made by a hacker to break into your network, as well as every successful intrusion, will leave a trace of packets that can be analyzed and searched upon.

Network administrators and security engineers should have intrusion detection or prevention systems deployed at every ingress and egress point in the network to not only watch for malicious incoming packets, but also outgoing packets. Free tools such as Snort provide a powerful system to quickly and cheaply deploy such a security solution.

Administrators should also be regularly monitoring their servers to ensure that they are operating in optimal shape. There are numerous products available, such as the free Nagios, to perform this duty.

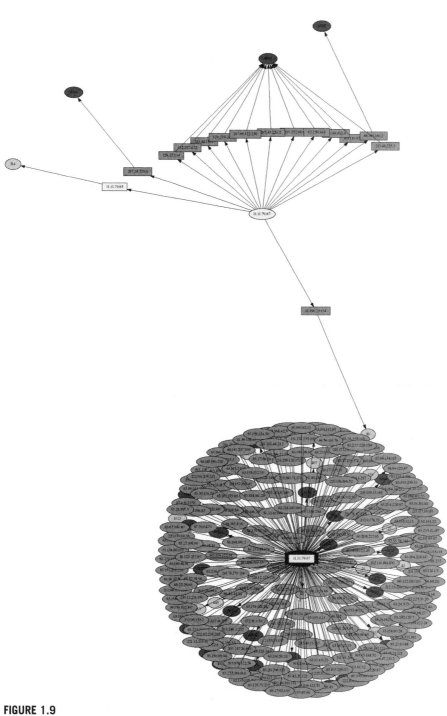

FIGURE 1.9

Visualization of a Compromised Host Beaconing

Although most applications will detail the traffic in a purely textual format, sometimes a more graphical display is required for intricate network captures or for display to nontechnical personnel. To accomplish this, various tools are available to visualize your network traffic. These graphics can then be printed through a plotter for large graphics that can be reviewed by teams and can be placed across offices for quick reminders of malicious traffic.

FOR MORE INFORMATION

The log analysis field is continually changing to defend against the latest malicious traffic and exploits. The material presented in this book provides a basic understanding of the field, but more detailed views can be found in the following publications:

- *Secure Your Network for Free* (ISBN: 978-1-59749-123, Syngress)

- *The Tao of Network Security Monitoring: Beyond Intrusion Detection* (ISBN: 978-0321246776)

- *Snort Intrusion Detection and Prevention Toolkit* (ISBN: 978-1-59749-099-3, Syngress)

- *Nagios 3 Enterprise Network Monitoring: Including Plug-Ins and Hardware Devices* (ISBN: 978-1-59749-267-6)

- *Applied Security Visualization* (ISBN: 978-0321510105)

DO IT YOURSELF: HACKING 3DNF

So now is the time to put on your hacker hat and follow along to see what kind of information we can collect about 3DNF. The first thing you need to do is to visit the Google homepage. Enter **3DNF** into the search box and click the **Google Search** button. You will see many results returned for 3DNF. The first few entries are likely related to the domain name 3DNF.net and among them is a 3DNF Twitter account. We will take note of both the domain name and Twitter account.

We will use the *site:* operator with "3DNF.net" to grab only results for the 3DNF.NET domain. Just type in **site:3DNF.net** into the search box and click **Search**. As you see in Figure 1.10, our search has returned some more information on 3DNF's Web presence. Of particular interest is the subdomain blog.3DNF.net, 3DNF's official blog, which could contain more information about the company for exploitation. If you notice the results for all of the pages have cached links, then this means you could look at the contents of their Web pages without directly accessing their Web site.

Now that we are able to gather information from the organization in an indirect manner, let us take a closer look at the information gleaned from this approach.

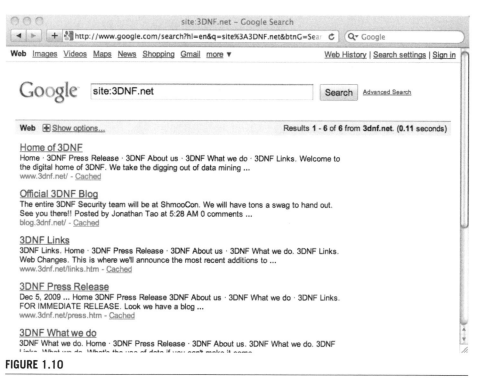

FIGURE 1.10

Google Search Results for site:3DNF.net

There are several contacts and an e-mail address in Figure 1.11. These contacts prob-ably have e-mail addresses on the 3DNF network.

The Internet contact e-mail address is "info@3dnf.net," which reveals that there is a high possibility that all of the e-mail addresses on the 3DNF network are a com-bination of employee names and the 3DNF.net domain. For instance, Mike Resol's e-mail may be mike.resol@3dnf.net, mresol@3dnf.net, or mike@3dnf.net. We could verify this by sending a couple of test e-mails. Once the e-mail structure has been verified, an attacker could phish everyone within the organization. Through a phish-ing attack, a hacker can construct a fake e-mail targeted directly toward the staff of 3DNF using internal information or terminology to make the victim feel as if the malicious e-mail is authentic. You will also notice that this page contains a physical address for the targeted organization.

Targeting Human Resources

For a quick example of how to target social networking, we'll look to see if Mike Resol has a Twitter account by typing in **site:twitter.com mike resol**. As you see in Figure 1.12, the top result is a Mike Resol. Mike's Twitter name is MResol and his account can be accessed right now at http://twitter.com/MResol. Try it in your own Web browser.

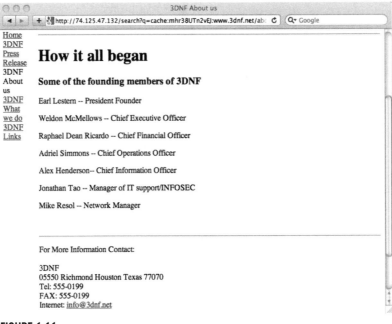

FIGURE 1.11

Google Cache View of 3DNF.net About Us Page

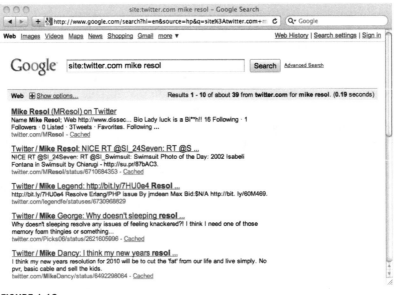

FIGURE 1.12

Google Search for Mike Resol's Twitter

The next Google Advanced Operator we'll use in this section is *intitle:*. This operator parses information from the titles of Web sites, the text that appears at the top of a Web browser, when viewing a page. We'll use this in combination with the *site:* operator from before. We will use these together to search for directories located on the 3DNF Web site. It is a common practice for organizations to leave files in directories for employees to download. Many think that these directories are hidden and that only the organization knows these files exist. It only takes a link to any of the documents to allow Google to discover the location of the documents.

Sometimes, Google indexes these directories, which can allow an attacker to download documents that are intended for employee use only. These documents may or may not be sensitive when viewed separately; however, reconnaissance is gathering all possible sources of information to provide intelligence. In Figure 1.13, you can see that there is a directory named "files" on the 3DNF Web site. At first glance, this directory seems to contain a couple of files worthy of our attention.

By clicking on the **Index of /files** link in the Google results, we are taken to the directory, which contains a couple of files, shown in Figure 1.14. Just by looking at the names, they appear to be contact lists for the 3DNF organization. This is

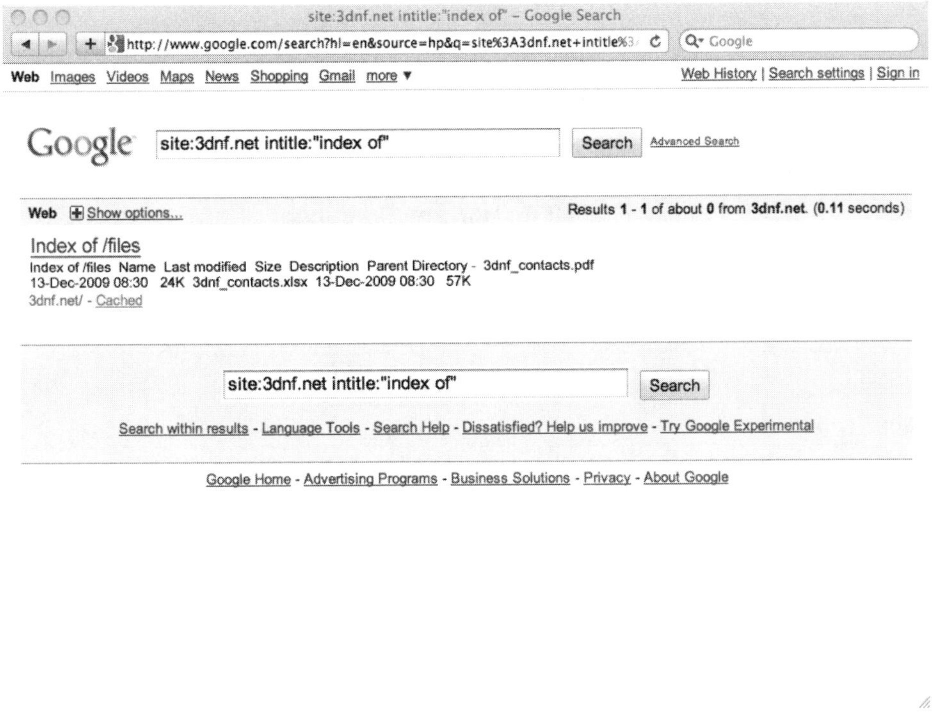

FIGURE 1.13

Google Search for Hidden Directories

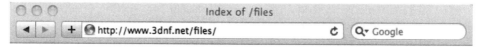

Index of /files

Name	Last modified	Size	Description
Parent Directory		-	
3dnf_contacts.pdf	13-Dec-2009 08:30	24K	
3dnf_contacts.xlsx	13-Dec-2009 08:30	57K	

FIGURE 1.14

3DNF Index of Files

◇	A	B	C	D
2		**3DNF Important Contacts**		
3	Name	Position	Phone	Email
4	Weldon McMellows	Chief Executive Officer	(713) 555-0201	weldon.mcmellows@3dnf.net
5	Earl Lestern	President Founder	(713) 555-0202	earl.lestern@3dnf.net
6	Raphael Dean Ricardo	Chief Financial Officer	(713) 555-0203	raphael.ricardo@3dnf.net
7	Adriel Simmons	Chief Operations Officer	(713) 555-0204	adriel.simmons@3dnf.net
8	Alex Henderson	Chief Information Officer	(713) 555-0205	alex.henderson@3dnf.net
9	Jonathan Tao	Manager of IT support/INFOSEC	(713) 555-0206	jonathan.tao@3dnf.net
10	Mike Resol	Network Manager	(713) 555-0207	mike.resol@3dnf.net

FIGURE 1.15

3DNF Contact Spreadsheet

exactly the type of information on which an adversary preys. Figure 1.15 shows the contents of the file named 3dnf_contacts.xlsx.

The spreadsheet has all of the important contacts from the organization listed. Now an attacker has the e-mail addresses necessary to launch a targeted phishing expedition, known as *spear phishing*, targeting high-value targets like executives and systems administrators.

You will also notice that this information is in a PDF file on the Web server, as shown in Figure 1.16. Adobe PDF documents are often targeted because they allow

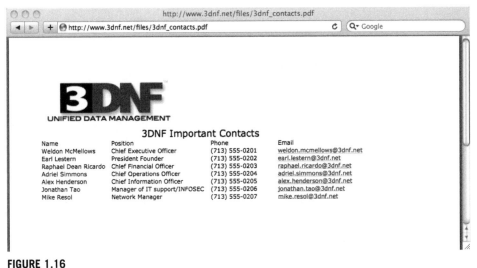

FIGURE 1.16

3DNF Contact PDF

attackers to embed malicious code in them. Attackers can take legitimate documents from Web sites, embed malicious code into them, and send them out to prospective clients of the actual company. In this case, if an attacker downloaded this PDF and sent it to 3DNF partners, then it could lead to the infection of a 3DNF partner. The victimized organization that trusts 3DNF content could be compromised. This could allow 3DNF to be compromised in return, using the compromised partner as an attack vector.

Google Apps

Many organizations use Google Apps for enterprise e-mail, chat, video, and document management. This is great for organizations because they can save tons of money by outsourcing these functions to Google. This could also be problematic because the information may be available to Internet users if they simply possess the credentials to a valid employee account. Although information on Google Apps is protected by basic account credentials, the security put in place by Google to protect their infrastructure may be more effective than the security placed on the local network of a company. There is a trade-off for placing information on Google Apps as your company turns direct control over hardware resources to an outsider, but benefits from having a possibly more secure network that reduces business costs. This debate frames the discussions of security on the recent evolution of cloud computing, a model where businesses services are hosted through an Internet-based provider instead of internally by the business.

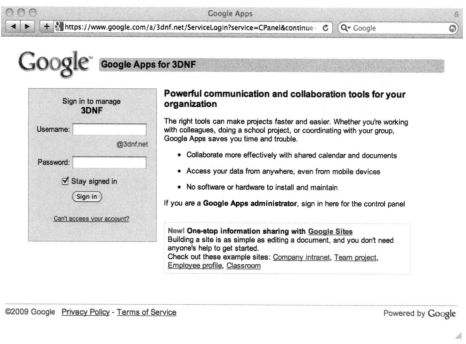

FIGURE 1.17

Google Apps for 3DNF

Finding out if an organization is using Google Apps is easy because you only need to append the domain name to http://google.com/a/. To access the 3DNF Google Apps login page, you would enter **http://google.com/a/3dnf.net**, as shown in Figure 1.17. As all of the communications content of 3DNF is stored in the Google "cloud," it makes it easy for an attacker to connect and siphon off material once he or she acquires valid account names and passwords.

Blog Recon

As we learned from our Google Hacking earlier, 3DNF has an official blog. You can visit the blog by going to http://blog.3dnf.net. Upon further inspection, we discover that Google also hosts 3DNF's blog. Corporate blogs can be a great source of information when studying a target. Looking at the blog, we can see that Jonathan Tao plays a major role in the organization's internal and external technology affairs. Figure 1.18 reveals Jonathan Tao's Blogger profile. An attacker will use blog information to establish quick rapport with corporate insiders.

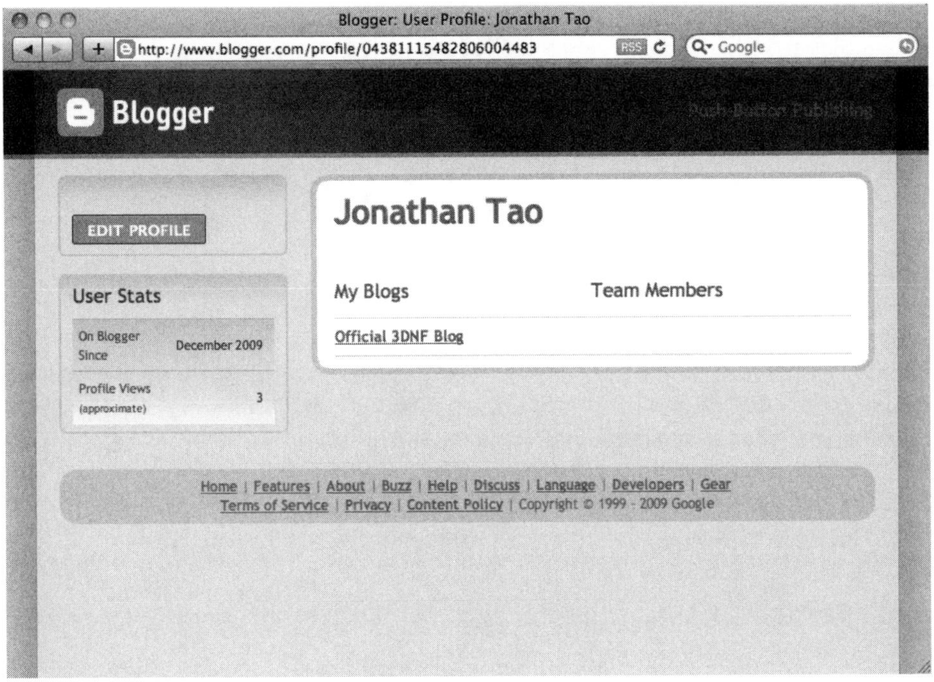

FIGURE 1.18

Blogger Profile for Jonathan Tao

Domain Information

One of the traditional methods of gaining quick information about a company is to attempt a WHOIS lookup on the company's domain name. There are many Web sites that provide this information. One such site is CentralOps.net. The output of a domain name WHOIS lookup for 3DNF.net is as follows:

```
Address lookup
Canonical name    3dnf.net
Aliases
Addresses         208.97.183.81

Domain Whois record
Queried whois.internic.net with "dom 3dnf.net"…
    Domain Name: 3DNF.NET
    Registrar: GODADDY.COM, INC.
    Whois Server: whois.godaddy.com
    Referral URL: http://registrar.godaddy.com
```

```
Name Server: NS1.DREAMHOST.COM
Name Server: NS2.DREAMHOST.COM
Name Server: NS3.DREAMHOST.COM
Status: clientDeleteProhibited
Status: clientRenewProhibited
Status: clientTransferProhibited
Status: clientUpdateProhibited
Updated Date: 01-dec-2009
Creation Date: 01-dec-2009
Expiration Date: 01-dec-2010


>>> Last update of whois database: Sun, 07 Mar 2010 01:55:40
   UTC <<<
Queried whois.godaddy.com with "3dnf.net"…


Registrant:
   Domains by Proxy, Inc.


   Registered through: GoDaddy.com, Inc. (http://www.godaddy.com)
   Domain Name: 3DNF.NET


Domain servers in listed order:
   NS1.DREAMHOST.COM
   NS2.DREAMHOST.COM
   NS3.DREAMHOST.COM
```

The 3DNF DNS information indicates that the domain name 3DNF.net was registered with GoDaddy. 3DNF also used the domains by proxy service to anonymize their contact information.

Twitter Recon

Twitter is versatile; everyone uses it a bit differently. Corporations use it to broadcast their latest news, to market new products, and to assist in customer service. Many people use Twitter as a self-branding platform, as well as a means to seek support.

During our Google Hacking, we found that 3DNF Inc. (Figure 1.19) and Jonathan Tao (Figure 1.20) both have Twitter accounts. Mike Resol (Figure 1.21) also has a Twitter account.

The real-time monitoring of Twitter could be important when your company experiences negative press or even a breach. Since Twitter has the potential for being an avenue of data leakage, it is suggested that your organization start monitoring your users. We have created several Twitter user accounts for the fictional characters. If you visit 3DNF's corporate accounts, you can see that it is following

FIGURE 1.19

Twitter Profile

FIGURE 1.20

Jonathan Tao's Twitter Profile

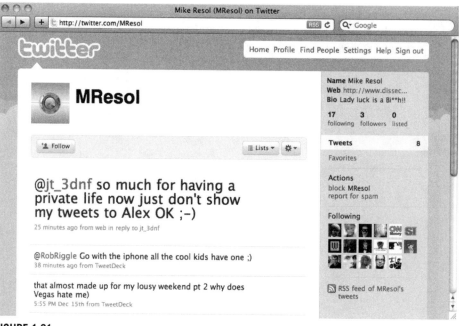

FIGURE 1.21

Mike Resol's Twitter Profile

several employees on Twitter. This information can be used to analyze connections for future attacks.

We encourage you to visit www.dissectingthehack.com for additional reconnaissance activities.

ENDNOTES

1. Pa. school webcam spying suit could be settled, Associated Press, ABC News, http://abcnews.go.com/Technology/TheLaw/wireStory?id=10070533; 2010 [accessed 11.03.10].
2. The Spy at Harriton High, Stryde Hax, http://strydehax.blogspot.com/2010/02/spy-at-harrington-high.html; 2010 [accessed 03.03.10].
3. Facebook Press Room Statistics, www.facebook.com/press/info.php?statistics [accessed 03.03.10].
4. Faculty on Facebook: Privacy concerns raised by suspension, Jack Stripling, USA Today, www.usatoday.com/news/education/2010-03-02-facebook-professors_N.htm; 2010 [accessed 03.03.10].
5. Rafe N, CNet News. How to fix Facebook's new privacy settings, http://news.cnet.com/8301-19882_3-10413317-250.html; 2009 [accessed 03.03.10].

6. Wesley F. The Hack the Planet Manifesto, http://hack-the-planet.felter.org/meta/manifesto.html; 1998 [accessed 04.03.10].

7. 17 Postal Service employee Social Security numbers end up on Internet, Ron Ingram, Herald Review, www.herald-review.com/news/local/article_ff02815e-b982-518d-87be-543ec55ce693.html; 2004 [accessed 03.03.10].

8. APPLE INC Search Results, United States Securities and Exchange Commission, http://sec.gov/cgi-bin/browse-edgar?action=getcompany&CIK=0000320193&owner=exclude&count=40 [accessed 03.03.10].

9. Richard B. Expert Opinion on Microsoft Source Leak, TaoSecurity, http://taosecurity.blogspot.com/2004/02/expert-opinion-on-microsoft-source.html; 2004 [accessed 03.03.10].

10. Windows Source Leak Traces Back to Mainsoft, Nate Mook, BetaNews, www.betanews.com/article/Windows-Source-Leak-Traces-Back-to-Mainsoft/1076674118; 2004 [accessed 03.03.10].

11. ViperLabs. Speaking at DefCon 17!, www.viperlab.net/wordpress/?p=124; 2009 [accessed 04.03.10].

12. SHODAN: Cracking IP Surveillance DVR, Praetorian Prefect, http://praetorianprefect.com/archives/2009/12/shodan-cracking-ip-surveillance-dvr/; 2009 [accessed 04.03.10].

13. Matthew K. Every Contact Leaves a Trace, http://mechanisms-book.blogspot.com/2008/06/every-contact-leaves-trace.html; 2008 [accessed 21.03.10].

Scan

In Chapter 1, "Recon," we focused on reconnaissance of targets. This allows for attackers to discover a worthwhile target. In the scanning phase of attack, attackers step forward to start singling out possible areas of attack against their target. This involves canvassing the target's defenses to search for small chinks in its armor that can be used for a later attack. This is also the first phase in which a target can identify that they have an attacker, assuming that the target has appropriate security in place.

WARDRIVING

> ### THE HACK DISSECTED
>
> *He had plenty of room for his pack-rat habits, including installing all manner of portable computer equipment in the car over the last couple of years. As he drove, he barely looked down the road while he turned on his old Toshiba Libretto laptop that was bolted to the dash of the car. Bob had a habit of wardriving whenever he could. He was constantly on the lookout for open wireless networks, and today was a good day to try out the new antenna he had installed the night before. (p. 28)*

While many may consider wardriving to be a typical commute along the Washington DC I-495 beltway, it is more commonly known as searching for wireless networks within a certain regional area. As the name implies, a person would drive around a certain regional area while a Wi-Fi-enabled laptop or other wireless device scans for wireless access points. All wireless access points are stored into a database with GPS coordinates so that they can later be found and accessed, if necessary.

Wardriving is a critical part of an attack against a company, and a very integral part to our story. As part of their Capture the Flag activity, Bob and Leon are wardriving around Houston looking for open wireless access points and networks to hide CyberBob flags in. It was through this wardriving effort that they discovered the "F0RB1DD3N" access point and got caught up in their deadly adventure.

Exploit Techniques

Wardriving is all about the ability to thoroughly scan an area and record every detail of each wireless network around. There are a variety of tools used for this purpose, even including the underlying operating system's wireless connection tools, depending on your goal at the time. For some, it's just to see if a known wireless network is still in the area and to trace its general location by following signal strength. At other times, the attacker may want to record hundreds of open or encrypted wireless access points and map them geographically onto a satellite map.

Operating System Scans

THE HACK DISSECTED

"Let me show you." Jonathan opened up the wireless options window on his Windows XP system and clicked the "scan for available networks" options. The three of them watched as it returned a blank window. "Nothing. I'm kind of surprised, I haven't picked up anything lately from some of the other businesses around here either." (p. 73)

Here in the story, Jonathan uses the basic Windows XP wireless connection software to scan for wireless networks in the vicinity of his company. This could be an appropriate response if the wireless access points were broadcasting their presence to the local area. However, earlier in the story, Vlad specifically told Michael to change the wireless router's network name (SSID) and to turn off public broadcasting. Jonathan's wireless scan is faulty because the wireless detection system in Windows will not display access points that have broadcasting turned off. There is a live wireless access point under their noses, but because he's using the wrong tool, Jonathan is oblivious to it. Tools provided to detecting live networks, such as Kismet and NetStumbler, would have picked up the presence of the network.

Kismet and NetStumbler

THE HACK DISSECTED

"You will get 20 riddles to solve. Each one will give you a clue about the location of the unsecured access point. All flags will be located in Houston proper, so don't worry about suburbs. You can use whatever equipment you think you need. I suggest a good GPS, a good external antenna, and a copy of NetStumbler." (p. 31)

***

Bob and Leon watched as several wireless networks appeared on the screen of the Libretto.

"Will any of these work?" Bob almost complained as he pointed to the NetStumbler display.

"I don't know yet. Let me look with Kismet. You don't see as much when you run just NetStumbler." (p. 39)

Unlike the tools built into an operating system, Kismet and NetStumbler are two applications that are geared specifically toward detecting and analyzing wireless networks in your area. While both serve the same purpose, each has a unique way of performing it.

Kismet is a free wireless scanner that is available at www.kismetwireless.net. It is predominantly a UNIX-based tool, running on Linux, Mac OS X, and BSD variants. While there is a Windows version available, it is able to fully function only with an AirPcap device (www.cacetech.com) due to the way most wireless device drivers for Windows are written.

What makes Kismet unique is that it is a passive scanner. It is able to sit quietly and monitor its surroundings without sending any packets to wireless access points and making its presence known. It is also able to log traffic traversing an open wireless network to a binary PCAP capture file that can be easily reviewed with Wireshark.

Conversely, NetStumbler is a tool that will actively probe local wireless access points to gather information from them. Like Kismet, NetStumbler is a free tool that can be found at either www.netstumbler.com or www.stumbler.net. However, it has a major limitation in that it will only run on older Windows operating systems, with Windows XP and Windows 2000 being the latest supported systems. As of February 2010, development is still in process on NetStumbler to make it compatible with Windows Vista and Windows 7, but an expected release date is not known. Although NetStumbler is a well-known application in wireless scanning, the results it produces are generally not as detailed or encompassing as other applications, hence the reason why Leon mentioned in the story that they should use Kismet instead.

The positive side effect to NetStumbler's inability to run in modern operating systems is the large number of alternative tools that have surfaced, such as inSSIDer from www.metageek.net. inSSIDer scans your local environment for wireless access points and plots them into an easy-to-read table, along with signal strength graphs, as shown in Figure 2.1.

WiFiFoFum

THE HACK DISSECTED

Bob had his iPaq running WiFiFoFum. The software gave him a radar-like display of wireless access points in the area. (p. 84)

WiFiFoFum is another Wi-Fi scanner used for detecting wireless access points available at www.aspecto-software.com/rw/applications/wififofum/. Unlike the other applications mentioned here, it is designed for handheld Pocket PC devices such as the iPaq. It has also been ported for modern handheld systems like the Apple iPhone. However, due to its use of undocumented iPhone application

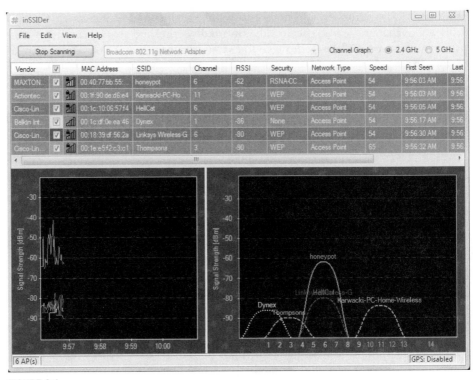

FIGURE 2.1

inSSIDer Wireless Network Scan

program interface (API) calls, it was pulled from the Apple App Store[1] in March 2010.

The radar-like display referenced in the story is shown in Figure 2.2.

Wireless Encryption Hacks

Locating a local wireless access point is only half of the battle, unless of course the access point is left open with no encryption and willingly gives an IP address to anyone that connects. For properly secured wireless access points, though, it is still possible to attack the security implementation to determine the secure passwords used by authorized laptops to connect.

When wireless security was first being implemented, the standard agreed upon was Wired Equivalent Privacy (WEP). It was even given a proper secure name, suggesting that its use was as secure as wiring your system directly into the router. This would prove false over the years.[2] WEP security was easily broken a few years after being implemented and is now considered deprecated. However, as you may notice in Figure 2.1, it is still popular among consumers. When given a choice of security

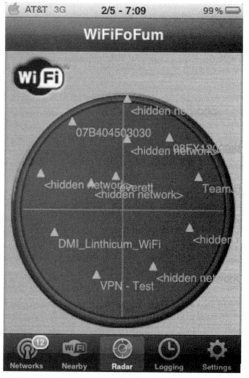

FIGURE 2.2

WiFiFoFum Wireless Radar Scan

protocols, a naive user will simply choose the first one shown or the one that is easiest to configure. The issue is also further complicated by hardware devices that are limited to only WEP security, such as older laptops and the Nintendo DS and DS Lite.

Wi-Fi Protected Access (WPA) was eventually released as the successor to WEP, but it also proved to be easily cracked. While WPA2 with Advanced Encryption Standard (AES) is the current best-practice security protocol, its day may eventually come when it is hacked. Though, it'll likely be many years off.

T.J. Maxx Exploit

When discussing wireless security, it is important to emphasize the attack against T.J. Maxx, a wireless intrusion that resulted in one of the largest breaches of consumer credit card information. In 2005, a group of hackers, masterminded by known computer criminal Albert Gonzalez,[3] was able to find an unauthorized, poorly secured wireless access point in a T.J. Maxx store by wardriving along highways in Miami.[4] They exploited the poor security for nearly two years before being caught; collecting over 45 million credit card and debit card numbers. Even after the public backlash of millions of credit card numbers being stolen, the same store was found to have lax wireless security a year later. This whole situation could have been avoided if T.J. Maxx would have conducted Wi-Fi audits of its stores and maintained proper security. Instead, they maintained poor security and fired employees who spoke out against it.[5]

Wireless Police Networks

THE HACK DISSECTED

The display showed sources of wireless network signals and estimated their distance. The Houston police department, like a few others around the country, had begun using wireless signals between their squad cars and repeater stations set on traffic signals. The resulting network gave them a high-speed data link back to their headquarters, so they could retrieve datalike lookups on license plates or pull up videos on certain public area surveillance cameras. The problem with the system was that they hadn't considered how easy it was to detect the wireless signal. Even though it was encrypted, it still warned of their presence. Even when they went on silent runs, they were emitting a Wi-Fi networking signal. (p. 84)

Due to the growing needs of the law enforcement community to have fast access to information, many police patrol cars are receiving high-tech upgrades. Customized laptop mounts and rugged laptops are equipped in thousands of patrol cars across the country in nearly every major federal and local law enforcement municipality. In 2009, I had the opportunity to tour the Brekford Corporation facility in Maryland that develops integrated computerized systems for law enforcement agencies, giving officers instant access to information through a rugged Panasonic Toughbook laptop. Officers can use integrated barcode scanners to instantly read information off a driver's license and transmit it to a centralized dispatch server to query for known aliases and outstanding warrants. Hand-typed errors into computers are virtually eliminated, and with a new electronic ticketing system, forms can be filled out automatically with cross-verification to reduce citation errors.

While the technology is sound, and much needed in the law enforcement community, the issue lies with how the data is transmitted between the patrol car and the centralized servers. While most major cities are using VPN tunnels over cellular broadband connections, there are still many areas that use standard Wi-Fi bridges to connect the in-car laptop to the cellular broadband network. One consumer example of this is the Autonet Mobile WiFi Router that can be installed into any vehicle. It then creates a small, mobile Wi-Fi hotspot that connects to the Internet through a cellular 3G signal, allowing for any device or laptop within the vehicle's proximity to have instant Internet access. Other low-tech solutions place a basic Wi-Fi transmitter in the vehicle that connects to Wi-Fi repeaters throughout the city.

In our story, it was this type of device that was being targeted by Bob in the parking garage. Using a Wi-Fi scanner, he was looking for the telltale Wi-Fi signal that is used by the local police department patrol vehicles. Not seeing anything appear on his screen, he declared the area free from law enforcement.

Best Practices

Establishing a wireless presence in your business is not for the faint of heart. Even with full buy-in from all departments in your organization, it will require extensive deployment, review, and auditing to ensure that it is safe from attack. We simply cannot help you plan a wireless network deployment in this book. However, you will find a few best practices that you should consider while you work with your security and networking teams in deploying a wireless solution.

> **NOTE**
>
> Even if your company does not have a wireless network, do not skip over this. You should have policies in place noting that wireless access points are prohibited within the facilities. You should also be performing regular wireless audits using the tools described here to see if you have your own Michael Resol in your office.

Wireless Security

When deploying a wireless network, you clearly do not want to blaze a new trail. There are established guidelines and case studies for nearly all business segments to assist in the process. Those in the commercial sector may need to rely upon Payment Card Industry (PCI) guidelines such as their Data Security Standards (DSS) to remain compliant. Defense contractors may need to be compliant with the US Department of Defense Directive 8100.2. Regardless, find a current and appropriate guideline for your company.

If you run an enterprise level company, or one day dream of running one, you should implement an 802.1X authentication system. This system provides each user a digital certificate to their device to authenticate with the network access controls as a valid system. All encrypted wireless networks should strive to be WPA2 with AES encryption enabled. One way of deploying this configuration is by creating a RADIUS server to authenticate and track all wireless users on your network. The most popular RADIUS server in use today is also free and is called FreeRADIUS from http://freeradius.org.

Hardware Compatibility

One of the biggest hindrances to wireless security is the prevalence of legacy hardware in many environments. There are many companies that still use legacy laptops and proprietary devices that are stuck to only recognizing WEP or WPA security protocols. These simply will not do in a modern network. The only way around this is to either replace the device or disable its onboard wireless and install a modern wireless PC card.

In the case of proprietary equipment, you may find yourself in a bind. In some cases, the vendor will no longer support the equipment and try to push extremely expensive upgrades to make your company compliant. In most cases, there is nothing you can do about it except to pay the cost to keep your business running. Ensure that equipment you buy today is, at a minimum, compatible with WPA2.

SUMMARY OF WARDRIVING

Every business in the world is in danger from wardriving, even if they do not officially use wireless technology. As shown in the book, employees can bring in their own wireless access points and create points of vulnerability for your internal network. A proper network administrator should be constantly vigilant about wireless security, even if it means regularly searching to see if there is a device on your network broadcasting wireless traffic when there shouldn't be.

We covered a few ways to determine if there is a wireless access point or device in the area. Using the operating system's wireless tools will give you a basic display of most wireless networks in the area but only for a casual glance. It cannot provide the technical information a good searcher needs to find a wireless network. Instead, tools like Kismet, NetStumbler, and inSSIDer can be used. While Kismet will sit quietly and soak up information off the airwaves, the other tools will actively talk to wireless access points to interrogate information from them. Mobile device applications, such as WiFiFoFum, can also be used for quick and easy scans of an area without attracting too much attention compared to someone walking around a building, staring at an open laptop.

Once a network has been found, attackers can then deploy many attacks to break the security in use, especially if the network is using archaic security protocols such as WEP or WPA. Failing to properly protect your network from an attack can lead to a massive intrusion, loss of customer data, and the potential to lose your future business.

Businesses that rely upon wireless infrastructure should deploy WPA2 with AES encryption to protect their network from most forms of attack. Administrators should also consider deploying a certificate-based authentication system, such as a RADIUS server, to protect their networks against unknown devices.

FOR MORE INFORMATION

Deploying a strong wireless network that can withstand routine wardriving and attack is a difficult endeavor. There are many drastic changes that would be required for your infrastructure and business policies. Even on the hacking side, the technology changes rapidly to address the changes in wireless technology. To gather more information about this topic, we recommend the following publications that explore wireless security in greater depth:

- *WarDriving and Wireless Penetration Testing* (ISBN: 978-1-59749-111-2, Syngress)

- *Kismet Hacking* (ISBN: 978-1-59749-117-4, Syngress)

LONG-RANGE WIRELESS SCANNING

> **THE HACK DISSECTED**
>
> *"Come on. I got that new directional antenna installed last night. I want to see if it works better than the Pringles can."* (p. 29)

In the prior section, we discussed the basics of wardriving to locate wireless access points. This is sometimes done with a basic laptop and built-in antenna to pick up signals within a few hundred feet. Here, in our story, Bob and Leon want to push the boundary of how far they can pick up a wireless network. This is performed through a directional antenna that can be targeted towards a specific target. Bob comments on trying out a new antenna to see if it works better than their Pringles can. While this may seem like a joke to many, the Pringles can antenna has become the icon of long-range wireless scanning.

Exploit Techniques

Long-range wireless scanning picks up on the skills learned from basic wardriving. The same tools come into play, with the same disclaimers. However, in this case we are discussing distances in the hundreds of yards and even miles. While one of the farthest distances clocked in for a Wi-Fi connection sits at 238 miles, this required specialty equipment and a direct line of sight for the entire distance.[6] The technologies here are a little more low-tech but can still allow for intruders to sit well away from their target and away from any physical surveillance.

Cantennas

The story made mention of using a Pringles can as a directional antenna. The Pringles can was actually discovered through experimentation to be one of the best conduits for most common long-range connections. However, you can also get by with a tomato can, if that's all you have. Any tin can should function as a cantenna as long as proper attention is provided to placing the wireless radiator in the correct spot.

A detailed list of instructions, as well as an online calculator for determining the best drilling locations, can be found at http://support.jefatech.com/cantenna. JefaTech, the company that provides these directions, also sells their own plug-and-play cantenna kits for the less adventurous hackers.

Yagi Rifles

> **THE HACK DISSECTED**
>
> *"I thought I'd start with Ohm and M00d1mus. They've been working on a Yagi rifle that we can use for a distant wireless hookup."* (p. 92)

Taking the enthusiasm of the hacker culture along with the need for a portable long-range Wi-Fi device has resulted in many interesting devices called *Yagi rifles*. These devices allow for reaching distant wireless access points while looking both stylish and deadly. Yagi rifles come in various varieties, with one of the most well-known ones being Mike Messick's (Cowboy Man) Sniper Yagi, unleashed in 2004. As reported, and commented upon by its creator,[7] the rifle was based on a standard M16 rifle, replacing the barrel with a 14.6 dBi antenna for Wi-Fi connections. His creation was a direct influence to the rifle used in our story, providing an effective long-range Wi-Fi device that looks and feels like a live weapon.

Another popular Yagi rifle, though geared for Bluetooth, is the BlueSniper. It was created by a private think-tank called Flexilis, now Lookout (www.mylookout.com), and was unveiled at DEFCON in 2004.[8]

Over time, Yagi rifles have grown in complexity and functionality. At ShmooCon 2010, John Dunning, known by his handle .ronin from www.HackFromACave.com, unveiled his newly built Yagi rifle called VERA-NG (Very Eccentric Radiofrequency Antenna – Nerf Gun). It sported two Pringles cans for Wi-Fi and Bluetooth connections, a GPS receiver, and a mounted, tablet Pocket PC. Even better, it shot real Nerf bullets and had a built-in flashlight for close quarters combat. John modeled his multipurpose rifle for us in Figure 2.3. Further details on the gun are available at www.hackfromacave.com/projects/vera-ng.html.

FIGURE 2.3

John Dunning with the VERA-NG

Best Practices

In terms of defending against long-range Wi-Fi scanning, you can only block access by simply reducing the strength of your wireless signals. Beyond that, it's best to implement proper wireless security into your network.

As mentioned in the earlier section on wardriving, it is recommended that you secure your wireless network based upon an agreed-upon set of guidelines pertaining to your industry and the sensitivity of the data housed within your network. For standard home networks and small office or home office networks, a wireless connection encrypted with WPA2-AES encryption would keep your network fairly secure. For enterprise networks, you should install a certificate authority server, such as a RADIUS server.

SUMMARY OF LONG-RANGE WIRELESS SCANNING

While typical wardriving is a threat in and of itself, a company can protect itself by limiting the signal strength of its routers, ensuring that the signal doesn't leak into parking lots, and by deploying surveillance cameras to watch for wardrivers. However, the existence of cantennas and Yagi rifles makes it incredibly difficult to protect your network through physical means. It places a stronger emphasis on your wireless security controls to ensure that unauthorized wireless devices do not gain access.

FOR MORE INFORMATION

The use of long-range wireless is a modern competition of technology and ingenuity. As the state of the art increases, it becomes easier and cheaper for consumers to implement their own long-range devices. To give you an idea of some of the research and competitions that go along with this field, we've provided a few additional reference Web sites below.

- Long Range Wi-Fi Guide: www.ab9il.net/wlan-projects/wifi1.html

- DEFCON WiFI Shootout 2005: www.unwiredadventures.com/unwire/2005/12/defcon_wifi_sho.html

SCANNING TOOLS

THE HACK DISSECTED

"Someone just scanned me!" Bob pulled his hands quickly off the keyboard as if he had been shocked. (p. 42)

After performing the basic reconnaissance steps to locate a target and discover its network and facility locations, an attacker will go into scanning the network to see what assets are available. Corporate networks typically have multiple external facing servers that continually listen for incoming connections. E-mail servers, Web servers, FTP servers, and even chat servers sit ready and willing for a lonely client to come and chat with them.

Exploit Techniques

There are a large variety of tools available from the Internet to assist you in scanning a network to look for available and active systems and services. These tools allow for an attacker to search within a particular network, or even the entire Internet, for active hosts. They can also be used to target individual hosts and determine which services may be running, as well as the operating system in use. In spite of the overwhelming amount of scanners available, we will mainly be focusing on those used within the story.

SuperScan

THE HACK DISSECTED

Bob went back to his "TOOLz" folder and clicked on the SuperScan icon. (p. 40)

SuperScan is a network scanner created by Foundstone, a division of McAfee, and can be downloaded from www.foundstone.com/us/resources/proddesc/superscan .htm. SuperScan is used to determine what computers and services are running on a network. This is similar to going to an office building and knocking on all the doors to determine what businesses are open. You wouldn't stop there; you would also want to know what services each business had to offer.

SuperScan runs along an entire block of IP addresses to determine if there is a host active and running on each IP. If so, it will then run through all of the available network ports to see if there are any external services running on the system. The results are then listed showing each active IP address, its hostname, and a list of its available listening ports as shown in Figure 2.4. These results will notify you if a particular server is an active FTP or Web server. In the network exploitation world this would be used to determine what hosts may be vulnerable to attack.

In our story, Bob runs SuperScan to canvas the 3DNF network to determine what hosts are alive on the network. Leon presses him that running the tool may be too aggressive, as it will certainly flag an alert on most network Intrusion Detection System (IDS) devices. Bob responds cleverly that if the company were dumb enough to have an open access point, they wouldn't know how to watch for a SuperScan. There's a certain logic to this, but the company didn't know about the open access point and was well equipped to see the SuperScan take place.

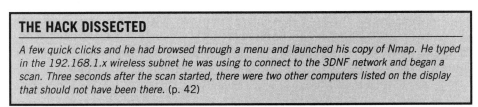

FIGURE 2.4

SuperScan Results

Nmap

> ### THE HACK DISSECTED
>
> *A few quick clicks and he had browsed through a menu and launched his copy of Nmap. He typed in the 192.168.1.x wireless subnet he was using to connect to the 3DNF network and began a scan. Three seconds after the scan started, there were two other computers listed on the display that should not have been there. (p. 42)*

In any discussion of network port scanners, Nmap is definitely one of the first and foremost applications that will come up. Nmap was one of the first fully-featured network and port scanners released and has seen continued development and improvement since its initial release in 1997, with releases covering every major operating

```
Select C:\Windows\system32\cmd.exe

C:\Program Files\nmap-5.21>nmap -P0 -v -O 192.168.25.5

Starting Nmap 5.21 ( http://nmap.org ) at 2010-03-04 19:33 Eastern Standard Time

Initiating ARP Ping Scan at 19:33
Scanning 192.168.25.5 [1 port]
Completed ARP Ping Scan at 19:33, 0.22s elapsed (1 total hosts)
Initiating Parallel DNS resolution of 1 host. at 19:33
Completed Parallel DNS resolution of 1 host. at 19:33, 0.03s elapsed
Initiating SYN Stealth Scan at 19:33
Scanning 192.168.25.5 [1000 ports]
Discovered open port 3389/tcp on 192.168.25.5
Discovered open port 445/tcp on 192.168.25.5
Discovered open port 135/tcp on 192.168.25.5
Discovered open port 139/tcp on 192.168.25.5
Completed SYN Stealth Scan at 19:33, 1.38s elapsed (1000 total ports)
Initiating OS detection (try #1) against 192.168.25.5
Nmap scan report for 192.168.25.5
Host is up (0.0015s latency).
Not shown: 996 closed ports
PORT      STATE SERVICE
135/tcp   open  msrpc
139/tcp   open  netbios-ssn
445/tcp   open  microsoft-ds
3389/tcp  open  ms-term-serv
MAC Address: 00:1F:D0:86:05:1C (Giga-byte Technology Co.)
Device type: general purpose
Running: Microsoft Windows XP
OS details: Microsoft Windows XP SP2 or SP3, or Windows Server 2003
Network Distance: 1 hop
TCP Sequence Prediction: Difficulty=264 (Good luck!)
IP ID Sequence Generation: Busy server or unknown class

Read data files from: C:\Program Files\nmap-5.21
OS detection performed. Please report any incorrect results at http://nmap.org/s
ubmit/ .
Nmap done: 1 IP address (1 host up) scanned in 4.15 seconds
           Raw packets sent: 1099 (49.068KB) | Rcvd: 1172 (49.204KB)
```

FIGURE 2.5

Nmap Scan Results

system in use. It is also completely free and open source, with the application and its source available at http://nmap.org. Nmap is capable of enumerating ports on thousands of targeted systems. It basically hits every possible port on a remote system and tries to identify if there's an application sitting and waiting for a connection, as shown in Figure 2.5. Information security professionals should use tools such as Nmap to identify unnecessary services running on networks. Otherwise, attackers will use the same tools to find the same potentially vulnerable, unnecessary services.

In the story, during their initial attack on 3DNF, Andrei takes a break while Pavel works his magic and walks to a convenience store for cigarettes. Seeing Bob and Leon behind laptops, he reports this to Pavel. Pavel loads up Nmap, his preferred alternative to SuperScan, scans the 3DNF network, and sees Bob's computer connected to the network.

Best Practices

At this point in the attack, the intruder is simply doing a few port scans across your external-facing servers to see what is awake and active. While an amateur running one of these tools would likely light up your alert logs like a Christmas tree, their use in the hands of an expert could virtually guarantee invisibility. However, you can implement protection plans to prevent any impact from the vast majority of attackers scanning your systems.

Intrusion Detection System

The first battle against a port scan is to detect that one is taking place. While some tools will actively block port scans, such as a well-crafted firewall or intrusion prevention system (IPS), a network IDS (NIDS) will easily allow you to review historical logs on port scans to create greater rule policies. If you review your port scan logs and notice that 95% of the traffic is coming from Asia-Pacific IP addresses (APNIC), yet your company is completely focused on internal US business, you may want to implement firewall and IPS rules blocking all incoming traffic from APNIC.

The most popular Network IDS in use today is Snort, a tool that is discussed in greater depth in the "Log Analysis" section in Chapter 1.

Intrusion Prevention System

While an IDS sits on the sidelines and monitors traffic flowing across a network, an IPS sits directly inline with the traffic and has the power to drop offensive data. It uses a similar rule structure as an IDS except that instead of simply alerting on a positive result, it can take action and drop the packet. As such, an IPS is much more effective in preventing the port scan from going forth, but the trade-off is that IPSes come at a much higher cost and they impact the performance of your network.

One exception to the "more expensive" rule is the ubiquitous Snort, which can be configured to act as both an IDS and an IPS, while remaining free and open source. However, consideration still must be made in placing the IPS into the correct network segments to reduce their impact on network performance while still securing your critical networks.

SUMMARY OF SCANNING TOOLS

After performing basic reconnaissance actions on a targeted network, an attacker will start scanning the network to get a general idea of what actual targets are available for further exploitation. Using many freely available tools, such as SuperScan and Nmap, attackers can canvass an entire range of IP addresses on a network to see which addresses are taken by live systems. Once an attacker has determined the machines that can be targeted, they can port scan each machine (including e-mail servers and Web servers) to determine which services are available for connections.

A network administrator can properly reduce the risk of a scan from seeing all of the devices and services within a network. The first defense is to simply have an active and up-to-date IDS in place that can monitor for scans and alert the administrator to their presence.

For a more automated defense, an administrator can also deploy an IPS that will sit inline with the packets and actively inspect the contents of each to determine if they are authorized or not. Unauthorized packets will then be immediately dropped, providing no feedback to the attacker.

FOR MORE INFORMATION

Scanning is not only the first line of attack against a company's network but also the first telltale sign of intrusion for the defenders. Many of the tools shown here have not changed dramatically over the years, but they are very powerful tools with great versatility. This book can only cover the basics of these tools and their usage. If you wish to add them to your toolbox for either attack or defense, you should gather more information from the publications below.

- *Nmap Network Scanning: Official Nmap Project Guide to Network Discovery and Security Scanning* (ISBN: 978-0-97995-871-7)

- *Nmap in the Enterprise: Your Guide to Network Scanning* (ISBN: 978-1-59749-241-6, Syngress)

- *Snort Intrusion Detection and Prevention Toolkit* (ISBN: 978-1-59749-099-3, Syngress)

BLUETOOTH SECURITY

> ### THE HACK DISSECTED
>
> *"R10t, did you bring the Bluetooth gear?"*
>
> *"Sure. It's working fine," R10t responded as he turned the small EeePC toward Bob. R10t picked up a small dongle cabled to the laptop. "With this and the Bluesnarf software we configured, you can use this either to detect a Bluetooth device in the area, or to even jack in on some of the older models." (p. 95)*

As technology develops, our society has sought new ways to integrate products together to improve our lives. Everyone has a cell phone but wouldn't it be nice to be able to synchronize our phone's calendar with our computer without having to dig out a cable? Or be able to talk to a coworker through our vehicle's internal sound system? Bluetooth was designed to create a personal area network (PAN) to allow your devices to communicate with each other within a close proximity without the need for cables. The devices vary in their signal power but most generally operate within a range of 10 m.

In our story, while at their 2600 meeting, R10t shows off his equipment to detect and hack into Bluetooth devices such as cell phones. He is using an Asus Eee PC netbook with a Bluetooth dongle to search for devices in the area.

Exploit Techniques

Bluetooth devices are typically very personal items to their holder, such as cell phones and handheld computers. As such, these devices are a treasure trove of personal information that could be of great use to an attacker including contact lists and text messages. Bluetooth can also be a vehicle for spreading viruses across mobile devices, as evidenced by the Cabir (www.f-secure.com/v-descs/cabir.shtml) and Lasco (www.f-secure.com/v-descs/lasco_a.shtml) worms.

Exploitation of Bluetooth devices can occur in a variety of ways. An attacker can simply set up a laptop to listen for Bluetooth devices in an area and can also go further by "jacking" into a Bluetooth device, sending unsolicited messages and content to surrounding devices. An equally impressive attack is through bluesnarfing, in which an attacker can copy off many of your personal details from your phone without you ever knowing.

Bluesniffing

While any Bluetooth device has the opportunity to search for other Bluetooth devices in the area, they are generally limited to devices that are in discoverable mode. Your own phone has to be set to discoverable mode for others to find it. With this setting disabled, or put into nondiscoverable mode, it will not respond to presence queries.

One of the biggest challenges for attackers is to find a way to detect when a nondiscoverable Bluetooth device enters an area and how to gain control over it. For the first part, Redfang was created in 2003 by Ollie Whitehouse with the former @stake organization, now owned by Symantec. The original Web site where the tool was hosted was eventually taken down due to their takeover by Symantec, but it can still be found on various mirrors around the Internet by the name "redfang.2.5.tar.gz."

Redfang was a simple, command-line utility that used brute force techniques to discover and enumerate nondiscoverable Bluetooth devices, a process that could take considerable time depending on the performance of the machine it was being run from.

To ease this procedure, Bruce Potter of The Shmoo Group released a graphical front end for Redfang at http://bluesniff.shmoo.com, which used the tool to efficiently display all available Bluetooth devices, discoverable or not, in a simple interface.

Bluejacking

Bluejacking refers to the act of sending anonymous Bluetooth text messages and images from your device to surrounding cell phones by creating a new contact and typing in a personal message in the Name field on the contact. Once created, the message is then sent to any Bluetooth device that you've discovered in the area and is immediately displayed on its screen. There is really no special software required for this action, and the legalities of it remain unclear. It has definitely become a vehicle for practical jokes by many in urban areas but can be used as part of a larger social engineering attack.

Bluesnarfing and Bluebugging

While bluesniffing and bluejacking allow for reconnaissance and practical jokes with Bluetooth devices, these quickly helped form a foundation for intrusion tools.

One of the first tools that hit the ears of the security industry was for bluesnarfing: the ability to silently connect to a Bluetooth cell phone and copy off data including calendar entries, contact lists, messages, and even stored multimedia. The exploit was originally discovered in 2003 by both Marcel Holtmann and Adam Laurie and carried over into many automated tools, such as Blooover (a portmanteau of Bluetooth and Hoover vacuum) at http://trifinite.org/trifinite_stuff_blooover.html, which can run directly from another cell phone.

Bluebugging takes this attack a step further by giving full control over the victim's phone. After a successful Bluetooth exploit, the attacker's phone can then tap into existing phone calls to record live calls and even initiate new ones. However, unlike other attacks, Bluebugging requires the two devices to be initially paired up, which would require a fair bit of social engineering.

Best Practices

The biggest step that an individual or a business can do is to set all phones and devices into nondiscoverable mode as a default. Phones should be locked down as much as possible to not interfere with business operations. While it may seem tempting to immediately lock down all Bluetooth capabilities on your employees' phones, that may not be a great solution. One of the advantages of Bluetooth is the capability to pair a phone with a Bluetooth headset or other hands-free talking device, allowing your staff to legally make phone calls while driving on the road. Many high-end vehicles have Bluetooth capabilities built into their stereo system, allowing you to sync your contact list directly to the car and scroll through your contacts through steering wheel controls. Some portable GPS devices also feature this ability, providing additional means for hands-free communications while driving. With a fully locked down phone, employees would no longer be able to field phone calls on the road in many states.

Most phones have the capability to switch between discoverable and nondiscoverable modes. Others are more sensitive, such as the Apple iPhone, which remains in nondiscoverable mode until you manually enter the Bluetooth configuration screen.

The Bluetooth Special Interest Group (SIG) also releases basic security precautions that should be taken with devices, hosted at www.bluetooth.com/English/Technology/Works/Security/Pages/Protecting.aspx.

SUMMARY OF BLUETOOTH SECURITY

Bluetooth provides for a personal angle of attack against the targeted individuals and their friends and associates. By attacking their personal communication devices, an attacker can listen in on confidential business transactions and even copy off text messages, e-mails, and calendar invites.

At the very least, poor Bluetooth security can allow an attacker to monitor for random devices that come near an established listening post. Depending on the target's device, further attacks could lead to a large cache of information. Much of this risk can be reduced by simply leaving a cell phone, or any other Bluetooth device, in a nondiscoverable mode at all times and only placing it into discoverable mode when you actually want to sync it with a device.

Advanced Bluetooth attacks such as bluesnarfing and bluebugging can allow an attacker to gain near-complete control over your cell phone. With a successful bluesnarf attack, a hacker can copy off all of the critical data from your cell phone without you even knowing it. Bluebugging, though it requires an additional step of being paired with the hacker's device, also allows for your phone to be controlled and listened in on by an attacker.

FOR MORE INFORMATION

Bluetooth attacks are fairly new ground for many in the information security field. As technology improves, Bluetooth is becoming more common in personal electronic devices and vehicles. This section covered some of the basic styles of attacks facing Bluetooth, but there are other threats that we haven't covered and many more in development. To learn more about other existing attacks, and general Bluetooth security issues, please check out the following Web sites:

- BluejackQ: www.bluejackq.com

- Intro To Bluesnarfing By Williamc and Twinvega: www.irongeek.com/i.php?page=videos/bluesnarf1

- They've Got Your Number …: www.wired.com/wired/archive/12.12/phreakers.html

- Car Whisperer: http://trifinite.org/trifinite_stuff_carwhisperer.html

- Bluetooth Crack (btcrack): www.nruns.com/_en/security_tools_btcrack.php

- Bluetooth Stack Smasher (BSS): www.securiteam.com/tools/5NP0220HPE.html

ENDNOTES

1. Rory P. WiFiFoFum Released for Free, in Cydia, iPhoneinCanada.ca, www.iphoneincanada.ca/iphone-news/wififofum-released-for-free-in-cydia/; 2010 [accessed 07.03.10].
2. Robert M. Whapped by WEP: Dangerously defective security still being sold, Computerworld, http://blogs.computerworld.com/14860/whapped_by_wep_dangerously_defective_security_still_being_sold/; 2009 [accessed 06.03.10].
3. Sharon G. Government informant is called kingpin of largest U.S. data breaches, Computerworld, www.computerworld.com/s/article/9136787/Government_informant_is_called_kingpin_of_largest_U.S._data_breaches; 2009 [accessed 06.03.10].
4. Tech Target, TJX hacking ring charged in federal indictment, http://searchsecurity.techtarget.com/news/article/0,289142,sid14_gci1324105,00.html/; 2008 [accessed 06.03.10].

5. Kim Z. 4 Years After TJX Hack, Payment Industry Sets Security Standards, Wired, www.wired.com/threatlevel/2009/07/pci/; 2009 [accessed 06.03.10].

6. Michael K. New Wi-Fi distance record: 382 kilometers, CNet News, http://news .cnet.com/8301-10784_3-9730708-7.html/; 2007 [accessed 08.03.10].

7. Peter R. Live from DefCon: The Sniper Yagi, Engadget, www.engadget.com/ 2004/08/01/live-from-defcon-the-sniper-yagi/; 2004 [accessed 08.03.10].

8. Humphrey C. How To: Building a BlueSniper Rifle–Part 1, Tom's Guide, www .tomsguide.com/us/how-to-bluesniper-pt1,review-408.html; 2005 [accessed 08.03.10].

Explore

3

Now that an attacker has found a worthwhile target, and has used scanning techniques to find angles of attack against the target, he will begin to build a strong attack profile. At this phase, the attacker has collected critical information on a target's infrastructure and presence and can move forward on exploring the company's assets to determine areas of weakness. In this phase, the attacker looks deeper into the network infrastructure to find actual weaknesses and vulnerabilities to exploit, based upon his or her research from the recon and scanning tactics discussed in previous two chapters.

AUTHENTICATION SECURITY

THE HACK DISSECTED

Stepan pulled out his access token and typed in the six-digit random number from the token and the four-digit PIN he had memorized. Soon he had established an encrypted connection to the office back in Zurich, Switzerland. He opened his e-mail software and found the message waiting for him. (p. 4)

In the prologue, Stepan used an RSA token to authenticate himself into his office network over a virtual private network (VPN) connection. A VPN allows for someone to connect into their home or office network from afar through a very strongly encrypted connection. A VPN allows people to check e-mails and view network files without third parties being able to view the network traffic.

Because a VPN connection allows Stepan into very important files back at the office, a simple username and password, like the one shown in Figure 3.1, would not provide enough security against hackers. So, an RSA token is used to provide a token value along with a PIN as his account credentials.

Exploit Techniques

With user authentication, the danger is always in the hands of the user. Nearly all computer systems in small offices, and even many large businesses, rely simply upon a user knowing a correct username and password to log in. With roaming profiles in

FIGURE 3.1

Cisco VPN Client Account Login

place, usually there isn't even a restriction on where the user logs into the network from. This information can be easily stolen or social-engineered from a user.

As password requirements become more complex and users start belonging to more online Web sites that require unique passwords, users will eventually start writing their passwords down. While a few users may realize it's prudent to store their passwords in an encrypted database, others may be just as willing to write them on a slip of paper and store them in their wallet. Unfortunately, there is still a larger percentage of users willing to store passwords under their keyboards and mouse pads.

Regardless of how a user stores his or her password locally, it is also stored somewhere on the Internet in a Web site's user database. Sometimes the database that contains your passwords may be encrypted, if you are lucky. If you are unfortunate and register a password at a less secure site that doesn't encrypt user passwords, your password could be used by the Web site administrator to log in as you on other sites where you registered the same password. Sometimes it doesn't take a hacker to compromise you, just an administrator out for a bit of fun or to make some money.

Once an attacker has the complete database including e-mail addresses, usernames, and passwords, the situation is pretty scary. The attacker can then turn and use that information to access e-mail accounts, Facebook, PayPal, and just about anything else that uses the same credential combinations.

There is an additional danger from criminals who set up their own sites to harvest user credentials. In early 2010, Twitter released details of a massive attack against many Twitter accounts.[1] These users were compromised by registering on a Web site that focused on the illegal trading of copyrighted software (warez) and using the same e-mail address and password that they use elsewhere. The owner of the Web site tested each of the accounts against Twitter and found that dozens worked.

Best Practices

If you ask an average person what they know about computer security, the first thing that they could probably tell you is to keep your passwords safe. Sure they may also know what antivirus is but that's usually the end of the road when it comes to security.

Passwords are the simplest form of security and if used alone can quickly lead to compromise. You see, passwords are known as *single-factor authentication* if used alone. The single factor being "something that you know." To increase your security, it would be wise to use a second factor; a device that displays a constantly changing number such as an RSA token that only the owner and the Web site would know.

NOTE

Strong security relies upon multiple factors of authentication. Most Web sites and basic applications require only single-factor authentication, such as your username and a password. Since this information is easily stolen or reproduced, more secure Web sites require additional factors. Factors are usually described as

- "Something you know" (password, PIN, pass phrase)
- "Something you have" (RSA token, identification card, badge, cell phone)
- "Something you are" (fingerprint, retina scan, voice print, DNA sample)

Withdrawing money from an ATM uses a two-factor authentication system because it requires something you have (debit card) and something you know (PIN).

Password Strength

The first defense against a password attack, if that is one of the factors in your authentication, is to simply have a strong password. Passwords are usually the first line of defense on workstations and network devices. A simple password by itself is weak security. A password is a series of characters that can be shared or cracked through brute force methods, so the best solution would be to create a password as strong as possible, but one that can still be remembered. Most organizations have found that merely making recommendations for employees to use stronger passwords isn't all that successful.

Consider the Password Policy from SANS,[2] which may appear to be the policy Stepan had fallen victim to, but is in fact a good policy. SANS defines a strong password as having the following characteristics:

- Contains both upper and lower case characters (e.g., a-z,A-Z)

- Has digits and punctuation characters as well as letters (e.g., 0-9, !@#$%^&*()_ +|~-=\`{}[]:";'<>?,./)

- Is at least fifteen alphanumeric characters long and is a passphrase (Ohmy1stubbedmyt0e)

- Is not a word in any language, slang, dialect, jargon, etc.

- Is not based on personal information, names of family, etc.

Passwords should never be written down or stored online. Try to create passwords that can be easily remembered. One way to do this is create a password based on a song title, affirmation, or other phrase. For example, the phrase might be "This May Be One Way To Remember" and the password could be "TmB1w2R!" or "Tmb1W>r~" or some other variation.

RSA Tokens

Using "something you know" (password or PIN) plus "something you have" (RSA token) makes it significantly harder for an attacker to compromise networks or systems. In this scenario, an attacker would have to coerce a password or PIN from a person and also gain access to the physical device. Most are familiar with ATM cards ("something you have") that have a PIN ("something you know"), which is a two-factor authentication. This is not a perfect solution but it's much better than someone leaving their password on their keyboards and somebody simply using a password to authenticate to the network.

There are many applications and hardware devices that take advantage of two-factor authentication. Many Web sites support RSA token devices, like the RSA SecurID.[3] This device displays a seemingly random six-digit number every 10 s. It is based upon an algorithm that is unique to its serial number. On receiving a token device, the serial number of the device is registered with the server. In this way, only two entities will know what number is displayed at any time: the server and the holder of the device. When logging into a remote site, the user inputs the six-digit number as part of their account credentials to further prove that they are a valid user. PayPal allows for users to purchase and use such a token device or to use their own cell phone to receive a token value that is used to authenticate during login. World of Warcraft players can even purchase one to provide additional protection to their gaming account from hackers.

However, this technology has its own weaknesses. In March 2010, news was released about a man-in-the-middle attack against World of Warcraft players who were using the Blizzard Authenticator token.[4] Even when the token was in use, accounts were being hijacked and used to steal in-game resources. The trouble came from users downloading malicious add-ons to their game from untrusted Web sites. These add-ons would work after the user logged in and then steal the transmitted token values. The value, along with the rest of the log-in credentials, is sent to an offshore site where hackers would immediately log in and do their damage. The end-user's client would purposefully crash and they'd be temporarily locked out of their account. This shows that no matter how strong a security solution you deploy, if your users have targeted, malicious software installed, it becomes useless.

Smart Cards

While many Web sites are starting to rely upon RSA tokens and other encryption mechanisms, many organizations are moving towards a smart card log-in system for workstations. These cards offer two-factor authentication to a computer system for a higher level of security. Instead of just knowing a username and password, users have to be in possession of a secure smart card and know the 6- to 8-digit PIN associated with the account. If the card is removed from the system at any time, such as when the user needs to step away from his desk, the session is automatically locked until the card is reinserted.

The US Government has implemented this concept with their Common Access Card (CAC). The card contains an integrated circuit chip (ICC) that holds the user's digital certificate and can also be used as a visual identification badge. Each card features a picture of the user, their department or affiliation, and an expiration date. In addition, as the card holds digital certificates for a particular user, the user's Web browser can be configured to store these certificates for secure Web sites. Many military Web sites are now requiring CAC certificates in order to log on. So, not only does a user require a CAC and its PIN but a CAC reader on their home and work computers as well.

SUMMARY OF AUTHENTICATION SECURITY

A number of exploits in the book were used against authentication security mechanisms. In real life, this is an area of information security that is always under attack, as attackers try to steal or bypass a user's credentials to gain access to a data source.

Such attempts can be greatly mitigated by using a strong password policy for your network and its various log-in sites. Users should use passwords that are not easily guessable or easily determined through a brute force attack.

For an especially secure log-in system you should implement at least two-factor authentication, which requires the user to be in the possession of an item to verify that he or she is the correct user. This could be an RSA token, which displays a unique six-digit number that only the user and the server will know. It could also be in the form of a smart card, a card containing digital certificates.

FOR MORE INFORMATION

As applications change and evolve over time, the ways in which users authenticate into them have also evolved. Authentication methods now implement additional factors of security to protect users from attack. Refer to the following Web sites and publications for more details on how to implement additional authentication security into your business infrastructure:

- RSA SecurID: www.rsa.com/node.aspx?id=1156

- DoD CAC: www.cac.mil

- Smart Card Basics: www.smartcardbasics.com

- Smart Card Alliance: www.smartcardalliance.org

- *Perfect Password: Selection, Protection, Authentication* (ISBN: 978-1-59749-041-2, Syngress)

PHYSICAL SECURITY

Throughout our story, there are many examples where the attackers exploit physical security precautions to further their intrusion. This goes beyond simply breaking into a building, and it includes hacking through security on a physical laptop or tapping into surveillance systems. This is the area of attack where we go beyond simple reconnaissance techniques and focus on setting the stage for our attack on actual resources.

Exploit Techniques

Once an attacker has physical access to a facility, or even a hardware device, they have the potential to completely exploit the resources available. There are many ways in which this can occur, but this section focuses on specific styles of attack from the story, from controlling a laptop once it is in your possession to covertly entering a company's physical facility.

Computer Basic Input/Output System Security

THE HACK DISSECTED

While Vlad walked around room, looking in drawers and sorting through Stepan's suitcase, Pavel lifted the computer deftly as someone who was comfortable with any device connected to a keyboard. He turned on the power and hit the default key combination to modify the boot settings. No power-on password. Pavel could always count on business types to not think of the basics. They always thought that spying was only targeted at governments. (p. 7)

In the information security industry, it has been mentioned that once an attacker has physical access to a system, security is gone. This has held true for many attacks, but there are ways that you can delay an attack against one of your company's devices.

In the story, as Stepan adventured around the city, Vlad and Pavel entered his hotel room to copy sensitive information from his laptop. Pavel makes note of the lack of physical security on Stepan's laptop system, with its lack of Basic Input/Output System (BIOS) passwords and basic security controls. This allows him to easily bypass the normal bootup procedure and start his own hacking tools.

In a computer system, the BIOS is used to control all interactions between the computer's hardware and its software until the operating system takes over. The BIOS controls which hard drives will be booted to load the operating system. The BIOS also allows for passwords to be set for various controls. At a secure level, the user will need to type in a password just to boot up the computer before the operating system is even loaded, as shown in Figure 3.2.

All of the settings controlling a system startup are managed in the BIOS configuration system, colloquially known as the *complementary metal-oxide-semiconductor* (CMOS) setup. From here, a user has control over the hardware assigned to the

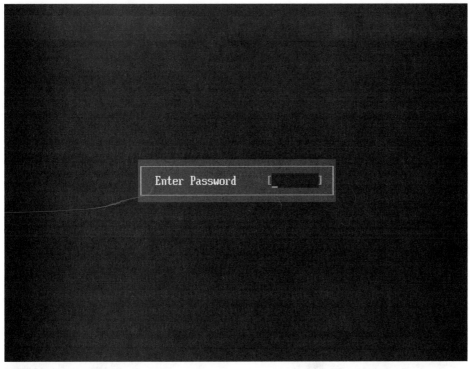

FIGURE 3.2

BIOS Boot Password

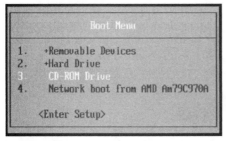

FIGURE 3.3

BIOS Boot Menu

system and can make major changes to how the system operates. By default, a hard drive is chosen in the BIOS to be the default boot device for the operating system. Pavel was able to bypass this by telling the computer to boot into his own USB thumb drive. This can be done by accessing the BIOS boot menu, such as the one shown in Figure 3.3, before the operating system loads, typically with the **F8** key.

Once attackers have the ability to boot from their own device, they can quickly skirt around most of the security controls within the operating system. A portable Windows distribution, such as BartPE (www.nu2.nu/pebuilder/) or ERD Commander, recently renamed to Microsoft Diagnostics and Recovery Toolset (DaRT) (www.microsoft.com/windows/enterprise/products/mdop/dart.aspx), can be used to create a live working environment completely based on a portable USB drive or CD. These environments can be used to change the administrator passwords on the installed system, as shown in Figure 3.4, or to just access and copy the files on the local hard drive.

If an attacker is truly desperate to get to the material on the hard drive, there is really nothing stopping them from just removing the hard drive and plugging it into another machine to pull the information off it. Well, except for full-disk encryption, which we discuss in Chapter 4, "Exploit."

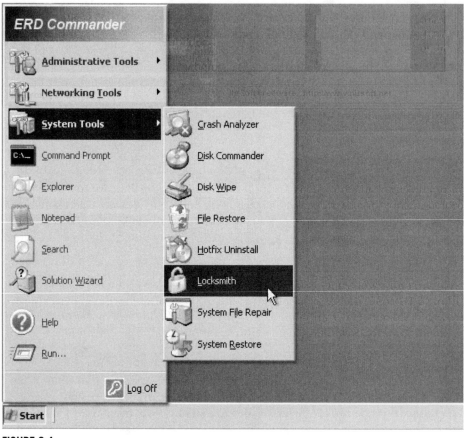

FIGURE 3.4

ERD Commander Locksmith

Fake Badges

The first line of defense against intruders into your physical workspace is typically a badge system. To cut down on the labor costs of security guards and man-trap operators, most facilities opt for a digital door access control system. Each employee is assigned a badge with a digital certificate that authenticates them into the building based solely on possession of the card. These cards are imprinted with a unique identifier that is compared against a database to determine if the card is allowed access to a particular door.

In our story, Michael Resol is able to obtain a contractor badge to use when entering the building over the weekend. This ensures that the security logs, upon review, will show that a generic contractor entered the building and not Michael himself. The contractor badge allowed him full access to the general work area while digitally hiding his identity.

While the physical security badges can be borrowed or stolen to allow access into secure facilities, the digital identification of the badge can also be stolen for reprogramming into a new badge. Using an attack known as *radio-frequency identification* (RFID) cloning,[5] an attacker can beacon to a security badge and request the badge's identification code from its RFID chip. All that an attacker requires to perform this attack is a specialized RFID reader and close access to the badge that they wish to clone. Once the identification is read from the badge, it can then be written to a brand new badge and used freely to enter the facility.

Other facilities that use common badges without RFID chips typically employ security guards that check for proper identification when someone is entering and leaving a facility. The main facility doors are wide open and all access control is maintained by a person. An attacker may gain access by impersonating a package carrier with a delivery. In other cases, by simply lounging at the employee smoking area, they may be able to just tailgate themselves into the building. In these cases, a fake badge can be created to fool the guards on duty. But, how does one find out what a proper badge should look like? Basic surveillance of employees in the parking lot and in their cars can provide this information. Johnny Long's popular book *No-Tech Hacking: A Guide to Social Engineering, Dumpster Diving, and Shoulder Surfing* (ISBN: 978-1-59749-215-7, Syngress) covers this concept in a chapter on badge surveillance.

Best Practices

For your own personal security, and that of your company, a few, simple precautions can be made to greater strengthen the defenses of your equipment and your facility. The changes covered here will not make great waves to upset users and, in fact, may work out in both the users' and the company's favor.

BIOS Security

Any controlled computer system owned by the company, whether it is a laptop or workstation, should be outfitted with BIOS security controls. The level of configuration may differ based upon the user and work location, but in many cases, there's no reason not to use the most secure settings.

Within the CMOS setup, like the one shown in Figure 3.5, an administrator can set basic password settings for the device. There are two password fields that can be set: user and supervisor. The user's password is used in conjunction with the "Password on boot" feature, forcing a proper password to be entered before the system can boot into the operating system.

The supervisor password can also be set here, using a different password than the user, to secure the CMOS setup from users. Administrators can then lock down the system's BIOS to their security policy and set a password to prevent regular users from being able to change settings.

One of the first settings that most administrators and owners should disable on their computers is the ability to boot to an external device. In a common work environment, there is no reason for users to boot to anything but the operating system

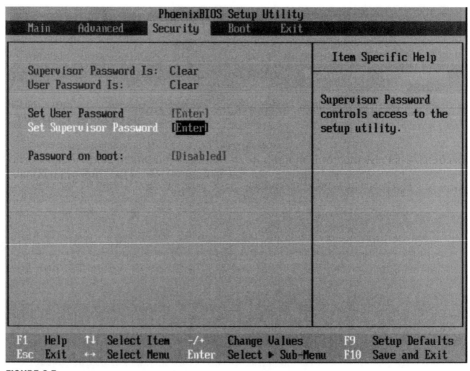

FIGURE 3.5

BIOS Boot Passwords

installed by the company. Common users know that tools such as the ones used by Pavel are easily found and used, and many are fully willing to hack their computer's administrator password just to restore Solitaire to the desktop.

However, any savvy technical user will know that there's a BIOS reset jumper right on the computer's motherboard, one that will reset all changes and remove all BIOS passwords. This, too, can be prevented by using computer chassis that feature chassis intrusion detection. Such cases feature a pushbutton on the sides that will be triggered if the case is opened. Once triggered, the system will not boot until an administrator types in his password to verify the intrusion.

Security Badges

Security badges are defensive items that, unfortunately, do not get much regard in many companies. Many businesses use a basic white badge with a photo ID and a name, with no other details provided. This may work well for the small company with five employees but becomes a security concern as the business grows larger.

With such a layout, it is too easy to create a forgery. Even with a valid badge, there is also no way to manage levels of exposure. The badge basically puts everyone onto the same plane, although some employees may be privy to higher classifications of data than others.

A color-coded system works well for most organizations. Each department or team can be given their own unique color, which is displayed prominently on their security badge. This allows employees to determine their department with a simple glance at their badge. In many government institutions, the badge color denotes the security clearance level of the individual. If a worker has open-secret material on his or her desk, he or she can quickly secure it when a "red badge," or uncleared, worker enters an area. In some organizations, a red badge is treated similarly to a scarlet letter, causing its possessor to be shunned from many locations and conversations.

The larger a company grows, the more common it is to find strangers in your vicinity. They could be new employees, contractors, or just family members visiting for the day. Your security should have plans in place for each of these people.

There should be uniquely identifiable visitor badges and contractor badges. There should be different designations with each as to whether an escort is required. You would definitely want an escort for a person coming in to repair your data center, but you may want to avoid requiring an escort for a partnering company's CEO.

If your facility uses badges with digital certificates, each badge should have its own unique certificate. Do not make a generic "visitor" group and apply every visitor badge with the same certificate. Make each badge have its own unique identifier, then imprint a unique, sequential number on the face of each badge. All badges should be stored in a locked safe box. All visitors and contractors should then sign out a badge in a log while noting the following: name, contact phone number, badge number, date and time of badge acceptance, and date and time of badge return.

Segmenting users based upon digital access control will help keep unauthorized employees from entering restricted zones. However, through RFID cloning, it is possible for an insider threat, or even an external attacker, to steal the badge identifier from a valid employee badge. This cloned badge can then allow the attacker to have access to areas typically beyond their reach. Such an attack can be foiled, though, through the usage of RFID shields. These shields are metallic card holders that block, or greatly reduce, radio signals from reaching the security badge. If an attacker has to clone the badge, they would have to have direct access to the card instead of merely being within a few feet.

Even with your own employees, badges should be treated carefully. Many workers may lose their workplace badge and request a replacement. Weeks later, they'll find their original badge and keep both on hand in case one goes missing or is left at home. This is a threat to your security. Each employee badge should have a unique certificate and identifier. If a badge goes missing, that certificate should be disabled from the system and a new, different badge should be issued to the employee.

SUMMARY OF PHYSICAL SECURITY

There is a belief that as soon as an attacker has physical control over your devices, all security is lost. This is true in many circumstances but can be somewhat mitigated by deploying a few basic physical security measures. These defenses do not protect against network attacks but rather from attackers at the keyboard.

One example is basic computer BIOS security. Secure systems are configured to only boot into a preinstalled operating system. An attacker can bypass the operating system by using the BIOS to boot directly to a USB device or CD-ROM that contains an alternative operating system with installed hacking tools, as Pavel did early in our story.

Such attacks can be mitigated by simply password-protecting the BIOS from a user level and an administrator level. While these passwords can be cleared by resetting a physical jumper on the motherboard of desktop computers, additional intrusion detection sensors on modern desktops can mitigate that risk by locking the system if the chassis has been opened. The machine will then stay frozen from booting until an administrator enters his or her password.

Another physical attack performed was using a contractor badge to gain physical access to the 3DNF facility. Due to poor security, Michael Resol was able to steal a contractor badge and use it to cover his tracks within the facility.

Security badges are items that should be treated with great respect and secured from theft and misuse. Badges should readily identify their wearer at an instant glance but be treated as a controlled security item, like a physical key.

FOR MORE INFORMATION

Bypassing physical security methods is definitely new territory for many hackers, as the risk of exposure is raised immensely. We covered a few basic topics on physical security in this section, but there are many more references available. The following material helps explain these topics in greater depth:

- *No Tech Hacking:A Guide to Social Engineering, Dumpster Diving, and Shoulder Surfing* (ISBN: 978-1-59749-215-7, Syngress)

- Why Bother About BIOS Security? www.sans.org/reading_room/whitepapers/threats/why_bother_about_bios_security_108 [PDF]

NETWORK TRAFFIC SNIFFING

THE HACK DISSECTED

"Load Wireshark. I want to see what else is running on this network," Bob suggested as he reached in the back seat and grabbed his backpack with his main laptop inside. Bob and Leon quickly settled into a zone of typing and reading. The only sounds were from the people in the parking lot walking in and out of the convenience store.

Leon made more progress at first since he had a head start on Bob. Leon followed Bob's suggestion and had Wireshark running. This program would give him an idea of the traffic running on the local wireless network he and Bob were investigating. Leon quickly saw that they were not alone on the network. Someone was transferring a large binary file. He didn't say anything at first. Instead, he changed the settings for Wireshark to do a packet capture so he would have a copy of what was flowing through the network. (p. 40)

One of the most dangerous attack methods on a network is the ability to simply listen in to other traffic and use it for your own purposes. In the early days of computer networking, applications would simply transmit usernames and passwords in clear text across the network. The File Transfer Protocol (FTP) still does this and is still used by thousands of sites, as does the Post Office Protocol (POP) for checking e-mails.

Network traffic sniffing also tells the watcher which machines are alive and active on a network and what type of traffic they are sending and receiving. By reviewing the logs, you can easily spot which machines are Windows users browsing eBay and which are UNIX servers sharing out corporate documents. This information is vitally important for planning an attack against the network.

Exploit Techniques

Half of the adventure of using a network sniffer is finding a way to integrate it into a facility and onto its network. But, once installed and running, it can prove to be a treasure trove of information for any attacker to use. User accounts, passwords, services, traffic flows, and application versions are continually sent across a local network for the careful sniffer to observe.

Placement of Sniffer

The first step in using a sniffer is to place it within the network that you want to grab traffic from. In the case of wireless networks, this can be done by just placing the laptop in a vehicle next to the facility and grabbing wireless information off the air. If an attacker is able to gain access to the inside of a facility, they can connect into an exposed and available network port. There have been a number of tales of laptops hidden within dropped ceilings or inside file cabinets, just plugged into a network and collecting traffic. When combined with the threat of someone using falsified security badges, this can allow someone to walk into the facility at night or on the weekend and install a sniffer within just a few seconds.

All a sniffer needs to be is a simple netbook running a Linux operating system for best performance. The size and design of this implementation allows for the machine to focus solely on capturing traffic, using a network diagnostic tool like tcpdump.

With a sniffer in place, it will start logging millions of packets of data to a local storage device for later review. This actually sounds easier than it really is. Many network capture tools will start to exhibit serious performance issues on some networks, dropping random packets if the sniffer's network card can't keep up with the flow across the network. Even reviewing the traffic could take hours if the capture files are too large. It's possible to put rules in place to only capture packets with certain identifiers, such as all FTP packets or all POP e-mail packets. This would reduce the amount of noise to filter through and allow the attacker to focus solely on exploitable traffic.

While switches will usually not allow a sniffer device to directly listen to all traffic on the network, a turned insider can help the attacker. Someone with access to the switches within a company can enable one of the ports to be configured as a switched port analyzer (SPAN) port (port mirroring), allowing it to see any or all traffic that crosses that device. A sniffer plugged into this port will then be able to see every single packet that crosses the device.

Traffic Review

While there are many tools available to capture network traffic, the de facto analysis tool is Wireshark, a free and open-source application available at www.wireshark.org. Wireshark, formerly known as Ethereal, has been the most popular traffic analyzer for years. It, too, can be used for capturing live network data but its strength lies in the ability to display the traffic and easily filter and sort the packets.

Once installed, an attacker can search for keywords within packets by customizing a search filter. To perform a keyword search, one just needs to filter for

```
frame contains "password"
```

The previous filter string will show only packets that have the literal word "password" within them. Wireshark also allows attackers to filter particular styles of traffic. You can filter for "smb", as shown in Figure 3.6, and be shown only packets involving Windows file shares. In this particular image, a graphic JPEG file is being copied from one machine to another across the network.

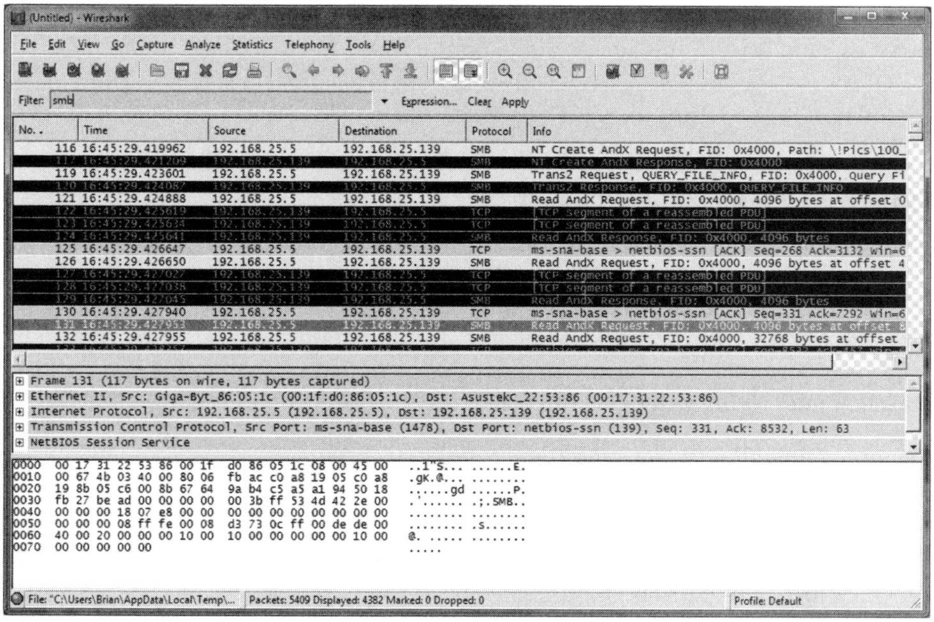

FIGURE 3.6

Wireshark Viewing File Sharing Traffic

Best Practices

Many people when faced with a network sniffer will offer little in the line of defense. To be honest, once a sniffer has been deployed and is active on your network, your best option for removing it is to physically search the entire facility for it. However, proactive steps can be taken to reduce the chances of a sniffer being deployed within your network.

Network Port Protection

One of the most basic steps that administrators can take today is to simply not allow hubs on their network. Hubs broadcast each and every packet to every connected device. As they are cheap and plenty, many companies still use hubs in their networking infrastructure, though the numbers grow less every day. Switches are the preferred device, as they send unicast packets from the source to only the intended target, with no other port being able to see the packet.

Switches should have Port Security enabled. All switches record the Media Access Control (MAC) address of the device that is currently plugged into each port. Port Security takes this another step by recording the MAC address and then only allowing that single device to continue to use the port. This prevents users from being able to unplug one computer and plug in another.

However, on some devices, an attacker can bypass this protection by basically unbinding the Transmission Control Protocol/Internet Protocol (TCP/IP) from their network card. Their machine will not be able to communicate, as it has no IP address, but it can still listen to broadcast traffic on the wire.

Of course, the simplest and cheapest solution is to simply disconnect every unassigned port in the wiring closet. The administrator should then only plug in ports to cubicles that require them and disconnect all other ports when not in use.

Watching for Inappropriate Traffic

As a network administrator, traffic sniffing is just as useful to you in defending your network as it is to an attacker. For one, you can determine if there is traffic indicative of vulnerable software on your network and secure it before it is found by an attacker. Search your network for plaintext information that should be sent in an encrypted format. Please ensure that you have notified your management and user staff that monitoring will be taking place to avoid upsetting your budget stream.

Develop Firewall and Intrusion Detection System Rules

In the event that you've noticed malicious traffic or an attack on your network segments, you can use Wireshark to help analyze the traffic to piece it together. You can also use Wireshark to quickly piece together filtering rules to start alerting on or blocking malicious packets.

For demonstration purposes, Figure 3.7 shows a basic Windows file share transmission. By viewing through the packets, you can attempt to find a common segment to each packet. This segment will be a stream of bytes that always exist at the same

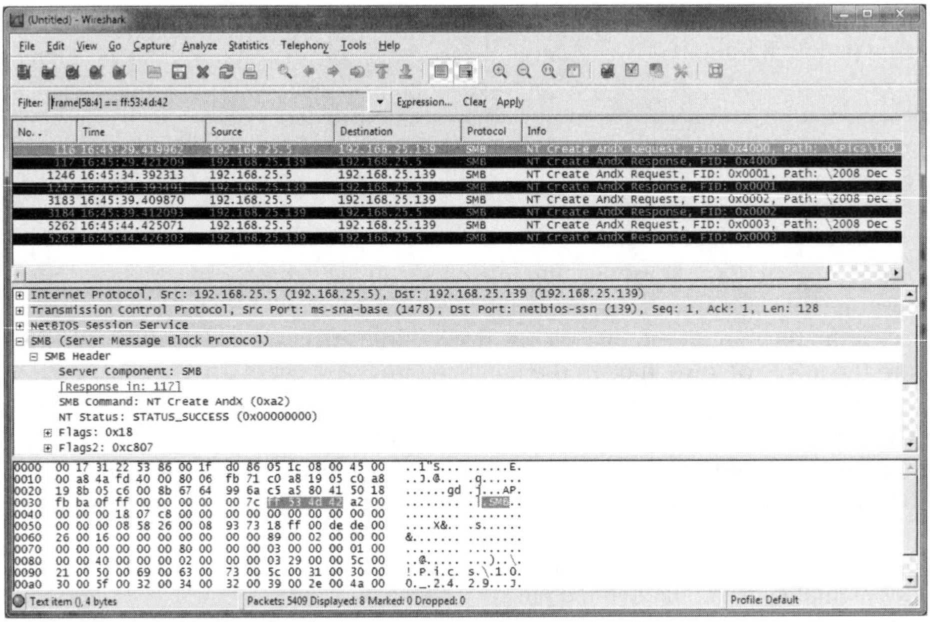

FIGURE 3.7

Searching for Packet Identifiers in Wireshark

location in each of the malicious packets, but not in normal packets. Once found, test the filter in Wireshark to ensure that it only matches on malicious packets, such as shown in Figure 3.7, where the following filter is used:

```
frame[58:4] == ff:53:4d:42
```

This filter tells Wireshark to look at the 58th byte in each packet and compare the 4 bytes beginning there to hexadecimal "ff:53:4d:42." If they match, Wireshark will show the offending packets in its display.

Using this information, we can then create a Snort filter to search for, and alert upon, these packets as they come in.

```
alert tcp any any -> any any (content:"|ff 53 4d 42|";
    offset:58; msg:"Unauthorized traffic!";)
```

SUMMARY OF NETWORK TRAFFIC SNIFFING

Once an attacker has a foothold within your network or infrastructure, a well-placed network sniffer can help provide them with the keys to the kingdom regarding your user's passwords and network usage habits. An attacker can simply place a device within your network to silently collect all information being broadcast across the network, or within a certain network segment. While a business can mitigate this risk by deploying network devices that do not broadcast packets, such devices can always be configured to allow for sniffer-friendly SPAN ports by a malicious insider.

Once an attacker has captured a few million packets, they can then search through the material for usernames, passwords, commonly accessed servers, and actual data files being transmitted across the network.

A network administrator can also use network sniffing for protective purposes. By using a sniffer to watch for and log network attacks, an administrator can easily construct custom filtering rules that can be implemented within an intrusion detection system (IDS) or intrusion prevention system (IPS).

FOR MORE INFORMATION

Network traffic sniffers can be an incredibly dangerous and silent tool when used by an attacker who has gained even partial entrance to your network. Creating and filtering through large amounts of packets is a skill that needs to be finely tuned by both attackers and defenders to look specifically for targeted data. While we've only shown the basics in this section, review the following references for more details:

- Writing Snort Rules: http://packetstormsecurity.nl/papers/IDS/snort_rules.htm

- *Wireshark & Ethereal Network Protocol Analyzer Toolkit* (ISBN: 978-1-59749-073-3, Syngress)

- *Penetration Tester's Open Source Toolkit, 2nd Ed.* (ISBN: 978-1-59749-213-3, Syngress)

DORMANT MALWARE

> **THE HACK DISSECTED**
> ___
>
> *"Here it is. The home computer is a Windows box and even has the SubSeven trojan running. I bet they have a teenage son who pulls down music on his dad's computer."* (p. 54)
>
> ***
>
> *Leon opened the client application and connected to the IP address.*
> *"Wow this version is old enough to have the 'not so secret' master password," Leon said.* (p. 54)

At this point in our story, our hapless heroes are in need of cash to live off as they try to plan their next steps. They drive to an affluent neighborhood to search for a vulnerable home computer in one of the expensive homes. They find a home computer that has been trojanized with SubSeven and further exploit it to grab financial account details that they can then sell for cash.

Bob and Leon are definitely acting illegally in this process, but they feel it is justified due to their situation. They promise to each other that every dime will be paid back once the crisis is over to ease their consciences.

Exploit Techniques

This is actually a often used tactic. It allows an attacker to avoid exploiting a machine and, instead, piggyback on the work of someone else. In this case, the owner of that home has inadvertently infected his own machine with the SubSeven trojan. Bob infers that there is likely a teenager in the home who infected the computer by downloading music. This is a nod to the presence of malicious software on many of the peer-to-peer (P2P) networks, including Kazaa and Gnutella. These programs then lie dormant on the victim's computer, patiently waiting for an attacker to come along and make use of them.

For this exploit, Bob simply started scanning home networks with open wireless access points, using the wardriving techniques discussed in Chapter 2, "Scan." Upon finding an open network, he scanned the computers for traces of malware and found a machine infected with SubSeven. He then exploited knowledge of a master password in the particular version detected to gain access to the malware.

SubSeven

The malicious software that Bob and Leon discovered on the home computer was the SubSeven trojan, a remote administration tool (RAT) that can be pushed out by malicious Web sites to unsuspecting users. SubSeven opens a TCP post to listen upon that varies based upon the version in use. It establishes a server port, allowing users with the SubSeven client application to connect and take over the system. Based upon the trojan version in use, Bob was also able to determine that it had a hardcoded master password, allowing for a complete backdoor in. This feature was implemented in earlier versions of SubSeven by its author but was removed from later versions upon its discovery. As discovered through a reverse engineering of SubSeven,[6] the master password was "14438136782715101980." By entering this password, Bob was able to gain full control over the user's computer and search for financial details stored on that computer.

While SubSeven is an older tool, don't rule it out for future exploitation. After years of stagnant development, the developers just recently republished the tool with new changes in February 2010[7] at www.subseven.org. While currently still limited to 32-bit Windows, by the time you're reading this, their 64-bit version should be available and targeting new Windows 7 home computers.

Best Practices

At any given moment, there are millions of computers across the world infected with all manner of malicious software. This vast collection of viruses, trojans, and botnet nodes can cause an otherwise healthy computer to be infected with vast amounts of illegal or unauthorized material. The best practice is to simply block such applications from being installed on your computer in the first place. However, this just isn't always possible, given the advanced social engineering by hackers and the general lack of security of the common user. Even when an infection takes place, systems should have methods in place to routinely search for, and remove, malicious applications.

Preemptive Protection

The best cure against disease is to never get sick in the first place. This philosophy is the same with malware on your computer. Besides the rare viral attacks on vulnerable applications, most malware is put into computers through drive-by downloads, a process in which applications are downloaded and installed without the user authorizing it. Much of this occurs by users visiting questionable Web sites. This is usually driven by desire. Sites featuring pornography, warez, software cracks, and video game cheat codes are particularly ripe for malware as their supposed content is in high demand.

> **NOTE**
>
> Recently, there has been a lot of effort to push malware through top Google links for certain search topics. Using advanced search engine optimization (SEO) code, malicious code sites can push infected sites to the top of a search result for the latest breaking news. Any time there is a global news story, you will inevitably find sites promising up-to-date news coverage hosted from very suspicious domain names within the first page of search results. This practice was detailed by Trend Micro in reviewing malware news sites from the 2010 Haiti earthquake,[8] with new malware sites popping up daily based upon the latest events.

The moral of the story: Don't rely on search results to provide you news. Manually type in the domain name for the home page of your preferred news source and follow their internal links to read the latest news coverage.

Because most users are unwilling, or unable, to change their surfing habits and because attacks are growing more advanced and intelligent, there should be additional automated buffers against an infection. Internet Explorer, Firefox, and Google Chrome all feature a safe-Web feature. This is basically a large blacklist of malicious Web sites. When a user attempts to view a site on this list, his or her browser will display large warnings that the site may be malicious and a connection should be avoided.

Many comprehensive endpoint security suites, such as Norton Security Suite, also offer the ability to monitor downloads that occur as part of their instant-scanning autoprotection.

Hopefully by the time you read this, a more adaptive tool named Block All Drive-by Download Exploits (BLADE) will be released by its developers at SRI International. As reported in early 2010 by Brian Krebs,[9] BLADE currently has a 100% block rate against thousands of attempted infections. To read more on this tool and to view its testing reports, visit www.blade-defender.org.

Malware Removal

Given that a malicious application has infected a computer, there is still hope in removing it to prevent any further damage. There is a large variety of spyware and malware removal tools available for download on the Internet. Before you jump off and start downloading applications, be aware that there are hundreds of fake and malicious malware removal programs. These programs will infect your computer while giving the impression that they are cleaning it. A master list of such programs can be found at www.spywarewarrior.com/rogue_anti-spyware.htm.

Removing most malicious applications can be as simple as running an automated tool, letting it find and delete the offensive files and then rebooting to scan again. It's recommended that you install a variety of removal tools to have available in case your computer starts acting unusually.

Recommended automated spyware removal applications include Spybot Search & Destroy (www.safer-networking.org), SUPERAntiSpyware (www.superantispyware .com), and Malwarebytes Anti-Malware (www.malwarebytes.org). These programs have the benefit of being free and completely automated. Although free, some have commercial versions available that provide real-time protection against malware and can help protect your computer from drive-by download attempts.

Some particularly advanced malware may require more manual intervention to completely remove it from a system. Some automated tools just can't keep up with their malicious signatures fast enough to protect you from today's malware. HijackThis (HJT) is an application that doesn't seek out malicious applications. Instead, it looks at areas on your computer where malware typically hides and blindly reports back everything it sees there, as shown in Figure 3.8. It requires extra skill in its use as removing every item reported could cause damage to your system. It's also a simple, portable application and can be downloaded from http://free.antivirus .com/hijackthis/.

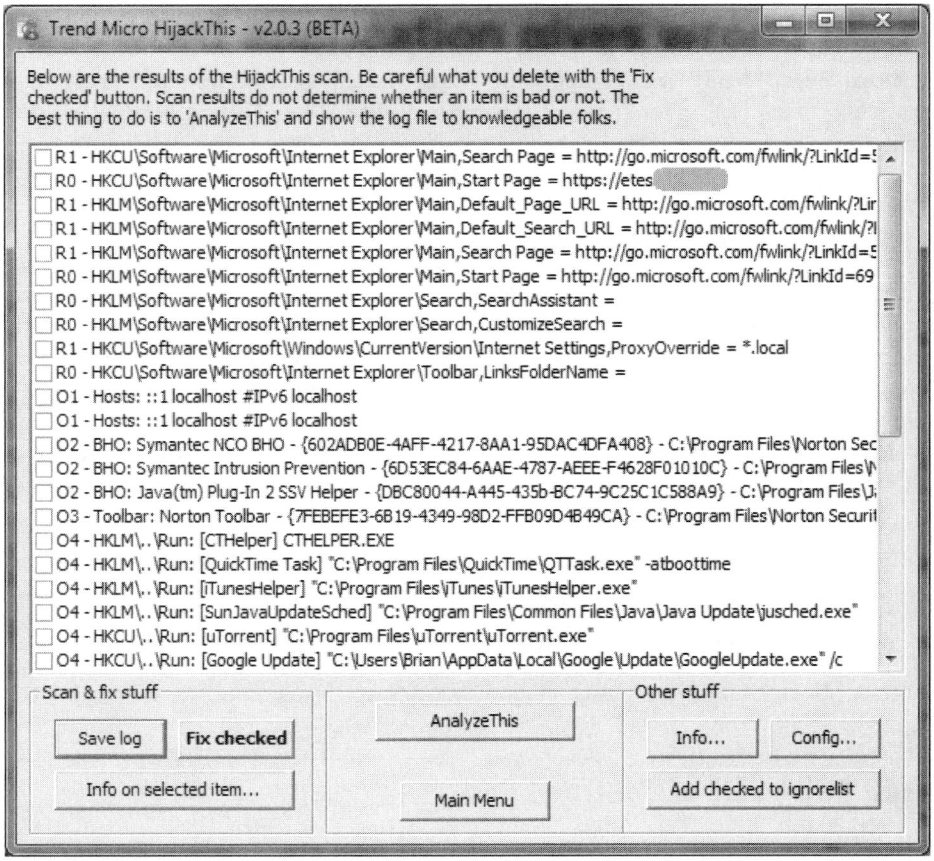

FIGURE 3.8

HijackThis Scan Results

SUMMARY OF DORMANT MALWARE

While an attacker will be looking for any possible way into your network, one of the simplest ways in is to simply ride along the attack of someone else. This is especially easy if a naive user has inadvertently infected their system by downloading malicious software from the Internet. This is particularly targeted towards users of early P2P applications like Kazaa and Gnutella and users who have little or no antivirus protection on their system.

In our story, the SubSeven trojan was installed onto a home computer through the actions of one of the computer owners. Bob and Leon were then able to attack the system and gain instant action through the trojan, which was laying dormant on the system and waiting for a connection from an attacker.

Such malicious software is a large threat to home users and businesses, but most can be easily cleared from a system with some effort. Automated tools can help remove the vast majority of malicious software and trojans on a system, but not all. A manual process can be implemented, using tools like HijackThis, to remove troublesome or zero-day infestations.

FOR MORE INFORMATION

Trojanized applications and other forms of malware are increasingly infecting computers on a daily basis across the Internet. While many of these applications will immediately start working to sniff your network traffic and steal your authentication credentials, others have the capability to be remotely controlled by a hacker for a personalized attack. In this section, we've only scratched the surface of malware attacks and how to remove them from your computer. The following references will show how to effectively mitigate installed trojans, as well as how to stay on top of the latest malware:

- *Combating Spyware in the Enterprise: Discover, Detect, and Eradicate the Internet's Greatest Threat* (ISBN: 978-1-59749-064-1, Syngress)

- F-Secure News from the Lab: www.f-secure.com/weblog/

- SophosLabs blog: www.sophos.com/blogs/sophoslabs/

WEB BROWSER SECURITY

> ### THE HACK DISSECTED
>
> *Leon quickly had a window open on Bob's computer that displayed the desktop of the computer in the target house. He browsed through several different directories and soon had a cached copy of the password used for an online brokerage account. A quick browser session confirmed that the password worked, and there was enough money in the account for their needs. (p. 54)*

With a need for quick cash, Bob and Leon find a vulnerable home computer in a very wealthy neighborhood. After taking over the computer with the SubSeven trojan that was already installed, they browsed through the directory structure to locate and view the saved password file for the computer's Web browser.

Every major Internet Web browser offers the ability to store the user's passwords for Web sites on the local computer. This allows users to quickly and easily log back into their sites without having to retype their passwords. However, this storage location for passwords is now a target of attack and can be used to locate each and every password used for online surfing. This was pretty disastrous in our story, where Bob and Leon were able to log into the victim's online brokerage account to siphon money out.

Exploit Techniques

When exploiting saved passwords, it is important to note that each client will save these credentials in unique ways. An attack has to be targeted towards a particular Web browser and, at times, a particular version of the Web browser. While browsers have made their password storage locations more secure over time, there are always many tools that can be used to break such protection.

Password Stores

While every Web browser has its own unique location and style of saving stored passwords, they all encrypt passwords and user accounts in some way. While we could go on with a dozen pages of technical reference material on how passwords are stored for every major Web browser, we'll focus solely on the attacks.

How did Bob and Leon grab the passwords in the first place? The storage location has to be readable and available for the Web browser to find it. These files are in known locations throughout the Windows Registry and hard drive. Older versions of Mozilla Firefox maintained text documents in the user's profile that stored all of the encrypted user accounts and passwords, which looked like this:

```
https://www.linkedin.com
session_key
MEIDEPgAAAAAAAAAAAAAAAAAAEwFAYIakVKcSL5IZxaKQe/9n+Fake+BBiRTruR
    KJXcWAkVKcSL5IZxaKQe/9PY6CQ=
*session_password
MAoEEPgAAAAAAAAAAAAAAAAAAEwFAYqVKcSL5IZxaKQe/92+NotReal+BDgO/
    4JoCdDauabcR41wvXm
https://www.linkedin.com
```

Another file in the same directory, key3.db, stored the encryption key that is used to protect the values. In the latest version of Firefox, this information is now stored into a small database file, signons.sqlite.

For cracking Web browser passwords, there is a suite of free Windows tools published by developer Nir Sofer at www.NirSoft.net. One of his specialties is a wide variety of "password recovery" tools for various Internet applications. A few that are relevant to our discussion are

- IE PassView: Internet Explorer password viewer

- PasswordFox: Mozilla Firefox password viewer

- ChromePass: Google Chrome password viewer

- OperaPassView: Opera browser password viewer

When running PasswordFox on a system, it will automatically seek out Firefox user profiles and display all password combinations to your screen, as shown in Figure 3.9. The results can also be searched and saved out to a text document.

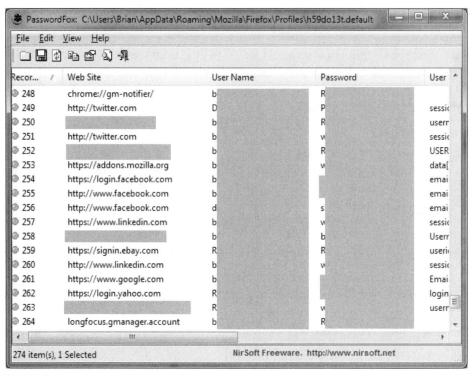

FIGURE 3.9

Displaying Saved Firefox Passwords with PasswordFox

With this information at their fingertips, Bob and Leon were able to test the user account and password for an online brokerage site to ensure that it worked, before contacting a carder to help them launder $10,000.

Best Practices

Much of the advice for protecting your online accounts comes down to basic password management skills. However, this is a topic that is greatly debated in information security circles. There is really no best solution for every person, but we'll present each side here for the reader to decide which would work best for them.

Commit Passwords to Memory

The simplest practice to keep your passwords protected is simply to not disclose them anywhere. Don't write them down and don't save them to your Web browser. Many would scoff at this idea and for natural reasons. A seasoned Internet traveler will have accounts on dozens, if not hundreds, of Web sites. If you think about it, though, you probably know someone who gets on the Internet to do just two basic things: check e-mail and surf eBay. For this person, it should not be hard to memorize two unique passphrases. Implement a strong passphrase based upon the guidelines shown in the "Authentication Security" section of this chapter, even one related to the site you're visiting. For example, your password to eBay could be IL0v3ebay.com. For longer passwords to more secure sites, like PayPal, you could use IR34LLYl0v3paypal.com.

For many of us, this practice is just unfeasible. Memorizing passwords will naturally lead to a person reusing the same password on multiple sites, one of the worst security mistakes that you can make. While you may trust the security at eBay and Twitter to not leak your password, you may use that same password at a less-secure site. Once your password is then cracked there, attackers can use it on every major Web site and eventually hit pay gold.

Password Safes

As we discussed earlier, your modern Web browser will include a basic password safe to secure the material locally. In some cases, like with Mozilla Firefox, you can even set a Master Password for the entire safe. This requires that you input a password, preferably a unique, strong password, for your browser to open the password safe.

There are also a number of products that will offer this ability for you. The Norton Security Suite, a commercial product located at www.symantec.com/norton/internet-security, offers an identity management system to lock all of your Web accounts into its own protected safe, as shown in Figure 3.10. For users of the Norton Security Suite, this is a painless and transparent security solution to maintain the security of their product. Norton's password safe also features plug-ins for Internet Explorer and Firefox, allowing it to completely take over password management from the browser. When in use, if an attacker attempts to pull passwords from your Web browser, they will simply receive no results.

Norton Security Suite is an excellent product for many homes and small companies. However, the more advanced user may wish for something more compatible with third-party applications and, well, free. One of the most popular password safes is KeePass, a free and an open-source application available at http://keepass .info. Being free and open source, KeePass has been ported to every major operating system and even most mobile devices.

By default, KeePass will encrypt your stored password into a database with Advanced Encryption Standard (AES) encryption, though it also supports Twofish encryption. If you already have a password safe within your Web browser and want to move to KeePass, you can use one of the importer plug-ins available at http://keepass.info/plugins.html to automatically import all of the usernames and passwords from your browser into KeePass. To pull in the passwords from Mozilla Firefox, you can use the ClockWork Firefox to KeePass Converter. This program will take all of your accounts and output an XML document. You can then install the

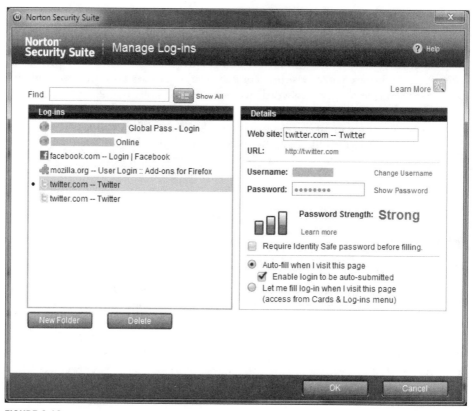

FIGURE 3.10

Norton Security Suite's Web Browser Password Safe

VariousImport plug-in and import the XML document into your KeePass database, as shown in Figure 3.11.

> **NOTE**
>
> If you use ClockWork Firefox to KeePass Converter to move your Firefox passwords into KeePass, make sure you note the XML document it creates. After the passwords are imported into KeePass, securely delete this XML document as it will contain all of your passwords in plaintext for anyone to read.

Another example of a comprehensive password vault is LastPass (www.lastpass .com). LastPass integrates into all major Web browsers and mobile devices and provides instant access to your passwords and secure information. Unlike KeePass, which stores the passwords in a database on your local hard drive, LastPass encrypts the password database and stores it directly on their own Web server. This allows users

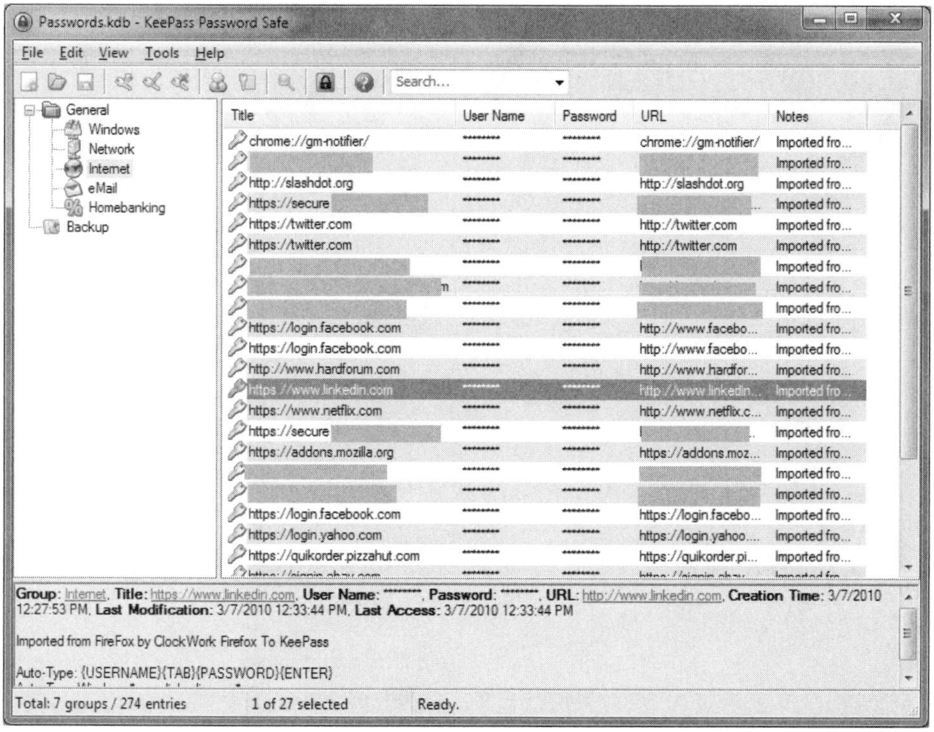

FIGURE 3.11

KeePass Password Safe

to synchronize their passwords from multiple computers and devices. Passwords can be randomly generated and automatically placed back onto a Web site form when logging in, allowing users to have extremely strong passwords that they do not have to worry about remembering. The company's business model is based upon a $1 per month premium account that allows you to install its mobile device application and allows for two-factor authentication into your password vault.

Randomly Generated Passwords

One of the best practices to implement to secure your accounts is to develop randomly generated passwords for each account. Many people use the same passwords across multiple sites, and even if using unique and strong passwords develop a sequential habit for passwords. Today's 1c4nhAzCh##z#burger1 can tomorrow be 1c4nhAzCh##z#burger2. If an attacker notices this trend, they can build a custom brute force password set geared for your password habits.

Obviously, creating random passwords is not for everyone. You will need to have a proper password safe in place to remember the passwords for you; it will be humanly impossible to remember your passwords at this point. Using KeePass, as described just above, is one of the best solutions for this. Inside KeePass is a random password

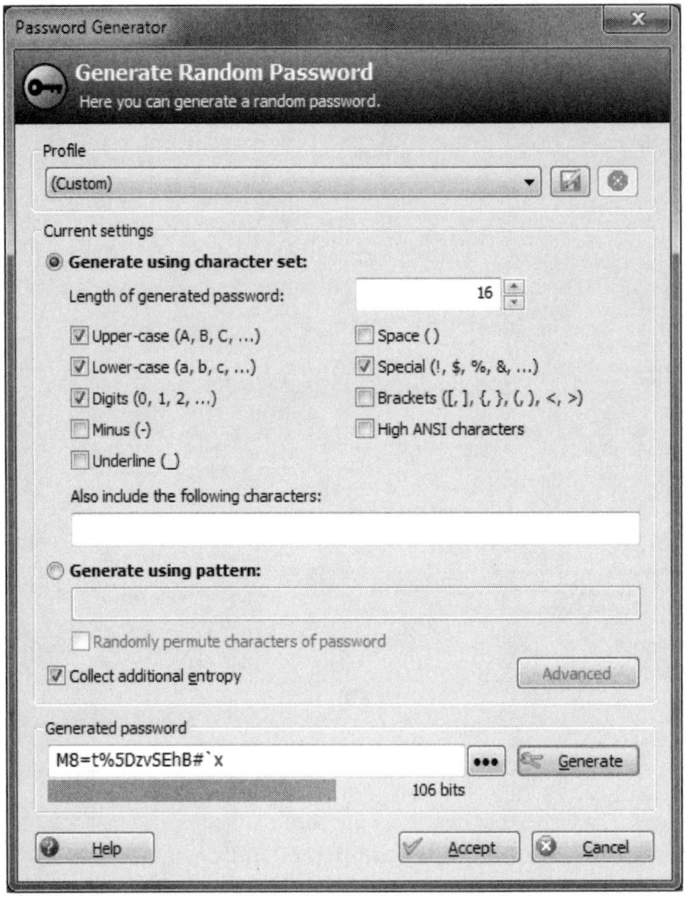

FIGURE 3.12

KeePass Password Generator

generator, as shown in Figure 3.12. You can set the various strength requirements of your password and even use entropic seeding (random keyboard presses or mouse movements) to improve its security.

Register an account onto a Web site, and when it asks for your password, note the password requirements. Enter them into the KeePass password generator to get your new password, then copy and paste it to the Web site to complete the registration and store the password into your password vault.

Mobile Password Safes

Password safes provide for incredibly secure Web browsing from your desktop computer. But what happens when you're on the road using a Web kiosk or travel laptop? What do you use when you're surfing from your mobile phone? You will need to have your password safe available on your mobile device for quick reference.

FIGURE 3.13

MyKeePass for Apple iPhone Password Safe

FIGURE 3.14

MyKeePass for Apple iPhone Password Copying

It is recommended that for a mobile password safe, you use a product like the KeePass application described above. The benefit of KeePass is that it is a free and an open-source application, allowing for public development of additional extensions and plug-ins for various devices. To focus on just one of these, we'll look at MyKeePass for the Apple iPhone, a $0.99 application available on the iTunes App Store.

After being installed to your iPhone, MyKeePass can accept your KeePass database from your desktop by setting up a Web server. You can then browse to your phone through your desktop Web browser and directly upload the database. After loading the database with a master password, you will then be presented with the same master list of Web sites as you would see on your desktop, as shown in Figure 3.13.

Upon selecting a site to visit, you will then be shown the stored account details for that site. From here, you can tap the password field to copy out the password value, as shown in Figure 3.14. You can also directly visit the Web site from here and have the application automatically enter your account credentials.

SUMMARY OF WEB BROWSER SECURITY

One of the biggest treasure loads for an attacker is to gain a user's valid set of credentials. Your username and password to even just one Web site can lead to your ultimate undoing, as many users habitually use the same account credentials for most, if not all, Web sites that they visit. While they may not care about their account on a small hobby forum, if hacked, that account's credentials could also allow an attacker right into their PayPal finances.

To protect against this threat, users should configure strong passwords across their accounts and not reuse passwords on more than one site. While this is difficult for many people as it requires memorizing multiple passwords, there are automated tools to assist.

Users should store and protect their unique passwords with a digital password vault. Most Web browsers feature a built-in password vault for just this purpose, but many feature poor security controls, allowing for anyone with access to the raw browser database to siphon out credentials.

Third-party applications, like KeePass, can help secure your data with strong encrypted databases. Such programs may also have support for mobile applications, allowing you to have constant access to your passwords when traveling on the road.

FOR MORE INFORMATION

The user accounts and passwords stored in a client application can be easy to grab by an attacker with the right tools and knowledge. To protect users from theft of their credentials, they will need proper training and an easy, effortless solution to manage their accounts. The following resources can help educate you, and your users, on the current issues with Web browser account security and ways in which it can be mitigated:

- Most consumers reuse banking passwords on other sites: www.theregister .co.uk/2010/02/02/e_banking_password_fail_survey/

- Reused Login Credentials Security Advisory: www.trusteer.com/sites/default/ files/cross-logins-advisory.pdf

- The Easy, Any-Browser, Any-OS Password Solution: http://lifehacker.com/5483119/

OUT-OF-BAND COMMUNICATIONS

THE HACK DISSECTED

He looked over his shoulder and watched as Bob loaded World of Warcraft. Soon his character was running down a stone road in the middle of a dark forest. There was no one around, but occasionally there was movement off to either side. Bob ignored the motion and kept running like he was on a mission.

"I thought we came here so you could get some help from Max," Leon asked as he pulled a chair up next to Bob.

"We did, and that's exactly what I'm about to do."

"It looks to me like you're playing a game when you ought to be making a phone call."

Bob didn't take his eyes off the laptop. "There's no way I'd call him. This has to be done out of band." (p. 61)

Out-of-band (OOB) communications is actually a concept that is familiar to even a four-year old and one that we use everyday. In certain situations, we may have a message that we need to relay to another person without letting everyone else hear it or know about it. In a casual environment, we would lean over and whisper the information or send it via an SMS text message that others can't read. The concept is the same: send a directed message that cannot be heard by eavesdroppers.

The OOB communication is actually a very critical part to both a network and a physical attack. If an attacker is working within a team, there needs to be a method of communication that can be hidden from police and the target and cannot be traced back to their source. On the Internet, this involves using encrypted communication channels. In the real world, encrypted shortwave radios and single-use cell phones come into play. It is essentially antireconnaissance. The better you hide your communications and plans, the harder it is for others to act against you.

In the story, Bob needs advice and help from Max St341, a correspondent that Bob virtually worked with earlier on developing an exploit. Later, Max will become an integral part to the story, but first the group of heroes needs to meet up and discuss the situation. Both Bob's and Max's paranoia precludes them from being able to just call each other or send a quick e-mail. Instead, they rely upon the World of Warcraft Massively Multiplayer Online Role Playing Game (MMORPG) to meet up. He determines the game to be safe from law enforcement (LE) individuals as he rationalizes that very few in the LE community would allow officers to spend their work day playing on a game server.

Exploit Techniques

Out-of-band communication is relied upon by many in the information security world, regardless of which team they're playing for. The goal is to establish covert communications with your team without your adversaries being able to listen to your conversations. Exploits come into play as attackers tap communication lines to read private messages. This concept also comes into play by attackers using non-standard communications protocols within your own network to coordinate their efforts, or exfiltrate data, without being noticed.

While many members of the information security world are familiar with Internet Relay Chat (IRC), and it is the central backbone for communication for many unsavory groups, it is based upon a plaintext network protocol. Each and every action and message is displayed proudly on the wire for any network administrator with a network sniffer to see.

Best Practices

The only real defense against out-of-band communications is to attempt to track and thwart them within your own environment. Most facilities do not have control over nonnetwork communications channels, as cell phone jammers are illegal in the United States.

However, as any good network security administrator should already be doing, you can monitor the traffic entering and leaving your network to attempt to find packets that may raise a red flag. If your network policy bans instant messaging communications, then you should have appropriate detection devices looking for such traffic to exit. However, with as simple it is for a developer to create a new obfuscated communications channel, administrators would have better luck looking for egress traffic going to unique and unusual IP addresses over nonstandard ports.

While it may be impossible to completely block the risk of OOB communications, proper outbound firewall rules and attentive log analysis can greatly reduce the risk.

SUMMARY OF OUT-OF-BAND COMMUNICATIONS

While an attacker either is in your network or planning an attack against it, he or she will need to use covert communications to avoid leaking their plans to the network defense group. Likewise, intrusion responders who are monitoring an active attack will also establish their own OOB communications to avoid leaking their plans to the active hackers. Even outside of a network environment, out-of-band communications are used to hide communications from LE, authority, and even public Web searches.

The tools that can be used for OOB communications vary, as there are many applications that have their own built-in chat functionality. Worst case, an attacker can always devise his or her own communications and exfiltration application to hide information from anyone on the network.

While the risk isn't completely eliminated, such traffic may be identified through proper log analysis and network perimeter security. Large amounts of continual data being sent to an unknown external server can be detected and followed up on to determine if there is an attack occurring or a threat of an attack.

FOR MORE INFORMATION

In any attack, out-of-band networks will be well used by both attackers and defenders to secure their communications from the opposing party. The channels used for these communications change on a rapid basis based on the technology and software available. The following reference goes in-depth on a unique, secure, OOB network that can be established:

- Authenticated Out-of-Band Communication Over Social Links: www.cc.gatech .edu/~avr/publications/wosn2008.pdf

ENDNOTES

1. Del H. Reason #4132 for Changing Your Password Twitter, http://status.twitter .com/post/367671822/reason-4132-for-changing-your-password/; 2010 [accessed 06.03.10].

2. SANS Institute, SANS Password Policy, www.sans.org/security-resources/policies/Password_Policy.pdf; 2006 [accessed 07.03.10].

3. RSA Security, RSA SecurID, www.rsa.com/node.aspx?id=1156 [accessed 09.03.10].

4. Boyd C. World of Warcraft authenticator users come under attack, http://sunbeltblog.blogspot.com/2010/03/world-of-warcraft-authenticator-users.html [accessed 07.03.10].

5. Annalee N. The RFID Hacking Underground, Wired, www.wired.com/wired/archive/14.05/rfid.html; 2006 [accessed 08.03.10].

6. O'Reilly Media, Windows Reverse Engineering, www.aspfree.com/c/a/Windows-Security/Windows-Reverse-Engineering/8/; 2004-07-27 [accessed 07.03.10].

7. SubSeven, www.subseven.org [accessed 07.03.10].

8. Mary B. Haiti Spam Leads to New Malware, Trend Micro, http://blog.trendmicro.com/haiti-spam-leads-to-new-malware [accessed 08.03.10].

9. Krebs B. BLADE: Hacking Away at Drive-By Downloads, Krebs on Security, www.krebsonsecurity.com/2010/02/blade-hacking-away-at-drive-by-downloads [accessed 07.03.10].

Exploit

4

At this point in the attack process, the attacker has canvassed your systems to find all of the points of weakness in your network and facilities. The attacker will weigh the pros and cons of each weakness to determine the most effective attack that will have the lowest risk involved. In this chapter, we will discuss the various styles of attacks that an attacker could use, while focusing on the ones specifically used within our story.

In this chapter, we will review some of the various angles of attack used by the characters in the story, including the areas which a hacker will directly target to obtain critical information.

ENCRYPTED STORAGE

THE HACK DISSECTED

He turned back to the main console. "This is a PGP passphrase screen – if he has anything valuable, it's going to be in this system, and we aren't going to get in." (p. 51)

Whenever a company has any information of critical value, it will virtually always be stored in an encrypted volume or device. This could be in the form of an encrypted storage archive or as an entire volume or partition. Because of the information typically stored within an encrypted volume, it is a highly sought-after target for attacks on a system.

This same concept is used for home users and hackers, like Bob, who use encryption to protect their own personal information on their own equipment. After Vlad and Pavel broke into Bob's home, Pavel noticed that one particular machine had a Pretty Good Privacy (PGP) passphrase screen on display, asking for a password to unlock it. The presence of this software implied to Pavel that it was being used to protect a critical system full of valuable data. He also expressed that it would likely be impossible to crack into it, based on PGP's strong encryption.

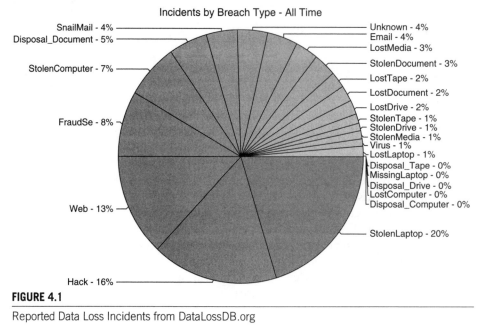

FIGURE 4.1

Reported Data Loss Incidents from DataLossDB.org

Courtesy: Open Security Foundation/DataLossDB

Encrypted storage is especially relevant to laptops and notebooks that can be stolen by an attacker and searched for private company information. The Open Security Foundation is an organization that tracks the exposure or loss of personally identifiable information (PII) and provides graphical reporting on these statistics. This information is found at http://datalossdb.org. By viewing a breakdown of all data loss incidents by the type of breach, as shown in Figure 4.1, you will notice a large amount of incidents are from lost or stolen devices. If you total all incidents by lost or stolen devices, it shows that 37 percent of all reported incidents were from an employee's laptop, desktop computer, or storage device being lost or stolen.[1]

The equipment that your company assigns to its employees, and even each employee's own devices, can be used as an attack vector in your network. This has become especially true in our society where motivated workers are encouraged to take their work home and be available at all hours of the day. This makes the physical employee a target of attack at work and at home.

Exploit Techniques

The strong advantage of encryption is that even if the data is stolen, it cannot be viewed without the appropriate key. The key that unlocks the data can be in the form of a digital certificate and is normally integrated with the encrypted data. The key, however, is password protected to prevent unauthorized access to the data. Once the user inputs the correct password, the key is unlocked allowing for the encrypted data to be viewed. This allows for another layer of defense against an attack, even after other physical and network defenses have been breached.

Most of the exploits that can be performed by an attacker are going to be focused on an encrypted storage container that the attacker already has in his or her possession. These exploits may require unfettered access to the equipment for long periods of time, or the ability to disassemble them with specialty equipment.

Additionally, there is also the concern that attackers themselves can use encryption to securely extract information out of your network without tripping an alert on one of your network security sensors.

Brute Force Password Attack

The most basic attack that can be performed against an encrypted storage container, and any password at all, is a simple brute force attack as they require no skill to perform. A brute force attack simply attempts each and every combination of characters until it can guess the correct one. Most brute force attacks can be scripted using basic command-line scripts that cycle through the available characters. A script for brute forcing a TrueCrypt-encrypted volume is written by running the TrueCrypt executable against the container for each possible password combination.[2] As the master key for the data is stored within the beginning of the TrueCrypt volume, outside of the encrypted data, the script can attempt to use the provided password to unlock the key until the correct password is found.

More information on this can be found later in this chapter under the section "Password Security."

Cold Boot Attack

It is common knowledge in the computer community that once a computer is turned off, all contents of Random Access Memory (RAM) will be wiped out to a null state. This is essentially true, but what most people fail to take into account is how long it takes before the contents are wiped. A group of researchers at Princeton University took advantage of this concept to publish a new attack marketed toward machines that have full disk encryption (FDE), such as computers with Microsoft BitLocker enabled.[3] With FDE, an attacker cannot access any file on the system without the password and encryption key. However, if the attacker is able to steal a computer that has already been booted, he or she can determine the encryption key through the cold boot attack.

The cold boot attack takes advantage of a known weakness in BitLocker, and a number of other FDE applications, where the encryption key is stored unencrypted in RAM while the computer is fully booted. Once power is removed from the RAM, the data that it holds is removed within seconds or minutes, based on the temperature of the RAM. The colder the RAM chips are, the longer they maintain their data. By spraying the RAM with the liquid contents of an upside-down can of compressed air, the RAM can reach temperatures that allow for 10 min of retained storage.[4] With liquid nitrogen cooling the RAM, the data can remain for hours. This allows an attacker to remove the RAM from a stolen computer, quickly freeze it, and then run a specialized tool to seek out, and extract, the encryption keys that remain in memory.

Exfiltration Container

The power behind encryption can also be used against a company that is being attacked. If a company is aware of a present and ongoing intrusion in their network, they will start looking for data being leaked out. Network traffic rules will be written for certain file signatures to determine if PDF documents, Word documents, or spreadsheets are being transmitted out of the network to the attacker's site. However, by using encryption in their process, the attacker can fool the victim by obfuscating the exact data that they are pulling.

The simplest way of encrypting data is to use any existing application that may already be installed on the target computer. The easiest way is to use OpenSSL, which is an application that is installed by default on many Linux and UNIX systems. The process is instantaneous and can be done with a command similar to the following:

```
openssl enc -aes-256-cbc -in /tmp/Customer_Data.xls -out /tmp/
    CD.enc
```

This command line will take the file "/tmp/Customer_Data.xls," encrypt it with 256-bit Advanced Encryption Standard (AES) with Cipher Block Chaining (CBC) and a typed passphrase, and output "/tmp/CD.enc." The attacker can then transmit CD.enc out of the network and decrypt it later. Decryption is done simply by using the *-d* option with OpenSSL, such as the following:

```
openssl enc -d -aes-256-cbc -in CD.enc -out Customer_Data.xls
```

Using a tactic like this, an attacker can covertly sneak information out of your network, a practice called *exfiltration*.

Best Practices

Protection against an encryption exploit is multifaceted. The important consideration is to prevent the attacker from gaining possession of an encrypted volume in the first place. Encrypted storage containers should be treated with a higher level of respect and caution than most other storage devices, as the data is obviously encrypted for a reason. As a company, there are a number of defenses that you can stand up to help prevent your protected information from being stolen or leaked out in the first place.

Password Strength

Although encryption may be the ultimate protection against data loss and theft, it is only as strong as the password used to access the key that is used to encrypt the data. Having a strongly secured encrypted volume is useless if your password is simply "1234" or "password," as a brute force application will crack open the container within minutes. As we'll discuss later in this chapter, having a strong password is the first line of defense against many attacks on the network and physical level. This is also discussed in greater depth later in this chapter under the section, "Password Security."

Passwords are also only the starting point to encrypted storage volumes. The password itself is used to unlock the master key, which itself decrypts the data stored within the volume. Although your users may have strong passwords, there are additional defenses that can be deployed to protect the key. Many encryption applications support the use of keyfiles, which are external files that can be chosen to be used as the master key. TrueCrypt, for example, allows the user to select a document or even an audio file to provide the key to the data. With this configuration, the user not only has to know the password, but also must have the correct keyfile in place.

Additionally, many encryption applications allow the use of smart cards to act as a key for an encryption volume. This is a more traditional form of two-factor authentication that some users may be familiar with. Not only does a user need to know the password, but they also must have their Smart Card inserted into the computer to access an encrypted volume. For information on how to provide these additional defenses within TrueCrypt, refer to www.truecrypt.org/docs/?s=keyfiles.

Data Protection Policies

Although strong technical measures can help protect against the disclosure of data after it is stolen, a strong business policy can be just as powerful to a business's security in that it can prevent the instance from occurring in the first place. Businesses need to establish strong guidelines about how equipment is consistently managed and maintained across the workplace.

Many businesses have a strict no-portability policy that prevents any information from being taken out of an authorized work location through laptop or thumb drive. In some places, employees are scanned on entry and exit to ensure that they are not sneaking material in or out of work. To really enforce this policy, a business should have clear and noticeable tags applied to all physical assets. This could be in the form of a bar code or company tag, but it should be something that is easily recognizable by employees and security staff. The business should also have a detailed asset database that includes every computer item with its manufacturer part number and serial number.

However, these same companies often leak the devices out themselves through repair work or charity work. For example, in 2009, the National Archives and Records Administration (NARA) sent a defective hard drive back to its manufacturer without first destroying the data contained within it. This data included database details for more than 70 million veteran accounts.[5] Many other companies will dispose of old equipment by simply throwing them into the dumpster, donating them to local schools, or selling them directly on eBay, all without taking the time to scrub the media clean of company information.

Finally, it is important for a business to understand that thefts do occur. Even while an employee strives to protect the equipment to the best of his or her ability, equipment does get stolen. It is important to establish an open and honest workplace where an employee feels comfortable notifying the management of the incident as soon as it occurs. In many instances, the employee will withhold details for days, or weeks, while he or she tries to formulate excuses and justifications, which makes the process of mitigating the risk more difficult. Management should be open and welcoming of the bad news and should avoid making harsh and knee-jerk reactions, such as immediately firing the employee. Stolen or lost equipment should be immediately reported to local law enforcement agencies, who can then start searching pawn stores. A record of the event should also be reported to the Federal Bureau of Investigation (FBI) National Crime Information Center (NCIC), which allows for nationwide law enforcement agencies to report if they recover the stolen equipment.[6]

Trusted Client Control

There are times when employees simply cannot perform all of their work from within a physical work location. An executive may need a laptop to finish reviewing documents while on a business trip, or a technical writer may be authorized to develop documentation while home tending to a sick family. Rather than trusting an encrypted resource to be taken out of the building, a business can implement a trusted client system to allow for employees to connect through a Virtual Private Network (VPN) so that they can accomplish work from afar.

One example of this concept is by deploying the Becrypt Trusted Client solution. An encrypted Universal Serial Bus (USB) thumb drive is inserted into the computer to open a dedicated, encrypted VPN interface back to the home office. The employee then works completely within a sandboxed environment with none of the information touching the host computer.[7]

SUMMARY OF ENCRYPTED STORAGE

As companies strive to protect their internal information stores, many have moved to place encrypted storage containers on desktops and laptops company-wide. As discussed in this section, large amounts of internal, proprietary data is lost or stolen every year through portable company assets. Many of these losses are preventable if the owners of the information had simply insisted on using basic encryption to protect their data.

Once an attacker has his or her hands on an encrypted storage container, he or she can attempt to break through the encryption to obtain the information within. This could be done through a simple brute force attack, although that can be the slowest method available, depending on the complexity of the password. Attackers can also attempt to perform a cold boot attack on a live and running machine to pull the encrypted keys straight out of memory. Besides being able to crack into your company's data, hackers themselves can also use encryption to exfiltrate their own stolen information out of your network without detection.

The best way to prevent such attacks is through proper policies and procedures. Strong passwords and proper handling of company devices can help mitigate many issues before the information is lost. External trusted computing platforms can assist your employees to safely and securely connect to your internal data and perform their duties from home or anywhere outside the office.

FOR MORE INFORMATION

Properly protecting your company's information is a hot topic in today's environment, and we could only briefly discuss some of the products and technologies available to help you succeed. We advise you to reference the following sites to read up on additional technologies available to you:

- Ironkey Personal Security: www.ironkey.com/

- Becrypt DISK Protect: www.becrypt.com/americas/Products/disk-protect

- Windows 7 Microsoft BitLocker Encryption: http://windows.microsoft.com/en-US/windows7/products/features/bitlocker

- TrueCrypt Free Open-Source On-The-Fly Encryption: www.truecrypt.org/

ATTACK RESEARCH

In our story, we discussed a number of various companies that research the latest exploits and trends. These companies offer actual cash rewards and prizes to attackers who exclusively sell them the details of new exploits. New exploits are discovered continually for applications and services that are run on millions of computer systems worldwide. Bob and Leon discovered that they can live a comfortable lifestyle by taking advantage of these services to fund their computer research.

Exploit Techniques

Why would a company wish to purchase current and popular exploits for their own use? This is done to avoid the dangers of full disclosure, a controversial stance within the security industry. Under full disclosure, once a researcher has discovered a vulnerability, the information is published in the Internet for everyone to see and respond to at the same time. Unfortunately, the hackers are usually faster at developing a working exploit than companies are to fix and patch their servers. Instead of risking a race against hackers, these companies work secretly with the vendors and large computing implementers to ensure that a patch can be developed and released well before a hacker can develop his or her own exploit. The cash rewards and prizes are used simply to dissuade the discoverer from selling the findings to a black hat group. Such groups collect the exploits and perform attacks against innocent users and companies to steal or extort money and data. In the security world, the black hats are the bad guys.

SANS Internet Storm Center

> **THE HACK DISSECTED**
>
> *[Pavel] just managed to turn back to his other laptop and pull up the SANS Internet Storm Center page before he heard the front door open. (p. 90)*

The Internet Storm Center (ISC) is a project run by the SysAdmin, Audit, Network, Security (SANS) Institute and staffed by volunteer Incident Handlers to monitor active exploits across the Internet. SANS ISC, found at http://isc.sans.org, openly accepts firewall logs and system logs from users and companies, and uses the details to correlate events across the Internet, showing current trends on attacks and exploits. ISC then publishes this information on security trends and incidents for companies to use to further secure their networks.

The ISC is a site constantly being monitored by hackers and defenders alike to gauge attack trends. In the story, as Pavel starts to discover his own danger in working with Vlad, his accomplice suddenly returns to their hideout. Pavel quickly brings up the ISC site on his laptop to hide his activities, as this is a page that he would be expected to view as the team's hacker.

Exploit Collection Companies

> **THE HACK DISSECTED**
>
> *"So where do you get the money for the lab?" Leon asked.*
> *"I sell vulnerabilities I find to iDefense."*
> *"You do? I've been selling to TippingPoint's ZDI!"*
> *Bob shook his head. "Dude, you should go with iDefense. They throw better parties at DEFCON." (p. 53)*

In our story, Bob and Leon are driving around the city, trying to put together a plan of where to go next and hideout. They quickly realize that they need cash while they formulate their plan of attack. Upon being asked about possible cash, Bob admits that all of his money goes toward improvements to his home lab. The pair reveals to each other at this point that they've been accruing money by selling exploits and vulnerabilities to competing exploit collection companies ZDI and iDefense Labs.

ZDI and iDefense Labs are two companies that collect vulnerability information and/or exploit code from hackers and security researchers. ZDI, short for Zero Day Initiative, is a program founded by TippingPoint. The iDefense Labs runs a Vulnerability Contribution Program (VCP) that is similar in focus to ZDI. Both companies offer cash rewards to security researchers for well-documented vulnerability information and/or reliable exploits. The actual cash amount is determined by how much impact the exploit has, and how well it has been researched and documented by the submitter, but typical rewards are in the thousands of dollars.[8]

These companies buy the exclusive rights to the materials, which they then research and provide to the affected vendors who turn them into fully functional patches that can secure enterprise networks. Each company has a client base that receives first notification of a new vulnerability, allowing them time to protect their own services from attack before the exploit is published. With the services of ZDI and iDefense, the "good guys" have a better chance of being able to patch their critical servers before the true "bad guys" get their hands on the vulnerability information or exploit.

TippingPoint, which runs ZDI, also runs the annual Pwn2Own contest at the CanSecWest security conference. The contest runs two events that focus on attacks that can exploit both Web browsers and mobile phones, with thousands of dollars dedicated to awards.[9]

Best Practices

For the modern business, there are many public Web sites available, such as the SANS ISC, to help you track and monitor the ongoing attacks and intrusions that are occurring to other businesses. This provides you the ability to proactively establish defenses on your own network before the attackers target you. This process is laborious, though, and is a full time job. For a purely automated approach, a subscription plan to one of the exploit collection centers can help you provide instant updates to your defensive infrastructure in real time, before the attackers can even create an exploit.

Exclusive Intrusion Prevention Systems

From a business perspective, your network infrastructure requires an intrusion prevention system (IPS) or intrusion detection system (IDS) to help discover and block network attacks before they can cause damage. Although there are many open-source tools available to help with this, the real protection comes from having a continual update plan with the latest threat signatures identified for you. Both TippingPoint (ZDI) and iDefense Labs provide comprehensive IPS implementations with cutting-edge signatures to help protect their clients from the latest attacks. The objective of purchasing the latest vulnerability details and exploits is to craft these signatures, providing instant protection to the IPS customers.

Free software applications also benefit from similar services. Although Snort is well known as the most popular IDS, and is free and open source, its developers also produce a live signature subscription plan. Snort is owned and operated by the security company, Sourcefire, Inc. Sourcefire employs their own staff of exploit experts called the Vulnerability Research Team (VRT) who research the latest exploits and develop zero-day Snort rules and signatures to protect business environments.[10] These latest real-time rules are given exclusively to commercial clients first and then made available to the public at a later date. One additional bonus to the Snort rules is that they are all open-source and easily readable and customizable by any client.

As a business with valuable information resources, you should have a dedicated IPS already in place. Although the standard free rule updates will help protect your network from the casual hackers, subscription to a real-time rule set will provide the best protection to your network and your data.

SUMMARY OF ATTACK RESEARCH

Computer vulnerabilities are risky business. Once found, how they're managed can prove just as dangerous as the actual exploit itself. While some researchers who discover vulnerabilities will release the information freely to the Internet, this can prove harmful to the infrastructure of many businesses. Instead, attack research companies such as SANS, TippingPoint, and iDefense Labs try to get the exploits off the streets and develop a safe defensive plan with the vendors to protect the resources of businesses. This business practice rewards vulnerability discoverers while protecting the systems in use by corporations and government agencies. Hackers have less of an opportunity to practice their exploits on unsuspecting networks and security researchers are not tempted to make deals with criminals to profit from their efforts.

As discussed earlier, companies purchase information on vulnerabilities and exploit code to hide the information before a proper patch can be developed to protect against it. Some exploit discoverers may work directly with the vendor to explore the vulnerability and assist in the creation of defenses while the details are kept secret from the public, a practice known as *responsible disclosure*. On the opposite side of the coin, some security researchers feel it necessary to exercise full disclosure and publish the details of their discoveries to the public as soon as it is discovered. Projects like ZDI and iDefense Labs make the assumption that only one person has discovered a particular exploit. While the details are being kept secret, additional researchers could discover the same exploit on their own and launch attacks. Full disclosure provides the ability for everyone involved to work from the same set of data. Although attackers may get a jumpstart in crafting exploits, proactive companies can also get a jumpstart in securing their infrastructure against the exploit.

FOR MORE INFORMATION

Vulnerability research and the disclosure of exploits are hotly-debated topics on the Internet, especially when there are cash prizes being introduced into the equation. For more details on active exploit development and the companies involved, we refer to you to the following sites:

- Full Disclosure Mailing List: http://lists.grok.org.uk/mailman/listinfo/full-disclosure
- SecurityFocus: www.securityfocus.com/

- The Open Source Vulnerability Database: http://osvdb.org/

- Exploit Database: www.exploit-db.com/

PASSWORD SECURITY

> ### THE HACK DISSECTED
>
> *Instead of the normal start-up screen that Stepan saw everyday, Pavel was greeted with a black screen with a few simple command options. This was a handy tool Pavel had picked up from a security Web site. It allowed him to reset any password on a Windows system as long as he could control how the system started. Pavel didn't bother giving the administrator account a new password. He set it to a blank password, disconnected his USB device, and rebooted the machine. Soon the Windows XP "splash" screen appeared. He typed in "administrator" for the ID and no password and pressed the "Enter" key. He was in.* (p. 7)

Passwords are the first line of defense, and the first angle of attack, against a known user account on a targeted system. Once a password has been compromised, it is extremely simple to use that account to dig further into a company's resources. After all, if an attacker has already taken over a valid account on a system, there is no need to launch an exploit and tip their hand.

In our story, after Pavel and Vlad snuck into Stepan's room, Pavel booted into a specialized tool that allowed him to completely overwrite and bypass the administrator password on the laptop. This allowed him instant access to the system with full rights to all of the data contained on it.

Exploit Techniques

As passwords are the most ubiquitous security defense used in computing, they obviously have numerous vectors of attack. In the encrypted storage section earlier in this chapter, we discussed the basics behind brute force password attacks. Brute forcing a password allows an attacker to cycle through every single character combination until they've guessed the correct one. This is the most straight forward attack, but it can take years to accomplish on sophisticated passwords. This section below will explore the basics of other styles of attack to show how each can occur.

Password Blanking

The most effective way to bypass a system password is to just remove it from play completely, and the method is known as *password blanking*. This is particularly effective on Windows operating system accounts, as a password is not required for access to the system. This was the attack used on Stepan's computer in our story. Pavel was able to use a password reset tool, such as chntpw[11] to gain access to the system and reset the system's administrator password to a blank password.[12] As

Stepan had his own, unique user account, and would not normally have access to the administrator account, this attack would have gone completely unnoticed until a company system administrator manually reviewed the laptop.

Password Reminders

Modern Web sites and online services are aware that many users routinely forget or lose their passwords. Virtually all online services now provide the ability to allow users to authenticate themselves without their password, in order to reset the password and regain full access. Early implementations of this concept were performed by sending the actual clear-text password back to the user through their registered e-mail address. This allowed anyone else with access to your mailbox to also see your passwords. Additionally, if an attacker did have access to your e-mail, they could request password reminders from all of your registered sites, record the passwords, and then delete the reminders from your inbox before you could see them.

Another protective system used by online services is to implement a series of personal challenge questions, asking questions that only the true user would know. Many sites use the same template questions. "What is your favorite color?" "What is your favorite food?" "Where were you born?" "Where did you meet your spouse?" Although these may have seemed like a great idea in the beginning, with the rise of social networking, it has become incredibly easy to find such details about someone else's life.

There have been two well-known account compromises that have occurred because of such challenge questions. The first was from 2005 when the T-Mobile cellular phone account of Paris Hilton was hacked, exposing her contact list to the Internet.[13] Hilton had established her challenge question as "What is your favorite pet's name?" However, due to her celebrity role, her pet's name, Tinkerbell, was widely known, and proved to be the correct response. This allowed the hacker to have complete access to Hilton's address list and text messages. A similar attack occurred in 2008, when United States Vice President hopeful Sarah Palin's personal Yahoo! account was hacked.[14] Not knowing the actual password, the attacker was able to successfully gain access to the account by answering three simple challenge questions: Palin's birthdate, ZIP code of residence, and where she met her spouse. Press releases and public details made by Palin were able to supply all of these answers.

Hacker Honeypots

Sometimes, it isn't even necessary for an attacker to seek out their target. Instead, they can sit back and wait for the target to come to them by creating a honeypot site to attract victims. As most malware authors have learned, easily exploitable Internet users are attracted to pornography and warez. Attackers have caught onto this trend as well and have generated their own discussion forums that pertain to these categories. As users create accounts for the hackers' forum all of the information is stored to a central database. The hackers can then cull e-mail addresses and passwords from the database and try them on various other Web sites. This was the exact method of attack used in early 2010 to hijack dozens of Twitter accounts[15] as we discussed in Chapter 3, "Explore," under the section "Authentication Security."

Even if the site isn't hosted by an attacker, it can still be an indirect target of an attacker. In this way, instead of the attacker going directly after their target, the attacker will exploit a shared resource and steal the target's credentials. This is done under the assumption that most users will reuse their accounts and passwords across multiple sites. While companies may put additional security defenses in place on their own networks, how sure can you be of the security on a random discussion forum on the Internet?

Once an attacker has the complete database including e-mail addresses, usernames, and passwords, the situation is pretty scary. The attacker can then turn around and use that information to access e-mail accounts, Facebook, PayPal, and just about anything else that uses the same credentials.

Brute Force Password Attack

The most basic attack that can be performed against a password is a simple brute force attack. This is a process by which an attacker will attempt each and every possible password combination until the correct one is eventually determined. The brute force application may start with the letter "a," then "b," then "c." After reaching "z," it will loop back and attempt the letters again in uppercase. After the letters are complete, it will attempt numbers and special characters. Once every known character is used, the application will then try two-character combinations. This process will then continue until the password is found which, for extremely long passwords, could take hundreds of years.

Brute force attacks are slow to complete because of the manner in which passwords are determined. When a user sets a new password to an account, their actual password is not saved directly into the site's database. Instead, the password is run through a mathematical algorithm, which produces a unique combination of characters, called a *hash*. For example, when using the popular MD5 hash algorithm, the password of "password" results in a hash of "5f4dcc3b5aa765d61d8327deb882cf99." Hashing is a one-way algorithm, meaning that if you have the hash, you cannot determine the original password that created it. Instead, a brute force application basically submits a password, the authentication system hashes it, and then it compares the hashed results to see if they match.

Many of the additional attacks covered in this chapter will be improvements made to speed up the process of brute force attacks.

GPU-Assisted Password Cracking

Using a computer's standard processor to crack passwords has improved through technological improvements to those processors. However, one Russian password recovery company, Elcomsoft, pushed the envelope for password cracking by taking advantage of the powerful Graphics Processing Unit (GPU) found in many high-end gaming machines.[16] As GPUs are designed specifically for mathematical computations, they naturally became a perfect choice for use in brute force password cracking.

Rainbow Tables

Earlier in this section, we discussed the basic brute force attack, a slow and methodical process of guessing the target's password. The negative performance impact due to brute forcing a password is caused by the system having to calculate the password's hash for each and every attempt. Understanding this concept, a new style of password guessing was created using what are known as *rainbow tables*. Rainbow tables are essentially huge lists of precomputed password hashes. Password hashes can then be directly compared against this list of known hashes until a match is found thereby greatly accelerating the process.

There are large rainbow tables already available for most forms of passwords including MD5 password hashes and even wireless encryption passwords.[17] Although an attacker gains significant performance improvements by using rainbow tables, the trade-off is that they occupy a very large amount of disk space. Each table is stored based on its targeted hash type and the types of characters used in the password, with some in the hundreds of gigabytes in size.[18] Because of their excessive size, some sites even sell 1 Terabyte external hard drives preloaded with rainbow tables to avoid bandwidth fees and delays.[19]

Once a hacker has obtained the rainbow tables for the attack, he or she can then use a tool to make the password comparisons. One such tool is Ophcrack, located at http://ophcrack.sourceforge.net, which cracks Windows account passwords using rainbow tables.

SSD-Assisted Password Cracking

The developers of Ophcrack, Objectif Sécurité, published details in early 2010 stating that with a solid state hard drive (SSD), they've been able process rainbow tables 100 times faster.[20] Their publication of this fact showed that the bottleneck in most brute force password cracking attempts is in reading the rainbow table data from the hard drive. As SSD storage drives do not feature any movable parts, they are exponentially faster than standard hard drives.

Best Practices

Password cracking will remain a vital offensive attack used by hackers for many years to come. However, attacks can be mostly mitigated through proper defensive approaches, although it may take years for the practices to be fully accepted by common users.

Strong and Unique Passwords

The single most effective defense against a password cracker is to simply use a strong password. Although any password can eventually be cracked, there are degrees of magnitude in the time it takes to crack a six-character password and a 20-character password.

There are many password strength meters on the Internet, some built into the sites in which you may be registering an account, which allow users to receive immediate feedback on the strength of their password. Generally speaking, the stronger a password, the harder it is for a hacker to crack it. With this as general common knowledge, you would assume that most users would prefer to use a strong password that is easy to remember for their accounts. One recent data leak from www.rockyou.com proves this to be wrong. In December 2009, a hacker gained access to the user database of RockYou and learned that all 32 million account names and passwords were being stored in plaintext in the database.[21] A follow-up review of the passwords showed that the vast majority of users chose weak passwords to protect their account.[22] In fact, the most common password, used by more than 290,000 users, was "123456."

Having such a simple password allows hackers to easily crack your password within mere minutes, if not seconds, even if it is encrypted. In practice, many people assumed that eight-character passwords were considered "secure enough" for the Web, but current recommendations are for passwords that are at least 15 characters long,[23] as recommended by the SANS Institute's Password Policy, which we reviewed in Chapter 3, "Explore." Additionally, passwords should also contain both upper and lower case characters along with special characters and should not be based on any dictionary term.

The simple practice of lengthening your passwords to 15 characters or more will disrupt most password crackers. At that length, with a good mixture of varying styles of characters, it would take years for most brute force applications to crack a password.

Although a strong password is critical to defending your data, it is useless if it is used across multiple sites. As soon as one site is compromised, and your password leaked, every other account that you have with the same password can also be compromised.

Automatic Screen Lock

THE HACK DISSECTED

Michael made sure that no one was watching and sat down at the desk. He right-clicked on the desktop and selected "Properties." His boss had a password-protected screen saver set to go off after 20 minutes – just like company policy. Michael disabled the screensaver and turned off the monitor, then quickly walked out. (p. 33)

In our story, Michael Resol had the difficult job of somehow installing a customized Trojan application onto his boss's computer system in 3DNF. Because of a family issue, Michael's boss suddenly had to leave his office and return home, but did so in such a rush that he forgot to lock his computer for the day. This allowed Michael to simply walk in and have access to the system.

Michael's boss likely left the building knowing that the company's automatic screen lock would protect his information. After 20 min of sitting idle, the computer would automatically engage the screensaver and lock his account out. If someone tried to log in after this period, they would be forced to type in the user's password. However, Michael was able to subvert the process by simply walking into the office before the 20 min had elapsed and disabled the screensaver.

Even if your company computers have mandatory account login policies, forcing each user to log into the computer to work, their data becomes at risk if they leave while the computer is unlocked. Insider threats, contractors, and office pranksters watch for coworkers who leave their computers wide open, allowing complete access to the data under the original user's account.

Setting an automated lockdown of a user's desktop is a very practical security procedure to protect a user's data if he or she leaves the computer unattended. Configuration can be as simple as setting the screensaver to launch every 10, 15, or 20 min and checking the **On resume, display logon screen** check box, as shown in Figure 4.2.

This configuration may work in most environments, but it proved to be exploitable in our story. With the setting stored on the client machine, Michael was able to access the screensaver settings of his boss's computer and simply disable this feature. In a more secure environment, an administrator will want to configure a network-wide group policy to enforce this setting. This will prevent a user from disabling it or altering its time-out duration.

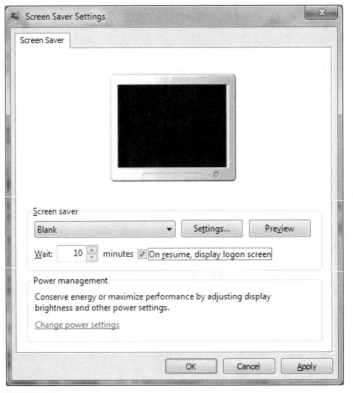

FIGURE 4.2

Setting a Windows System to Automatically Screen Lock

SUMMARY OF PASSWORD SECURITY

We focused a lot of attention on passwords in this section of the book, but for good reason. Passwords are the front line defenses that many users and companies have against attackers. It is also a topic that is universally accepted and understood by technical and nontechnical users. By implementing strong password policies, and using encrypted password vaults, computer administrators can help protect users from the many varied attacks that currently exist. As shown here, technology definitely works in favor of the attacker, as new devices allow for faster brute force capabilities. However, those advances can be mitigated through a few basic changes to a person's password usage.

FOR MORE INFORMATION

Even with the focus that we placed on password security and cracking in this section, we've barely scratched the surface. There are a variety of specialized password-cracking tools available to assist attackers with their efforts. However, there are just as many tools available to the consumer and business owner to protect their resources by making password cracking unfeasible. The following Web sites refer you to some of these tools and additional best practices:

- Bruce Schneier: Choosing Secure Passwords: www.schneier.com/blog/archives/2007/01/choosing_secure.html

- The Default Password List: www.phenoelit-us.org/dpl/dpl.html

- Project Alecto: Default Password Database: www.helith.net/projects/alecto/

- John the Ripper: www.openwall.com/john/

- Cain and Abel Password Cracker: www.oxid.it/cain.html

- ElcomSoft Password Recovery Tools: www.elcomsoft.com/edpr.html

- Mnemonic Password Formulas: http://uninformed.org/?v=7&a=3&t=sumry

E-MAIL SECURITY

THE HACK DISSECTED

Vlad ignored Pavel and kept his attention on the laptop. He looked in the default folder and quickly found the file he wanted. He copied the "outlook.pst" file to the pocket knife. This would give him a copy of all the e-mails Stepan had stored locally. With the e-mail secured, he looked up at Pavel. (p. 8)

In modern businesses considerable stores of information can be found in simple e-mail communications. E-mails typically include security policies, password reminders, personnel changes, internal product details, and other information vital to an attacker. In our story, Vlad and Pavel hacked into Stepan's laptop to obtain information on the job they were being hired to fulfill. To gather additional details about his employer, Vlad located and copied off the laptop a Microsoft Outlook e-mail Personal Storage Table (PST) archive containing information about their attack plans.

Microsoft Outlook allows users to store their personal data into PST files. This information includes e-mails, calendar entries, task items, and journal entries. This is the type of information an attacker would love to obtain in order to exploit a business. By compromising e-mail information, an attacker can quickly gain a foothold into an organization's assets.

Exploit Techniques

The most common and straightforward way to exploit an employee's e-mail is simply to hack into the mail server itself. Whether it is Microsoft Exchange, Sendmail, or Postfix, each type of mail server has versions that are vulnerable to particular exploits. Once an attacker has exploited a server, they can siphon off all of the e-mails for their own use.

A recent story of such an attack involved a situation coined "ClimateGate." In November 2009, hackers broke into the e-mail servers of the University of East Anglia's Climate Research Unit and stole 160 MB of e-mail archives.[24] These files were then placed onto a public Russian Web server and mirrored across the world. Thousands of people reviewed the e-mails in an attempt to find conspiracies with the controversial global warming research. Even though an inquiry in February 2010 showed no wrongdoing, it still put the organization under heavy scrutiny for many months.

Password Cracking

Although Outlook offers the ability to password encrypt your archived e-mail PST files, Microsoft actually admits that this protection is easily cracked and is not trustworthy.[25] PSTs are implemented with such lax security that they can easily be broken with basic tools. In fact, Microsoft released their own PST upgrade tool, "pst19upg .exe," to convert older PST files into the modern file format, which had the side effect of completely removing the passwords.[26]

E-Mail Redirection

An attacker can still get his or her hands on your e-mail contents even without having possession of your archived PST files by simply exploiting e-mail forwarding locations. Modern e-mail systems are designed to keep e-mail contained within an organization so that it can be controlled for security and auditing reasons. However, because of convenience, many employees will setup e-mail rules to automatically forward all of their work e-mail to a secondary address, possibly one that they can access from home. In an employee's mind, this is a good strategy. Employees can stay on top of issues at work even from home and be able to respond to questions as soon as they come up. From a security standpoint, this is a bad strategy.[27] This move places all of the company's internal e-mail out into the wild where they can be stolen. Or, in a worst-case scenario, the information can be sold or given away to a competitor.[28]

An infamous example of this was the MediaDefender e-mail leak of 2007. MediaDefender, Inc. was a company that performed peer-to-peer investigations for copyright owners, especially recording and motion picture industries. Unfortunately, one employee automatically forwarded all of his e-mail to his personal Google Mail (Gmail) account. He then later signed up onto one of the warez sites that his company was investigating using the same account credentials as his Gmail account. The owners of the warez site were then able to use his password against him by logging into his Gmail. This compromise leaked out thousands of e-mail messages detailing internal company strategies, and it was further used to extract their applications' source code, as well as telephone recordings.[29]

Best Practices

E-mail is a core source of information to your company's assets, daily operations, and future plans. The loss of such information into a competitor's hands, or even those of an attacker, can spell financial ruin for many businesses. However, there are ways in which your business can help protect e-mail resources to reduce the amount of data available to an attacker or competitor.

E-Mail Retention Policy

In reaction to electronic discovery (e-discovery) laws, many companies are now implementing retention durations for all e-mail. By setting a retention rate, the mail server will automatically remove all e-mail messages older than a certain period of time, such as 30 or 60 days. This lessens the amount of documentation that can be discovered by an opposing council in a court of law.[30] This option can be set within the Microsoft Exchange configuration, as described by Microsoft at http://technet .microsoft.com/en-us/library/bb124524.aspx.

Prevent PST Usage

As mentioned earlier in exploitation techniques, an e-mail PST file has very little defense against attack. If an attacker is able to acquire one of these e-mail archives, he or she can easily crack the passwords and encryption to read all of the user's backed-up messages. The easiest way to prevent this from occurring is to simply not allow users to create and read PST files. This would force them to read their mail directly from a mail server and not be able to store it locally where it can be stolen. This can be done by adding a simple entry into the user's local registry, as shown in Figure 4.3, to disable Outlook from accessing the PST files.[31]

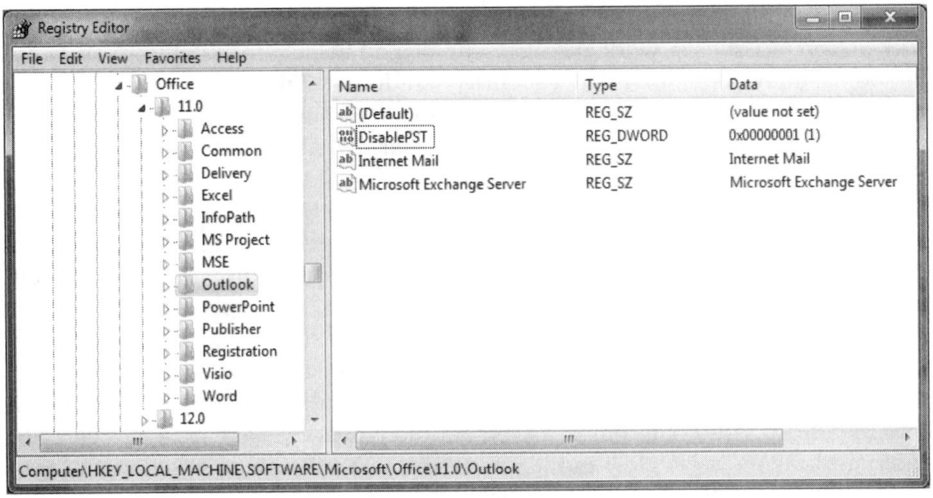

FIGURE 4.3

Disabling PST Access In Microsoft Outlook

SUMMARY OF E-MAIL SECURITY

E-mail security should be a focal point for any business or organization. Much of your critical data is likely stored within e-mail, and because of its nature, e-mail is heavily portable outside of your organization. Not only can e-mail be automatically forwarded to external mail accounts, which may have poor security, but also the archive formats used by Microsoft Outlook have historically weak security allowing for easy password cracking or removal by attackers. By exploiting e-mail archives, hackers can gain critical insight into your business. However, this can mostly be mitigated through retention policies and prevention of archives. By preventing the creation of archives and reducing the retention time for individual e-mail messages, companies can greatly reduce the amount of information that could be leaked out.

FOR MORE INFORMATION

With the changing laws governing courtroom discovery, e-mail retention and collection has recently proven to be a very hot topic with many businesses. Those with the need to address the issues of e-discovery should have dedicated staff and resources available to assist in providing proper defense against lawsuit discovery. The following Web sites provide basic information on e-discovery rules and legislation for further reading:

- E-Discovery and Microsoft Technology: http://blogs.technet.com/ediscovery/default.aspx

- The Electronic Discovery Reference Model: http://edrm.net/

WINDOWS NULL SHARE EXPLOIT

THE HACK DISSECTED

It took Bob only a few moments to produce a list of computers on the network he was scanning. He left the scan to run and opened a new window from his "Run" box at the bottom of the screen. He typed the first name of a computer that looked like a server followed by the default root path \\3D-FS1\C$. (p. 41)

After running his initial scan of the 3DNF network over the backdoor wireless router, Bob started scanning for a server he could easily place the CyberBob icon onto. He scanned through the list of computer names shown to him and picked the first that looked like a server name, 3D-FS1. Knowing the company and typical naming conventions, we can assume that this server name stands for "3DNF File Server 1." Bob was then able to access the server's filesystem by using one of the simplest exploits ever discovered: the Windows Null Share exploit.

Exploit Techniques

In a Windows environment, a user can share out folders for others to access across a networked environment. However, what many people don't know is that an entire volume, by default, can be shared out. Windows will automatically share out each volume, or partition drive letter, on your system for other users to access, as shown in Figure 4.4. These shares are typically hidden from view by the presence of the trailing dollar sign at the end of the share name, a character that tells Windows to hide the share from view. When Bob connected to \\3D-FS1\C$, he was literally connecting to the C: volume of the file server.

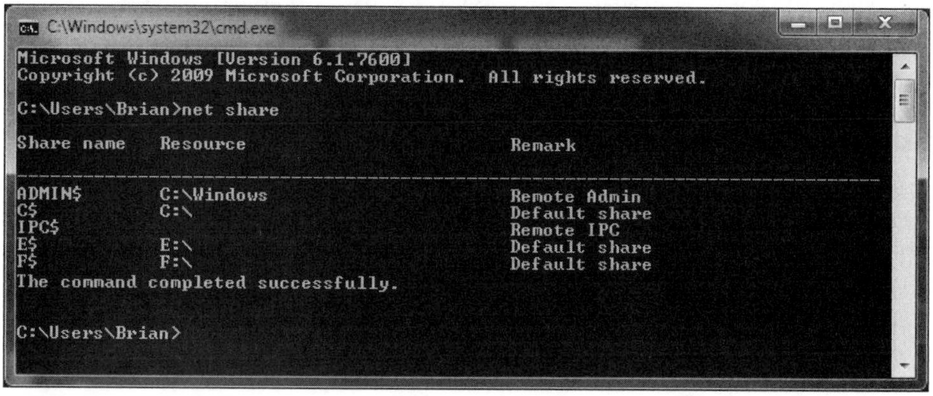

FIGURE 4.4

Windows Hidden Shares

When discussing Windows shares, "null" refers to the authentication ID in use. When a user attempts to connect to a remote share as an anonymous user, by supplying no user account for authentication, he or she uses a null identifier. Otherwise, a user would use his or her account name as the identifier to determine if he or she has appropriate permissions. In our story, the 3DNF file server was freely allowing Bob to connect to the system's primary partition to access all of the files contained within it.

For Bob to pull off the attack, he had to notify the remote server that he would be connecting through the Inter-Process Communications (IPC) socket, IPC$, with a null user account.[32] This is accomplished on many systems by running the following command:

```
NET USE \\3D-FS1\IPC$ "" /USER:""
```

This command will tell the attacker's computer to make a temporary IPC connection to the server with a null username and null password. Once completed successfully, the attacker can then simply make a connection to the server and have full access to the files contained on it.

Best Practices

The exploit discussed here and in our story is one that takes advantage of a default configuration with many Windows-based systems. Fortunately, the issue has become very well known, and the modern versions of Windows are no longer susceptible to such a simple exploit. The exploit requires that the remote server has NetBIOS installed and running on Transmission Control Protocol (TCP) port 139, a protocol that is no longer enabled by default on computers.

Based on Microsoft's own security bulletin,[33] it is advised to simply "disable NetBIOS and verify that ports 139 and 445 are closed." By locking down these ports and disabling NetBIOS, a user cannot make a null authenticated IPC session to a Windows computer. To view system shares, such as C$, the user would have to submit a valid user account and password that has the permissions to view the information.

SUMMARY OF WINDOWS NULL SHARE EXPLOIT

The Windows Null Share exploit shown in our story was a critical exploit targeting older Windows machines. The attack is simply done by taking advantage of default Windows shares that allowed for null users to have read and write access to critical system files and folders. With this exploit attackers have full access to all information stored on a system drive, which can include company files along with user accounts and passwords. Although the exploit can be mitigated, it has mostly been secured through recent revisions of the operating system. Computers running modern operating systems will no longer be vulnerable to this attack.

FOR MORE INFORMATION

We discussed a basic example of how to launch this attack in this section, but there are additional methods. To read more about the topic, and ways in which it can be exploited, we refer you to the following Web site:

- Microsoft MSDN: Null Session Vulnerability: http://msdn.microsoft.com/en-us/library/ms913275(WinEmbedded.5).aspx

CREDIT CARD FRAUD

> ### THE HACK DISSECTED
>
> *Next Leon opened an IRC session and was quickly logged into a carder site.*
>   *I need a quick cash out. $10K guaranteed 30/70 split. No rippers. No Nigerians.* (p. 54)

Carders are individuals who exchange stolen credit cards for cash. The carding business has easily grown to be one of the most lucrative cyber crime markets on the Internet. It evolved into a very complex and segmented industry as well, with a single credit card number exchanging between multiple hands before finally being used.

In our story, Leon contacts a carder chat room to find someone who can fence the financial account that he stole from an unwitting home owner. Leon gave over the computer owner's own brokerage account to a carder, who filed an electronic transfer for $10,000 into one of their own accounts. Of this, the carder gets $3000 (30 percent), a hefty sum for such a quick and easy transaction. But, as the fence, the carder holds all the risk and is fundamental in making the transaction successful.

Leon makes a few additional comments in his initial post like "No rippers." A ripper is simply someone that will rip you off. They will take the money and then just disappear. And many in the community feel that Nigerian carders are untrustworthy because of the ubiquitousness of Nigeran 419 scammers and shun them from transactions.

Exploit Techniques

There are many ways in which an attacker can obtain a credit card number, or any other financial account, to exploit for money. The most direct way is to simply just hack into a store's point-of-sale system and collect the credit card numbers that are being stored there. There have been numerous large credit leak outs in the recent past, such as the infamous T.J. Maxx attack[34] that we discussed in the "Wardriving" section of Chapter 2, "Scanning." In other cases, hackers go directly for corporate credit cards and accounts by attacking hotels and business-friendly restaurants. The *Wall Street Journal* reported that hotels are currently the most targeted industry for hackers who steal financial accounts.[35] In March 2010, Wyndham Hotels suffered a third breach of its security in just over a year, exposing the account details of guests at 37 of its hotels.[36] These breaches not only endanger the financial details of guests but also the future business capabilities of the company. Ironically, this latest breach at Wyndham also disclosed the guest details of an annual hacker convention, Notacon, which was hosted at one of the hotels.[37]

There are numerous other ways in which an attacker can gather financial details and turn them into cash for their own needs, as we'll discuss here.

Skimming

One increasingly popular way for attackers to gather credit card and debit card information is to record the card details at the point of transaction. One venue in which credit cards are occasionally stolen is in a formal restaurant. This is one of the few times in which a card holder willingly relinquishes their card to a stranger, who leaves with the card to scan it at a remote credit card terminal. During this process, it is easy to see that a waiter or waitress can use their own card skimmer to steal your details, with a number of documented cases already encountered.[38] To combat this issue, many restaurants are moving toward a "pay-at-table" system that allows for a credit card to be scanned and authorized while the card remains in the possession of the card holder.[39] Besides having someone manually scan your card, attackers are now exploiting Automated Teller Machines (ATMs) to capture bank card information as it is being inserted. Criminals attach customized skimmers to the front of an ATM that would be unnoticeable by the common customer.[40] Small cameras are also covertly attached to the ATM to monitor users as they type in their account PINs.[41] Beyond ATMs, any kiosk device that accepts a credit or debit card is at risk. Recently, skimmers were used on gas pumps in Utah to record credit card information and wirelessly transmit it to a nearby Bluetooth receiver.[42]

Once an attacker has gained a database of credit card numbers, they may be used for the attacker's own personal use. Others find it more lucrative to simply sell off their lists of credit card numbers to others, such as with the advertisement posted in Figure 4.5. The financial result may be less than actively using the stolen numbers, but it guarantees a regular source of income, not to mention less risk, and is a sign of the specialization of roles within the carding community.

Money Mules

Even when an attacker has successfully stolen a series of credit card numbers, there is still the difficulty of somehow getting the stolen money out of its legitimate account and into the hacker's hands. Hackers recruit money mules to unwittingly take stolen money and transfer it out of the country. Such mules are usually regular people looking for a quick buck without realizing that they are doing something illegal.[43] They are normally recruited online through "get rich quick" advertisements. Others are approached by criminals through popular career and job search sites, offering opportunities to work from home.[44]

> **ATM DUMPS**
> *February 10, 2010 - 12:39 PM*
>
> We are selling fresh skimmed ATM dumps from Canada and USA ONLY (101/201) with PIN number, all dumps are skimmed on Atm`s with dial pad (Pin Pad). We are selling the dumps w/pin USA, CAN ONLY for 180 USD each for Amex USA/CAN (050,041,040...) 250 USD each. No other countries at this time.
> Everyday fresh dumps and never sold twice. No tests and no rippers (rippers will be posted), minimum order from $ 900 USD and up.
>
> Minimal order amount for Payment, W-U and Money Gram.
>
> US Dumps:
> US Classic = 70$
> US MC Standard = 80$
> US Gold = 120$
> US Platinum = 120$
> US Business/Corporate = 180$
> US Purchasing/Signature = 200$
> US MC World = 200$

FIGURE 4.5

Advertisement for Stolen ATM Card Numbers

The sole role of a money mule is to establish an online financial account, such as with www.paypal.com, and wait for money to appear in the account. Once deposited, the money mule then withdraws the cash and wires it to the criminals while keeping a small percentage for themselves. However, when the police catch up to the crime, it's the mules that take the fall.

Best Practices

Many of the best practices that can be followed by a company or consumer fall into basic defenses. Companies need to secure any financial information that they store within their network. If a company collects payment card information, then they will typically have to follow the guidelines and compliances of the Payment Card Industry Data Security Standard (PCI DSS). PCI DSS compliance is an incredibly detailed security strategy that impacts every layer of your network infrastructure and business model and, as such, cannot be described in detail here. For more information on PCI compliance and how to follow security standards for your commercial business, review *PCI Compliance: Understand and Implement Effective PCI Data Security Standard Compliance, Second Edition* (ISBN: 978-1-59749-499-1, Syngress).

Consumer Protection

From a consumer standpoint, the best protection against having your credit card information stolen is to simply protect the numbers from being exposed. For online purchases, this can be accomplished by the use of a "controlled payment number," or a one-time credit card number. Many banks offer this service, although under various names, which allows users to create a unique credit card number with a capped dollar amount.[45] Once used to purchase goods, the card will only accept additional charges from that same merchant, and only up to the capped amount that the user chose. The process requires a few additional steps on behalf of the consumer, but if their credit card number does get leaked out, it will prevent any excessive use by criminals.

When making ATM transactions, consumers should attempt to use teller machines in well-lit and public locations. Criminals installing skimmers tend to seek out machines off the beaten path to avoid surveillance cameras. Most skimming devices are simply attached onto the ATM with glue or double-sided tape. Before inserting your bank card, physically nudge the card reader to ensure that it is the one built into the machine and not a skimmer that has been attached. If you notice exposed wiring or loose panels, then avoid the ATM and move on to another one.

Consumers should be vigilant about their bank account details. Check your bank card transactions often and check for suspicious entries. At the first sign of a suspicious transaction notify your bank to start an investigation and cancel your bank card. Consider enrolling into a credit protection service, which will alert you if new accounts and cards have been generated under your name and assist you in refuting unauthorized accounts.

SUMMARY OF CREDIT CARD FRAUD

As cyber crime evolves, criminals seek more than just to cause mischief and harm computers. It is now more prevalent for hackers to directly profit from attacks, and many do just that with attacks focused on financial data on the Internet. The issue has risen in urgency in recent years because of a number of notable, large-scale attacks, such as the one on TJX, Inc. Although there are basic steps that can be taken by the common consumer to protect his or her assets, the core focus of defense should be laid on the businesses that store financial information. For these groups, there is the Payment Card Industry body of regulations that help protect critical financial data.

FOR MORE INFORMATION

Financial crimes are some of the most common attacks promulgated on the Internet today. As such, defenses against them need to be deployed throughout your company's entire infrastructure. For the purposes of this book, we provided basic coverage of the risks associated with credit card fraud on the Internet. Financial data security is an evolving field, and we recommend the following publications and Web sites to gather more information that you can use to protect your customers:

- *PCI Compliance: Understand and Implement Effective PCI Data Security Standard Compliance Second Edition* (ISBN: 978-1-59749-499-1, Syngress, companion Web site at www.pcicompliancebook.info)

- Krebs on Security: www.krebsonsecurity.com/
- PCI Standards Council: www.pcisecuritystandards.org/

TRAFFIC OBFUSCATION

THE HACK DISSECTED

Hannah jumped in. "Whatever you guys caught, it wasn't amateur. I found references to IPs that tie back to Germany, Russia, Switzerland, and China. There's no way to know where the command and control for this is. I tried looking at these IPs and they are all black holes. They either don't exist or they have some good source filtering." (p. 81)

In our story, we make references to obfuscating the source of communications across the Internet. As Bob and Leon brought Hannah into their team, they asked her to review the code that they had retrieved from the 3DNF attack in an attempt to determine where it originated from. After reviewing the Trojan code in their shared hotel room, Hannah admitted that there were numerous Internet Protocol (IP) addresses that relayed information back to multiple countries across the world.

As Hannah traced down the IP addresses, she noticed that they were all pointed to nonresponsive computers. As she admitted, either the addresses didn't exist or they were using source filtering. Since it seems unlikely that Pavel would deploy a Trojan that was not functioning, it is more likely that the end node computers were choosing not to respond to Hannah's interrogations because she was connecting from a hotel network. Using well-crafted firewall rules, a server can appear to be completely offline except to a white list of certain IP addresses, notably those used by 3DNF and the government networks in which the Trojan was ultimately inserted. So, the only way for Hannah to get a response from the remote servers would be to do her scanning from within 3DNF's network or from the targeted government networks.

Alternatively, Hannah could have modified her request packets to these servers to appear as if they were coming from 3DNF and attempted to get a response that way. That process is just one of the methods we'll discuss here for obfuscating traffic across a network.

Exploit Techniques

In terms of obfuscating traffic, an attacker is generally looking to send packets into a network without them being traced back to their original location. If the victim notes the attacker's actual IP address, then the victim can set up firewall rules to block the traffic and have a solid lead for law enforcement to follow up on. Instead, there are a number of ways in which an attacker can alter their traffic flow to the victim.

IP Spoofing

The most basic way of altering an attacker's source location is to simply spoof some-one else's IP address. In this process, the attacker uses specialized software to edit the individual packets leaving his or her machine and replaces every instance of the actual IP address with another.

However, while spoofing was very popular in the early days of the Internet, it is much less effective today. For one, modern Microsoft operating systems no longer allow the process to work, as they do not allow applications to access raw network sockets.[46] This prevents any Windows operating system from XP Service Pack 2 to current from being able to spoof TCP packets. However, they can still spoof User Datagram Protocol (UDP) packets.

Additional limitations are placed on spoofing because of large network providers blocking outbound packets that do not appear to have originated within their net-work. In laymen's terms, if an Apple employee spoofs a Microsoft packet, the Apple router will drop the packet since it did not appear to have originated from Apple. Based on a continually running study of the state of IP spoofing at the Massachusetts Institute of Technology (MIT), found at http://spoofer.csail.mit.edu, less than 20 per-cent of all IP addresses and Internet netblocks allow for spoofed packets.[47]

Traffic Relaying

Although using a spoofed packet can help throw off the trace to your original machine, it is virtually impossible to use spoofed packets in a two-way communica-tion. How can the server respond back to an attacker's actual computer if it thinks they're at a different IP? A hacker needs a solid path of communication between his or her computer and the target while remaining anonymous. This is done by relay-ing the packets between intermediary hosts between the attacker and the target. Anyone who has seen a visual Hollywood reenactment of a network attack would recognize screens of a hacker bouncing his or her network traffic through servers all over the world. This is accomplished by the hacker installing a relay application, otherwise known as a *bouncer*, on various servers across the Internet. An attacker connects to the first relay point, and then uses that computer to connect to a second, then to a third. Each relay adds another degree of separation between the attacker's actual computer and the one used to connect to the target, as shown in Figure 4.6.

Tor

THE HACK DISSECTED

Bob gave her an incredulous look. "Of course, not. I don't carry a phone – and I'm not going to use Leon's and give them a way to trace us. I'll use a VMware browser appliance through Tor to a Web site that sends texts." (p. 83)

Although creating manual relay points across the Internet is a good defensive move for an attacker, it is a laborious job, and one that isn't always reliable or secure. Using relays will separate an attacker's IP address from the victim but does not do anything

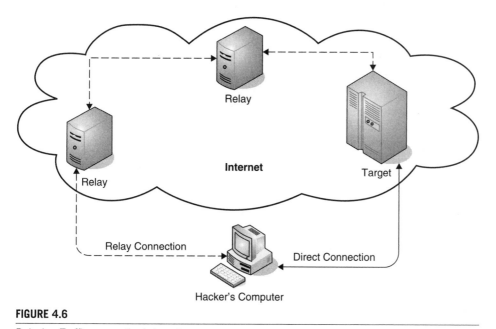

FIGURE 4.6

Relaying Traffic across the Internet

about the flow of traffic. If an incident responder finds 50 MB of data going to a relay and then 50 MB of data leaving the relay, then the incident responder can follow the packets until the original source is found. One way around this is to use Onion Routing (OR). The Electronic Frontier Foundation (EFF) provides an implementation known as Tor, The Onion Router, a traffic anonymity application from http://tor.eff.org.

In our story, Bob mentions Tor when discussing how he would properly back-stop his connection to the FBI. The group of heroes decides to finally contact Agent Jackson, known to them as Jeb, and work with the FBI. Bob mentions that they should send a text message to Jeb to start a line of conversation, but Hannah warns him not to use his own cell phone so that the line couldn't be traced back to their physical location. Bob, obviously aware of this, said that he would send a text message from a texting Web site, through a virtualized machine, over the Tor network.

Bob's plan places his actual computer such that there is four degrees of separation between himself and Agent Jackson. His text message is typed into a texting Web site over Tor, from within a virtual machine. The texting Web site sends the text message to the cell phone SMS server, where it is then relayed to Jackson's cell phone. Each layer of separation is designed to provide additional security to Bob. By using a texting Web site, they do not have to use their own cell phones and give up their personal phone numbers, or potentially their location. By visiting this Web site through a VMware browser, they leave no traces on the actual laptop host operating system showing that they visited the Web site. A forensics examiner would have to dig into the virtual environment to find this, but most VMware browsers wipe their history logs after their use. The message is then sent from Bob's laptop to the texting Web site over Tor.

Onion router (OR) proxies are a unique innovation in the proxy world. Instead of a single proxy server relaying your data, OR takes advantage of a network of multiple proxy servers, as shown in Figure 4.7, through which data is seemingly bounced around to random hosts before it reaches the intended target.[48]

Tor operates by building a circuit through the OR network. Each client has a database of all available Tor servers on the network, and the client plans out a circuit through the network using this list. The data is then encrypted into multiple layers of encryption (hence the onion reference), and passed on to the first Tor server. Each server uses a symmetric encryption key to decrypt their "layer" of encrypted data, which gives them the data for the next server and instructions on which server to next send that data to. Once the data reaches the last Tor server and is decrypted, it is sent out directly to the target system. From the time the packet leaves the hacker's computer until it reaches the "exit server" on the OR network, it stays encrypted. The only time in which it is ever unencrypted is when

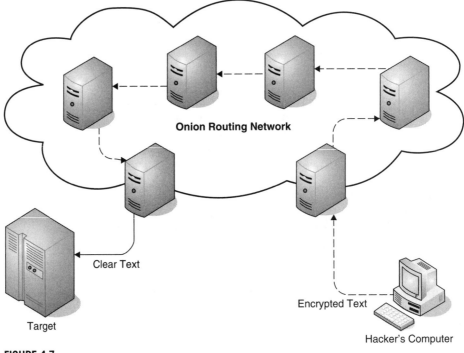

Onion Routing Network

Clear Text

Encrypted Text

Target

Hacker's Computer

FIGURE 4.7

Relaying Traffic across the Internet through Tor

it is transmitted from the exit server to the target system. Additionally, since the Tor servers are geographically spread out, and communicating through encrypted packets, it is impossible to sniff traffic at one point and determine who sent the packet or who it is ultimately intended for.

Best Practices

For a standard business there should be very few reasons, if any, to allow employees to use obfuscation techniques in their daily jobs. These techniques are generally limited to bypassing detection. For example, Tor is particularly useful for bypassing a corporate network's monitoring software, allowing a user to visit eBay or other sites that may be against their network policy. The best protection against clients like Tor is to simply prevent users from having administrative rights to their computer and being able to install the Tor application.

Many relaying applications will create traffic that may be difficult to track down and block. As the software is designed to be completely configurable, the packets may enter and leave on any TCP port and may even be encrypted to protect against monitoring. Catching an internal relay within your network will require a close eye on your network statistics to find any servers that are directly receiving the packets from the Internet and then transmitting the same-sized packets to another Internet, or internal, host.

SUMMARY OF TRAFFIC OBFUSCATION

Traffic obfuscation techniques, such as IP address spoofing, help attackers in committing attacks while remaining anonymous from pursuit. Apart from modifying their packets, which has become more difficult in modern Microsoft Windows operating systems, attackers can also bounce their traffic between intermediate relay points before they make contact with your network. These can consist of relay points that a hacker has constructed across the Internet, or through the encrypted Tor network. These allow an attacker to hit your network from multiple outside IP addresses, bypassing your basic firewall blockades.

FOR MORE INFORMATION

Traffic obfuscation techniques change regularly over time as attackers adopt new technologies to help bypass firewall rules and basic defenses. We've reviewed the most common methods in use, but there are a variety of tools that provide additional capabilities for attack. Below are references to such tools, as well as additional reading on how to read into encrypted network communications.

- Intrusion Detection FAQ: What is the Q Trojan? www.sans.org/security-resources/idfaq/qtrojan.php

- Pivoting BOUNCEr: www.hackinthebox.org/modules.php?op=modload&name
  =News&file=article&sid=19325

- Peeling the Onion: Unmasking Tor Users: www.fortconsult.net/images/pdf/
  tpr_100506.pdf

METASPLOIT

THE HACK DISSECTED

Leon loaded nmap and began a profile scan of the single IP address. It didn't take long for the application to identify the target host as an unpatched installation of Fedora Core.

"Look, they've got SNMP running on the box," Leon again pointed triumphantly at the screen. Before Leon could get the mouse over to the folder to get his next tool, Bob pronounced "Use Metasploit."

"Just a sec," Leon sounded mildly annoyed as he pulled up the app and directed an exploit at the target. It took just a few seconds for the remote shell to launch. Soon Leon was typing away as he explored the directory structure of the system. (p. 100)

Near the end of our story Bob, Leon, and Hannah revisit 3DNF to try and collect the rest of the Trojan code used by Pavel in his attack. After performing an nmap scan of the network, Leon points out that one box is running Simple Network Management Protocol (SNMP). SNMP is a management protocol that is used for remote configuration of systems, as well as for performing vitality checks on various systems and services across a network to notify an administrator when a system goes down or is acting unusual, similar to a Nagios server. The trio is not looking to use SNMP; instead, they recognize that it may be vulnerable to an exploit for SNMP that is contained within Metasploit.

For a hacker to perform an attack, he or she will need access to a vast repository of exploit code. An exploit will work on a particular application and version, requiring hackers to gather every exploit that they can find and methodically catalog them for easy reference. The core act of exploitation then comes down to choosing the correct exploit to run against a vulnerable computer and determining how to correctly run the exploit code. The process is even further complicated by exploit code that is poorly written, has no documentation, or is in a foreign language. Not only does a hacker have to learn which exploit to use, but he or she has to learn exactly how to run that exploit code to make it functional.

Metasploit, found at www.metasploit.com, is an open-source software project that aims to make exploit development and delivery much easier for everyone involved. For hackers who are exploiting systems, Metasploit provides a clean and simple interface where the same command line syntax can be used for hundreds of varying exploits, as shown in Figure 4.8. Additionally, by using a common framework for development, exploit writers can quickly and easily develop new exploits that

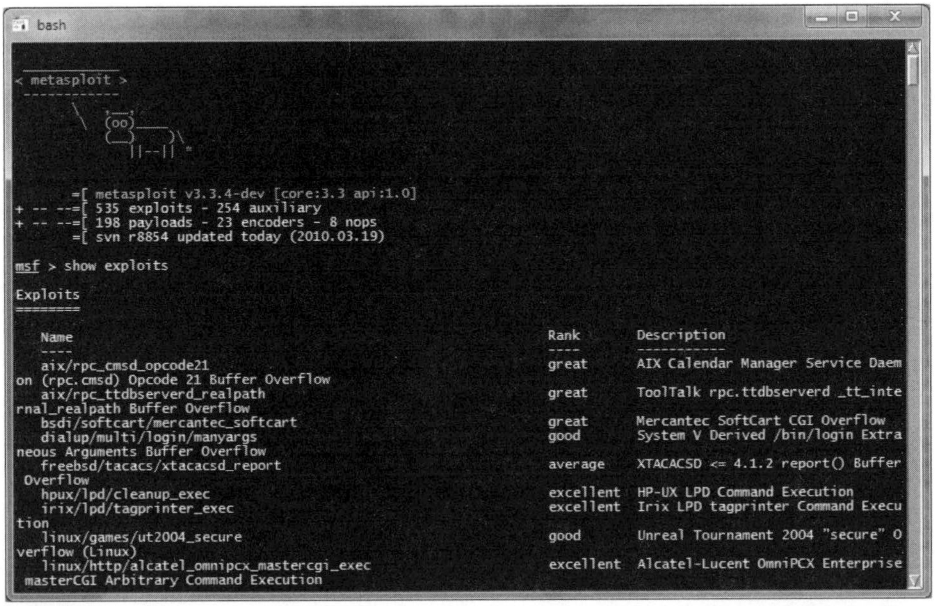

FIGURE 4.8

Metasploit Command Line Interface

plug into the overall system. This allows developers to focus solely on the exploit code without having to write debugging code or a user interface.

Exploit Techniques

Metasploit is easily available to any budding hackers in the community, and it provides a simple interface that makes exploitation easy to pull off. The optional Web-based interface, shown in Figure 4.9, allows for hackers to point and click their way through an entire attack. From here, its user can pick from a list of hundreds of included exploits. Along with exploits, users can also choose from auxiliary modules that perform additional tasks, such as scanning a network for active computers, searching for misconfigured services, or setting up a fake service to capture credentials.

Metasploit has been both praised and criticized for its interface and automated functionality.[49] Metasploit is considered by some to be an evolution in tools for a "script kiddie," a hacker with very little technical ability who runs automated scripts to hack into systems. However, by making attacks easier to perform, Metasploit has allowed authorized network administrators and internal security auditors to easily scan their network for vulnerable systems that need additional security defenses. Upon knowing which exploit to pick, the attacker simply has to pick which type of payload, or exploit deliverable, that he or she wishes to have associated with the attack. These payloads can vary from opening

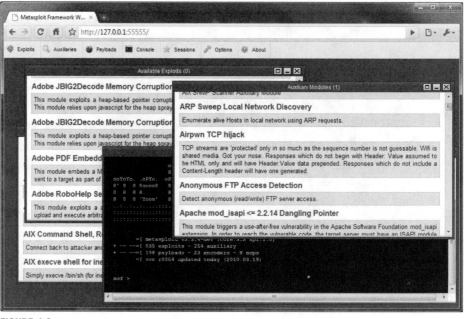

FIGURE 4.9

Metasploit Web Interface

up a command line terminal to adding a new user with administrator rights. The hacker then simply types in the target's IP address and service port, as shown in Figure 4.10, and launches the attack.

Best Practices

There are few defenses against an attacker who runs Metasploit itself. As Metasploit is simply an interface to hundreds of various exploits and scanning routines, your business's network must be properly secured against any vulnerability that Metasploit may exploit. This may initially sound daunting, especially when you consider that many of the Metasploit developers research and develop their own exploits specifically for use in the tool. Using vulnerability information released under full disclosure, exploits can quickly be researched and integrated into Metasploit.

An active internet network security team can take advantage of Metasploit for use in its own defense. By proactively scanning and testing the machines within their network, authorized security engineers can address security issues and rectify them before they are found by malicious attackers. Additionally, monitoring newly developed Metasploit exploits on a regular basis allows security teams to discover new vulnerabilities that they can defend against.

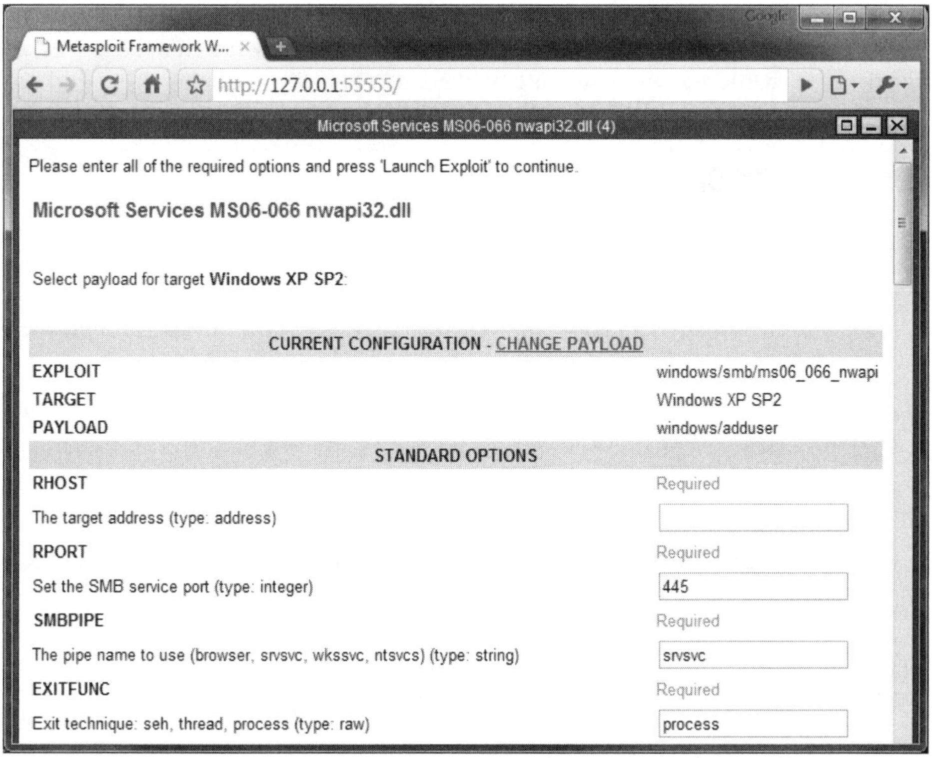

FIGURE 4.10

Configuring an Attack with Metasploit

The best defense against a tool such as Metasploit, and most exploit attacks in general, is to simply maintain a routine system patch policy. This allows your security team to work with network administrators to apply security patches to vulnerable systems before they can be targeted by an attacker.

SUMMARY OF METASPLOIT

For many attackers, a successful intrusion means having an available cache of exploits to use at a moment's notice. However, the major failure of such exploits is that each is written in a nonstandard format with differing interfaces and controls. Metasploit solves this issue by providing a standardized framework by which all exploits are executed in the same manner, making it easier for an attacker to launch them against targets. By using a structured exploitation environment, with standard variables and command structures, Metasploit allows attackers to quickly and easily launch exploits against their targets. This effectively lowers the skill requirement for launching exploits, which allows more attackers, but also allows for greater use within network defense teams. The ease of use allows internal network security teams within large organizations to routinely test their own defenses before an attacker can, while staying up to date on the latest available exploits.

FOR MORE INFORMATION

Metasploit is an ever-evolving application that benefits from a dedicated team of developers. Although we covered the very basics of its use here, Metasploit features an amazing level of depth that can benefit both attackers and network defenders. For more information about this versatile tool, we recommend the following publications:

- *Metasploit Toolkit for Penetration Testing, Exploit Development, and Vulnerability Research* (ISBN: 978-1-59749-074-0, Syngress)

- *Penetration Tester's Open Source Toolkit, Volume 2* (ISBN: 978-1-59749-213-3, Syngress)

- *Writing Security Tools and Exploits* (ISBN: 978-1-59749-997-2, Syngress)

ENDNOTES

1. DataLoss DB. Data Loss Statistics, http://datalossdb.org/statistics?timeframe= all_time; 2010 [accessed 14.03.10].
2. Truecrypt, a variety of bruteforcing options, http://diablohorn.wordpress .com/2009/01/01/truecrypt-variety-of-bruteforcing-options/; 2009 [accessed 11.03.10].
3. Ed Felton. New Research Result: Cold Boot Attacks on Disk Encryption, http:// freedom-to-tinker.com/blog/felten/new-research-result-cold-boot-attacks-disk-encryption; 2008 [accessed 14.03.10].
4. Halderman JA, Schoen SD, Heninger N, Clarkson W, Paul W, Calandrino JA, Feldman AJ, Appelbaum J, Felten EW. Lest We Remember: Cold Boot Attacks on Encryption Keys, http://citp.princeton.edu/memory/; 2010 [accessed 14.03.10].
5. Singel R. Probe Targets Archives' Handling of Data on 70 Million Vets, Wired, http://www.wired.com/threatlevel/2009/10/probe-targets-archives-handling-of-data-on-70-million-vets/; 2009 [accessed 14.03.10].
6. National Crime Information Center, NCIC, http://www.fbi.gov/hq/cjisd/ncic_ brochure.htm; 2010 [accessed 25.03.10].
7. Becrypt. Trusted Client – Bootable USB for Secure Remote Access, http://www .becrypt.com/americas/Products/trusted-client; 2010 [accessed 25.03.10].
8. Zero Day Initiative – Program Benefits, http://www.zerodayinitiative.com/ about/benefits/; 2010 [accessed 25.03.10].
9. Portnoy A. Pwn2Own 2010, TippingPoint DBLabs, http://dvlabs.tippingpoint .com/blog/2010/02/15/pwn2own-2010; 2010 [accessed 25.03.10].

10. Sourcefire, Inc., Snort® Rules, http://www.sourcefire.com/products/snort/rules; 2010 [accessed 25.03.10].

11. Freshmeat. chntpw, http://freshmeat.net/projects/chntpw/; 2010 [accessed 25.03.10].

12. Remote-Exploit. Chntpw, Remote-Exploit.org, http://forums.remote-exploit.org/tutorials-guides/10876-chntpw.html; 2008 [accessed 25.03.10].

13. McWilliams B. How Paris Got Hacked? http://macdevcenter.com/pub/a/mac/2005/01/01/paris.html; 2005 [accessed 13.03.10].

14. Zetter K. Palin E-Mail Hacker Says It Was Easy, Wired, http://www.wired.com/threatlevel/2008/09/palin-e-mail-ha/; 2008 [accessed 13.03.10].

15. Harvey D. Twitter. Reason #4132 for Changing Your Password, http://status.twitter.com/post/367671822/reason-4132-for-changing-your-password; 2010 [accessed 14.03.10].

16. Ricker T. Elcomsoft turns your PC into a password cracking supercomputer (gulp), Engadget, http://www.engadget.com/2007/10/24/elcomsoft-turns-your-pc-into-a-password-cracking-supercomputer/; 2007 [accessed 13.03.10].

17. RenderLab. Church of Wifi WPA-PSK Rainbow Tables, http://www.renderlab.net/projects/WPA-tables/; 2010 [accessed 25.03.10].

18. ophcrack XP Rainbow tables, http://ophcrack.sourceforge.net/tables.php; 2010 [accessed 25.03.10].

19. Tables for this hash routine, Free Rainbow Tables, http://www.freerainbow-tables.com/en/tables/ntlm/; 2010 [accessed 25.03.10].

20. Leyden J. SSD tools crack passwords 100 times faster, The Register, http://www.theregister.co.uk/2010/03/12/password_cracking_on_crack/; 2010 [accessed 25.03.10].

21. O'Dell J. RockYou Hacker: 30% of Sites Store Plain Text Passwords, The New York Times, http://www.nytimes.com/external/readwriteweb/2009/12/16/16readwriteweb-rockyou-hacker-30-of-sites-store-plain-text-13200.html; 2009 [accessed 14.03.10].

22. Gabbatt A. As easy as ABC! Hackers reveal easy-to-crack passwords, Guardian News and Media Limited, http://www.guardian.co.uk/technology/blog/2010/jan/21/rockyou-hackers-reveal-simple-passwords; 2010 [accessed 14.03.10].

23. SANS Institute. SANS Password Policy, http://www.sans.org/security-resources/policies/Password_Policy.pdf; 2010 [accessed 25.03.10].

24. de Souza M. 'Climategate' inquiry shows scientist didn't falsify data, Montreal Gazette, http://www.montrealgazette.com/technology/Climategate+inquiry+shows+scientist+didn+falsify+data/2518522/story.html; 2010 [accessed 14.03.10].

25. Microsoft Support. XLCN: Improving the Security of PST Files, http://support.microsoft.com/kb/143241; 2006 [accessed 24.03.10].

26. Jerry B. 'pst19upg.exe' For Removing PST Password, Article Alley, http://www.articlealley.com/article_719835_11.html; 2008 [accessed 24.03.10].

27. Mosey BM. Why are .PST files a security threat to Exchange Server mailboxes, Search Exchange, http://searchexchange.techtarget.com/generic/0,295582,sid43_gci1320572,00.html; 2008 [accessed 24.03.10].

28. Paton N. Fowarding emails home puts security at risk, workers warned, Management-Issues,http://www.management-issues.com/2007/1/11/research/forwarding-emails-home-puts-security-at-risk-workers-warned.asp;   2007 [accessed 25.03.10].

29. Paul R. Leaked Media Defender e-mails reveal secret government project, Ars Technica, http://arstechnica.com/software/news/2007/09/leaked-media-defender-e-mails-reveal-secret-government-project.ars; 2007 [accessed 25.03.10].

30. Spencer JJ. Prepare for E-Discovery Before a Lawsuit Is Filed, Baseline Magazine, http://www.baselinemag.com/c/a/Legal/Prepare-for-EDiscovery-Before-a-Lawsuit-Is-Filed/; 2009 [accessed 20.03.10].

31. Microsoft Support. A network administrator can add the DisablePST registry value to a registry key so that all the users of a computer cannot create or access Outlook .pst files in Outlook 2003, http://support.microsoft.com/kb/896515; 2009 [accessed 25.03.10].

32. Exploiting The IPC Share, GovernmentSecurity.org, http://www.overnmentsecurity.org/articles/hack-exploit-ipc-share.html; 2009 [accessed 14.03.10].

33. Null Session Vulnerability, Microsoft MSDN, http://msdn.microsoft.com/en-us/library/ms913275(WinEmbedded.5).aspx; 2006 [accessed 14.03.10].

34. Zetter K. 4 Years After TJX Hack, Payment Industry Sets Security Standards, Wired, http://www.wired.com/threatlevel/2009/07/pci/; 2009 [accessed 13.03.10].

35. Nassauer S. Data Breaches Are Heaviest at Hotels, The Wall Street Journal, http://online.wsj.com/article/SB10001424052748704743404575127674094249164.html; 2010 [accessed 14.03.10].

36. McMillan R. Wyndham: 37 hotels were hit in latest hack, CSO Online, http://blogs.csoonline.com/wyndam_37_hotels_were_hacked_in_latest_hack; 2010.

37. Froggy. Wyndham security breach, part 2, Notacon, http://blog.notacon.org/?p=310; 2010.

38. News Tribune. Credit card skim-scam waitress arrested, http://blog.thenews-tribune.com/tntdiner/2008/02/21/credit-card-skim-scam-waitress-arrested/; 2008 [accessed 20.03.10].

39. Fabricant F. After the Meal, the Credit Card Scanner Is Served, The New York Times, http://www.nytimes.com/2007/11/21/dining/21hand.html; 2007 [accessed 20.03.10].

40. Krebs B. Would You Have Spotted the Fraud? Krebs on Security, http://www.krebsonsecurity.com/2010/01/would-you-have-spotted-the-fraud/; 2010 [accessed 20.03.10].

41. Krebs B. ATM Skimmers, Part II, Krebs on Security, http://www.krebsonsecurity.com/2010/02/atm-skimmers-part-ii/; 2010 [accessed 20.03.10].

42. Goodin D. Payment card skimmer secretly planted in gas station pump, The Register, http://www.theregister.co.uk/2010/02/23/card_skimmer_scam/; 2010 [accessed 20.03.10].

43. Krebs B. Data Breach Highlights Role of 'Money Mules,' The Washington Post, http://voices.washingtonpost.com/securityfix/2009/09/money_mules_carry_loot_for_org.html; 2009 [accessed 20.03.10].

44. Krebs B. 'Money Mules' Help Haul Criminals' Loot, The Washington Post, http://www.washingtonpost.com/wp-dyn/content/article/2008/01/25/AR2008012501435.html; 2008 [accessed 20.03.10].

45. The Finance Buff. One-Time Credit Card Numbers for More Security, http://thefinancebuff.com/2009/01/one-time-credit-card-numbers-for-more-security.html; 2009 [accessed 21.03.10].

46. Microsoft MSDN. TCP/IP Raw Sockets, http://msdn.microsoft.com/en-us/library/ms740548(VS.85).aspx; 2010 [accessed 25.03.10].

47. Spoofer Project: Spoofer Main, http://spoofer.csail.mit.edu; 2010 [accessed 25.03.10].

48. Dingledine R. Tor: The Second-Generation Onion Router, Nick Mathewson, Paul Syverson, http://tor.eff.org/doc/design-paper/tor-design.html; 2010 [accessed 25.03.10].

49. Feid A. Easy Pentesting: Metasploit's db_autopwn, http://allanfeid.com/content/easy-pentesting-metasploits-dbautopwn; 2009 [accessed 26.03.10].

Expunge

5

Expunging is the process of destroying information to cover the tracks of the attacker. These steps allow a computer user to remove traces of their activity from a computer so that someone else cannot determine what was done. Every modern computer system features a logging ability that tracks when certain activities take place. These logs could encompass all of the activities taken by users on the system, and they could also log activity from the attacker. This chapter will cover a few of the basic methods to erase information and help obscure an attacker's presence on a computer system.

REMOVING WINDOWS LOGIN TRACES

> ### THE HACK DISSECTED
>
> *Pavel took Stepan's laptop from Vlad and blanked the three Windows event log files. Next, he changed the "last logged in user" registry key so that it would appear that Stepan's account was the last one used.* (p. 8)

Early in our story, Pavel and Vlad hack into Stepan's computer to gather details on their employer and the job that he has for them. Pavel used a Linux bootable operating system on a Universal Serial Bus (USB) drive to change the password of the Administrator account and gain control of the system. However, when he was done siphoning off the information from the laptop, he went the extra step of cleaning up after himself and removing traces that he was on the computer at that time.

Exploit Techniques

There are many ways in which an attacker can remove the traces of his or her actions after the attacker's work is done on a hacked system. All modern operating systems have account auditing and logging enabled in some form to log information on when users log in and log off of the system, which can help place a physical person at the keyboard during an investigation. In other cases, the computer may log all of the activities that a person performed while he or she had logged in. There may be additional locations in which data is stored, but only if the attacker knows where to look for it.

Event Logs

Microsoft Windows stores all notable events into a collection of log files called the *event logs*. These logs store information about events that occur on a regular basis from within the Windows operating system and from the applications that run on it. When viewed through the integrated Windows Event Viewer application, event logs are commonly the first area that a system administrator monitors when something goes amiss. Assuming that Stepan would return to work with the laptop in tow, Pavel expunged the records of his work on the system by completely removing the three event logs on it.

Although Windows stores events into a collection of event logs, each log stores a particular type of data. There are three main log files that have been in use since the event logs first appeared in Windows NT: Application, Security, and System.[1] We'll explore the details of these individual logs in the "Best Practices" section under "Event Logs", but suffice it to say at this point that these three logs store many types of information that a hacker would want erased.

In the Windows NT and XP environments, these logs are stored in the %SystemRoot%\System32\Config directory or, for most computers, C:\Windows\System32\Config. Here, they are named as AppEvent.evt, SecEvent.evt, and SysEvent .evt. Although most computer systems have the operating system installed onto the C: volume, there are a rare few that choose another volume; the %SystemRoot% is automatically replaced by the actual drive letter to make it work on all systems.

In a Windows Vista or Windows 7 environment, these logs are stored in %SystemRoot\System32\winevt\Logs, normally seen as C:\Windows\System32\winevt\Logs. They have a different naming convention of Application.evtx, Security .evtx, and System.evtx.

Typically, these files are locked by an Event Logger service running on the system, preventing a user from simply deleting the file outright. However, in a hurry, their contents can always be cleared from within the Event Viewer application itself. This is done by highlighting the log that you wish to be cleared and selecting from the pull-down menu the **Action | Clear Log...** item, as shown in Figure 5.1. This will immediately remove all entries from the specified log, but it will leave a trace event that shows that the log was cleared at the current date and time.

Last Logged-In User Key

Immediately after cleaning out the event logs, the story notes that Pavel cleared the "last logged in user" registry key. This is an actual value in the Windows registry that stores which account last logged into the computer. This information is stored in the following registry key:

```
HKEY_LOCAL_MACHINE\SOFTWARE\Microsoft\Windows NT\CurrentVersion\
   Winlogon\DefaultUserName
```

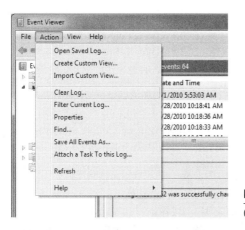

FIGURE 5.1

Clearing a Windows Event Log

FIGURE 5.2

Windows Last Logged-In User Key

This registry key, shown in Figure 5.2, will record the last user name that was manually logged into the system.[2] As Pavel logged into Stepan's laptop as Administrator, that name would show up in this registry entry. To clear his trails, as Stepan would not have been able to log in as Administrator, Pavel changed this entry from "Administrator" to Stepan's account name.

Best Practices

When an attacker reviews the logs shown here, he or she finds the information stored directly in Windows by the operating system itself. As this data is needed for system purposes, it may not be possible to either block its usage or modify it. For example, any user who has the administrative rights to the system can open the Registry Editor and change the DefaultUserName field shown earlier. There is nothing to prevent this as long as the attacker has administrative rights to the machine. Your defenses will have to be set well ahead of this point to prevent a hacker from obtaining administrative rights in the first place.

Event Logs

Unlike protecting against a registry edit, there are steps that you can take to maintain the event logs in your Windows systems, even when they have been deleted or modified. But, first, let's look at what data is contained within these files.

The Application log stores events created by applications running on the system. This file normally logs errors and warnings given by applications, such as when they crash or exhibit noticeable errors. An example of this is shown in Figure 5.3, where an entry is shown for a Mozilla Firefox crash. The event records the exact time and date when the application crashed, as well as basic debugging information. This information shows that Firefox crashed because of a faulting module named FOXITR~1.OCX.

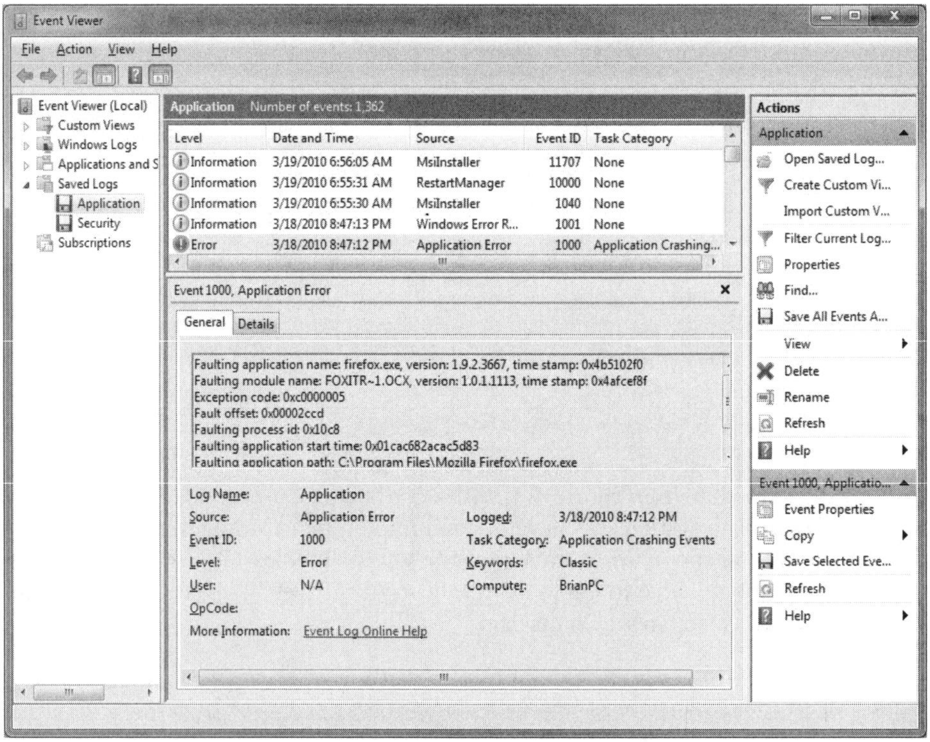

FIGURE 5.3

Windows Application Event Log

Tracking down that file leads to the FoxitReaderOCX.ocx plug-in for Firefox, part of Foxit Reader, a free PDF viewer from www.FoxitSoftware.com. This event coincided with the Web browser opening a corrupted PDF document and subsequently crashing.

The Security log is used by Windows to track security events such as account logins and logoffs, as shown in Figure 5.4. It also notes when accounts attempt to read, modify, or delete protected audit files. On a properly configured system, this log reports any activity that would trigger a security audit for suspicious behavior.

The System log deals with system-level errors and warnings, such as those produced by device drivers and system services. This log will detail hardware issues, as well as when services are started and stopped. Additionally, it will display any error messages that appear at the service level, such as the DNS errors shown in Figure 5.5.

While the Application, Security, and System logs are the primary source of data for system events, Microsoft has included additional new logs with each recent

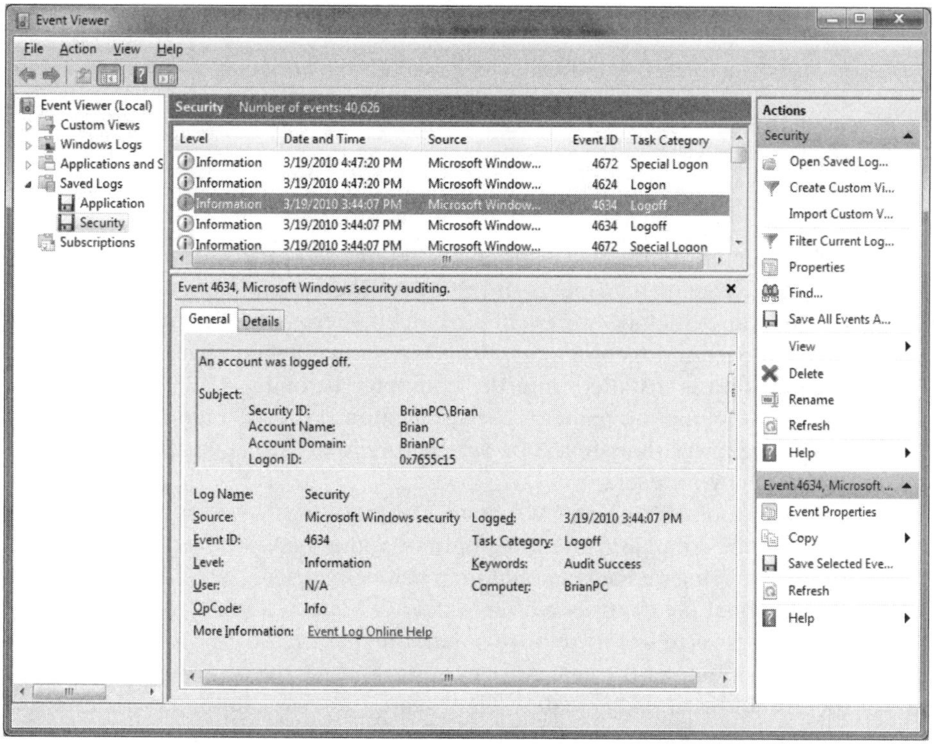

FIGURE 5.4

Windows Security Event Log

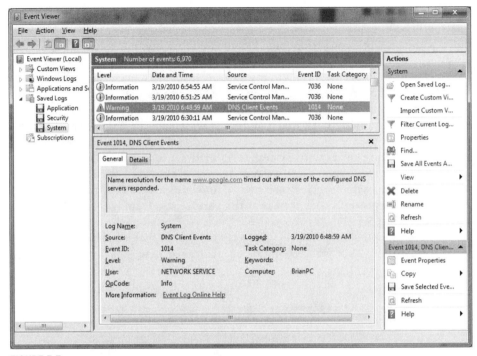

FIGURE 5.5

Windows System Event Log

release of Windows. Windows Vista and Windows 7 feature dozens of various event logs that cover many aspects of the operating system. For example, recent versions of Windows include one event file named Microsoft-Windows-Application-Experience%4Program-Inventory.evtx. This log, shown in Figure 5.6, will log every time an application is installed onto the computer through official setup scripts. Each entry will include the name of the application installed and its version number. This is a log entry that should be scanned regularly to audit the applications being installed by your users.

In earlier versions of Microsoft Windows, the event logs were vulnerable to deletion easily from the command line. By simply stopping the Windows services associated with the event logs, a hacker could then manually delete or rename the entries. However, additional file controls within Windows Vista and Windows 7 have made it difficult for hackers to simply remove or edit the files. In the case that a hacker has cleared event logs, one of the best ways to mitigate the issue is to simply have backups of the event logs already created. The backup process can be completed using the integrated command line tool "wevtutil.exe."

To create a regular backup using the wevtutil utility, you can create a new scheduled task in the Windows Task Scheduler. Create a new task inside Task Scheduler

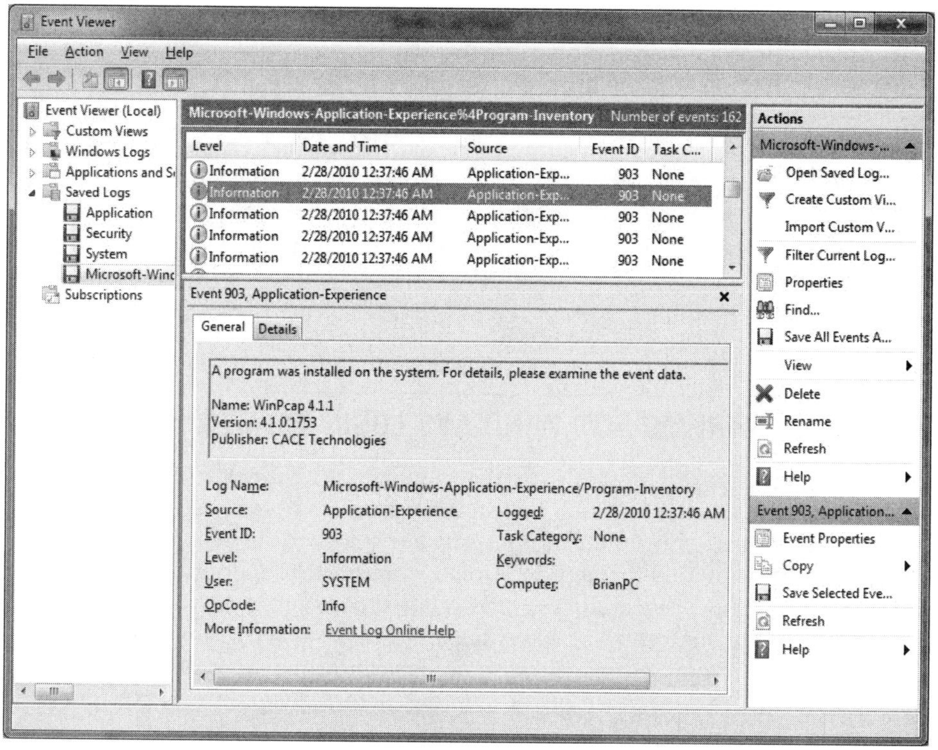

FIGURE 5.6

Windows Application Inventory Log

and set the trigger to occur on a daily schedule and to repeat every 5 min indefinitely. For an action, start a batch file similar to the following:

```
@echo off
for /f "tokens=2-4 delims=/" %%a in ('date /t') do (set
   mydate=%%c-%%a-%%b)
for /f "tokens=1-2 delims=/:" %%a in ("%TIME%") do (set
   mytime=%%a%%b)
:Above code takes the current date and time and strips out the
   illegal
:filename characters, from http://stackoverflow.com/
   questions/203090

wevtutil epl Security C:\Users\_Hidden\SecurityBackup-
   %mydate%_%mytime%.evtx
```

This batch file, which is saved with a .bat extension and placed anywhere on your system, sets a foundation for creating your own customized script. Currently, the script retrieves the current date and time and strips out the illegal colon and slash characters, allowing these values to be placed into the filename. The wevtutil utility is then run to export the Security log into the file C:\Users_Hidden\SecurityBackup-%mydate%_%mytime%.evtx, although the folder location can be changed to meet your needs.

Ensure that the task is configured to run at the highest elevated privileges, to allow the script to access the Security log. After being enabled, the task will then start creating backups of your Security log in 5-min intervals. Naturally, this will eventually fill your hard drive, so you will need to modify the script to place limits or run clean-up routines. However, this is a basic example to show that it can be done.

SUMMARY OF REMOVING WINDOWS LOGIN TRACES

Performing an exploit is only the first step in attacking a network system. Once an attacker has gained a foothold and stolen the resources needed from a system, the attacker will attempt to clean up his or her traces to throw off any investigative efforts. We saw this through multiple examples throughout our story, and it is a tactic used widely by attackers. It is relatively easy to remove basic traces of a normal login through the Windows Registry Editor, as we discussed in this section. Although removing the basic system logs can prove more difficult, they are targeted by attackers because of the copious details they store on system-wide operations.

System administrators can perform basic mitigation to help prevent many of these attacks through proper security and backups of their system logs. With a proper backup strategy, an administrator can still retrieve details of an attack even if the logs are wiped clean.

FOR MORE INFORMATION

For this chapter, we've covered the basics on log scrubbing to remove traces of an attack. There are a variety of dedicated tools for this task and additional ways to protect against them. For more information, we refer you to the following Web sites:

- WinZapper tool: http://ntsecurity.nu/toolbox/winzapper/

- ClearLogs tool: http://ntsecurity.nu/toolbox/clearlogs/

- How to Delete Corrupt Event Viewer Log Files: www.windowsnetworking .com/kbase/WindowsTips/WindowsNT/AdminTips/EventLogs/HowtoDelete-CorruptEventViewerLogFiles.html

- Back Up Your Event Logs with a Windows PowerShell Script: http://technet. microsoft.com/en-us/magazine/2009.07.heyscriptingguy.aspx

BROWSER CLEANUP

THE HACK DISSECTED
The sound of a car door out front announced Vlad's return. Pavel surfed to the Black Hat conference site and then cleared his browser cache before Vlad walked in. (p. 115)

In our story, Pavel is just beginning to worry about his working relationship with Vlad. He fears that his life may be in danger and starts creating a contingency plan for escaping the area. At that moment, Vlad returns to their hideout and Pavel quickly cleans up his traces. He switches to the Black Hat Web site, a site that Vlad would expect him to be on, and clears his browser cache.

By clearing his browser cache, Pavel removes all traces of his Web surfing history. He hides the airlines and car rental Web sites that he was browsing just minutes before. If Vlad did attempt to view Pavel's history, he would see a blank slate.

Exploit Techniques

Clearing the history of a Web browser has become a common technique in the daily browsing of many people. It allows for privacy while surfing the Web by removing a user's activity log so that others can't see it at a later point.[3] Additionally, by clearing away the large amount of cached data on your hard drive, clearing the history can improve Web browser performance.

The typical Web browser records many aspects of our daily Web-browsing activities. Every individual Web page that you view is stored, as well as copies of every page, image, and movie that you viewed. Additionally, all typed user names and passwords and every file downloaded is also stored. Modern Web browsers give you the ability to clear out this information, as shown by the Delete Browsing History window for Internet Explorer 8 in Figure 5.7.

Although these options are normally buried within the multiple pull-down menus of their respective browsers, all modern browsers feature a universal keyboard shortcut to quickly bring up the history deletion function: Ctrl + Shift + Del. Upon pressing these three keys simultaneously, the browser's history deletion window will appear. While each browser has a slightly different style to their functions, they all operate the same way. Internet Explorer 8's feature is shown in Figure 5.7 while Mozilla Firefox and Google Chrome's are shown, in respective order, in Figure 5.8.

Private Browsing

Although modern browsers allow for users to clean up their browsing history before signing off, they also offer a feature to prevent the system from logging this information in the first place. Known as private browsing, though with differing names between Web browsers, the feature blocks cookies and Web browsing history from being stored to the local system. It will also not store the information you type into online forms nor cache any of the data to the hard drive.

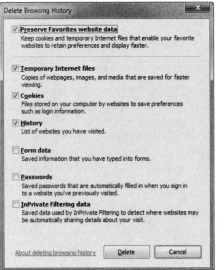

FIGURE 5.7

Internet Explorer 8 Delete Browsing History Window

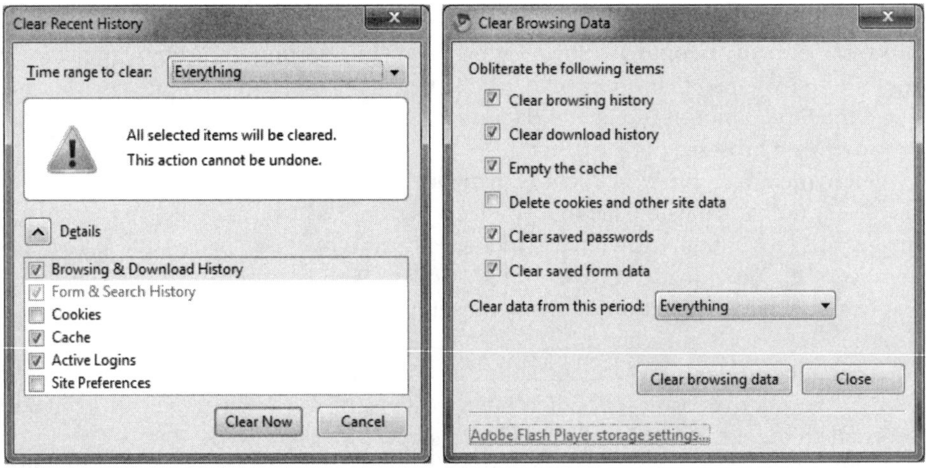

FIGURE 5.8

Mozilla Firefox and Google Chrome's Respective History Delete Windows

In Internet Explorer, this feature is known as *InPrivate Browsing*. Although InPrivate Browsing will not store search entries or Web sites, it does cache data to the hard drive. This cached data is deleted when you close the browser, but it can be recovered through basic forensics. InPrivate Browsing is enabled by selecting **Safety | InPrivate Browsing** from the pull-down menu. Details on Internet Explorer's InPrivate Browsing can be found at http://windows.microsoft.com/en-us/Windows7/What-is-InPrivate-Browsing.

Mozilla Firefox also offers a Private Browsing feature with many of the same abilities. Its Private Browsing also blocks cookies and browser history from being stored to the local system. It is enabled from the pull-down menu under **Tools | Start Private Browsing**. Greater detail on Firefox's Private Browsing is found at http://support.mozilla.com/en-US/kb/Private+Browsing.

Google's Chrome browser has the same feature set as the other major Web browsers in a feature they call Incognito Mode. Their implementation of private browsing is slightly different from Internet Explorer and Firefox. Upon selecting **Tools (wrench icon) | New Incognito Window** from the pull-down menu, a new browser window will open in private mode. Google Chrome then allows you to have a simultaneous Incognito window and a normal browsing window. Additionally, while in Incognito mode, Chrome disables all of your browser extensions and add-ons. This prevents your private information from being leaked through third-party applications.

Best Practices

As these options are controlled by the browser itself, it is difficult to control their use as an administrator. The one exception is Internet Explorer 7 and later versions, for which there is a group policy that allows you to disable the ability to delete browsing history. This setting can be found in the Group Policy editor under **Administrative Templates | Windows Components | Internet Explorer | Delete Browser History**. Under this final folder is a setting to **Turn off "Delete Browsing History" functionality,** along with various other deletion controls.[4]

For serious infractions that absolutely require determining the browser history, it may be possible to forensically recover the deleted browser cache files after they've been erased. This would assist in helping to see what content the user downloaded, and some sites, but may be limited. For instance, in Mozilla Firefox, all history details are now stored in miniature databases that are scrubbed clean after a user has deleted his or her browsing history.

SUMMARY OF BROWSER CLEANUP

As many attacks are beginning to use the Web browser as an attack vector, criminals have more of a need to clean their tracks on the browser itself. Additionally, even basic research and reconnaissance activities exist within the Web browser cache that can incriminate an attacker or a researcher in the middle of their tasks. The information stored within the browser cache can pinpoint the Web pages that a user browsed, as well as the content that he or she had viewed and downloaded. Not only can this store private data but also potentially embarrassing information for the user. For basic privacy reasons, all of the major Web browsers now support the ability to scrub browser history files and statistics, although this is also taken advantage of by attackers. Although users can easily clear their personal browsing history, an attacker can also scrub the history on their own computers in the event that their equipment is seized by law enforcement. For businesses, your employees are also able to clear their browsing history to remove evidence of activity on unauthorized Web sites. There is little that can be done by a company to protect against this action, though. Forcing users to use a modern version of Internet Explorer, blocking any alternative browser, and disabling the ability to remove the browsing history can maintain the cache on a system that the company controls. Beyond this, the risk is always present.

FOR MORE INFORMATION

We've covered much of the ability to scrub a user's history and activities from a Web browser in this chapter, as well as how to enter private browsing mode. There are a few topics that we were not able to cover here, especially in the realm of best practices. The following Web sites cover some of the various aspects of recovering data from a Web browser, as well as some of the ways in which data can still be leaked out even while private browsing is enabled.

- Web Browser Forensics – Part 1: www.symantec.com/connect/articles/web-browser-forensics-part-1

- Web Browser Forensics – Part 2: www.symantec.com/connect/articles/web-browser-forensics-part-2

- Why Private Browsing Isn't...: http://ouseful.wordpress.com/2009/07/15/why-private-browsing-isnt/

ENDNOTES

1. How to view and manage event logs in Event Viewer in Windows XP, Microsoft Support, http://support.microsoft.com/kb/308427; 2007 [accessed 18-03-10].
2. DefaultUserName, http://technet.microsoft.com/en-us/library/cc939710.aspx; 2010 [accessed 18-03-10].
3. Rick B. Erase Internet Explorer 8's Browsing History, The Washington Post, www.washingtonpost.com/wp-dyn/content/article/2010/03/03/AR2010030302628.html; 2010 [accessed 18-03-10].
4. Prevent users from deleting IE browsing history, Online Tech Tips, www.online-tech-tips.com/internet-explorer-tips/prevent-users-from-deleting-ie-browsing-history/; 2009 [accessed 18-03-10].

Hacker Culture

6

This part of the story – for the real-world steps are as much a part of the story as the fiction of Bob and Leon – will also introduce you to the underlying hacking culture. Unlike most Hollywood movies, the line between the good guys and the bad is not clearly defined; there are no black and white motives. Everything is in shades of gray. To be able to fully understand a hacker, you must understand the culture they thrive in. What makes a person want to attack a remote computer? What information are they trying to collect? Are they even trying to collect information or are they in it for sport? These are difficult questions that change dramatically over time. As we've seen in our story, it is very easy to tempt a good guy into doing bad work. It is also just as easy to convince a bad guy to help out the good guys. It all comes down to understanding the roles that each person has in an attack situation and their ultimate expected outcomes.

HACKING CELEBRITIES

THE HACK DISSECTED

Bob turned to Leon. A smile spread across his face as the enormity of the story he had just told sunk in. "Dude, do you know what we just did? We just saved the United States! That's bigger than saving the Internet! That means we're bigger than Dan Kaminsky! Or Tony Watson!"

Leon looked exasperated. "Bob, we aren't even up there with GOBBLES. Or n3td3v for that matter."

Bob's shoulders dropped a little and he asked almost plaintively, "Well then won't we at least get an interview with Stephen Colbert?"

"Sorry, Dude, I wouldn't be expecting a call even from Letterman," Leon responded with a satisfied smile as things got back to normal. (p. 125)

As the story draws to a close, our heroes reflect back on their adventures and ponder their own impact in the events. After realizing that they stopped an advanced team of cyber criminals, Bob states that they're now more popular than Dan Kaminsky and Tony Watson.

Leon takes a more cynical view of their situations, thinking that Bob is overplaying their work. Leon counters that they won't even be as popular as GOBBLES or n3td3v.

Dan Kaminsky

Dan Kaminsky is a well-known security researcher that is known for his work with the Domain Name System (DNS) protocol and security issues related with it. Kaminsky had success in performing penetration testing on business networks and software products and was an author of *Hack Proofing Your Network, Second Edition* (ISBN: 978-1-928994-70-1, Syngress) and a contributing author to *Stealing the Network: The Complete Series Collector's Edition, Final Chapter, and DVD* (ISBN: 978-1-59749-299-7, Syngress). Kaminsky didn't fully become a celebrity until his disclosure of a large security flaw within the DNS in 2008. The flaw that Kaminsky discovered allowed for a DNS server's cache of addresses to be poisoned, or altered, to redirect traffic meant for a legitimate company to an attacker's personal server.[1]

Kaminsky worked with a small team of DNS experts in secrecy to generate a patch for the flaw, which they then released to the public without any details on the flaw itself. Many computer security experts were concerned at installing a patch without knowing why it was needed,[2] as the details were intended to be kept secret until Kaminsky's scheduled talk at the Black Hat security briefings later that year. But this was likely the best method to ensure that the vulnerability could not be exploited by hackers before proper defenses could be stood up. However, the information was eventually leaked out to the public,[3] allowing for an exploit to be quickly developed and released for Metasploit.

Tony Watson

Before Kaminsky a similar story played out with security researcher Paul "Tony" Watson. Watson discovered a flaw within the Transmission Control Protocol (TCP) across the Internet, which allowed attackers to inflict TCP Reset attacks against victims.[4] By using particularly spoofed packets, an attacker can cause a denial of service (DoS) against another computer on the Internet by terminating an already established TCP connection.[5] When used en masse, the attack could decimate large portions of the Internet backbone. Watson worked with developers and vendors to craft a patch to mitigate the issue before his presentation at the 2004 CanSecWest security conference. Ever since his discovery and its subsequent patching, Watson has been known as *The Man Who Saved the Internet*,[6] prompting Bob's comment of "That's bigger than saving the Internet!"

GOBBLES Security

GOBBLES is the name of a security research group[7] that released regular security advisories on Internet security issues.[8] The group was most publicly notable for a press release where they announced that they were working with the Recording

Industry Association of America (RIAA), a copyright protection group reviled by many in the hacking community. GOBBLES stated that they had released a Trojan that would spread across peer-to-peer (P2P) networks, inventorying audio files on computers and reporting the results back to the RIAA.[9] The GOBBLES group later recanted the story, noting that it was simply a tactic to attract attention.[10]

n3td3v

In the long line of Internet trolls, none may be as well known as n3td3v. For a number of years, n3td3v frequented the Full Disclosure mailing list at https://lists.grok .org.uk/mailman/listinfo/full-disclosure, posting controversial arguments and counterpoints to discussions on the forum.[11] There have been extensive studies into the background of the n3td3v account to determine the actual person, or persons, behind the account,[12] but the account owner continued to enjoy their anonymity until late in 2009 when details of the alleged n3td3v were released to support his defense.[13]

Stephen Colbert

Stephen Colbert is a widely popular entertainer who hosts a political satire program called *The Colbert Report* (pronounced "cole-bare re-pore") on the Comedy Central television network. Colbert is an admitted technology junkie who revels in new gadgets and was noted as one of the first consumers to use the new Apple iPad when he showed it off at the 2010 Grammy Awards[14] weeks before its release. Colbert is well known for his viral attacks on Wikipedia content through his own term *wikiality*, where false information posted to Wikipedia can be considered reality if enough people agree with it.[15] He is also well known for his orchestrated social attacks, where he commands a large army of Internet volunteers to perform online anonymous actions in his honor, such as voting for his namesake on the Hungarian Megyeri Bridge[16] and on a NASA space node for the International Space Station (ISS). Although he won both of these competitions, his name ultimately wasn't chosen, though the ISS treadmill did receive his namesake as the Combined Operational Load Bearing External Resistance Treadmill (COLBERT).[17] Colbert is a modern example of how a single person can social engineer the masses in order to influence change on the Internet.

CONFERENCES

In the security industry, much of the ideas and concepts that are implemented by practitioners are shared through annual or one-off security conferences. There are dozens of security conferences held each year that vary in their scope and focus. Some attract only a few hundred visitors while others attract thousands, with a handful keeping strict capacity limits to keep their attendance to a manageable amount. The most attractive reason to attend security conferences is the opportunity to network with other security professionals. Information security professionals can develop relationships that bolster professional development and assist in future collaboration. Organizations benefit from the knowledge that their employees gain by attending conferences by being able to stay on top of the latest trends and security threats facing the industry.

Below is a list of a variety of security conferences that may be of interest to you.

- ARES, The International Dependability Conference (The International Conference on Availability, Reliability and Security): www.ares-conference.eu/conf/

- Best of Open Source Security (BOSS) Conference: www.bossconference.com/

- Black Hat: www.blackhat.com/

- BlueHat: http://technet.microsoft.com/en-us/security/cc261637.aspx

- BruCON: www.brucon.org/index.php/Main_Page

- CanSecWest: http://cansecwest.com/index.html;   http://cansecwest.com/dojo.html

- Chaos Communication Congress (CCC): http://events.ccc.de/congress/

- Computer and Communications Security (CCS): www.sigsac.org/ccs/CCS2010/

- Computer and Enterprise Investigations Conference (CEIC): www.ceicconference.com/

- Computer Forensics Show: www.computerforensicshow.com/

- Computer Security Institute Annual Conference (CSI): www.gocsi.com/

- Computer Security Institute Security Exchange (CSI-SX): www.csisx.com/

- CONFidence: http://confidence.org.pl/

- DeepSec In-Depth Security Conference: https://deepsec.net/

- DEFCON: www.defcon.org/

- DojoSec Monthly Briefings: www.dojosec.com/

- Ekoparty Security Conference: www.ekoparty.com.ar/

- EUSecWest: http://eusecwest.com/index.html

- ExcaliburCon: www.newcamelotcouncil.com/

- FRHACK International IT Security Conference: www.frhack.org/

- Hack.in: www.security.iitk.ac.in/hack.in/

- Hack in the box (HITBSecConf): https://conference.hackinthebox.org/

- Hacker Halted: www.hackerhalted.com/

- IPTComm: Principles, Systems and Applications of IP Telecommunications: http://iptcomm.org/

- Infosecurity Europe: www.infosec.co.uk/

- International Conference on Security and Cryptography (SECRYPT): www.secrypt.org/

- International Workshop on Fast Software Encryption (FSE): https://www.cosic.esat.kuleuven.be/fse2009/

- Internet Security Operations and Intelligence (ISOI): www.isotf.org/isoi6.html

- Kiwicon: www.kiwicon.org/

- LayerOne: http://layerone.info/

- PH-Neutral: http://ph-neutral.darklab.org/

- PacSec: http://pacsec.jp/

- RSA: www.rsaconference.com/

- Rocky Mountain Information Security Conference (RMISC): www.issa-denver.org/RMISC.htm

- SEaCURE.it: www.seacure.it/

- SecTor, Security Education Conference Toronto: www.sector.ca/

- SecureWorld Expo: www.secureworldexpo.com/

- Shakacon: www.shakacon.org/

- ShmooCon: www.shmoocon.org/

- SOURCE Conference: www.sourceconference.com/

- SyScan: www.syscan.org/

- Techno Forensics and Techno Security Conferences: www.thetrainingco.com/

- THOTCON: http://thotcon.org

- ToorCamp: www.toorcamp.org/

- ToorCon: www.toorcon.org/

- uCon: http://ucon-conference.org/

- USENIX Security Symposium: www.usenix.org/

- Workshop on Collaboration and Security (COLSEC): www.univ-orleans.fr/lifo/Manifestations/COLSEC/

- XCon: http://xcon.xfocus.org/
- You Shot the Sheriff: http://ysts.org

The Four Points of the Hacking Compass (From BruCON to DEFCON and Beijing to Brazil)

Jayson Street, the author of our fictional story, has been ingrained in the security industry for many years. He regularly attends dozens of conferences each year worldwide and has written his thoughts on conferences he has personally attended. Below are his thoughts on a variety of conferences offered throughout the year.

BruCON

I was lucky enough to be able to speak at the 1st BruCON Conference in Brussels, Belgium. I was impressed right out of the gate how easy it went. I am sure there was a lot of chaos. What was impressive was that this chaos was not apparent to the attendees or speakers. This conference brings speakers from all over the world and all disciplines of Information Security. I have been to a quite a few conferences around the world but this was the template to follow. The reason was how quickly the speakers and attendees mixed and interacted with each other. Information was not a one-way street but it was a place to learn as well as teach. This is a conference to keep an eye on because if they can keep that atmosphere and energy it will soon be one of the must-attend conferences in Europe.

PH-Neutral

It is my firm belief that a lot of the research you see at conferences like CCC or DEFCON was conceived over drinks between attendees at PH. If you have ever asked yourself what would happen if you got all the smartest and creative minds in the field of hacking and INFOSEC in one place PH is the answer. FX started this conference as a small get-together and he has watched it grow beyond expectations every year. If you are lucky enough to be able to get invited to this conference in Berlin there is NO excuse for not making the trip! Prepare for great conversation, talks, and awesome dance beats!

XCon

One of the things that struck me as most disconcerting about the XCon hacking conference held in Beijing was the porcelain china tea cups for everyone. No matter what the topic you never forgot you were expected to be on your best behavior. This was a great hacking conference but it was subdued and formal. There was no mixing or much interaction between strangers at the event. There were speakers speaking then people discussing with their close associates what they heard during the breaks when you left.

ShmooCon

Imagine a small (compared to other mega conferences that get such big names) con where you not only get to hear great talks but you get to speak and discuss with the speakers afterwards. That is ShmooCon. Of course the 2010 con had a nice wrinkle of snowing everyone in so now you also have the "we are all in this together" atmosphere.

ShmooCon brings a lot of people from all over the world and the mixture of games and multiple approaches to hacking (hardware, software, and biological). This gives you an actual chance to not only see great talks but also the chance for you to interact on a one-on-one basis with a lot of cool people who more likely than not share your same interest. Bruce and Heidi Potter and the Shmoo Group have put in a lot of work to make sure that the con stays not just small but manageable and personal and to make sure you just don't have a great time but you take away some good knowledge you didn't have before.

SYSCAN

SYSCAN Shanghai was one part conference one part CORE training class. It was an interesting concept to listen to some really great and educational talks. Then you were able to take some of that and try to implement it. Being just a regular attendee and not a speaker I was thankful to Thomas Lim who invited me to the dinners and just generally hung out with the SYSCAN crew. Shanghai has a more Western casual setting, where it was acceptable to speak with strangers, making it nice to be able to hang out with others. If you live in Asia and are not able to travel too much then the SYSCAN conferences are for you.

ExcaliburCon

In full disclosure I have to state that I am one of the founders and organizers of this conference. There are other conferences in China but Excalibur-Con right out the gate has proven to be the most Western and open of the INFOSEC conferences in China. I was questioned, "Why bring so many speakers to China?" The answer was simple: if they can't get to the information bring it to them! From the heart of the hacker credo, "Information wants to be free" and hackers do not recognize race, politics or religious beliefs. If I do so say myself it turned out to be one of the biggest conferences in China. It will only grow and bring more information to those who are willing to learn and willing to share it.

DEFCON

By reading the story you can see that DEFCON holds a special place in my heart. I am not the only one who has been blown away and overcome with the energy and experience that is DEFCON. It is wild, crazy, and a safe kind of dangerous all rolled into a multi-educational party. If you can take the lack of sleep and a year of exploits coming at you in 3 days you will be thankful you made the trip. There is after over 17 years something for everyone. If you want to pick a lock, program a robot, or just play CTF and watch the sheep scrolling along the wall DEFCON has it.

CCC

Taking place every year for over 25 years the week between Christmas and New Years in Berlin is the Chaos Communication Congress. This is the biggest and oldest hacking conference in Europe.[18] I do mean HACKING; this conference is not for the INFOSEC cert. carrying crowd. This is a conference for the hacker wanting to get his hands dirty and actually do the things he sees being talked about onstage. This is also a place where politics are not just discussed but acted on. With so many people hiding in the shadows not willing to take a stand on any issues it was inspiring to see so many hackers take to the streets in a march supporting the abolition of laws that threaten privacy and individual rights.

UCon

In a land where hacking laws are notoriously weak[19] it was interesting to see how the hacker community in Brazil was dealing with the issue. So I went there for UCon Conference. It was a small one-day affair that had speakers from all over the world. It was worth the trip to see and meet people I have read about. I am not sure if this conference will continue. Though, if not, there are two other conferences in Brazil, H2HC and YSTS, that are still going and getting bigger and better every year.

Security Meetups

While annual, formalized conferences have proven to be a focal atmosphere for information exchange, there has been a recent movement toward a more informal and regular set of security meetings. One example is CitySec, a movement where groups of volunteer organizers from various metropolitan areas conduct a monthly meeting for regional security professionals to casually discuss their work and personal projects. CitySec meetings are unique in that there is no scheduled agenda or presentations and typically no sponsors. They simply allow professionals and hobbyists to mix and discuss the pressing needs of the day. A sample listing of the CitySec meetings is featured below:

- BaySec (San Francisco, CA): www.baysec.net

- BeanSec (Boston, MA): www.beansec.org

- CharmSec (Baltimore, MD): www.charmsec.org

- ChiSec (Chicago, IL): www.sockpuppet.org/chisec/

- NYSec (Manhattan, NY): www.sockpuppet.org/nysec/

Alongside CitySec meetups, there is also the Austin Hackers Association (AHA!). AHA! and its shoot-off groups typically revolve around short and relevant dinner presentations by peers in the community. In fact, participation is mandatory for membership in the group, ensuring fresh briefings and discussions every month. While the Austin association is the largest and oldest, with meetings tracing back to 2006, others have appeared across the country to emulate its successful design. Additional details on AHA! and its kin can be found at http://wiki.austinhackers.org/ our-spawn. As of April 2010, the following groups exist:

- AHA! – Austin Hackers Association

- CSHA – Colorado Springs Hackers Anonymous

- DOH! – Dallas Order of Hackers

- HAHA! – Houston Area Hackers Anonymous

- NoVAH! – Northern Virginia Hackers

- SAHA! – San Antonio Hackers Association

Also notable are the infamous 2600 meetings that occur on a monthly basis in many cities. We will cover these in Chapter 7, "Bit Bucket."

FOR MORE INFORMATION

As shown here, there are dozens of security conferences that are of great importance to practitioners in the field. Choosing which conferences to focus on for yourself and your group is a personal decision, but there are a wealth of choices available. To help with your own scheduling of these conferences, there are also a variety of online Information Security calendars available that show the dates and durations of each major conference. These calendars can be found at the following Web sites:

- Calendar maintained by Dustin D. Trammell (a.k.a. I)ruid): http://lists.grok.org .uk/pipermail/full-disclosure/2008-April/061359.html or www.dustintrammell .com/projects/

- Information Security Events: http://infosecevents.net/calendar/

PODCASTS

Besides traveling to expensive conferences around the world, it is possible to receive the same critical information in regular formats in your home every week. There are a large number of information security podcasts that cover technology, vulnerabilities, exploits, and legal challenges faced by the industry. Below is a list of the regular podcasts, each with a different focus and style, which may be of interest to you.

- CyberSpeak: http://cyberspeak.libsyn.com
- Exotic Liability: www.exoticliability.com/
- EuroTr@sh: www.eurotrashsecurity.eu/
- Hacker News Network (HNN): www.hackernews.com
- PaulDotCom: http://pauldotcom.com/
- Securabit: http://securabit.com/
- Security Justice: http://securityjustice.com/
- Southern Fried Security: www.southernfriedsecurity.com/

BLOGS

Looking for the latest and greatest information to use today? While security researchers are still working out the details of their latest conference talk or interview session on a podcast, they may detail their notes and research on their personal blogs. By following the work of security researchers, you can proactively watch for upcoming vulnerabilities and help patch your network before the issue becomes widespread. More proactive community members can also jump in and assist in research efforts to provide for better defenses for everyone. We've collected a list of blogs maintained by some of the most innovative and influential minds in the information security industry below.

- Adrian Lamo: http://pax.vox.com/
- Alex Sotirov: www.phreedom.org/
- Anthony Gartner: http://grassrootssecurity.com/
- Benny Ketelslegers: http://blog.security4all.be/
- Chris Gates: http://carnal0wnage.attackresearch.com/
- Chris John Riley: http://blog.c22.cc/
- Christophe Veltsos: http://blog.drinfosec.com/
- Cody Pierce: http://codypierce.com/
- Dale Pearson: www.headhacker.net/

- Dustin D. Trammell a.k.a. I)ruid: http://dtrammell.wordpress.com/

- Felix FX Lindner: www.phenoelit.net/lablog/

- Jayson E. Street: www.dissectingthehack.com/

- Joanna Rutkowska: http://theinvisiblethings.blogspot.com/

- Joe Grand: www.kingpinempire.com/whatsup/

- Joe McCray: www.learnsecurityonline.com/

- Johnny Long: www.hackersforcharity.org/

- Kevin Poulsen: www.wired.com/threatlevel/

- Leon van der Eijk: http://lvdeijk.wordpress.com

- Marcus J. Ranum: www.ranum.com/

- Richard Bejtlich: http://taosecurity.blogspot.com/

- Richard Stallman: www.fsf.org/blogs/rms

- Rob Fuller: www.room362.com/

- Rsnake: http://ha.ckers.org/

- Saint Patrick: www.l1pht.com/

- Tim Berners-Lee: http://dig.csail.mit.edu/breadcrumbs/blog/4

Along with the great insights given by private researchers in the field, many security corporations are also maintaining their own blogs to openly discuss the latest vulnerabilities and risks that impact the industry. Below is a selection of corporate blogs that are useful to information security practitioners.

- BreakingPoint: www.breakingpointsystems.com/community

- Fast Horizon: http://fasthorizon.blogspot.com/

- Google Online Security: http://googleonlinesecurity.blogspot.com/

- Independant Security Evaluators: http://securityevaluators.com/content/blog/

- Matasano Security: http://chargen.matasano.com/

- McAfee Security Insights Blog: http://siblog.mcafee.com/

- McAfee Labs Blog: www.avertlabs.com/research/blog/

- Metasploit Blog: http://blog.metasploit.com/

- Microsoft Security Research & Defense Blog: http://blogs.technet.com/srd/

- nCircle: http://blog.ncircle.com/

- Saecur: http://blog.saecur.com/

- SourceFire Vulnerability Research Team (VRT): http://vrt-sourcefire.blogspot .com/

- Symantec Security Blogs: www.symantec.com/connect/blogs

- Tenable Security Blog: http://blog.tenablesecurity.com/

- TippingPoint Digital Vaccine Laboratories: http://dvlabs.tippingpoint.com/ blog/

- Voice of VoIPSA: http://voipsa.org/blog/

HACKER INTERVIEWS

In the world of information security, it is important to understand the motivations behind all of the players. While you can appreciate the difficulties of protecting a network against hackers and criminals, the job is easier to manage when you can understand exactly what the hacker is looking for and why.

Jeff Moss (Dark Tangent)

Jeff Moss has long been known as the founder and director of both the DEFCON and Black Hat security conferences. DEFCON is famously known as the largest hacker conference in the world, with over 10,000 attendees at DEFCON 17 in 2009.[20] DEFCON has been a staple in hacker culture since its inception in 1992 and has experienced tremendous growth over the years as the community also grew. Though Black Hat is a slightly younger conference, started only in 1997, it has become a premiere global training venue for information security defenders.

Q: *I want to get your opinion on the use of the word hacker and how it pertains to bad guys only. Can you please talk about that real quick?*

A: *Jeff Moss*: Yeah, this is an old topic that never dies, kind of like vulnerability disclosure and the semantics of the word, meaning of the word hacker, to the people who have been around a long time, and by a long time I mean 70s onward, I got involved in computers in the early to mid-80s.

In fact, then, hacker was a positive term. It had been popularized in Silicon Valley (it wasn't Silicon Valley yet) where I grew up in the Bay area and Steven Levy wrote a book called *Hackers* that explored the early hackers that started the computer revolution and the people from DEC and Apple and the idea there was that hackers have a very wide breadth of knowledge, look at problems differently, solve complicated problems, are very inventive, constantly curious and trying to figure out how to take things apart and make them work.

When the Internet grew up and criminals started committing crimes using computers, I think the media needed a name to describe these people. The only name that was around that they weren't really familiar with was the term *hackers*. So they borrowed it and applied it to people committing crimes using computers. Well, instead of just calling them computer criminals, which seems very descriptive, they had to take a term from us – hacker.

So when my mom learned about computer criminals, she learned about these hackers. That really screwed things up because people in the underground and in the industry would still compliment each other like "yeah, he's a really good hacker." But if someone outside the community heard that, they'd be all confused and might think we're talking about criminals.

So, it's very confusing. And then, to make matters worse, before the Web was popular, I remember these debates on bulletin boards and on the Internet, "Well, we need a new name for hackers and maybe we'll call them crackers, no let's call them spiders because they crawl around the Internet looking for things." And then the World Wide Web was invented so the spider analogy wasn't going to work because there was this World Wide Web. That caused more confusion.

Okay, so let's call them crackers, then, because they crack into systems and that has this negative connotation. But they didn't realize that in the piracy world, in the warez world a cracker is a reverse engineer that circumvents copy protection. So the people are calling computer criminals crackers are doing the same thing the media did with hackers. They misappropriated a term from a different community they weren't familiar with.

So I stick with "computer criminal." It keeps everything clear, just like you can have a criminal plumber or non-criminal plumber, or good plumber or bad plumber, whatever, same thing. Good hacker, bad hacker, criminal hacker, whatever. One denotes a skill set and one denotes intention.

Q: *Okay, okay, I like that. My next question is, I read some stuff recently about the sharing of information. After 9/11, the U.S. government was supposed to be able to share information more, and now recently in the last couple of years there's come to light all these computer intrusions of government networks. But it doesn't seem like the government is sharing information with each other. It seems like we didn't learn from 9/11 that lesson, especially as it applies to the computer world. I know you have some strong feelings about this. Could you please let us know where you are at on it?*

A: *Jeff Moss*: Well, I don't know about strong feelings but generally the way you combat that crime, whatever the crime is, is through information sharing. You can see this with community watch programs and publicizing statistics of what are high crime areas, you know, you publicize vehicle recalls, you publicize everything to make people aware because what happens is people are afraid of what they don't understand.

Also if you're a decision maker, either for the military or the government or a teeny little company, how can you make an informed decision about the future of your company if you don't have the real facts? You end up making all kinds of weird, distorted decisions that might lead you astray.

So I'm a believer that you should share more information than less. No doubt, granted, there might be national security exceptions to that, but generally speaking I think it should be easier rather than harder to share information. You see a little bit of this with these disclosure laws started in California and now in 20-some-odd states where these breach notification laws sometimes they're called. So I'm a big fan of federal breach notification laws hoping that the Feds or the Congress can pass a law that will create a standard across the nation because what's happening now is let's say you're a company and you're doing business in all 50 states and you get broken into now you have to comply with 20-something different notification laws.

It's a nightmare. You need one standard. So, I think once you have one standard, then you can start gathering statistics and you can start having a better understanding of the breaches that are out there. I can't think of too many other instances where the Feds should step in with any other legislation to mandate information sharing but that's the most obvious.

Q: *Okay, real quick, inside the security community, there's a big debate about what's cyber warfare and what's not. You mentioned before you think a lot of things can fall under the umbrella of computer criminals or computer crime. What's your idea on cyber warfare?*

A: *Jeff Moss*: I don't have a clearly articulated vision, but I'll make a couple distinctions. One is there is a difference between what criminals want and what nation-states want or intelligence wants. So generally criminals go after money and nation-states go after secrets or information so they can know what their potential adversaries may or may not do. Or they may take it for economic reasons to bolster their nation's companies.

Well, I don't think we've seen a cyber war yet. It's not technically impossible to have a cyber war, I just don't think we're in the middle of one now and I think that a lot of things that are happening, because we can't attribute attacks very easily it makes kind of getting into a fight really difficult for us. You know you can't apply the theories of deterrence if you don't know who's attacking.

How can you deter someone who's not identifiable? It's more difficult, right? And so you can see after the "aurora attacks" on Google and Adobe and such that all of a sudden everyone's crazy trying to figure out how to attribute attacks. Adversary characterization models, statistical models and software analysis – tools where you try to figure out the pedigree of the malware, the evolution of it. How many times have you seen this code snippet? Where was it used? How has it been modified? Does that match how other groups have used it? And so on, and so forth.

You try to attribute, but it's going to be, in my mind, a combination of old-style, gumshoe, feet on the ground investigation and some high-tech forensics, because you never can get a 100% answer, you're going to have to supplement it with this sort of pattern of behavior. All indicators point to this country or this group. But you're not going to catch, like, Colonel Mustard in the library with the candlestick.

It's going to be too difficult, I think, against a savvy adversary. And I think when we do get into a cyber war, you'll pretty much know it because things will come crashing down on both sides. That could lead very rapidly to a sort of electronic war, a kinetic war. There are some people who would say we're in a cyber war now and I'm not going to say that. No, no, no. We're in a sort of electronic Cold War. Everybody is posturing, everybody's angling for advantage.

Q: *What makes it interesting is that some people are saying that a Chinese company broke into an American company, the Chinese company is owned by the government of China and trying to correlate, it's all wishy-washy, isn't it?*

A: *Jeff Moss*: Yeah, right. So how do you attribute it? And the thing I keep pointing out is that the defenses against this are the same defenses you have for pretty much anything. Which is still better systems, monitoring your systems, increase your defenses because if they can't break into you in the first place, who cares? Its like, if you stuck an IDS, say, on the outside of Amazon's network on the external perimeter and you plugged in that IDS, guess what? It's going to go bright red! And Amazon probably doesn't really care because none of those attacks are getting through.

If you were able to monitor behind their first line of defense they'd probably care a whole lot more about what gets through. They have to stick their limited resources in the areas that count most. Pay attention to the ones that get through. Amazon's not a university or the military that might spend a lot of time on research analyzing new attacks. They want to sell books and other things and the smartest thing for them to do is have a quick capability to respond, you know, when an attack happens, recover from the attack and get on with doing business.

And it would be great if you could prosecute someone who steals from you but what they do to build those capabilities – forensics, system recovery, disaster recovery, hardening their systems – is the same thing that everybody should do. There is nothing magical, I think, to really defend against a cyber attack, outside of a military situation or continuity of government. I'm talking about 90% of the population.

Q: *One thing I've noticed, and this will lead to my next question, is how the government funds people to go to Europe for DEFCON or Black Hat and to get training. I see a big movement in the government requiring certification for security professionals. Do you think these certifications are providing adequate cyber defenders for the U.S. government?*

A: *Jeff Moss*: Yeah, I don't think it's adequate, but unfortunately I think it's necessary cause the problem is in the government that likes check boxes. It's very hard for them to understand who has appropriate experience and who doesn't.

It's sort of like do you have to have a college degree to be a good programmer? No. Do you have to have a college degree to be a good security guy? No. But good luck trying to get a really top job anymore without a college degree. It's more difficult than it was 10 years ago. But on certifications, I'd say about 80% of them out there are crap. The ones that are valuable are the ones that task specific skills. For example, the Cisco, I forget the name of it – CCNA, CCNE.

Q: *CCIE where you have to do the labs, the intense labs?*

A: *Jeff Moss*: Yeah, the CCIE. That has great respect in the industry because, you know, I don't know if any of the readers are familiar with the "goat lab" in the special forces medic program but it sounds a lot like a small version of "goat lab" where people come in at night and they screw up your router configs and, you know, they mess things up. Then you come in the next day and you only have a certain amount of time to figure out what just happened to your routing infrastructure, find it and fix it.

They're touching everything from your ability to set it up, once you have it set up they mess with it, you have to learn how to troubleshoot, you have to recover, they're touching the whole spectrum. And when you get this certification, you know that this guy can walk the walk where a lot of these other paper certifications, it's testing their understanding of the lingo, they understand some of the concepts, but maybe they don't know how to apply them or when to apply them or where to apply them.

So I think as a profession, we need to move more toward skill-based testing. If you look at how accountants operate or doctors, or plumbers, or anything, they have an apprenticeship program; they have some sort of certification. This is a model that a lot of people are talking about moving to. It took decades for accountants and doctors and plumbers to figure out their profession. We're essentially a 20-year-old profession.

Q: *I know the security community is quite diverse with many different devices and technologies. What core competencies do you think we should start with?*

A: *Jeff Moss*: I think you would start with the fundamentals. Think about how people are getting broken into. It's happening through insecure web apps – so you might want a certification for secure web development; someone who can analyze source code and edit perl, PHP, Python, and try to figure out how to protect these on the front end. You want to have somebody who is competent in designing filters for user input into SQL databases. These are the fundamentals. The part I am unsure about is how do you get corporate America, which doesn't really understand this, to spend a lot of money paying for their people to get these certifications? It's unclear.

You can understand "If I want to become a plumber I better get a plumber's license." But there's no such economic forces in the security industry that drives the approach "I want to hire three programmers so I better be sure that they are X, Y, or Z programmer certified."

Q: *There are a couple of the SANS GIAC certifications that are approved by the DoD, there is the CISSP, and recently there is the Certified Ethical Hacker.*

A: *Jeff Moss:* Sure, and they're all under the one program of trying to get a minimal level of acceptable certification. Just like ten years ago when I was working in Minneapolis. If I wanted to touch the state of Minnesota's government systems, I had to have a CISSP. That's kind of silly, but I can see what they were trying to do. They had to have something. They had to filter out some group. Ten years ago the only real game in town was the CISSP or there was an auditing certification so they went with CISSP. You can argue about that all day long, but if you own those networks and you need to write the specifications on who gets to touch them, they had to do something to show that they had people that were adhering to a code of conduct and were the "good guys." It took a bit of liability off of them.

Q: *Okay, then real quick – one more question. There has been this explosion of security conferences. You're known as the godfather of organizing security conferences. What do you have to say about all the ones that are popping up now?*

A: *Jeff Moss:* I think it's great. DEFCON and later on Black Hat were started for slightly different reasons. But really what we are trying to do is spread knowledge. If you think about it, we are sort of in the knowledge transfer business. So the more conferences you have, the more knowledge transfers are going on and that's great. Like we talked about earlier, the more education and awareness we can generate, the better it is for everybody.

From a business standpoint, all these extra cons haven't hurt the business. I think that points to the size of the demand. There is so much need for this kind of information that you can have hundreds of security conferences and sometimes it seems that it's still not enough. It makes me really happy.

Another thing is that imitation is the sincerest form of flattery. I love watching new conferences pop up in places like Pakistan, Afghanistan, Egypt, or wherever it is. I get emails from these people who say they are starting these conferences and do I have any advice for them. It's really exciting to see the global reach these conferences have become. People sometimes say I'm the godfather, but really it was the CCC in Germany. They've had the longest running hacking conferences. Different groups have organized it and different people have been involved, but the Europeans did it first and best.

In the States I think we have put our own twist on it. I think it's great. I love going to other shows and seeing what they are up to. I'm always thirsty to see what's new – how people look at things differently.

I never thought this was going to be my job. It was just a hobby. Kind of like everyone else in the hacking world, we got into it because it was exciting and fun. You're learning a lot and the next thing you know the dot com bubble came along and we all had jobs. Then our jobs became professions.

Q: *It's like a kid playing basketball not expecting to get into the NBA.*

A: *Jeff Moss:* Yeah, but back then we didn't even realize the NBA was ever an option! There weren't any jobs for hackers. There was no money involved, so why would anyone hire you? Soon as companies started hooking up on the Internet and they started having money involved, then they suddenly needed to secure it. Once that happened, jobs started getting crazy.

When it became a profession, a lot of my friends were like "Crap, it's a job now!" "It's no longer fun!" "They took all the life out of my hobby!" So then hacking becomes a job and then they have to go get a new hobby.

Q: *What seems to be missing now in security is the passion. When people were doing it for no money, people learned just to learn. Now people are learning to get paid. It's not the same.*

A: *Jeff Moss:* No, then it becomes a formula. "What are the certifications I need?" "What books should I read?" "Okay, I've done all that I'm good for my job." I think it's a symptom of the industry growing up.

Q: *There are some really talented people that may not have the degree or the certification, but they can kick butt on most people I know with the proper boxes checked. Places like the government need to start recruiting those people.*

A: *Jeff Moss:* I think you are right. But once you bring those people into the government or into any company, and they start having to exist within bureaucracy, their effectiveness is going to go way down. Now they have to fill out the HR forms, deal with Legal, do the conference calls. Suddenly their effectiveness goes way down. Think about when you are most effective. Is it when you are at work? Or is it when you are at home on the weekend with your phone turned off?

I remember people would say that the best time to hack is on the weekend. That was always the common wisdom because all of the serious administrators would be home with their families. So around the Fourth of July or whenever was always the best time. As you grow up you realize there is a reason why that is common wisdom – because it's true. Unless it's a really big company like a Microsoft that has a 24-hour SOC or NOC staffed up, that's just the nature of it. We need to stop hoping that the next silver bullet is going to come along and save us. We have to realize that this is an awareness, education, and skill-based problem. It's partly political and partly organizational and partly technological – and you can't solve the problem by fixing just one of those pieces. They all need to come into play.

We are starting to see that with more and more federal regulations.

Dan Kaminsky

As we discussed earlier, Dan Kaminsky is a computer researcher well known for discovering an Internet-wide vulnerability within the DNS protocol. We were able to catch up with Kaminsky at ShmooCon 2010 to discuss his thoughts on hacking culture. To see the original interview, visit www.dissectingthehack.com/video/dan-kaminsky-dissecting-the.

Q: *Is there a double standard when it comes to hackers? People complain about organizations like NSA and AT&T wiretapping people and disclosing information. And then you have organizations like EFF that defend hackers. Do you think it is a double standard that hackers openly promote compromising of data and EFF appears to support those things?*

A: *Dan Kaminsky*: No, no, no. At the end of the day it's the difference between capabilities and actions. Hackers are at their core, no matter what side of hacking you're on – even if you have nothing to do with security – hacking is about seeing the difference between what a system is capable of versus what it was designed to be capable of. This is a fork and we are supposed to use it to eat food, but you can also use it as an antenna. This is the sort of shifting of objects and shifting of creations that is at the heart of the hacker ethic. It's also at the heart of the invention ethic. It is ultimately how we get new things.

Now this is totally alien from the question of how does society and law enforcement function? Like, at the end of the day it's a question of capability. Obviously there is the question of capability to spy on everyone. In fact, at the end of the day this is something that no one has really dealt with. There is a crossover point where it is cheaper to spy on everyone than it is to selectively choose who you do or don't spy on.

Now this is new. When you had to actually send someone out to watch a guy, the more people you watched, the more it cost. Now, because of technological advances, the less people you watch, the more it costs. Because you have to have all these filters and these exception pieces and "oh it's the lawyers" and "oh it's the non-American citizen" and "oh it's the American citizen." And figuring out rules, now the technology has shifted, and figuring out the rules of how it is to be used by the agents of the state – it's just a new debate.

The debate of what should the legitimate purview of law enforcement be – I'm sorry, it just has nothing to do with "so should people be looking into what things we are capable of or not."

Q: *Are you trying to say that the technology side is totally different from the use of what you do with it?*

A: *Dan Kaminsky*: I'm saying nobody is surprised that you can log data. This is not a hack. No one is saying, "Oh my God, you can record my phone call?" Yes, you can record phone calls. There is nothing about hacking in it. It's a question of should the state be doing this or not. I'm just saying the debate about wiretapping is about the written rule of law enforcement. The debate in hacking is should you be able to see what things are capable of – what they're really capable of. They're just two different debates.

Q: *You can go to several talks this afternoon and people are cracking GSM encryption and that stuff, monitoring 3G. So many of these things you have to break the law to do.*

A: *Dan Kaminsky*: Let me explain. What you're seeing here with "Look, you can crack GSM." Whether that is good or bad isn't part of the discussion. And frankly, you know, one group will say, "Look, you can break GSM. This is a problem and we need to go fix it" and that is a totally reasonable reaction. Another group might say, "You know what, this is awesome! I can spy on people and it's fun." Neither of those have anything to do with the law enforcement question, which is, "How do you find bad guys?" It is a different scene.

One thing is, "Hey, what can the technology do?" and the other thing is, "Well, what should the state be doing with the technology?"

Q: *I know a little bit about your background and how you became a big name. What do you recommend for people that are trying to get in the game? What should they do? Networking, know programming, what should they do?*

A: *Dan Kaminsky*: Play. Play. Play with toys. Look, there is so much software out there, so many systems out there, so many hacks out there – I mean, we are inundated with technology. Computers – they're not just for geeks any more. Everyone uses this stuff. Really, the best piece of advice I can give is to just become passionate about something. It doesn't matter if it's the controller of a Nintendo Wii. It doesn't matter if it's the firmware on an Intel SSD. At the core of hacking is "Okay, this thing is awesome and it does X. What else can I make it do? How does it work on the inside?"

Find the man behind the curtain. And say, "Hi." That's what it's about. Don't worry or think that everything has been found. Because I'm telling you, it hasn't. Don't think that you can never beat the big guys because you probably have more time than the big guys. The big guys get really busy and in the end you are seeing the results of some number of weeks or months of work. There's new stuff coming out every day. Play with it. See what you can make it do.

Q: *Cool. I've got one more question. Talk a little bit about what do you think the relevancy of all the security conferences and the information sharing at conferences is?*

A: *Dan Kaminsky*: I think that that's a very interesting question. I began my career in the late 90s. That was the end of an era. Through the end of the 80s and 90s we thought we knew how security worked. We thought the answer was cryptography. If you encrypt everything we will be safe. Maybe a little bit of Java, but mostly cryptography – applied cryptography was supposed to save the world. So the 200s hit and we found out "oh my God, we're all wrong." Implementation bugs are everywhere. Design bugs are everywhere. We have to completely re-think how attacks work because we are getting destroyed.

The spread of conferences really is about all of us talking to each other. "This is how attack actually happens." It broke out from a small thing that a few people knew into an actual field. We are very, very good at talking about attacks. I think, my suspicion is that we need to talk more about defenses as well. We're just not that good at it. We don't really know that much about what it really means to protect ourselves.

I was on this great thread and someone said, "Oh, that IE is a terrible browser." So I asked, "What's a good one? Really, which is the safe browser?" And of course the answer I got back was, "Well, Telnet – you can Telnet to a port." And it's like, "Hey, look, you're joking, but you notice how you don't have a serious answer." What you have is a hammer and you've been going around bashing nails in. And that's great, and you've got your hammer, but you've got to make some walls.

Q: *One follow-up question on that. What do you think about compliance and do you think that is what the industry is going to?*

A: *Dan Kaminsky*: I'm worried. I'm worried about compliance. The reason I'm worried – the grand challenge is how do you operationalize security? We have some group of people who run around and we know how to break stuff and we do our pen testing and we get people into what I call "Pen Test Hell." We show up. We break everything and then we say, "Go fix it." Then we come back in six months, we show up. We break everything, and then we say, "Go fix it." And you repeat ad nauseaum until the budget is exhausted. That sucks.

The compliance guys have their hearts in the right place. They are trying to make a series of operational rules that say, "This is what you do to make yourself safe." The problem is we don't think what they are recommending is sufficiently concrete or frankly, effective. I would like to see data that says compliant operations get hacked less. I haven't seen this data.

In fact, as an industry, we love operating on the rumor. We do. We are all very good at keeping secrets. Whatever we pick up, we don't dig, or challenge, or demand backstory because we are kind of finding out on the down low anyway. So what this means is we don't know much of what's going on and we really don't know much about protecting ourselves. So, to have compliance programs are the right idea. But to come out of an industry this steeped in rumor and poor data – it's garbage in garbage out.

I'm not saying any specific compliance program is bad. I'm just saying I'm concerned that what we have is either too vague to do anything, or specific in ways that we know don't actually make a difference.

Johnny Long

We were able to catch up to Johnny Long via Skype while he was performing volunteer work in Uganda. Johnny has been the driving force behind the Google Hacking movement and has spent much of his professional life as a penetration tester. He is currently the head of Hackers for Charity and is assisting in implementing technical learning environments and classrooms into impoverished areas of Africa.

Q: *First of all, could you please introduce yourself and tell us who you are?*

A: *Johnny Long*: Sure, my name is Johnny Long, and I'm a professional hacker. I've spent about fifteen years in the security field, and currently living in Uganda, East Africa focusing on the work for Hackers for Charity.

Q: *Okay, Johnny, could you please describe for me what the "hacker culture" is in your opinion?*

A: *Johnny Long*: Boy, that's a heavy question. Um, "hacker culture" has always been this thing that has lots of myths and folklore around it. But over the past ten years or so, it's become an actual thing through conferences and gatherings and things like that where hackers are getting together in semi-public places and outwardly talking about the things that they do. At first glance most people would think, "Okay, so this is a bunch of criminals getting together and talking about how to commit crimes." But hacking is mostly mental – it's a state of mind. It's looking at a problem, coming up with a creative solution for it, it's looking at a technology and looking for clever ways to use it, and it just so happens that a whole lot of that work focuses on security, you know, because security is the pinnacle or one of the top levels of technology where things get really difficult and the hacker mentality is all about figuring out that really difficult stuff.

So the culture is really a collection of very bright people that come from a lot of different disciplines. You know, you've got programmers, you've got network guys, you've got all these different types of disciplines that get together. And interestingly enough, share an awful lot about stuff that they know. One thing that's cool about the hacker culture is that if you are willing to do a little bit of research, and you are willing to read the manuals, and put in some sweat equity, and to figuring some things out, there's lots of people out there that will help you with the next step as long as you're willing to do some of the research on your own. So it's a really amazingly open group of people from all over the world that don't know anything about geographic boundaries, that share a common love of technology and figuring out some of the most difficult problems around it.

Q: *That's a good explanation, thanks. Okay, the next thing I want to talk about is if you can explain the difference between "white hats," "black hats," and "grey hats" to me?*

A: *Johnny Long:* (Laugh) I'll explain it as best I can. I mean I get lost somewhere in the middle myself. So, on paper at least, a white hat goes back to the old black and white movies where you could tell the protagonist and antagonist, the good guy and the bad guy, from the color of their hat. Before you had audio in movies you had a sinister character that was all dressed in black and that was the bad guy. The hero would be all dressed in white and you could tell the difference between them. And there was the campy piano music to help you figure out who was who. So it's a holdover from those days.

So the black hats are looked at as the bad guys and the white hats are looked at as the good guys. But in technical terms, it's generally accepted to call someone who does computer security work, whether it's pen testing, reverse engineering, and all that sort of stuff – the white hats are the ones doing it professionally. Those guys get a salary for doing that work. But they also have this level of trust about them where they have worked for some companies. They've gained the trust of a client base, and they have a proven track record that they do this stuff ethically.

Black hats on the other hand, they also make money in some cases, but their motives are often completely different. Either their motives are purely malicious, they intend to do damage, or they intend to gain access to systems that they have no business messing with. They haven't gotten permission from the target. So you've got this dividing line, which boils down to your motives.

If your motives are to help secure a system, then you are looked at as being a white hat. If your motives are to explore or to just build up your knowledge – you are not doing it to help the problem, but you are a part of the problem, then you are generally looked at as being a black hat.

Now you get pretty deep into the weeds if you have a guy that's done nothing but pen testing and has been a white hat his whole career, but then maybe crosses a line for one gig or gets angry about something or does something that's malicious or uses his powers for evil – what's that? Some people would say we need another classification because that's like a "grey hat." You're mostly white with a little bit of black. The whole thing is up for big time discussion. To use a really bad pun – there is no black in white. There is no solid line. It's really just a bunch of people's opinions; unfortunately it's sometimes the hacking community that will make that decision for you.

You look at someone like Dan Kaminsky who has been a professional his whole life and has worked for companies doing legitimate security work. He gets beat up pretty badly about one release that he makes and how he handles the problem that he discovers. Suddenly people start throwing him over the fence and calling him a black hat and things like that. Sometimes it's really just up for grabs.

Q: *Okay, now I'm going to ask a quick follow-up question. Do you think that the hacker community is perceived as bad because it seems like a lot of people want to pretend that they're black hats even if they are white hats? It seems that everyone wants to have an outlaw persona. Can you talk about that?*

A: *Johnny Long*: I think there's a couple of questions here. I think the first one you lean towards is, "What is the perception from the outside?" I think the perception from the outside is what the media makes it. The hacking community is essentially a bunch of criminals, a bunch of black hats. There's nothing good that will come of it. There's only a bunch of people that screw around with your credit reports and steal your stuff and give you viruses. So I think the perception is almost across the board, the people that you talk to, there is a negative connotation when you talk about hackers and you talk about the community.

So I think that is the first part of your question. The second part of it is when you start talking about this outlaw persona and the people that have these skills wanting to be perceived as renegade or something like that. I think that's fairly valid. It's hard to paint in such broad strokes, but I think that hacking is this mysterious thing. Twenty years ago computers were – there was a little bit of magic to computers. And in those days if you knew a programming language you were absolutely considered someone who was like a wizard. Well that was twenty years ago and today really high-end stuff like security work is perceived that way as well. A lot of people look at hackers as being very mysterious. In an effort to sort of keep that persona – if that is why you are in the game is to be known as someone mysterious and has these "superpowers" – then you are going to do these oddball things to make you look a little bit like a renegade or an outlaw or some type of magic wizard with these little parlor tricks. But I think it comes with what you bring into the industry. If that's what you are trying to get out of it, then you're going to create an environment that looks a lot like that.

Q: *I know you have been to a lot of security conferences. You spoke at tons of them. From an organizational perspective, from management, or even from a new person trying to learn security, can you please tell us the benefits of a security conference?*

A: *Johnny Long*: The conferences are a mixed bag these days. If you want to talk in generalizations, most conferences have mixed attendance. There are some conferences that lean particularly one way or the other. You look at something like the Cyber Crime Conference run by DoD and that's primarily good guys. You know you get to some of the smaller, lesser known conferences and you're gonna find that it's primarily black hats. But across the board it's generally a mix. So when you go to a conference, what you get is a taste of a culture. If you go to something like DEFCON in Vegas, you're gonna definitely get a mixed bag these days. The vast majority of the talks in the old days were by black hats. These days you're gonna have talks from people that work for the Department of Defense, federal agents. You are gonna have the "meet the Fed" panel. But you also have people that are a little more mysterious. Maybe grey hats. And there are definitely black hats. So what you are going to see – you are going to get a taste of the culture – what it looks like when the black hats and the white hats get together. You are going to pick up some lingo. But the most important part if you go through the tracks, you are going to get security from both sides. You are going to learn offense and you're gonna learn defense. When you go through a lot of college curriculums, you don't tend to get that good balance. And anyone that knows anything about warfare – you can go back to amazing books like *The Art of War* – you have to understand how offense and defense works. To have really good offense you have to have really good defense. When you get to the point that you've mastered the art of war, offense and defense blurs together. There really is no difference. It's a lot like that with computer security. If you only study the defensive angles without studying how the offensive angles work you can't completely understand security. You're gonna be pretty much a failure at your job because won't understand what the bad guys are capable of. Conferences give you the chance to pick up both sides of the fence – to learn about the culture. You get to rub elbows with the future. The people at these conferences are the future for good or for bad. The average age of the attendees is fairly young. Most of the people are "up and comers" in the industry. This gives you the chance to rub elbows with them and talk with them on a personal level.

Q: *If you were giving someone advice on where to start in security – I know you talked earlier about finding out information for yourself and there are other people that are willing to help you – but what do you advise for someone just starting off? Do they start offensively or defensively?*

A: *Johnny Long*: First of all you are asking someone who spent a career on offense. So if you are asking the striker on a football team which is the way to go – offense or defense – the answer is offense. For me, I'll be quite honest with you, my skills lie in the offensive side. I can configure a firewall and do some defensive work. But to be perfectly honest with you, when I am doing it for real and it really matters, I'm going to call in someone who really knows what they are doing with defense. For me, the allure was in offense. For a lot of people they find that to be pretty sexy. But the way the industry is right now, there are so many specialties. The first thing you have to do is figure out what you enjoy. Some people really romanticize the offensive stuff. They've seen movies and whatever and they think the offensive hacking stuff looks really sexy and they go down that path. Then they find themselves ten years down the road going "This isn't exactly what I thought it was going to be." It's a lot of long hours sitting in front of a computer screen where you can spend weeks or months working on one problem where you get to the culmination and it lasts for all of ten minutes. It's not a constant adrenaline rush.

You really have to spend some time figuring out what you love. I can program, a little bit – if you want to call it that. Some people would look at my code and argue that point. I don't enjoy it and it shows in my work. I'm an evil person whenever I'm programming because I just absolutely hate it. While I wasn't cut out to be a programmer, some people live and breathe that stuff. Some people go to the grocery store and they're standing in line writing a routine in their head – maybe some pseudo code on how the line process could be improved and putting some error correction in there. They're doing this crap in their head and that's just how they are wired.

So you need to spend some time getting exposed to a few different things. That's going to take some playing. You need to play around with some technologies. It's going to take taking some 101 kind of classes – maybe through organizations like SANS that do really good training – and maybe get introduced to a lot of different technologies in this field. Then you need to really narrow it down even further.

Offense and defense isn't really the dividing line any more. The lines are really starting to blur. My best advice is to work. We work to live. You don't live to work. So at the end of the day find something that you really enjoy. And as you go down that road, start asking yourself, "If this was free, would I still do it?" If the answer is "yes" then you have probably found exactly the right field.

Q: *That's pretty much what I have for you.*

A: *Johnny Long*: Well thanks Marcus, it was good talking to you.

Q: *How's that Internet café thing going?*

A: *Johnny Long*: Dude, the place is just crazy. The new property – like I said in the post – it's like walking into medieval times. It's going to be absolutely incredible. We have the potential to make an awful lot of money and create a revenue stream to fund the work that we're doing here. But I'll be perfectly honest with you. Writing the check for six months of rent in that place just absolutely broke us. So at this point we are operating on an awful lot of faith that this is the right path. I really feel led that this is for a lot of different reasons. We had no business looking at that property. It was handed to us on a silver platter for much less than what a lot of other buildings are going for in the area. I have faith that we are going in the right direction, but my bank account right now speaks otherwise. It's going to be an interesting few months. I'm excited about it. It's a little bit like the rush you get when you are in a start-up and things are really basic and grass roots.

For more information about this last part of the conversation with Johnny, go to his Web site for Hackers for Charity and see pictures of the Internet café they have started in Uganda as a funding source for their work at www.hackersforcharity.org/long-journey/buy-a-piece-of-the-hfc-internet-cafe/.

Marcus Ranum

Marcus Ranum is a security researcher currently employed by Tenable Network Security as their Chief Security Officer. Ranum has had a long career in the information security industry, which includes establishing the initial whitehouse.gov Web site and infrastructure.[21]

> **Q:** *What is your reaction to the Google vs. China situation?*
>
> **A:** *Marcus J. Ranum*: I am mystified by some of the claims that are being made about the Google vs. China situation. I just finished reading Gerald Posner's "Daily Beast" article about it, and I consider Posner to generally be a solid and thoughtful journalist. I think that I'm not reading between the lines when I say that he also appears to be a bit skeptical about some of the claims being made. For one thing, the FBI (according to Posner) is claiming that the Chinese government has an army of 180,000 cyberspies. I find that claim to be literally surreal.
>
> First off, the claim is supposedly from a senior FBI agent, based on a classified report – which would mean that someone is deliberately leaking classified material to the press – but that number is just flat-out laughable. How did they compute the number of cyberspies, anyway? Did they total up the number of Chinese IP addresses that bounced a probe off a U.S. Government site? The number 180,000 is completely disproportional to anything I think a security expert would expect.
>
> If you were running the cyberwar operations for China, what would be your ideal force size? I'd say about 400 people, max? And that would be pretty heavy on the research and development side, without counting intelligence analysts to sift the data. Adding analysts, maybe, what, 1000 people? For the FBI to have come up with 180,000 they must be smoking something they confiscated from one of those boats in Miami, or something.
>
> Consistently, our government's claims about Chinese cyber attacks have been incredible and sensationalistic. For example, they claim 90,000 "identifiable attacks" originating from China. Depending on how you count it, that's either a couple of Nessus scans, or that's a great big thundering herd of script kiddies.
>
> What I think is going on is exactly that – it's a great big thundering herd of script kiddies. In China, they have executed people for hacking. I'm guessing that the typical Chinese script kiddie is going to direct his attention elsewhere than Chinese government systems. Considering that the Chinese Internet

population is now larger than the U.S.'s, we have to assume that they have a pretty good thundering (but utterly chaotic) herd of script kiddies and they

A. Know they can safely poke U.S. government machines
B. Know they'd better, in fact, not poke Chinese government machines

So – yeah – I think there's a threat but it's probably just that the Chinese government sees no reason to stop their thrill-seeking idiots from having some fun at our expense, especially considering that it would be hard and expensive for them to do so.

The one part of the whole story that I am very skeptical of is the "sophisticated and targeted attack" bit. Considering how poor our government's awareness of computer security has historically been, I'm guessing that any advanced script kiddie looks like a robo-cyber-ninja-death-squad to our guys. I think this whole kerfuffle is just a hand being held out for bigger budgets for our cyber defense efforts. Which is sad, because mostly what those have amounted to, so far, is a waste of money.

Q: *Do you think the emphasis of security compliance is due to a failure on the part of the software and security vendors? Where will they spend the money at next?*

A: *Marcus J. Ranum*: I think the emphasis on security compliance is due to a failure at the executive management level. You know as well as I do that the techniques and tools that bring good security are not expensive and that they're widely available and have been well-understood for a long time. They just haven't been being used effectively, and the blame for that rests entirely on executive management. They're the ones who approve the Flash-app streams through the firewall, the active content, the downloadable code, the mobile blah blah – you get the picture.

I'm afraid that what they're going to do is spend the money by giving it to the same guys who built the current disaster. Which will result in a bigger, worse disaster.

Q: *What is the best way to communicate risk to executive level management? Who should tell them? It almost seems like a chicken and the egg scenario.*

A: *Marcus J. Ranum*: I don't have an answer to that one. Seriously, it seems to be exactly as you say – chicken and egg. One of the things that I hope will happen is that the current generation of executive management (the ones who play golf instead of WOW (World of Warcraft), and who read Gartner reports instead of Dr Dobbs) are going to have to die. I don't propose that we take steps to kill them off, but they're going to have to evolve out of the workforce before we can have a chance of making progress. The new generation of technical executives that I work with grew up understanding password-guessing is a problem, social engineering is a threat, etc. So just time and evolution is going to help us out a lot.

Q: *I've never really thought of it as cultural thing. Do you think that secure programming is a cultural thing also? Do we have to wait until old code goes away instead of patching it?*

A: *Marcus J. Ranum*: Ultimately, the problem is that our executive managers are expected to make smart decisions based on partial information. That's their job. So they're comfortable listening to some code monkey who says, "Hey, Web 2.0 cloud mashups RULE!" and making a snap decision to go with it. So, what I usually do is explain that I understand that their strength is exactly that, but it's a weakness, too, and they need to learn to be a bit more skeptical about the promises of new technologies and the assumption that there is no risk in doing a given thing. I always like to remind them that the neophile pundits said wireless computing was never going to be a big deal because FDDI (Fiber Distributed Data Interface) was going to be a lot better. The best way to get executive managers to think about this stuff is not to lecture them; it's to gently challenge the basis by which they think they know something. If they're a good executive that will stimulate them to go do some research. If they're a bad executive, they'll decide based on what Gartner says and everyone gets screwed.

The practice of coding needs to change dramatically. Right now, however, all the change I see is moving us in the wrong direction. And the movement in the wrong direction is accelerating rapidly.

Let me give you an example of what I mean – imagine you're the CTO of a company that is going to develop some software that your business must rely on. Got that? You're betting the bank on it, and your career along with it.

Now, someone says that they want to code that application using programming environments in which – not only is there no such thing as a "debugger" but the only way programmers can analyze code is to just beat it with a spoon until it stops crashing. The Web 2.0 programming model not only does not have a software reliability component, it is actually impossible to build one, because the code execution happens all over the place and there isn't even a line between data and execution-state anymore.

It is utterly, totally, insane, and everyone is cheering "rah! rah! rah!" and jumping on the bandwagon as it heads faster and faster toward the cliff.

Q: *Final Question: Please give your advice to a new information security person on what they should know in a general sense. Better yet, if you were creating a curriculum, what would you include?*

A: *Marcus J. Ranum*: My ideal information security curriculum would be a superset of network management, military strategy, and business administration. Seriously, those are the skills that you need – you need to have the technical chops not to get snowed in by BS from vendors, coders, and co-workers – combined with the management skills to work the organizational chart to find the right pressure points.

In other words, you need to be Musashi with TCP/IP skills and have the person-skills, which Musashi clearly lacked, to convince your enemies that you're right without having to draw your sword.

> **NOTE**
>
> Miyamoto Musashi was a famed Japanese samurai and is considered one of the greatest warriors in history.[22]

In my mind, a purely technical path is the best place to start. If you don't have the technical chops to hold your own with the geeks, you're always lunch meat. You need to know enough, for example, when someone starts talking your boss into shifting development to some shovelware framework, to poke a smoking hole in it right in front of everyone. Because otherwise the decisions get made and once they're made your whole career consists of fighting rearguard battles.

SUMMARY

As we discovered in this chapter, the hacking community is not cleanly divided into good guys and bad guys. Many of the people involved are not evil villains. Instead, many are inquisitive researchers that want to push the boundaries in order to better secure digital assets in the future. A defensive security posture is only half the story. Great security comes about through knowing what vulnerabilities exist on a system and how they can be exploited by an attacker. But what ultimately encourages these attackers to want to attack our systems? Many attacks are for malicious purposes though, sometimes, they are performed because of pure curiosity. Understanding what product your company develops, what information it stores, and what value this could hold for an outside attacker can help build better defenses against an attack.

You just can't take our word for it, though. We've brought in experts from the information security industry to give you their thoughts on the current state of the hacking community and culture. By knowing and understanding these various viewpoints you can craft a better image of who the typical hacker is and what they strive for.

For further information about the hacking culture, we invite you to visit www.dissectingthehack.com, where you can engage in online discussions and listen to the recorded interviews that were provided exclusively for this book.

ENDNOTES

1. Davis J, Secret Geek A-Team Hacks Back, Defends Worldwide Web, Wired, www .wired.com/techbiz/people/magazine/16-12/ff_kaminsky; 2008 [accessed 21.03.10].
2. Steve F. An Illustrated Guide to the Kaminsky DNS Vulnerability, www.unixwiz .net/techtips/iguide-kaminsky-dns-vuln.html; 2008 [accessed 21.03.10].
3. Zetter K, Details of DNS Flaw Leaked, Wired, www.wired.com/threatlevel/ 2008/07/details-of-dns/; 2008 [accessed 21.03.10].

4. Watson PA. SLIPPING IN THE WINDOW: TCP RESET ATTACKS, www.osvdb .org/ref/04/04030-SlippingInTheWindow_v1.0.doc; 2003 [accessed 21.03.10].

5. US-CERT. Technical Cyber Security Alert TA04-111A Vulnerabilities in TCP, www .us-cert.gov/cas/techalerts/TA04-111A.html; 2004 [accessed 21.03.10].

6. Lemos R, CNet News. Net's 'savior' sets the record straight, http://news.cnet .com/2100-7355-5198853.html; 2004 [accessed 21.03.10].

7. Phrack. SIGINT Confidential Report on GOBBLES, Issue #58, www.phrack .com/issues.html?issue=58&id=3; 2001 [accessed 20.03.10].

8. GOBBLES Security Advisories, Attrition.org, http://attrition.org/security/ advisory/gobbles/; 2010 [accessed 20.03.10].

9. Orlowski A, The Register. Is the RIAA "hacking you back"? www.theregister .co.uk/2003/01/14/is_the_riaa_hacking_you/; 2003 [accessed 21.03.10].

10. McWilliams B, Hackers Humble Security Experts, Wired, www.wired.com/ techbiz/it/news/2003/01/57229; 2003 [accessed 21.03.10].

11. Neal K, Hacker Factor. I am who I am, www.hackerfactor.com/blog/index .php?/archives/2006/11/01.html; 2006 [accessed 20.03.10].

12. Hacker Factor Solutions. Who is 'n3td3v'? www.hackerfactor.com/papers/ who_is_n3td3v.pdf; 2006 [accessed 20.03.10].

13. Kaibelf. Impersonation is a against the law. Full Disclosure mailing list, lists.grok .org.uk/pipermail/full-disclosure/2009-November/071521.html; 2009 [accessed 20.03.10].

14. Colbert Shows Off His iPad At The Grammys, Mocks Jay-Z, Huffington Post, www.huffingtonpost.com/2010/02/01/stehen-colbert-ipad-at-gr_n_444210 .html; 2010 [accessed 21.03.10].

15. McCarthy C, CNet News. Colbert speaks, America follows: All hail Wikiality! http://news.cnet.com/8301-10784_3-6100754-7.html; 2006 [accessed 21.03.10].

16. Bridges of Budapest. Megyeri Bridge, www.bridgesofbudapest.com/bridge/ megyeri_bridge; 2010 [accessed 29.03.10].

17. Jake C. NASA: Colbert name on treadmill, not room, Associated Press, MSNBC, www.msnbc.msn.com/id/30217550/; 2009 [accessed 29.03.10].

18. Toralv D, McAffee Labs Blog. Here Be Dragons: The 26th Chaos Communications Congress, Part 1, www.avertlabs.com/research/blog/index.php/2009/12/29/here-be-dragons-the-26th-chaos-communication-congress-26c3-part-1/; 2009 [accessed 22.03.10].

19. Michael M, Foreign Policy Journal. Brazil's Next Battlefield: Cyberspace, www .foreignpolicyjournal.com/2009/11/15/brazils-next-battlefield-cyberspace/; 2009 [accessed 29.03.10].

20. Lingefors E, Reliant Security. Defcon 17, Eiwe Lingefors, http://blog.reliantsec .net/2009/08/defcon-17/; 2009 [accessed 29.03.10].

21. Who's Who in Infosec: Marcus Ranum, SearchSecurity.com, http://searchsecurity .techtarget.com/news/article/0,289142,sid14_gci906598,00.html; 2003 [accessed 29.03.10].

22. Daniel D. One of the Greatest Warriors in History, www.danieldimarzio.com/ miyamotomusashi.htm; 2010 [accessed 29.03.10].

Bit Bucket

In the course of our story, we've laid quite a few Easter eggs and obscure comments for our readers to find. Some of the more obvious ones we've referenced in this chapter. In the computer world, the bit bucket refers to the place where lost data goes – a virtual afterlife for all computer data, sometimes known as "/dev/null." In other situations, it refers to a catch-all for data that does not fit in any defined category. In our story, we've used real examples from real people to show how the events that play out here can actually occur.

An *Easter egg* is a term applied to a hidden surprise that a careful reader may notice or find after closer investigation of a book, image, or video. Easter eggs populate many stories, television shows, movies, and video games that we interact with in daily life, although we may not realize it. To get an idea of what you've been missing, check out The Easter Egg Archive at www.eeggs.com. We've made references in our story to many of the celebrities and notable events of the Information Security world, as well as to popular culture items. An observant reader may have picked up on some of these references in our story. This chapter will explore some of these lesser topics and Easter eggs to give you an additional understanding of what they are and how they tie into the story. Although some Easter eggs will be covered here, we won't cover them all. The rest are for you to find in the story, and on our companion Web site at www.dissectingthehack.com.

COVERT PHYSICAL DEVICES

THE HACK DISSECTED

Vlad seemed to have had enough of the conversation. He removed a Swiss Army knife from his pocket. He opened a small connector from the knife, which fit neatly into the Universal Serial Bus (USB) port on Stepan's laptop. Soon he was copying the "My Documents" folder from Stepan's laptop to his "pocket knife." (p. 8)

***

Vlad opened the sealed envelope. It contained a pen.
   "What is the pen for?"
   "It's a data storage device. If you pull the top off, you will see a USB connector for your computer." (p. 11)

As technology has improved, manufacturers have found ways to squeeze more data storage into smaller containers. When combined with normal household items, it is incredibly easy to hide data storage devices for infiltration into secure companies and government agencies. With newer flash memory cards, such as the MicroSD, it is now possible to hide gigabytes of data on a device smaller than a coin, as shown in Figure 7.1. This strategy was highlighted in the 2003 movie, *The Recruit*. In the movie, a female operative for the United States Central Intelligence Agency (CIA) hides a USB flash drive in her coffee mug, allowing her to sneak it past security officers at the facility.

Our story references a USB Swiss Army knife, an actual product that incorporates a USB flash drive within a functional Swiss Army knife.[1] For novelty purposes, USB flash drives have also been incorporated into a multitude of innocent items, including in the handle of a hair comb.[2]

The story also makes mention of an ink pen with a hidden USB connector. This is a real item, such as the nondescript pen shown in Figure 7.2.

FIGURE 7.1

Comparative Size of a MicroSD Card

FIGURE 7.2

Ink Pen with Hidden USB

OYDSSEUS

> ### THE HACK DISSECTED
>
> *Vlad took Pavel's laptop and looked over the list of files they had just acquired from Stepan's laptop. He didn't have much time, so he sorted the files by "Last Modified Date" and scanned the list. One file caught his eye immediately. It was called "Odysseus.doc" and was last updated just one day before. (p. 9)*

The term Odysseus is used at multiple points in our story as file names and passwords for certain data. This is directly in reference to the leader of the soldier army in Virgil's epic *The Aeneid*. This poem described the famous story of the Trojan Horse, a hollowed-out statue wheeled to the gates of the city of Troy. Although the main Greek army retreated, a small group of soldiers, led by Odysseus, hid inside the horse as it was carried into the city. At night, the soldiers left the Trojan horse and opened the main gates of the city, just as the main Greek army returned to overtake the city's defenses.[3]

As we discuss the term Trojan Horse in today's terms, it refers to a malicious program hidden within a more innocent program. You might not have known that the original Trojan Horse would have not been successful if not for a social engineering attack by Sinon, a Greek deserter who had pretended to defect to Trojan. He was a little more committed than today's social engineer as he knew he had to sell the idea that he was no longer a part of the Greek army. Sinon disfigured himself in such a gruesome way that it would be believable that he turned against the Greeks and that the Trojan Horse left behind was actually something that would be beneficial to the Trojans. This shows us that even centuries ago social engineering attacks were very effective. Hacking is not something new. The spirit of hacking has been around for thousands of years, although it may manifest itself in new names and technologies.

VOLKSBANK

> ### THE HACK DISSECTED
>
> *Vlad took a pen and small piece of paper from his coat pocket and wrote "Volksbank, 111-8-18-1-13-15-27-1" from memory. "Have the first half of the payment deposited here. I'll start as soon as I have confirmed the funds, and by the way, don't complain if you see any extra charges on your American Express card. I'll expect you to cover some of my travel costs." (p. 11)*

If you have seen or read *The Bourne Identity*, you may recognize this reference. The number structure is based on the Swiss bank account that is integrated into a device in Bourne's body.[4] The account number is his only clue to his real identity.

The significance to this Easter egg is to show the importance of identity theft and how just one set of numbers can be the key to your existence. We have so many numbers that are tied to our identities that we often overlook what would happen if we no longer had those numbers. It took only one sequence of numbers, and sheer persistence, to give Jason Bourne his life back. We should also wonder what numbers we may have that could take everything away from us. Identity theft is getting more prevalent and the average person's identity and credit rating is being sold on the black market in bulk. Those who have seen SyFy's television series *Caprica* may have a unique outlook about information stored on the Internet. In the show, scientists are able to create online avatars, whose identities closely resemble specific actual people by culling all of the publicly available information of a particular person, until they virtually become that person.[5]

TIGER TEAM

THE HACK DISSECTED

"More muscle is the last thing I need. I had my fill of jarheads when I was on the Tiger Team in San Antonio. I bet all Agent Battle could do with a hard drive is use it for target practice." (p. 17)

A *Tiger Team* is historically a military-run team that tests the defensive securities of friendly bases and encampments.[6] Long before the American public became familiar with the white-hat penetration testers in the 1992 movie, *Sneakers*, the military was using the concept to test their own security, although not always information security, as Agent Jackson suggests in his quote. *Tiger Team* was also the name of a television series on TruTV, which highlighted a group of security experts led by Chris Nickerson performing penetration tests of select businesses.[7] The stars of this show went on to host the popular Exotic Liability podcast.

ONLINE VIGILANTISM

THE HACK DISSECTED

"We got a tip from Perverted Justice. They're today's online version of the Guardian Angels from the 1970s. They got into a discussion with this pervert in a chat room. He claimed he had some "content" that he had personally created, and they talked him into giving a sample. When they got that, they called us. Jamison had given Perverted Justice a Yahoo! e-mail account." (p. 18)

In the story we are introduced to the Perverted Justice group from an early case that Agent Mark Jackson was wrapping up. Perverted Justice is a volunteer group that operates to combat the constant presence of potential online child predators. Volunteers sit in online chat rooms, pretending to be underage females, and wait for propositions to meet for sexual encounters. The group has been in operation for many years and, as shown by their Web site www.perverted-justice.com, they've now claimed more than 500 convictions since 2004.

For the early part of their existence, Perverted Justice sought to simply post the inappropriate chat history logs online to shame the offender, and they still do. However, they gained greater fame when they started working directly with law enforcement to stage larger sting operations.[8] Perverted Justice would notify local law enforcement when they found an online predator who wanted to meet in person. The police would then sit and wait for a proposition to be made before rushing in to arrest the perpetrator. These efforts eventually led to the creation of the National Broadcasting Company (NBC) show "To Catch a Predator," where host Chris Hansen waits to question the predators about their motives before the police haul them off.

In our story, Perverted Justice had an online run-in with a potential predator, Randolf Jamison, and sent the details to the Federal Bureau of Investigation (FBI) Houston field office. There, Agent Mark Jackson was able to decrypt Jamison's hard drives and uncover evidence about his crimes stored there.

SPOT THE FED

THE HACK DISSECTED

"What does 'I am the Fed' mean?" Battle asked as Jackson reclaimed his drink and took a swallow of the now-warm Pepsi.
   "I was 'spotted' at DEFCON this summer." (p. 20)

***

"It looks like word got out since our last meeting. I don't recognize quite a few faces. If anyone here spots a Fed in the group, speak up." (p. 31)

In a number of places in our story, we refer to "Feds" being spotted. This refers to a casual "game" played out every year at DEFCON. DEFCON is known as one of the most popular hacking conferences in the world. Because of the population that it attracts, the conference started seeing attendance from law enforcement agencies and FBI agents. This was not so that the law can bust a few hackers, but more so to allow law enforcement to stay up on the latest technologies and attacks to watch for in their own case work.

This mixture of law enforcement and hackers led to the traditional game of "Spot the Fed." If an attendee at DEFCON notices someone who he or she thinks is a law enforcement agent, then they can "out" this person to a member of the DEFCON staff. If the agent is indeed a member of law enforcement, then they receive a T-shirt labeled "I am the Fed," while their spotter receives an "I spotted the Fed" shirt.

In the story, Agent Jackson was successfully spotted while attending DEFCON. While his new partner would be mortified at being identified as an agent in public at a hacking conference, Jackson displays it in his workspace with pride.

BOB FALKEN

> ### THE HACK DISSECTED
>
> *For the uninitiated, Bob Falken's bedroom looked like part-NASA control room and part high-tech junkyard. To Bob, it was both lab and sanctuary – the one place where he was in control of his world.* (p. 27)

Falken is a direct reference to the artificial intelligence researcher that created the War Operation Plan Response (WOPR) supercomputer in the 1983 movie, *WarGames*. Dr. Stephen Falken developed and programmed WOPR to perform war simulations, including the Global Thermonuclear War program that started the events of the story.[9]

HONEY POTS

> ### THE HACK DISSECTED
>
> *"We're planting 20 flags. One of them is going to be at my house."*
> *Leon turned with a surprised look. "Why would you want to have all of the 2600 hackers pounding on your network? Are you setting up a honeypot to track someone?"*
> *"No. I need plausible deniability," Bob responded. "And don't you ever tell anyone I said that."*
> (p. 29)

A *honeypot* is simply an application, computer system, or network that appears to be something vulnerable to attack. However, the system is actually monitoring itself for signs of an attack and will log and record all actions taken against it by a hacker. As its name symbolizes, a honeypot is a system that looks tempting from the outside, but traps its victims inside, such as with the stories of Winnie the Pooh.[10] As Bob is planting a CyberBob icon on his own computer, Leon asks if Bob is setting up a honeypot. In this context, if Bob was doing so, he would have a computer system logging all intrusions into it. This would give Bob detailed information on the attackers and the exploits that they attempt.

Honeypots are in use across a wide variety of industries, although generally they are relegated to computer intrusions. For example, it was recently detailed how the CIA had worked with the Saudi government to create a honeypot Web site that logged terrorist recruits.[11]

There is also a periodical challenge called the *Honeynet Project*, in which actual honeypot systems are intruded upon, and then the information collected during the intrusion is released to security researchers to determine how the exploits were made. To join in on one of the Honeynet Project challenges, visit www.honeynet.org.

2600 CLUBS

> ### THE HACK DISSECTED
>
> *Soon they were inside and making their way down to the food court. As they approached Ninfa Express, they could see that the usual crowd was supplemented with extra people this time. This was the monthly 2600 club meeting. Leon and Bob were regular attendees. Today, they were leading the prep for the first Capture the Flag war drive put on by the Houston chapter. (p. 30)*

The 2600 club has been a long-term pillar of the hacker community. It was originally formed around regular periodicals that spread information on security, phone hacking (phreaking), and various subculture subjects. It is currently produced as a quarterly magazine available by subscription at http://2600.com.

There are numerous 2600 club meetings held across the world every month that bring together hackers and enthusiasts. In the story, the local 2600 club met in the Houston, Texas Galleria Mall next to Ninfa Express. This is actually the real location where 2600 club meetings take place in Houston on the first Friday of every month. Houston 2600 maintains its own Web site at www.hou2600.org, while an official list of all club meetings can be found at www.2600.com/meetings/.

CAPTURE THE FLAG

> ### THE HACK DISSECTED
>
> *"Hey everybody! Looks like we've got a pretty good crew. Today we're going to set the rules for Capture the Flag," Bob started. Slowly the talking stopped and everyone looked up from many different sticker-covered laptops to watch Bob. (p. 31)*

Capture the Flag refers to a hacker competition in which competitors attempt to exploit computers to gain points, while other competitors work to control and protect their own servers from attack. These competitions are normally designed to test the skills of the competitors in a fun venue.

In our story, Bob and Leon developed a Capture the Flag competition that directly placed them into the path of the bad guys. The two were driving around the city, locating computer systems that had open Wi-Fi access. On these systems, Bob would upload a CyberBob icon, which acted as a "flag." After teams compete in their goal to locate and retrieve these flags, they turn in their cache at the end of the competition. Flags are normally created in the form of simple text files or graphics that can be easily collected by competitors. Some flags may be placed in plain sight on an open system, whereas others may be hidden on secure systems that need to be exploited.

MD5 HASH

> **THE HACK DISSECTED**
>
> *Leon stood up again to add a little more. "Don't try to be clever and bring your own copy of the icon files. We're going to give each its own MD5 hash, so I will know if you have the genuine file."*
> *"And no hacking the judge's PC for the MD5 hash files, or trying to work out a collision on your PS3," Bob added. "The contest will begin next Friday at 5:00 p.m. Meet here at noon next Saturday with the files you find. Leon and I have some more flags to drop still. We'll post the riddles on the Web site at the start time. But I'll give you one now to get you started." (pp. 31–32)*

MD5 is used as an integrity checking mechanism to verify information that is sent across a network or other channel. MD5 refers to Message-Digest algorithm 5, a mathematical hash function that takes raw data and outputs a set-length string of text, known as a *hash*. In many ways, this can be seen as fingerprinting of data.[12] If any value of the original data changes, the hash will also change. This allows for a computer user to quickly and easily detect if the data has been changed or altered.

In the Capture the Flag competition in our story, Leon warns the competitors not to bring their own flags from home. Bob and Leon had created an MD5 hash of each of their flags. When the flags are turned in at the end of the competition, Bob and Leon can calculate the hashes of the submissions to ensure that they match the originals. This prevents competitors from creating their own flags.

And while Bob jokingly refers to using a Sony PlayStation 3 (PS3) to work out an MD5 collision, this is an actual attack that has been proven to work. A team of security researchers presented a demonstration at the 2008 25th Annual Chaos Communication Congress on how to perform collision attacks against Web Secure Sockets Layer (SSL) security certificates that were signed with signatures created using the MD5 hash function. They performed their tests on a distributed network of more than 200 PS3s and were able to successfully create a fictitious security certificate that would redirect user traffic to a malicious server.[13]

SYDNEY BRISTOW

> **THE HACK DISSECTED**
>
> *Michael froze and listened…just someone at the copier down the hall. He took a deep breath, got slowly back into the chair, and scanned the cubicles around him. Nothing. "Where is Sydney Bristow when you need her?" he muttered to himself as he looked back to the monitor. (p. 33)*

Michael Resol is cautiously making his way through 3DNF's offices, attempting to install malicious software on his boss's desktop computer. However, his nerves are on edge and he jumps at any little noise that he hears in the office.

At this point, he would love the assistance of Sydney Bristow to help him with his task.

Sydney Bristow would definitely be up to the job, as the fictional CIA double-agent from the TV series, *Alias*.[14] Bristow finds herself in very dangerous situations as she takes upon multiple identities to break into secure facilities to carry out her missions.

In the hacking culture, you will find a different standard for heroes and heroines. Looks are not as prized as much as brains. Sydney Bristow was the ideal woman for hackers and geeks. Not based on her looks but the combination of brains, brashness, and fighting skills (although her looks did not count against her). One hero you will find admired is David Tennant, known better as Dr. Who #10. He is admired not for his gun wielding, swash buckling, and lady swooning ways, but instead for his ability to resolve conflict without using a firearm and the prowess to outwit his opponents.[15]

CYBERBOB

THE HACK DISSECTED

"Like anyone would want to watch a couple of unemployed nerds drop CyberBob icons," Leon mumbled as he turned back to his monitor..."Of course." Bob went back to his "TOOLz" folder and clicked on the SuperScan icon. If someone was transferring a file to the .200 box, then there must be other interesting things in that network. This would be a good bonus site for the CyberBob icon. Once the program loaded, Bob started the scan to explore the 10.24.53.x network and see what he could find. (p. 40)

***

He was quickly rewarded with a listing of files and folders. He wasted no time in dragging a copy of the CyberBob icon from his desktop to this new window. (p. 41)

***

Hannah complied and turned right off of the access road just before the small shop where Bob and Leon had sat just a couple of days before dropping a CyberBob icon for a game. She drove down the street and pulled to the front of an empty three-story office building. It was dark outside, so once she turned off the headlights, they were well obscured by shadows. (p. 96)

In our story, CyberBob is a direct reference to a fictional character from the 1995 movie, *The Net*, starring Sandra Bullock.[16] In the movie, CyberBob was the handle of one of the star's online friends, though someone she had never met in person. This fact was exploited by the movie's bad guy killing the real CyberBob and taking over his identity. Although the movie covered many aspects of Internet identity and Trojan malware, it was not well received by the hacker community and was used sarcastically by Bob and Leon in their Capture the Flag competition.

For every positive portrayal of hackers in movies and television, you will find even more horrible mischaracterizations of them. It is a sad state of affairs today when we need to learn about cyber-crime and people are murmuring about cyber-warfare. The entertainment industry still skews the perception of hacking and the culture so badly that it is hard to tell the truth and fiction apart! Here is a list of some of the top offenders that this book's author has compiled and published in the Syngress mailing list Phishwrap[17]:

10. *FireWall*

    iPod + fax machine (even if you coded OCR software) = fail!

9. *Transporter 2*

    A guy being able to launch his car off a ramp and do a barrel roll to knock off the bomb on the bottom of his car is more believable than taking an iPod, grabbing a screenshot from a security camera, and then jacking it into your car to send automagically to the U.S. Marshals office! Not even Jack Bauer has the audacity to try to get away with that (yet).

8. *Independence Day*

    Option 1: Hardly anyone on Earth is using a Mac, so of course it would be able to interface with an alien OS.

    Option 2: These are vastly superior beings, so of course they would use a Mac-like OS. (Let the OS flame war begin!)

7. *The Net*

    I know Sandra Bullock played an über-elite hacker but not even Neo was leet enough to be able to telnet to an e-mail address and connect to a computer network no less.

6. *Swordfish*

    All the positive or negative reinforcements in the world are not going to make it possible to visualize the encryption passphrase, even to government systems. (+5, though, for best gratuitous use of monitors in a movie. This made the *Matrix* seem reasonable.)

5. *The Recruit*

    Spartacus: great name to cheer? TRUE. But Spartacus as a protocol that takes over every computer system to broadcast video? FALSE. (This is less likely than a virus that spreads through your power outlet.)

4. *Transformers*

    Let me get this straight: Access to Cray supercomputers and geniuses from around the country? Epic Fail. Take it to a guy with a laptop, and in between a game of Dance Dance Revolution, the Decepticon's alien stream is deciphered. I thought the talking truck more plausible.

3. *National Treasure 2*

    Yes, it was cool, but sorry you cannot set up a command center in the loo and take over a government facility security system. (Yes it may be the Queen's house, but it's still run by the government.)

2. *Sneakers*

    You create a device that can decrypt and break into any firewalled, secured, and encrypted system in the U.S. in mere seconds, but only the U.S. because it only knows English encryption methods? Start programming in a Rosetta Stone™ plug-in and you could take over the world.

1. *The Core*

    What's worse than an unneeded hacker character? An unneeded hacker character that does bubble gum origami and then utters, "Here, you now have free long distance on this phone. Forever." Ugh!

LINKSYS

> ### THE HACK DISSECTED
>
> *"You'd think people would figure out to encrypt all of these older Linksys networks that everyone still uses," Leon commented as Bob waited for his browser to load the page from one of his Web servers.* (p. 49)

As Bob and Leon drove through a wealthy neighborhood, looking for a victim to "borrow" money from, they decided on a home with an open Linksys Wi-Fi connection. Leon comments that people should know by now how to configure their old Linksys networks to be encrypted. Linksys is one of the largest producers of wireless access points for the home. However, earlier Linksys models were designed to plug-in and start working without any configuration. This ease of setup allowed for nontechnical users to quickly get on the Internet, but it also kept the access points insecure and with a default configuration. A report from RedSpin showed a wardriving analysis that discovered that 10 percent of all networks located still had "linksys" as their network identifier.[18] Of all access points with default configurations, 80 percent were from Linksys, and 33 percent had no encryption enabled.

INFRAGARD

> ### THE HACK DISSECTED
>
> *"Hey, uh hello. This is Jonathan Tao at 3DNF. We met at the InfraGard meeting a couple of weeks ago."* (p. 66)

When Jonathan Tao noticed unusual behavior in his network, he knew that he needed help. His first call was to FBI Agent Jackson. He had first met Agent Jackson at a local InfraGard meeting, a collaboration group between the FBI and private sector organizations. It allows for those responsible for protecting the nation's critical infrastructure to build relationships so that when an emergency does occur, a line of communication can be easily established. InfraGard is a free, nonprofit organization that, as of March 2010, has more than 36,000 members.[19] For more information on InfraGard visit www.InfraGard.com.

ECHELON

> **THE HACK DISSECTED**
>
> *Mark gave up. "Chris, this is Dobbs. He's a friend of Bob from the 2600 meetings."*
> *"I knew it!" Dobbs exclaimed. "You guys and your Patriot Act are watching all of us!"*
> *Mark revealed a look of exasperation and annoyance as he raised both his hands slightly towards Dobbs. "I'm just a tech who has learned it's best not to tell everyone where I work."*
> *"That's crap! I bet you are part of a whole program made just to watch people like us. You just need to put some faces with all the data you've been scraping with Echelon!"* (pp. 77–78)

As FBI Agent Jackson tries to innocently question Dobbs about the whereabouts of Bob Falken, Dobbs becomes very paranoid. He is shocked to learn that a member of his 2600 club is a federal agent, and believes that he is being watched for signs of criminal activity. As Mark tries to calm Dobbs, Dobbs responds that the agents are just seeking to gather more information to supplement their Echelon data. Echelon refers to Signal Intelligence (SIGINT) that is being collected by a government or military organization. SIGINT refers to the collection of data over any electronics line including telephone calls, cellular calls, text messages, faxes, and e-mails. Some believe that Echelon has been collecting and storing information on American citizens for decades for government purposes.[20]

PERL SCRIPTS

> **THE HACK DISSECTED**
>
> *"Dobbs is one of the smartest ones at the 2600 meetings. I swear if you put a keyboard on a '57 Chevy he could write a Perl script to improve the gas mileage."*
> *"What's a pearl script?" Chris asked.* (pp. 78–79)

Perl is a scripting language for multiple operating systems. It is pronounced the same as pearl, causing Chris to be confused over the terminology. Although traditional, compiled programming languages require a programmer to write the code, compile it, and then run it, scripting languages remove much of the complexity of coding and the need for compilation. Once a program is written, it can be run immediately by an interpreter. Perl is well regarded for its level of depth, allowing its programmer to perform many advanced functions normally not found in a scripting language. It is also known for being an extremely complex language to read and understand, as demonstrated by the short-run Obfuscated Perl Contest and one of the entrants at http://perl.plover.com/obfuscated/. Perl is also highly regarded for usage in computer forensics and network intrusion analysis, with regular SysAdmin, Audit, Network, Security (SANS) blog postings on using Perl for data analysis.[21] An additional book that goes in further depth with using Perl for forensics is Harlan Carvey's *Perl Scripting for Windows Security: Live Response, Forensic Analysis, and Monitoring* (ISBN: 978-1-59749-173-0, Syngress).

Those who master the Perl language are held in high regard in many computer circles as evidenced by Mark's statement of Dobbs being able to write a Perl script for a '57 Chevy.

GHOSTRAT

THE HACK DISSECTED

"Good, that will be what you target as soon as we arrive. Next, we need a more standard malware that we can drop on a couple of systems inside 3DNF."

"Won't this just set off alarms?" Pavel protested.

"I just want a couple, and they will be enough to make it look like they were sloppy with their surfing habits – which I'm sure they are. That way they won't be looking for external activity."

"All right. I've got a copy of the gh0stRAT," Pavel offered.

"Good – everyone loves to blame the Chinese. The Americans will spend their time looking in the wrong place," Vlad agreed. "It is usually easy to make them look for the wrong enemy." (p. 93)

As Vlad and Pavel plan their return attack on 3DNF, they realize the need for misdirection. If someone noticed suspicious activity within the 3DNF network, an investigator may come across their Trojan and remove it. So, they plan to install a normal Trojan on some of the systems to attract attention away from their own code. In this approach, they're assuming that once investigators find the simple malware application gh0stRAT, then they'll stop looking and pass over their custom malware.

The gh0stRAT tool is Remote Access Trojan (RAT) developed by a group named C.Rufus and known to be used by groups of Chinese hackers against American targets. Pavel's use of gh0stRAT is also a very political move. As cyber tensions grow between the United States and China, many are looking at China as an obvious culprit.[22] If there is evidence of a Trojan on the system that has been seen in similar incidents, then investigators may jump to include the 3DNF attack as part of a large grouping of attacks. This could cause investigators to look for the wrong evidence on systems and overlook Vlad and Pavel's custom Trojan.

LOCK PICKING

THE HACK DISSECTED

Bob knelt on one knee and began to rummage through his backpack. "I've been playing with bumping locks and I'm getting pretty good at it." (p. 97)

In an industry that has been around for generations, bump keying is a fairly recent tactic that is used by many certified locksmiths and budding hackers. A specially designed bump key is inserted into a lock and given a slight tap, or bump. This jarring motion will strike the internal lock tumblers, causing them to retract as if the proper key was inserted, and allow the attacker to open the lock.[23] This is a very basic explanation of the attack, and as with all lock picking, the technique requires extensive practice and specialized tools.

When a hacker is really after a specific target, sometimes a strict network-based attack will not be enough. This is a time when you need to take the attack into the physical world. Breaking through a firewall can sometimes be easier than breaking into a back door. However, sometimes breaking through a physical door is the only way to achieve your goals as more companies harden their digital perimeter. If an attacker gains physical access to a computer on your network, then he or she can easily exploit it and your network. Lock picking is no longer some obscure, mysterious art. DEFCON hosts one of the largest lock-pick villages, a casual practice environment that teaches how to pick locks ranging from handcuffs to padlocks. The DEFCON lock-pick village is voluntarily run by Deviant Ollam, a well-known figure in the lock-picking world who is on the Board of Directors for the U.S. division of The Open Organization of Lockpickers (TOOOL).[24] Ollam has also written the soon-to-be-published *Practical Lock Picking: A Physical Penetration Tester's Training Guide* (Syngress). Some people in the mainstream may find this a dangerous or bad skill to be teaching everyone. Once again, we emphasize the fact that skills and tools are not inherently evil. The tools and skills are morally neutral; it is what that their possessor intends to use them for that determines their context.

ENDNOTES

1. ThinkGeek. Swiss Flash USB Knife, www.thinkgeek.com/gadgets/tools/ad41/; 2010 [accessed 21.03.10].
2. TechChee. Comb USB flash drive keeps your hair neat always, www.techchee.com/2009/10/12/comb-usb-flash-drive-keeps-your-hair-neat-always/; 2010 [accessed 21.03.10].
3. Gill NS. The Trojan War and the Trojan Horse, About.com, http://ancienthistory.about.com/cs/troyilium/a/taleoftroy_3.htm; 2010 [accessed 21.03.10].
4. Anthology of Swiss banks in fiction. The Bourne Identity Photo Gallery : Laser device projecting a Swiss numbered account number on the wall, http://swiss-bank-accounts.com/e/fiction/bourne-identity/account-number.html; 2010 [accessed 21.03.10].
5. Striphas T. Where the Cylons will come from, http://striphas.blogspot.com/2010/02/where-cylons-will-come-from.html; 2010 [accessed 21.03.10].
6. Washington Technology. Want to win big? Call in a tiger team, http://washingtontechnology.com/Articles/2009/08/10/Upfront-Tiger-Teams.aspx; 2009 [accessed 22.03.10].
7. Bruce S. "Tiger Team" Reality TV Show, www.schneier.com/blog/archives/2007/12/tiger_team_real.html; 2007 [accessed 22.03.10].
8. Rob S. Dateline NBC. Your kid's cyber secret, www.msnbc.msn.com/id/9878187/; 2006 [accessed 23.03.10].

9. Brown S. *WarGames*: A Look Back at the Film That Turned Geeks and Phreaks Into Stars, Wired, www.wired.com/entertainment/hollywood/magazine/16-08/ff_wargames; 2008 [accessed 21.03.10].

10. Richardson WTG. Honey Pots, www.witiger.com/ecommerce/honeypots.htm; 2007 [accessed 21.03.10].

11. Nakashima E. Dismantling of Saudi-CIA Web site illustrates need for clearer cyber-war policies, The Washington Post, www.washingtonpost.com/wp-dyn/content/article/2010/03/18/AR2010031805464_pf.html; 2010 [accessed 29.03.10].

12. Rivest R. The MD5 Message-Digest Algorithm, http://tools.ietf.org/html/rfc1321; 1992 [accessed 25.03.10].

13. Sotirov A, Stevens M, Appelbaum J, Lenstra A, Molnar D, Osvik D, et al. MD5 considered harmful today; Creating a rogue CA certificate, www.win.tue.nl/hashclash/rogue-ca/; 2008 [accessed 27.03.10].

14. Robert B. Super 'Alias' will bowl you over, USA Today, www.usatoday.com/life/television/reviews/2003-01-23-alias_x.htm; 2003 [accessed 26.03.10].

15. Aislinn S, Telegraph Media Group. Dr Who's David Tenant joins other 10 Time Lords for one-off show, www.telegraph.co.uk/culture/tvandradio/doctor-who/5609141/Dr-Whos-David-Tenant-joins-other-10-Time-Lords-for-one-off-show.html; 2009 [accessed 26.03.10].

16. Passwall. The Net: Suspense, http://mike.passwall.com/uselesstrivia/thenet.html; 2010 [accessed 29.03.10].

17. Top Ten Most Ridiculous Movie Hacks of All Time, Jayson Street, Syngress Phishwrap, www.elsevierdirect.com/Phishwrap/Top_10_Most_Ridiculous_Movie_Hacks.html; 2009 [accessed 29.03.10].

18. Nathan D, Redspin Inc. War-Driving, www.redspin.com/securityadvisory/securityadvisory_march2009.html; 2009 [accessed 25.03.10].

19. InfraGard. About InfraGard, www.infragard.net/about.php; 2010 [accessed 21.03.10].

20. Duncan C, ZDNet. Echelon: Sigint under the spotlight, www.zdnet.co.uk/news/security-management/2000/06/30/echelon-sigint-under-the-spotlight-2079876/; 2000 [accessed 21.03.10].

21. Michael W, SANS Institute. Forensics and Perl-Fu, http://blogs.sans.org/computer-forensics/2009/04/17/forensics-and-perl-fu/; 2009 [accessed 21.03.10].

22. Cathal K, Toronto S. Cyberspies' code a click away, www.thestar.com/news/world/article/610860; 2009 [accessed 21.03.10].

23. Tobias M, Engadget. The Lockdown: Locked, but not secure (Part 1), www.engadget.com/2006/08/24/the-lockdown-locked-but-not-secure-part-i/; 2006 [accessed 21.03.10].

24. Deviant O. Lockpicking, http://deviating.net/lockpicking/bio.html; 2010 [accessed 29.03.10].

Index

Page numbers followed by *f* indicates a figure and *t* indicates a table.

329